TOKELAU

TOKELAU

A Historical Ethnography

Judith Huntsman & Antony Hooper

UNIVERSITY OF HAWAI'I PRESS
HONOLULU

Published in North America by
University of Hawai'i Press
2840 Kolowalu Street
Honolulu, Hawai'i 96822

First Published in New Zealand by
Auckland University Press
University of Auckland
Private Bag 92019
Auckland, New Zealand

Royalties from this publication will be used in support of Pacific Island education.

JACKET DESIGN Christine Hansen
JACKET ILLUSTRATIONS
FRONT Photo by Marti Friedlander
BACK (Bottom) Alfred T. Agate (1841) 'Cocoanut Grove and Temple: Fakaofo (Bowditch Island)', oil
on canvas, 10 x 14 inches. *National Academy of Design, New York*
(Top) Meeting house: photo by Marti Friedlander
AUTHOR PHOTO Neville Peat

Typeset in New Caledonia by Auckland University Press
Printed in New Zealand by GP Print

Library of Congress Cataloging-in-Publication Data
Huntsman, Judith.
   Tokelau: a historical ethnography / Judith Huntsman and Antony Hooper.
      p. 18.5 x 26 cm.
   Includes bibliographical references and index.
   ISBN 0-8248-1912-8
   1. Ethnology—Tokelau. 2. Villages—Tokelau. 3. Folklore—Tokelau.
4. Tokelau—History. 5. Tokelau—Social life and customs. I. Hooper, Antony. II. Title.
GN671.T46H86   1996
305.8'009615—dc20
                                                                                        96–27748
                                                                                             CIP

CONTENTS

PREFACE

There are long and distinguished separate traditions of both ethnographic and historical research in Polynesia; none the less, anthropology and history in the region have always been closely allied with one another. In recent decades, for example, Polynesia has been the setting for a substantial academic tradition of 'island oriented' narrative histories: Davidson (1967), Gilson (1970, 1980) and Newbury (1980) are a few of the better known. All were written by historians with some anthropological sophistication, using both European and indigenous historical texts to produce informed portraits of the indigenous polities as they were at the time of European contact, both as baselines for their narrative accounts, and to inform their interpretations of change.

Anthropologists have also made good use of historical sources for their own purposes, reconstructing aspects of culture and schemes of significance which are gone from the present and are now accessible in no other way. Valeri's analysis of Hawaiian sacrifice (1985) shows perhaps better than any other recent work in the field the use of wholly historical sources for a characteristically anthropological project—the depiction of an alien practice in terms of its motivating cultural logic. Again, Sahlins's recent studies (1985, 1990, 1992) of Hawaii and Fiji use historically documented myth, ritual and tradition not simply to extend the historical record but to explain it. Both these works have considerable analytic power, suggesting analogues right across the Polynesian region.

We have learned much from anthropologists and histories such as these, and have drawn freely from all of them in writing this book—even though none of them directly addresses the central problem which has confronted us. Our concern here has been the ways in which an *ethnography* of the present might be conjoined with history. That, as we have found, is a special kind of enterprise, involving not only the connection of the past to the present, but the integration of two powerful but logically independent interpretive modes of dealing with the past.

Ethnography gives privileged access to a people's contemporary representations of the past, to the ways in which knowledge about that past is constructed, passed on and invoked in everyday social life. This is the past as it appears in the present, which can be related to present-day structures of social and cultural significance. It matters little whether such representations are 'objectively' true or not: myths, legends or fabulous genealogical structures can all be seen as part of the symbolic structures by which reality, both past and present, is perceived and understood. By comparison, narrative histories do not give such matters much attention. Historians commonly have less direct experience of such representations than ethnographers, are less concerned with their significances, and certainly less inclined to give them credence in their evaluations of data about the past 'as it really was'—or can plausibly be made out to have been.

Ideally, one would think, these ethnographic and historical modes of interpretation might be placed side by side, evaluated and conjoined within a single narrative structure. There have, however, been few opportunities for this to be done in island Polynesia. Ethnographies are generally placed in relatively small, restricted local settings, where the significances of social action can be more readily grasped within a wide range of economic, political and ideological contexts. Such interpretations do not depend upon fictions of 'closed' or insular systems, as some critics have maintained. They do, however, imply grounded, localised communities through which wider regional, national and even international systems of power and significance may be viewed; and that in practice has generally meant villages, districts and small islands, in which both discourse and social action are direct and largely face-to-face.

Other social scientists quite commonly regard such approaches as unnecessarily restrictive, if not quaint, and focus instead on settings of wider range. The narrative 'island oriented' Pacific histories, for example, have been concerned primarily with the ways in which indigenous societies have been gathered into European protectorates, colonies and economic systems, and with their later transformations into independent or self-governing states. They have, certainly, connected the past with the present. But the present which is depicted is typically on a national rather than an ethnographic scale, with all traces of an ethnographic past elided by the broad sweep of history.

Ethnographies are not in any way incompatible with historical studies of this kind. They may at times provide illuminating perspectives on various aspects of national life, but the social and cultural realities which they depict are mainly of local scope and marginal to newer, more pressing national concerns.

If ethnographies of the present have generally only tangential relevance to national narrative histories, they have generally even frailer connections with the ethnographies of the past constructed wholly from historical sources, simply because the linkages between past and present have been broken by depopulation or the overwhelming force of circumstance. The kings, priests and the conceptual structures of Hawaiian religion are effectively gone. The Pomares are merely 'history', irrelevant and largely unknown to the general modern Tahitian cultural consciousness. The Tahitians of Oliver's two monumental ethnographies of past and present inhabit radically different worlds, and by comparison with its crowded past, the Marquesas that Dening actually saw was a 'silent land'.

These are sweeping generalisations, contestable, no doubt, at various levels. We introduce them simply to point up the special circumstances of Tokelau and the approaches to its ethnography and history which we have taken here. Time, 'real time', is of direct relevance to both. As recently as 25 years ago, roughly the period that we have taken as our 'ethnographic present', the three atolls were relatively self-contained places, remote from one another as well as removed from many of the social, economic and political changes that had already taken place in neighbouring groups. Although unified to a degree by simple propinquity and a common past, language and culture, they were in no sense a 'nation', and few people considered the possibility that they might ever become one. They were, at classic ethnographic scale, three villages provisioned largely from their own atoll resources, self-governing to a marked degree and very much concerned with their own affairs.

Although they had all undergone the violence of depopulation through disease and displacement, as well as being subjected to missionisation and colonial rule, they were by no means a silent land. They remained connected to their common and individual pasts. The significant past was an ethnographic past, largely oral, tied very much to the local communities and expressed in myth, *tala* or 'historical accounts', and genealogy; these narratives of the past were also relatively copious, and could be related readily enough to the ongoing structures of their social lives. It was a past that, as we came to understand it, was also very much apparent in the present.

There was at the time no narrative history of Tokelau, no record of the atolls based on archival sources which allowed for their essential *historicity*, exploring the relationships between events over periods of time in a plausible 'causal-temporal-logical line' (Errington 1979:239). Historians of the Pacific, understandably, had been concerned with larger, more populous and significant places. Yet, as we found, the archival sources were there, and furthermore, they contained an appreciable amount of detail that had no place in the local, ethnographic past.

That, of course, is not at all unusual; the past commonly enough appears as a foreign country, full of surprising details. What is unusual, though, is the extent to which the most plausible interpretation of much of this historical detail, including its inherent historicity, replicates the categories and conceptual structures of the ethnographic past—which in turn are also manifest in everyday life of the ethnographic present.

This book thus has two possible beginnings, set in either the ethnographic present or the remote historical past. Beginning with the present, one might proceed through ethnographic comparison of the social organisation of the atolls back through the ethnographic past of myth, genealogy and tradition, establishing the distinctive structures encompassing both past and present reality. Historical details, real archival 'facts', might then be conjoined, with their historicity 'put on hold', either to give some depth to the ethnography, or employed to explicate salient 'structures of the conjuncture'. Or alternatively one might begin with the 'real' past, patching it in as far as possible with mythological, traditional and genealogical accounts to produce (with strong authorial control) a general narrative history culminating in the ethnography of the present.

We have in fact done a bit of both—governed, so we like to think, by the logic of the particular situation, as well as in the interests of clarity. The ethnography, however, comes first, mainly because although there might be a familiar logic in moving from past to present, there are also difficulties in relating the past of a place like Tokelau to an audience wholly unfamiliar with its present life and circumstances. For the benefit of readers who might want their history first, we have sketched Tokelau's post-contact past in Chapter 1. One could of course read Part II before Part I; but those who have any impulse to do this might be better advised to turn to the Tokelau-authored book *Matagi Tokelau*, which is set out in the order of past to present—simply because both the authors and their main audience were familiar enough with the present.

Introduction

One village can teach us nothing. It is only when we have the variations that we can begin to theorize.

—Hocart 1952:viii

When we first went to Tokelau to begin our research three decades ago, everyone, it seemed, wanted to tell us the same story. It concerned two spirits, one named Fenū who lived in Fakaofo, and the other a spirit of Nukunonu named Hemoana. The story went something like this: Fenū went and stole the fresh water from the well which used to be on land where the Nukunonu village now stands, and set off back to Fakaofo with it held in a half coconut shell. Hemoana discovered the theft and took off in pursuit, overtaking Fenū at the Nukunonu islet of Motu Akea. Hemoana struck at the shell, causing a little water to fall on Motu Akea, but Fenū escaped to Fakaofo with all the rest. Not long thereafter, Hemoana thought one day of the fine *kie* pandanus which grew on Fakaofo but not on Nukunonu. Hemoana went off to Fakaofo and, unseen by Fenū, stole the pandanus and brought it back to Nukunonu.

We heard this story again and again, in both Fakaofo and Nukunonu, told by sages, by ordinary men and women with no particular pretensions to learning, even by children—in fact everyone who knew something of the purpose of our visits and felt inclined to help with a first lesson, an essential primer of what was, somehow, the nature and truth of Tokelau. We did not, however, realise this at the time. We were grateful for the attention, listened distractedly, made notes, and got on with what seemed to us more important matters.

In a very direct and what seems to us now a very obvious sense, this book is about how we came to discover the relevance of that simple story of reciprocal theft. We did not really appreciate it until we had spent several years in the atolls. Even then, its significance came upon us piecemeal, as we gained better understandings of very diverse areas of Tokelau life, and as we argued through various other interpretive leads—none of which seemed to lead anywhere in particular. History, as it turned out, was crucial. It was a complex and drawn-out process, best understood perhaps through a straight-forward account of what happened.

We did not set out to write a history of Tokelau. Our concerns at the outset were more narrowly ethnographic, focused on variations between the three atoll communities and how they might be accounted for—the familiar 'microsociology' of what is now another era. We had of course other research interests as well, some derived from what Gordon Macgregor (1937) had previously published about the atolls, and others which we took from the general anthropological air of the 1960s. Macgregor had spent two months in Atafu during 1932. His documentation and description of Tokelau material culture was superb, but by his own admission (pers.comm. 1969), he had only a tenuous grasp of institutional structures and social relations. We were also concerned to explore the relevance of what Sahlins had written (1957, 1958) about atoll societies and their socioeconomic complexities, and to make whatever contributions we could to the still ongoing debate over cognatic descent systems (Davenport 1959 & 1963, Firth 1957 & 1963, Goodenough 1955). These, however, were all peripheral concerns. For most of our periods in the atolls between 1967 and 1970 we were occupied with gathering comparable data from each of three atolls—on mundane matters such as household composition, land holdings, distribution patterns and family genealogies. We always went to different atolls, and though we joined in similar sorts of meetings and gatherings, we were also, in the nature of Tokelau sociality, each thrown more with people of our own gender; and partly through that we came to acquire different sorts of information on many things, and different perspectives on Tokelau gender relations. That was interesting, though our discussions of the topic were obfuscated by the different ways in which gender relations were institutionalised in the three islands.

The Tokelau that we experienced and came to know was clearly a single sociocultural entity. The language of everyday life was Tokelauan, spoken throughout the three atolls with no significant variations that we were aware of, or that anyone drew attention to, except perhaps in jest. It was also a single political domain, a dependency under a New Zealand administration based in Western Samoa which dispensed the same laws, followed the same policies and generally dealt equitably with the three separate island authorities. Everyone was either Roman Catholic or Protestant, and no other religions were established. From the outside, Tokelau was clearly 'one people', even one body of custom throughout, based upon a common heritage from the past. That was, indeed, the way that Tokelau people regarded themselves, and the way they presented themselves to the outside world.

There was, we found, also a profound sense in which islands had the 'same' social organisation, constructed from the same basic elements and concerned to carry out the same repertoire of tasks. Each had a variety of 'activity systems' or social configurations which could be used at different times for doing different things (cf. Howard 1963 on Rotuma). The most regular configuration balanced communal village activities with those pursued by households and descent groups. But then for extended periods a village might operate as two separate halves, with the competition between the halves dominating all aspects of daily life, and at other times, a village would do all things communally, as a single giant household—before disbanding again into routine activity groups.

Beyond these extraordinary and transient 'sets' each village had very much the same range of social groups. Yet they were obviously not clones, nor were the variations that we noted and fixed attention upon merely random. The most fundamental difference between the villages lay in the organisation of local authority. Each village had a council of some sort (called the *taupulega* 'ruling body' or *fono toeaina* 'elders' council') to coordinate and direct community activities and to speak for the atoll as a whole, but they differed significantly from one another in composition and in the ways in which they were articulated with other local groups and organisations. Of this we became aware early on, thanks to the intercession of Nukunonu's wireless operator, Tiō. In the course of our weekly exchange of information via wireless one evening late in 1967, Hooper in Fakaofo insisted that Huntsman in Nukunonu had it all wrong: the *taupulega* was not composed of representatives of 'families' within the village, but rather was a self-selected group of elderly men. An argument did not even begin, for Tiō, in Nukunonu, said with a grin: 'Fakaofo is different.'

Fakaofo indeed has a *taupulega* made up of a dozen or so elderly men. As its individual members age and either lose interest or become incapacitated they simply stop attending meetings, and their places are taken by others—chosen by the council itself. Age, then, is what makes a man eligible for selection and, in turn, underpins the council's authority. The Nukunonu council, by contrast, is made up of representatives of all the descent groups on the island, regardless of age, but also includes elderly men who for one reason or another were not (or had ceased to be) descent group representatives. Essentially, the Nukunonu council derives its legitimacy from the fact that it speaks for all the descent groups of the island. Atafu's council, like Nukunonu's, is made up of descent group representatives, but does not include any others.

The common elements in the make-up of the three councils are obvious enough, yet the slight differences contribute to each island's particular preoccupations and tone, especially as the councils articulate with other village organisations and oversee many aspects of daily life. In Fakaofo, virtually everything depends upon decisions taken by that small group of elderly men, 'the elders', and their decisions are final. They speak for the entire island, over and above the descent groups and other local organisations and enthusiasms. Nukunonu appears as basically a coalition of distinct corporate descent groups; decisions in the council are affirmed by consensus and its members are charged with transmitting them to the groups they represent. Although Atafu's council is again representative, its role is more often one of surveillance, monitoring and overseeing the activities of other semi-autonomous village organisations that initiate and plan their own activities, but nonetheless characteristically include the whole village.

INTRODUCTION

To those people (perhaps the majority, but by no means all of the adults) who, like Tiō, have experienced life on other islands of the group, these different institutional structures are known, but generally unremarkable. People follow the ways of their own island or village, and simply put the differences down to something in the *uiga*, the 'nature' or 'habit' of the islands concerned.

For us, however, this did not seem a sufficient explanation, and we worried the problem through a number of stages. At first, we wrote independently on topics that were of interest—social organisation, land tenure and resource distribution (Hooper 1968, 1969a, 1969b, Huntsman 1969a, 1969b, 1971)—using data from the particular islands on which we had worked. Ignoring the differences between the islands, we either implied or stated directly that our findings were 'generally applicable to all Tokelau'. Later, however, when we began to collaborate on joint publications (Hooper and Huntsman 1973, Huntsman and Hooper 1975 & 1976) drawing on our research in all three atolls, we could no longer elide the differences. In confronting them, we had many disagreements, most of which centred on our doubts as to whether the differences were 'real' or simply artefacts of our different perceptions, gender biases or the different roles we had established with our hosts on the separate islands.

Eventually, however, we concluded that the differences were real enough. In terms of social organisation, Tokelau was made up of three quite distinctive atoll communities. That settled, we turned our attention to accounting for the differences. Given the common language, the profusion of common elements of social organisation and Tokelau's very explicit sense of its own distinctiveness, we assumed that the differences must have arisen gradually over time by processes of steady, cumulative accretions in three different directions from a common and presumably undifferentiated source. We even invoked the distinct though minor geographical and ecological differences between the atolls to account for the social differences, reasoning that the exploitation of resources on one atoll might favour economic cooperation among extended family units with little need for centralised direction and control, while another called for exploitation by smaller groups requiring control to articulate their efforts.

As a theoretical argument, a three-finger exercise in practical reason, this seemed inherently plausible. Yet we came to regard it as misguided, for all that. In the first place, it was a wholly speculative argument, and given the nature of the evidence available, would have to remain so. Second, while the argument was perhaps tenable in comparing two of the atolls, it was very tendentious when we tried to add the third. We also looked closely at the separate contact histories of the atolls, thinking that the differences we sought to explain might have been generated by external social and economic pressures—but that too proved to be unfruitful.

So we tried to put these comparative concerns to one side, and began in 1979 to write a generic Tokelau ethnography. Yet in writing that we confronted and worried the differences almost daily, and the more we wrote, the

4

more salient they became. How were we going to avoid writing three ethnographies (which was patently absurd), and how, if we wrote a single ethnography, might the differences be expressed and explained? Nagging though these concerns were, the single ethnography was drafted and put aside, and we turned our attention to the past.

We had by that time gathered together a fair number of historical documents on Tokelau, and we knew the most widely told oral tales of the hostilities between the islands. But we were still inclined to think of these as 'history', 'legend' or 'folklore'; interesting as such, but of no obvious relevance to the problems which preoccupied us. However, as we turned to putting together all the historical sources, oral and written, local and foreign, it became clear that they all were transformations of one another, repeating the same basic message about both the 'nature' of each island and the relations between the islands.

As depicted in the historical tales, Fakaofo, Nukunonu and Atafu were at the outset three independent polities. They fought and Fakaofo became dominant, subjugating Nukunonu and driving off the entire original population of Atafu. Later, Atafu was settled by a man of Fakaofo and a woman of Nukunonu, and their descendants repeopled the island. All this tallied closely enough with what was reported of the islands by the earliest European accounts: Atafu at first deserted and later home to a small, socially unstratified community; Nukunonu timid and retreating before all overtures of contact; Fakaofo at first aggressive and overbearing and later, having experienced the power of European firearms, cautious, stand-offish and reserved. The later reports of the United States Exploring Expedition (1841) amplified many of these observations, depicting the wider dimensions of Fakaofo's domination in terms of rank and religion.

Once we realised these distinctive patterns, the differences between the genealogies of the three islands fell into place. They gave not only the records of distinct ancestries, but also, by the very ways in which they were structured, distinctive views of the nature and dimensions of the past: Fakaofo centred on a chiefly patrilineage; Nukunonu a complex, enduring coalition of four separate stocks; and Atafu a single constantly expanding stock derived from the original founding couple. In their different ways, all of these records threw light on the simple story of reciprocal theft which everyone had seemed so eager that we should record and understand: Fakaofo as male and the aggressor, stealing Nukunonu's water, the source of life and productivity; Nukunonu responding by the appropriation from Fakaofo of the *kie* pandanus, women's pre-eminent valuable and a prefiguration of both the Nukunonu woman taken as a wife by the first conquering Fakaofo chief as well as the later woman who went with a Fakaofo man to repopulate Atafu.

As these patterns emerged, we were led to revise our notion of differentiation from a common source. Myth, genealogy and historical tales are the distinctive idioms of traditional Polynesian intellectual discourse. In the Tokelau case, it seemed that all of them, in their separate ways, were concerned with the establishment and differentiation of an entire cosmology and social order. This was not set forth in terms of a practical logic of gradual, adaptive modification, but was instead proclaimed as an 'original' differentiation, deeply embedded in the nature of the culture itself. Tokelau, 'from a Tokelau point of view', was never one entity which differentiated into three. It was three right from the beginning.

From that point on, our comparative sociological project became absorbed by a cultural one. And since the Tokelau views of the past seemed to be speaking plainly to the distinctions we had noted in the present, we realised that history was also integral to our project.

On the ground/In the field

Huntsman spent an initial year in Nukunonu doing field research for her doctorate, while Hooper, constrained by teaching duties at Auckland, had only an initial three months in Fakaofo over the summer; this was 1967–68. Hooper's previous field experience in French Polynesia allowed him to become conversant with both Tokelauan and the outlines of Fakaofo social life relatively quickly, while Huntsman had time and opportunity to delve into more detail. We each returned to the atolls in 1969–70. Hooper spent nine months in Fakaofo, expanding and enriching his previous brief study, and Huntsman spent three months in Nukunonu extending her previous work, and six months in Atafu, exploring at first hand the third atoll and its variations on Tokelau life.

By the end of 1970, we each had what we considered to be a fairly comprehensive understanding of life in the atolls. By then, however, we had also committed ourselves to a somewhat different research agenda, working in collaboration with medical epidemiologists on a project concerned with the relationships between migration and health. This proved to be more than a diversion. It was a comprehensive study in its own right, and because it was supported by medical research funding, it allowed us to spend considerably longer in Tokelau than would otherwise have been possible. The guiding hand was Ian Prior, director of the Epidemiology Unit at Wellington Hospital, which had been monitoring the health status of recent Tokelau migrants in New Zealand for a number of years, and had also undertaken a medical survey in the atolls during 1968. For epidemiologists it was a valuable opportunity to study many aspects of the health changes associated with migration and with what was conceptualised as 'modernisation'. Attracted by what appeared to be a unique 'natural experiment'—people involved in a rapid transition from an atoll diet and a 'traditional' way of life to modern cities—the World Health Organisation became involved, and convened a seminar in Wellington in early 1970. We were invited to that gathering, and persuaded to create a conceptual framework for detailed studies of the 'modernisation process' as it pertained to Tokelau. Less than a week later, what had previously been simply friendly consultations and exchanges of information between ourselves and the epidemiologists had been transformed into a collaborative and expansive research project.

In 1971 we spent a further nine months in Tokelau, at first working closely with Prior and his colleagues during their intensive and rapid medical survey of the population, but then engaged in collecting the project's 'baseline' sociological and cultural information. The medical survey data referred to individuals, and our social and cultural information had to conform to this format. This involved gathering information on the whole adult population in the atolls at the time, organised in a way that each individual could be given a 'sociological–cultural' profile which could be monitored and extended through time with further surveys and interviews.

This first encounter with survey methods and quantitative research was, for both of us, an abrupt sink-or-swim, hands-on introduction, forcing us to translate virtually all that we had learned about Tokelau social life into new formats and unfamiliar conceptual frameworks. Nevertheless, we did it, and in the process learned several things. We interviewed privately all the lucid adults then resident in the atolls, using a questionnaire designed to elicit basic sociological and economic data as well as attitudinal data or 'personal opinions' about some of the basic moral precepts of Tokelau culture.

We spent considerably briefer periods of time in the atolls after 1971, returning at five-yearly intervals (in 1976, 1981 and 1986) to collect further data with our medical colleagues and to monitor changes, as well as following up on some of our other research interests. During 1972, we extended our survey study to the Tokelau people and communities in New Zealand, using a modified version of the questionnaire that we had used in the atolls the year before. This exercise was repeated in 1977 and again, in a much abridged form, in the early 1980s. By that time, though, the wider study had grown to almost unmanageable proportions as the data accumulated and as circumstances in both the atolls and among the migrants had broken the bounds of what was originally conceived as a straightforward and controlled longitudinal study of Tokelau life in two environments. We turned to writing it all up (Wessen et al. 1992).

The epidemiology project gave us many opportunities and some new perspectives on Tokelau life. We gained other insights from another longterm project, this time on culture and history, that occupied us intermittently throughout the 1980s. During the late 1970s, development projects of various kinds proliferated in Tokelau, new opportunities became available, and both the United Nations Committee of Twenty-Four and the New Zealand Government began to raise the possibility of eventual self-government for Tokelau. All this led to widespread discussions in the atolls about questions of identity, custom and tradition, and a general quickening of a self-conscious (though very tentatively proclaimed) nationalism. One of the outcomes of this was that when the University of the South Pacific put forward a suggestion that a book might be written by Tokelau authors about their history and lifeways, the idea was taken up with cautious enthusiasm. Shortly afterwards, we found ourselves engaged by the quickly formed national Book Committee as the honorary consultants, 'facilitators' and editors for the project. These were novel roles for us, and work of collating, editing and translating took much time. There was, however, little to be done in the way of consulting since both we and the authors concerned knew what kinds of material would be included. History and traditions were the main concern, with the tales of warfare between the islands as a centrepiece. What we had not expected was the extreme circumspection with which the representatives of the three islands approached these tales. Each, it seemed, expected that the others might come forth with their own novel versions, and dreaded dealing with the disagreements that might result. As things turned out, these fears proved groundless. Other concerns were the division of topics between the islands and the question of their authorship; but there again these were amicably resolved, especially once it had been decided that almost all contributions should be anonymous, as befitted a truly Tokelau cooperative undertaking and a reflection of a generalised 'Tokelau' persona.

Ethnography

At the end of 1971 we had spent approximately half our days since late 1967 in the atolls. There were certainly changes which were taking place during that period, most of them related to emigration to New Zealand (Hooper and Huntsman 1973). During our first period in Tokelau, in 1967–68, most people in the atolls knew very little about New Zealand. They reminisced about their kin who had departed and speculated about their fate, sending long letters and sound recordings full of urgent instructions about holding fast to the old principles of *fealofani* 'mutual compassion' and obedience to God's directions. The older adults of the time perceived New Zealand as a remote and even dangerous place. Several years later, however, many of these same older people had spent brief periods in New Zealand with children and grandchildren, and numbers of younger people were travelling to and fro, bringing new ideas and awarenesses to the atolls.

Nevertheless, Tokelau remained during those years very much its own place. Local concerns predominated, daily activities were attuned to fishing and other subsistence activities, few people had paid employment and remittances, although growing, were still windfalls, with little lasting effect on the basic rhythms of life. Most importantly, the local authority structures remained secure and basically unquestioned. Much of this was to change in the later 1970s, more particularly after 1976 with the introduction of widespread paid government employment, more comprehensive social services, and ideas of development. These changes have been comprehensive and cumulative, so that Tokelau of the 1990s is a quite different place from a generation ago.

For all these and other reasons, we have chosen to locate our ethnographic description of Tokelau in the period between 1967 and 1971. This is our 'ethnographic present', a historical moment, but not by any means a timeless one. It is the time when we were most intensely involved with the daily activities of the villages where we lived. Before that period, things were doubtless different, but it was still a time when people spoke with some certainty about the nature of 'the Tokelau way'; a decade later, people made conscious distinctions between the *poto tuai* and the *poto fou*, the 'old understandings' and the 'new'.

Several other features of our ethnography also call for comment. We begin with the exposition of several commonly articulated Tokelau 'sayings', wise saws which gather up and express, either directly or metaphorically, some of the basic precepts on which custom is based. Following this, we have concentrated on giving portrayals of the major institutional structures of village life, both those centred on the *nuku* or village itself, and those which are embraced by the concept of *kāiga* or 'kinship'. It is very much an ethnographic sketch, dwelling on none of the details which we have elaborated in other, shorter publications. Furthermore, the institutions are portrayed rather narrowly in what used to be called their 'jural aspect', concerned with the explicit 'rights' and 'duties' on which participation is based, and which link them to other social units.

This, we realise, is hardly an innovative approach. It also one which pays but little attention to the reflexive, interpretive nature of our separate undertakings. We share an enthusiasm for such interpretive accounts, but only up to a point—which lies roughly where a concern to understand the worlds that others inhabit gives way to a preoccupation with the ethnographers' own exquisite sensibilities.

For all this we make no apologies. Our ethnography has been put together to serve our particular purposes here. And besides, there is much in the approach which we have adopted which sits easily with the manner in which Tokelau people themselves portray the distinctive features of atoll life. Tokelau villages are crowded places, organised by a dense array of crosscutting social groups. Individual initiative is not frowned upon, but since all the business of daily life is allocated to appropriate groups, that initiative is more properly expressed in group context. Everything is morally better done together than alone. Perhaps because of this, Tokelau adults are extremely conscious of the ways in which interaction is constrained by particular roles. Every group or undertaking has its internal structure and authority, and in a great deal of interaction (especially of the more formal kind, as in the innumerable fono or meetings) people speak only from appropriate *tulaga* or 'positions'. They can depart from these fixed roles, but generally do so only by first marking the fact that they are speaking now as 'themselves' and from the 'heart'. In the dense net of interactions that make up the round of village days, people are constantly confronting one another in varying roles—all of which places an emphasis on a certain formality, with the etiquette of space, address, time and location all clearly marked.

The point we wish to stress is the explicit Tokelauan consciousness that social life is moral, constrained, and comprises a system that is balanced, finely tuned, and entirely capable of rational explanation. When speaking of institutions, they know the rules and can articulate them—using terms which translate almost exactly into the vocabulary of Radcliffe-Brown's functionalism: rights, moral obligation, coherence, ownership, covenant and so forth. (We record this as an ethnographic observation, not as a statement of our theoretical allegiance.) A consciousness of this sort is not merely acquired in the business of daily living. It is explicitly taught. Again and again we heard elders speaking to assembled villagers, preachers addressing their congregations and parents lecturing their children, all using the same phrases and explanations in the interests of ensuring harmony. They told us as well, many times. Such homilies do not by any means constitute all that there is to Tokelau life, but they do establish an outline of some of its most significant concerns.

History

As ethnographers fortunate enough to have had both ample time, and congenial and accommodating hosts, we have had an abundance of detailed information from which to construct the ethnographic account which we present in this book. We are fairly assured about it. We are less assured about our history, partly because the basic archival sources have not been as available as our ethnographic informants, and partly because we do not attempt to present a 'strong' narrative account of the kind that historians (even those who do not themselves 'do' this kind of history) might feel generally comfortable with. In spite of the relative paucity of sources, such an account could be written, and we have in fact described a number of the events, the foreign incursions, the decisions taken in far-off places and the epochal changes, from which such a narrative might be constructed. But they appear here largely as background; the foreground is made up of details of what was actually happening (or seemed to be happening) in each of the three atolls, during roughly the same stretches of time. This approach, of course, has been dictated by our comparative purposes, and we can only apologise if it seems at times to do a violence to narrative flow. Quite different things were happening on the separate islands at various periods, and were often unconnected with what was happening on the others; furthermore, at times when the archival sources are copious for one island they are silent about the others. We have in some instances relied exclusively on other sources such as genealogy, reminiscence or historical *tala* to make up for the absence of archival information—to varying effect; in others, we have just had to accept a silence.

When we began our search for records of the Tokelau past, the atolls, from the perspective of historical scholarship, were little more than a footnote in the history of the Pacific. Take, for instance, Scarr's (1967) history of the Western Pacific High Commission in which the only mention of Tokelau is a paragraph in a long footnote (p.290) which ends: 'Although their comparative isolation in respect of both the Protectorate and Suva made them a source of some administrative embarrassment, they presented the High Commissioner with no other major problems.'

Initially we intended to record the Tokelau past as fully as possible by collecting every document we could find, and in the intervals between our several periods in the atolls we sought to link the stories of the past we had heard there with what we could learn from foreign records. A historian might have set about this more systemically. As it was, we just looked in what seemed to be the obvious places at first and followed what leads came our way (see below). We envisioned a continuous, if perhaps fragmentary, narrative record of the past informed by what we had learned and experienced in the Tokelau present. We were after all ethnographers reading what others had written about Tokelau from brief encounters or more extended sojourns or even from far away. We could visualise the places referred to, and we 'knew' the people named, even if they were long gone, because of their connections to people we knew. When writers remarked on 'strange' behaviours and practices, attitudes and reactions, we usually had some idea of what they were about.

Our story of the Tokelau past is still a record, but has become more than a singular narrative, as will become apparent. It falls, however, into three broad eras, defined as much by the nature of the information about them as by the events and changing situations that mark their beginning and end. The first era (chapters 4 & 5) is about what is referred to in Tokelauan as 'in the beginning' (*i te kāloā*) and 'ancient times' (*aho anamua*), and to tell about it, we draw heavily on Tokelau narratives and genealogies and on documents describing the very earliest European encounters in Tokelau. When this era began is unknown; it ends in 1841. The second era (chapters 6 & 7) bridges 'ancient times' and 'these days' (*na aho nei*) ending about the turn of the century. For it, the Tokelau accounts are second-hand, told by elders to us as they had been told by their elders who were eyewitnesses, and the documents were mainly composed by missionaries. The third era (chapters 8 & 9) is truly of recent years, years experienced by the same people who reminisce and tell stories about them, and the records about them are primarily from colonial or government archives. To these eras we add a post-Second World War 'Postscript' to bring the record up to the ethnographic present.

We have purposely composed an intensely local story of the past, one that is concerned more with what Tokelau people have done than what has been done to them, and structured more often by thematic juxtaposition than by chronological causality. Tokelau is our focus and how foreigners and their ideas and ways have impinged, intruded and retreated are viewed from Tokelau, rather than as world movements or great forces.

The story of the Tokelau past that we have constructed has turned out to be more than the record we originally envisaged when we were assiduously gathering in all the possible sources of information: Tokelau narratives, genealogies and anecdotes, foreign records and documents, and a grounded ethnographic familiarity with Tokelau places, people and ways. The shape that this story has taken has been motivated by its own history, by the situations we encountered and the change in our own research agenda as it gradually shifted from a comparative microstudy of social variation to an appreciation and exploration of a cultural logic of difference. Along the way we have come to fully appreciate the wisdom of Hocart's words with which we began this introduction: 'One village can teach us nothing. It is only when we have the variations that we can begin to theorize.'

Acknowledgements

We have incurred many debts to diverse people and institutions during our lengthy research enterprise and are pleased to acknowledge them here.

Our first expression of gratitude must be to the late Ropati Simona, one of the first Tokelau schoolteachers, who in 1967 was settled in Auckland. He was our first Tokelau teacher, giving us introductory lessons in Tokelauan and a general primer in Tokelau manners before we ever went to the atolls. He remained a close colleague in many of our other Tokelau projects, most significantly as the lexicographer of the *Tokelau Dictionary*.

In Nukunonu during 1967–68, Huntsman began her explorations of Nukunonu's past with four knowledgeable elders—Manuele Palehau and Ioakimi Paselio, who remained in Tokelau, and Peato Tutu Perez and Alosio Kave, who would shortly afterwards move to New Zealand. During periodic sojourns in Nukunonu for well over a decade, her discussions about the past with Ioakimi and Palehau took up where they had left off the time before, each time providing further insights into that island's complex, sophisticated historical discourse, and over time becoming more interactive, as shared knowledge was discussed and interpretations exchanged, until in 1981 they became something in the order of a seminar on the Tokelau past. In New Zealand Alosio was always delighted to comment on our queries about the past, and indeed provided a crucial interpretation, which his more elderly counterparts in Nukunonu found particularly illuminating. Likewise, Peato followed our work with interest and was particularly generous with his own works, which focused more on Fakaofo, where he had been raised. Using an antique typewriter, he had been setting down Tokelau texts since the 1940s. In New Zealand he spent a considerable time editing and expanding them, and generously allowed us to make copies of two of them (cited here as n.d.1 and n.d.2). We were also fortunate in being able to stimulate his interest in the value of his own long experience as a catechist in Fakaofo, and he eventually presented us with an autobiographical account of those years which we cite as Perez 1977. Peato Tutu Perez passed away in the early 1980s and we have acknowledged his singular 'words of the sea' in an essay (Hooper and Huntsman 1991). Ioakimi Paselio, Alosio Kave, and Manuele Palehau were 'lost' in 1986 and to them a volume of Tokelau songs and stories has been dedicated (Thomas et al. 1991). They all wanted their knowledge to be widely shared; that is why they were such willing and patient teachers.

Over the years, several people kindly allowed us examine and study treasured 'family books'. The most comprehensive of these is a 136-page manuscript which, from internal evidence, seems to have been written during the 1930s, and which we cite simply Fakaofo (n.d.). It is written in Samoan, which was until the early 1980s the common language of literacy in Tokelau. The first and much the longest section of the manuscript is a historical account organised under thirty-two headings dealing with classifications of the natural world, the origins of the people, institutions of heathen times, Tui Tokelau, the slavers and the events of the later nineteenth and twentieth centuries associated with the ministries of successive Protestant pastors. This is followed by a 58-page genealogy of the *kāiga aliki* through seventeen generations from Kava, the first aliki. The manuscript relates the master narrative of the traditional history of Fakaofo, and is a key document on the nature of the unified Tokelau polity. From it Hooper gained a host of insights into contemporary issues on the island and a springboard for discussions of historical events with Fakaofo elders.

When we were first en route to Tokelau (and for what was not to be the first time, delayed in Apia), Paul Gabites, then New Zealand High Commissioner in Western Samoa and Administrator of Tokelau, generously gave us access to administration files. We were able to learn much from them, both about distant nineteenth-century events and more contemporary policies; and we continued to do so on other trips as various Official Secretaries: Neil Walter, John Larkindale, Tony Browne, Adrian Macey, and Casimilo Perez, allowed us the same generous access.

It was after our initial visits of 1967–68 to Nukunonu and Fakaofo, that we began a determined search for whatever historical sources there might be on Tokelau, and at different times over the years we had opportunities to search or access several archives. It seems appropriate for us to detail something of what we found with the willing and necessary assistance of librarians and archivists at the Mulivai Catholic Mission in Apia, the Western Pacific High Commission Archives in Suva, the Alexander Turnbull Library and New Zealand National Archives in Wellington, the United States National Archives in Washington, the New Zealand and Pacific Collection at the University of Auckland Library, and the Auckland Institute and Museum Library.

The Roman Catholic Mission at Mulivai in Apia holds records of Tokelau baptisms back to 1863 (and more recent records of marriages and deaths). These proved invaluable historically in conjunction with local genealogical accounts, have provided source material for demographic studies of fertility (Molloy and Huntsman 1996).

A week or so delay in Suva (waiting this time for a seaplane instead of a ship) gave us the chance to seek out Tokelau material in Western Pacific High Commission Archives, and opened our eyes to the complexities of Tokelau's relationship with the British Empire. We did not have enough time then, in 1970, to sort out the tangle of misunderstandings involved, but we were fortunate in that when the archives were later transferred to Britain, microfilm copies were deposited in the University of Auckland Library. (Some of the documents that we initially perused in Suva were subsequently refiled. We have attempted to cite them all as they are now listed.)

For mission documents, we had access to microfilms of London Missionary Society records held in the Alexander Turnbull Library in Wellington, and combed the published Catholic records in the *Annales des Missions de l'Océanie*.

During 1969 Huntsman located the unpublished journals and other documents of the United States Exploring Expedition (1838–42) in various east coast libraries from Virginia to Connecticut, and also searched public and private collections in Rhode Island and Massachusetts for relevant whalers' logs and journals, helped by the compendium of American 'sightings' and 'landings' held in the Peabody Museum at Salem (see Ward (ed.) 1967). (This was before the logs and journals were microfilmed and indexed by the Pacific Manuscripts Bureau.)

The New Zealand National Archives in Wellington were thoroughly explored in 1972, and many relevant documents were located and copied. The Archive's holdings have been relocated twice since 1972; we have checked and cited the current file identifications.

Our last major source of historical records was United States Consular Despatches from Apia, which we obtained on microfilm from the National Archives in Washington.

Although we have come to know the delights of serendipity in our searches, we must acknowledge that most of our more arcane sources have been gifts. Our historian colleagues have been indispensable sources of information and advice. Senior among them is, of course, H.E. Maude, who shares our devotion to tiny Pacific atolls and passed on whatever documents or leads he had about Tokelau—the one island group in the South Pacific, so he said, he had never visited. J.D. Freeman, when he learned of our research, provided us with copies of the meticulous notes he had taken from the London Missionary Society Archives in London. These notes helped us to locate items relevant to Tokelau that we would otherwise have missed. When we visited E.H. Bryan, jr. at the Bishop Museum, he provided us with copies of his notes and photographs taken during the Whitney Expedition's visit to Fakaofo in 1921. Robert Langdon also kindly referred us to some particularly recondite sources, and Doug Munro forwarded us copies of Tokelau material that he came across in the course of his historical research on Tuvalu. Then there is Niel Gunson, who turned up one day in Auckland with a manuscript recording a European–Tokelau encounter earlier than any that we had previously known about.

In the early 1980s, Hugh Laracy, who had been helping us with references to Marist historical sources over the years, put us in touch with the late Father Th. B. Cook SM, who was then indexing and microfilming the documents in the several Marist Provincial Archives in the Pacific (Cook 1984). Father Cook very generously sent us typed and annotated copies of many invaluable documents—including extracts from the journals of Father Padel ('a kind of Coastwatcher *avant la lettre*' as Father Cook characterised him). These extracts enabled us to settle the complex comings and goings of people to and from Tokelau in the 1840s and 1850s, and his extracts of Tokelau baptismal entries from the records of the Uvean parishes told of the fate of many Fakaofo people who ended up there in the early 1850s. Francis Zeger, Josephine Baddeley and Judith Macdonald all helped us at different times in translating the Marist published and unpublished records from the French.

We have received both joint and separate funding support, but because all the sources contributed to our collaborative project, which of us particularly received each grant or fellowship is not herein specified. Our initial ethnographic research was financed by the United States National Institutes of

Health (1967–69, 1970), the Auckland University Research Grants Committee (1967–68), the Wenner-Gren Foundation for Anthropological Research (1969–70), Society of Sigma Xi (1969), and the Nuffield Foundation (1969–70). In the early 1970s, we received research fellowships from the McCarthy Trust (1971–72) and Sunderland Trust (1971–73), and field research funding from the New Zealand Medical Research Council through the Wellington Hospital Epidemiology Unit. In 1981, we again received research support from the Wenner-Gren Foundation for Anthropological Research and also from the New Zealand Social Science Research Funding Committee. The Auckland University Research Grants Committee repeatedly aided us directly in funding travel, research, and consultation, and the New Zealand Medical Research Council regularly did likewise via the Wellington Hospital Epidemiology Unit. Finally, we received a grant from the New Zealand Lottery Science Committee (1992) that greatly aided the completion of this text.

In 1969, Huntsman arranged to meet Gordon Macgregor, the original ethnographer of Tokelau, in Washington DC. A delightful luncheon was the beginning of a collegial relationship that continued by correspondence until his death in late 1983. Macgregor kindly arranged for us to have copies of his fieldnotes and handed over to us a collection of photographs he had taken. He also handed on the field notebooks that he had been given by Andrew Thomson, a meteorologist, who spent several months in Tokelau during 1928. Macgregor's own notes are a most valuable addition to his published ethnology, and an impressive ethnographic record of his brief and concentrated period of fieldwork.

On two occasions in the course of writing this book we have enjoyed lengthy sojourns at North American universities among North American colleagues. We wish to reciprocate their warm hospitality with warm thanks to William Simmons, Paul Kay, Laura Nader and others of the Anthropology Department at the University of California–Berkeley in 1979; and Marshall Sahlins, Bernard Cohn, Terry Turner and others at the University of Chicago in 1986.

It is impossible to separate the research that informs this book from the research we were engaged in as parties to the Tokelau Island Migrant Study, because they have so enriched one another. During two decades of collaboration we enjoyed the collegiality of Ian Prior, creator and director of the Wellington Hospital Epidemiology Unit, and his diverse staff, most especially Cara Fleming, the late Rosemary Rees and Henry Tuia. The late John McCreary throughout provided invaluable and sound oversight—keeping the Study from straying too far afield, and Al Wessen provided key leadership at the beginning of the Study and kept us on track at the end.

More directly involved in our own studies from the outset has been Robin Hooper, companion and ever-present linguistic consultant. Fulimalo Pereira and Kelihiano Kalolo have been our students and as colleagues have helped create this book. Michael Goldsmith, Valerie Sallen Green and Allan Thomas are other 'students' of Tokelau that we have advised in their research and who in turn have contributed to our own. Then too we must acknowledge with warm appreciation our more remote mentors, those who guided us in our own studies by their advice and example: Douglas D. Oliver, Frederica de Laguna, and Jane C. Goodale.

In preparing this work for publication, Greg Dening, Elizabeth Wood-Ellem, Ann Chowning and Niel Gunson provided wise counsel, and in editing and crafting the volume Gillian Kootstra and Elizabeth Caffin of the Auckland University Press proved to be masters of their profession and of diplomacy. Hamish Macdonald, photographer, and Joan Lawrence, illustrator, were most generous with their time and expertise, sometimes in times of stress and duress.

Our picture of Tokelau has been enhanced by the photographs of many others. The late E. H. Bryan jr and the late Gordon Macgregor simply gave us the now historical photographs they took in 1921 and 1932 respectively. We acknowledge with thanks the Providence (Rhode Island) Public Library for photographic copies of illustrated pages from a 1839 whaling journal in the Nicholson Collection, the Museum of New Zealand Te Papa Tongarewa for photographs taken by Mr Andrew in 1886, the Royal Anthropological Institute for permission to include photographs of Fakaofo taken in 1889, the Public Records Office (Kew) for photographs of the 1914 Cyclone, and the National Archives of New Zealand for photographs taken during the first official New Zealand visit to Tokelau in 1925. The New York Academy of Design provided us with the transparency of Thomas Agate's painting in its collection which appears on the back cover, and Neville Peat responded instantaneously to the request for his picture of us in 1981. Finally, and most especially, we thank Marti Friedlander for allowing us to adorn this book with some of her photographs of Tokelau 1971 (now archived in the Anthropology Department at the University of Auckland).

For over a generation, we have not only come to know many Tokelau people very well, but also we have developed new interests and grown older together, so that we have all come to look at things from changed points of view. Age gives both more wisdom and greater knowledge in the Tokelau scheme of things. Be that as it may, events and developments during the past twenty-five years have made all Tokelau people—whether living in the atolls or in New Zealand—increasingly aware of alternative ways of living, and consequently more self-conscious about their own distinctive way of life. Many have consequently come to see relevance in our studies that they did not see when we began them. Some have contributed and shared in our discoveries; a few have even studied anthropology. So in many ways this has been an inclusive enterprise, though the significances of it have not been precisely the same for all concerned. Above we have singled out particular Tokelau colleagues who have worked and studied closely with us for sustained periods. Our wider debts to Tokelau friends and communities who have welcomed and hosted us are immeasurable and unaccountable. We cannot name everyone, and so we do not name anyone in particular, but we must say: *ki nā toeaina ma lōmātutua kua gagalo, ki toeaina ma lōmātutua koi ōla, ki tāulelea ma fafine, ki te tupulaga fou ma tupulaga koi hau—faka-fetai lahi lele ki toutou ālolofa kia te kimatou*—'to elders who have departed, to elders who are still living, to men and women, to the younger generation and for generations to come—our immeasurable thanks for your support and generosity to us all'.

Conventions

• Throughout this volume, single quotes are used for English glosses following italicised Tokelau words, phrases and sentences, or when the gloss takes the place of the Tokelau form. Tokelau words or phrases that follow English equivalents are italicised and placed in parentheses.

• Our journalistic portrayals of recurrent events, both specific and composite (i.e. derived from several, but not all, instances), are italicised and indented in Part I.

• Tokelauan text passages in Part II are italicised, indented and acknowledged when appropriate. Unless otherwise indicated, English translations are ours.

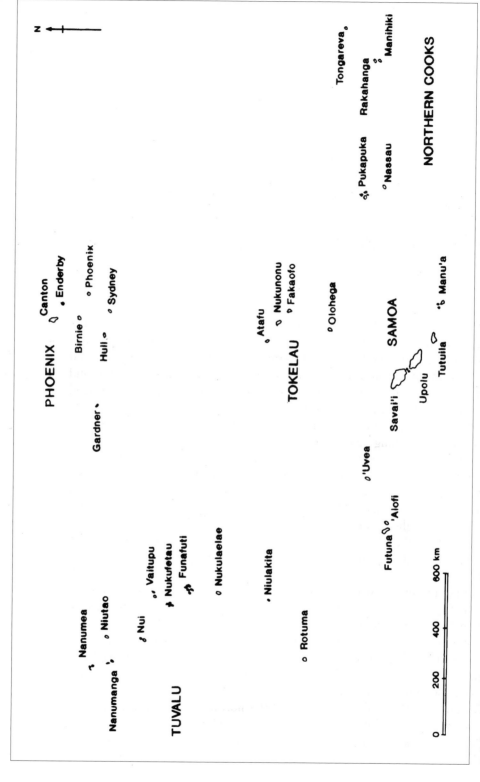

Tokelau and its closest neighbours in the central Pacific. The islands to the south and southwest—Samoa, Uvea, Futuna with 'Alofi, and Rotuma—are high volcanic islands. All the others—of Tuvalu, Phoenix, and the northern Cooks—are atolls like Tokelau.

ONE
Atolls and Villages

The Atolls

Atolls are special kinds of places. Unlike other islands, whose shores and headlands cut off and oppose the surrounding seas, they are more a growth from the sea itself, built of structures more marine than geological, and subject to the winds and weathers of the ocean which both surrounds and washes over the enclosing reef to form a lake within. The patterns of land and water are all horizontals: seawards, the rank grey-brown reef rising to a slight crest at its outer margin with its silver-white line of breaking water; beyond, the long mid-ocean swells rising and falling almost at eye level, their course barely deflected by the slight bulk of the island; within, the more gentle lake of the lagoon meeting with the far islets and their walls of vegetation appearing as an irregular line of low smudges under the huge equatorial skies. The land is no more than these low islets, which rise, at their highest points only five metres or so, above the level of the reefs on which they rest. Their bulk is sand and coral rubble thrown up by the sea, whose storm-driven surges from time to time claim a bit of them back.

Among the widely scattered, small islands and island groups of the Central Pacific, the three atolls that comprise contemporary Tokelau are remarkable perhaps only in being so very small and rather more isolated than most.[1] They lie between latitudes 8° and 10° south and longitudes 171° and 173° west, about 500 km north of Western Samoa, and on the way to nowhere in particular. The scattered, infrequently inhabited atolls of the Phoenix group are some 600 km further north; to the west it is about 1000 km to the atolls of Tuvalu;[2] and Pukapuka, the closest of the northern Cook Islands, is about 600 km to the east. The atolls have long been called Tokelau by their inhabitants, and this is their name on recent maps. On older maps they are named the Union Group.[3] The atolls lie along a northwest to southeast axis of some

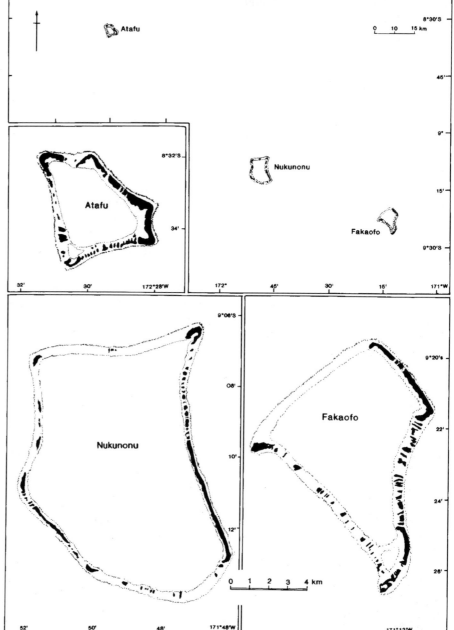

The atolls of Atafu, Nukunonu, and Fakaofo are distant enough from one another to discourage regular travel between them, and are distinctively different in size and configuration. The dry land portions (indicated in black) are approximate only, and in places only mark areas of raised reef and coral rubble with no vegetation.

150 km and together have a land area of only 12.2 km². Atafu, the northern-most and the smallest, has a land area of 3.5 km² and a particularly small lagoon covering only 19 km². Nukunonu, some 90 km southeast of Atafu, has the largest land area, 4.7 km², and an extensive lagoon of 109 km². Fakaofo, with 4 km² of land and some 59 km² of lagoon, is about 60 km further to the east–southeast.

In many respects the three atolls are much the same. Each is set upon a coralline base which rises very steeply from the ocean depths, so there are no offshore anchorages, and they are all surrounded by an unbroken barrier reef, awash to depths of a metre or more at high water but bare and exposed during lower tidal phases, so there are no deepwater passes to the open sea.

The eastern shore of each atoll, facing the prevailing southeast winds and current, has the largest land mass, with some islets extending for several kilometres along the reef and in places being over 200 metres wide. Characteristically these islets have their highest ground along the ocean side, where there is a crest of heaped-up coral boulders and rubble sloping steeply down to a narrow ocean beach and the rough limestone of the reef. Towards the lagoon there is a much longer and more gentle slope of coral rubble, with patches of exposed hard-pan soils and softer, even swampy ground, down to the tranquil lagoon shore. The vegetation is characteristically dense, the ubiquitous coconut palm spreading a high canopy over the profusion of other growth. The dominance of coconut has been achieved by purposeful clearing and planting of many areas for food and copra production—followed by virtual abandonment, except for the hacking back of undergrowth to clear paths and work spaces. Though mixed here and there with organic debris in various stages of decay, the skeletal soils have very low fertility and rain washes straight through the porous surface. Only in more fortunate areas is the rain retained as fresh groundwater. There are no streams.

Flora and fauna

The outer beach crests are typically lined with a thick growth of salt-bush (*Scaevola taccada*), well above head height, forming a solid wall against the

Plantation properties are marked by Xs inscribed on the palm trunks at the stand margin. Similarly marked palms face them. The boundary runs somewhere in between the two marked stands. Photo: J. Huntsman

salt-laden winds. Here too are stunted growths of *Messerschmidia argentea*, straggly pandanus of the less valued varieties, some tough growths of *Pemphis acidula* thriving on what appears to be nothing but beach rock, and a few specimens of other trees which generally do better in the more protected interior. A tangled mass of the creeping *Cassytha filiformus* is the common ground cover, and becomes in some places parasitic on smaller trees. Inland, there is denser, more luxuriant growth and the ground is typically covered with moist accumulations of leaves, logs and other debris and growths of mosses, lichens and various epiphytes. The more valuable edible varieties of pandanus, most of which are said to have been introduced from Tuvalu, are to be found here, and are cultivated to the extent of some planting of branch cuttings and the casual pruning away of competing species. The most valued tree is *kānava* (*Cordia subcordata*) which has a dense, wide-spreading crown studded with delicate orange flowers, and a dark heavy heartwood which is used for the construction of canoes and houses. There are also well-developed specimens of *Guettarus speciosa* and *Pisonia grandis*, and, in between them, smaller seedling specimens mixed with taller shrubs such as *Morinda citrifolia* and *Ficus tinctoria*, the fruits of which are occasionally eaten. The ground cover is mainly ferns, of which the most common is decorative clumps of bird's-nest ferns.

In this stifling setting, swarms of flies and mosquitoes swarm in concentrations high enough to drive off the casual spectator. There are two common species of housefly in the atolls, and one larger bush-fly which dominates in the outer islets. The mosquitoes are all the common day-biting *Aedes polynesiensis*.[4] Other insects also abound, in what Tokelau people regard as an unremarkable and largely unnamed profusion. The only one which presents a threat to life in the islands is the rhinoceros beetle (*Oryctes rhinoceros*), which is highly destructive of coconut palms.[5] Small Polynesian rats (*Rattus exulans*) are the only rodents in the atolls. They are a minor nuisance in the villages but far more numerous in the plantations, where they nest in the coconut palms and gnaw the young green nuts, causing them to fall before they are of any use (Wodzicki 1969). Of much more interest (because they are a delicacy) are the numerous land crabs and birds. There are ten species of land crabs in the atolls, including the large coconut crab (*Birgus latro*) and other edible varieties (Yaldwyn & Wodzicki 1979). Twenty-six bird species have been recorded in Tokelau (Wodzicki & Laird 1970), fifteen of which are sea-birds. Of those which nest in the atolls, the most common are the elegant fairy tern, the brown noddy and the white-capped noddy, which are special culinary treats when captured as fledglings. Larger boobies and frigates also nest in restricted localities. So much for the creatures of the land; of far more import are the creatures of the sea.

In Tokelau everyone is interested, if not obsessed, with fishing, from children just old enough to play in shallows around the village overturning rocks to collect gobies and other small fish, right through to the oldest and most infirm men—repositories, many of them, of arcane knowledge and fishing lore—who totter to the shore to welcome fishing parties and hear the

Some women's fishing speciality is identifying octopus lairs in the reef by the arrangement of disturbed stones at the entrance and enticing or extracting their denizens. The woman with octopus in hand is locating the point between its eyes where a sharp bite will kill it. The woman looking on carries their fishing gear: a half-shell of coconut meat, which is chewed and then spat in the reef shallows to clear the water and make the lairs more visible, and an iron rod to extract the octopus from the lair.
Photo: Marti Friedlander

latest fishing news. Women specialise in capturing octopus—locating their lairs and enticing them out or extracting them. They also occasionally join their menfolk in detaching clams from the reef, in fish drives and interceptions on the reef, and in line fishing. However, women's major role, as of right, is to distribute the catches made by men through the tangled crisscross of customary obligations and expediency. Fish are the important food in Tokelau, perhaps even the staple food. Fish also figure prominently in folklore and hospitality; fishing is central to male prowess and accomplishment and the focus of a good deal of customary etiquette; and, overwhelmingly, it is the constant topic in the ongoing discourse of village life, particularly among men. Fishing is organised around seasonal and monthly movements, which are spoken of in terms of both star cycles and the European calendar, and the local lunar cycle of three sets of ten nights. When discussions of these are combined with observations on the weather, currents, recent catches and the demands of the many special occasions which need provisioning, it is hardly surprising that fish are so much talked about.

Stone traps, positioned in key spots, are tended on appropriate days at the

Right: Kakahi 'yellowfin tuna' are fished with 100–150 metre handlines of 45–90 kilogram breaking strain. The average weight of a landed kakahi is about 20 kilograms. This is a rather small specimen.
Photo: J. Huntsman

Below: Canoes returning to the lagoon shore from communal fishing, netting fish on or crossing the reef. The catch from such communal expeditions is shared throughout the village (see chapter 2).
Photo: Marti Friedlander

right tide to capture fish on their spawning runs from the lagoon across the reef to the open ocean. The most frequently taken species are the common jack and rabbit-fish, although emperors, half-beaks and others may also be caught. Spawning aggregations of other fish are also liable to appear, sometimes in tremendous numbers, at almost any point on the reef, calling for the immediate deployment of nets and large numbers of people to surround and control them. Of these the most common are scad, and up to 10,000 of them may be taken. Large netting drives involve up to a hundred men surrounding

several acres of reef flat and gradually closing in to chase whatever species are present into a net set in a gullet at the lagoon margin. Good catches of marbled sea bass are obtained by line-fishing in the lagoons during the early months of the year, and some men, using private knowledge and personal techniques, are well known for their lagoon catches of emperor, perch and wrass at practically any time. Tridachna clams are prised from the reef, especially during stormy weather.

Although only about half the weight of fish caught in Tokelau comes from waters outside the reef barrier (the proportion varies between the three islands—see below), ocean fishing is generally considered more challenging and exciting. There is the chance of larger fish and a greater element of sport. Skipjack, turtle,[6] marlin and sailfish are especially valued, and the catching of them is subject to some elaborations. Pacific yellowfin are taken by trolling and also by handlining at depths between 40 and 100 fathoms. Other pelagic species are flying fish (taken at night using flares and long-handled scoop nets), barracuda (*Sphyraena picuda*) and wahoo (*Acanthcybium solandri*). Tokelau fishermen also have developed ingenious techniques for exploiting the demersal zone, catching oilfish, the nocturnal black jack, sharks and many other species.

The different atolls

There are no marked environmental contrasts between the three islands. Each atoll is made up of the same elements and has the same resources. There are, however, some differences in the availability of these resources, and it is this, combined with more subtle local variations in the manner in which the resources are controlled and used, that gives each atoll its distinct ecological character.

Atafu is small and compact, all its resources close at hand. Within its shallow lagoon and upon its short stretches of open reef, inshore resources are relatively limited and there are fewer opportunities to trap spawning aggregations at their reef crossings. However, from the village there is easy access to productive ocean fishing grounds, so Atafu understandably specialises in ocean fishing. Along the southern margin of the atoll the numerous small and separate islets have never been cleared for coconut plantations and, as a consequence, there are good stands of various other trees, which are favoured nesting sites for several varieties of sea birds, many of which are taken for food. Here too are good specimens of *kānava* (*Cordia subcordata*). The people of Atafu have husbanded this supply, both for local use and for presentations to others, so that *kānava* timber is the emblematic resource and marked valuable of Atafu.

The plantation lands on Atafu's eastern and western margins are intricately divided among landholding families, and access to these lands is tightly controlled by village authorities, but only very small areas of land in Atafu are held in the name of the village. At the southeastern corner of the atoll, pits have been dug where groundwater is available, and *pulaka* or 'elephant ear taro' (*Cytosperma chamissonis*) is grown.

Felled kānava *timber trimmed and being sectioned for a hull piece of a canoe. The section will be rolled and inspected to determine the best lie, roughly shaped and then floated to the village.*
Photo: J. Huntsman

Nukunonu appears huge in contrast to Atafu, mainly because of its broad, more open lagoon and extensive stretches of open reef. The lagoon is relatively rich, and large catches of fish are made there as well as on the reefs during regular spawning runs. Ocean fishing is less productive because access to the sea is difficult and the good fishing grounds at point reefs are not close at hand. All of the eastern islets are extensively planted with coconuts, and for most of this century Nukunonu has produced more copra than either Atafu or Fakaofo. Lap-streaked whaleboats, which were originally imported and are now locally built, greatly facilitated copra-making. They are more capacious than traditional canoes and large enough to cope with rough lagoon waters even when heavily loaded, and they can sail closer to the wind. Groundwater is virtually absent, being confined to a small well on one small islet on the southeastern margin of the atoll, a considerable distance from the village. Two islets of the northwestern margin, which have fewer coconuts and greater forest cover than other islets, are directly under the control of the village council. There are, however, two extensive tracts of plantation land (one of them comprising the whole northern section of the village islet), which are given over to the Catholic mission, and from which the village

Canoe hull being fashioned in Atafu, 1932. The hull pieces are shaped and lashed, and then the sides are built up with irregular planks shaped to precise joins and lashed to the hull sections.
Photo: G. Macgregor

derives some benefit. Nukunonu's distinctive and highly valued resource is *kie*, a non-fruiting pandanus (*Freycinetia*), used for plaiting fine mats, and intensely cultivated by women in a single, finely divided plot close to the village. It is said that this special variety simply 'does not grow elsewhere in Tokelau'. Though this is not strictly true, the statement is validated by a widely known myth (see introduction and chapter 4), and it is certainly the case that it is not cultivated to any extent in either of the other two islands.

Fakaofo's distinctive resource is *pulaka*, which is grown in large humus-enriched pits dug down to the freshwater lens on many islets of the eastern shore. *Pulaka* is emblematic in signifying that Fakaofo, unlike the other two islands, has extensive supplies of groundwater, and furthermore has always had a reliable well right in the village. The village itself is also distinctive, being confined to a relatively small islet on the western shore that has been artificially built up over the years and extended over the adjacent reef flats. Alongside the village there is a gullet across the reef which allows canoe and small-boat access from the lagoon to open sea during all tidal phases and in all but the most contrary weather. Fakaofo's lagoon and reef produce considerable yields, and the ocean fishing grounds off the point reefs are relatively close to the village. There are extensive land areas controlled directly by the Fakaofo village council. Some of these areas were formerly associated with chiefly office; others, owned at one time by extended families but appropriated by foreigners during the late nineteenth century, came under village control when ownership was restored to the island. All except one, which has large trees and is maintained as a bird sanctuary, are extensively planted in coconut.

Top left: *A* kie *mat to be presented to a newly-wed couple on behalf of the new husband's father's sister. The fringe material is processed from* kānava *bark.* Photo: J. Huntsman

Right: *Stands of* kie *'fine pandanus' in Nukunonu. The area of* kie *plantings is intricately owned and closely controlled by senior women of the village. The dry leaves are collected to make durable, pliable sleeping mats, and the green leaves, after complex processing, become the delicate white fibres used to plait fine mats and* malo, *garments made of 20 cm wide strips of plaiting, now fringed and worn as dance or ceremonial costumes.* Photo: J. Huntsman

27

Above: Tauga 'a bunch of four or more coconut shell water containers' is the only receptacle permitted in the Fakaofo village well. The containers are carefully hung in an airy place, away from any source of contamination. Photo: Marti Friedlander

Right: Fakaofo's fresh-water well in the middle of the village now has a tiered concrete surround. A century and a half ago, the well 'was . . . about fourteen feet deep, neatly walled up, and surrounded by a high fence' (Hale 1846:158), 'and great care was taken to preserve it clean and pure' (Wilkes 1845:15). Photo: Marti Friedlander

The Villages

In spite of the many changes that have occurred over the past 130 years or so, the Tokelau village settlement pattern has remained as it was in the early nineteenth century—although each has expanded over the years to accommodate new types of buildings and an increased population. Each atoll has only a single village, located on the western margin of the atoll where, according to the common view, it has always been and sensibly should be. From here fishermen have access to the more sheltered waters of the lee side of the island, and the laden sailing vessels returning from the plantations on the opposite shore have a straight downwind run. In Atafu and Nukunonu villages growth has been readily accommodated by expanding the settlement into contiguous lands, but in Fakaofo expansion has been hampered by the restricted size of the village islet. For many years the people simply inhabited the islet more and more densely, until by the late 1960s there was just not the space available to build a new school and hospital. These were eventually built on a larger neighbouring islet, and some families moved to the new settlement area that was developed around them. The new settlement remains a suburb, however, and Fakaofo continues as one village in the socio-political sense.

Tokelau villages have a particularly open and intimate air, appearing more as a series of interconnected shady rooms and places than as a collection of separate domestic establishments. This effect comes largely from the distinctive style of Tokelau houses, defined by their elevated foundations and overhanging roofs rather than by external walls. From outside, one can look into every house—and through it, beyond, through the neighbouring houses, to

ATAFU VILLAGE

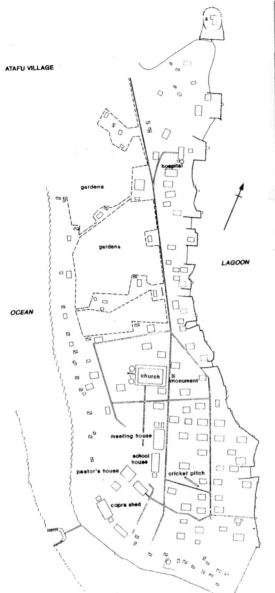

hospital

gardens

gardens

LAGOON

OCEAN

church · monument

meeting house

school house

pastor's house · cricket pitch

copra shed

dwelling house
cookhouse
former house site
outhouse
paths

0   100 m

Part of the Atafu pastor's compound and the open sports field in front of it at the southwest periphery of the village. Photo: J. Huntsman

Atafu village is relatively spacious and open. There is a concentration of dwellings in the vicinity of the public buildings—the church, meeting house, schoolhouse, etc.— but many houses are scattered at the ocean shore where most of the cookhouses are located, within the gardens, and along the lagoon shore on the way to the hospital and beyond. The homestead at the northern tip of the village is built on reclaimed land. Mapped by J. Huntsman, 1970

TOKELAU

Nukunonu village is laid out in a grid, the houses filling the centre and public buildings at the peripheries. Beyond the church to the northwest is the precinct of the Catholic mission, excepting the area where the kie *pandanus stands are and 'have always been'. The houses outside the grid are still aligned to it, and to the church as well. All is rectangular. Southward, across a channel, residence is more recent and houses are scattered among (unmapped) pigsties. This southern extension of the village occurred when the open cricket pitch was created by filling in, with thousands of baskets of coral gravel, a stagnant, smelly saltwater lagoon.* Mapped by J. Huntsman, 1968

Below: Viewed from offshore, Nukunonu village is dominated by its lofty Catholic church (centre). Immediately to the left is the school compound of thatched classrooms, and then the burial ground and stands of kie pandanus. Immediately to the right is the iron-roofed meeting house, further right the copra shed and cookhouses, and behind them, just visible, are dwelling houses. *Photo: Garth Rogers*

From the air, Fakaofo village is a circle of vegetation surrounded by sea, reef, and lagoon, with plantation islets afar. To the left of the village is the papa 'reef flat' where pigs wander, and at its edge the hospital compound. Photograph 1966, courtesy of New Zealand Government Publicity Division, now in National Archives of New Zealand, Wellington (AAQT 6401/A81144)

Fakaofo village is the smallest in area—approximately 4.7 hectares—but throughout the twentieth century has had the greatest number of residents. Despite the straight paths and houses aligned to them, the village is concentric; the public buildings surround the open centre occupied by the cricket pitch and well, the houses and adjacent cookhouses form a middle circle, and the ocean, reef, and lagoon shores, with their overhanging latrines and canoe bays, form the outer circle. Mapped by A. Hooper, 1968 glimpses of shoreline, sea and sky. Breadfruit trees, some of imposing girth and height, provide a canopy above the houses, giving in places the effect of a large airy hall filled with shade and dappled light. The villages are sweet and restful places by comparison with the glare and harsh blues of the surrounding waters.

Living spaces

Typical Tokelau dwelling houses (and as late as the early 1970s they were almost all 'typical') are rectangular, single-roomed structures, with coral-pebble floors covered with coarse coconut-leaf mats, which serve as underlay for finer pandanus sitting and sleeping mats. The low platforms upon which most houses are set extend more than a metre beyond the interior space, sometimes marked by low perimeter walls breached by several entrances. The steeply pitched gabled roofs are covered with pandanus thatching. Beneath the overhanging thatch of the roof coconut-leaf blinds are secured ready to be let down to shield the interior from wind and driving rain. Most houses have little furniture apart from a few lockable wooden trunks for clothing and valuable possessions, and perhaps a homemade wooden armchair or a bed, neither of which is necessarily used, since most people prefer to sit, lounge and sleep on the floor. Mats and fishing gear are stored in the rafters.

Within these open dwellings adult household members customarily have their own loosely defined areas in which they sleep, sit about, and store their belongings. Separate nuclear families may inhabit different ends or corners of the house, and the elderly have set, clearly defined places for themselves. Meals are generally eaten within the house, though food is prepared in separate cookhouses, which are smaller structures, a good deal more roughly constructed and more casually maintained than the dwelling houses. Some are immediately adjacent to the dwellings which they serve, while others are at some distance, even on the far side of the village, so as to minimise the nuisance of smoke from their fired ovens. Cookhouses are often shared by adjacent or related households, but whether shared or not, they are generally open and convivial places, the focus of much casual sociability as women, men and children come and go.

A lot of domestic activity also takes place on the low platforms upon which the houses stand. Clothes are washed and household members bathe there, undressed to the extent that modesty and the time of day or night allow. Here people sit around chatting with neighbours and calling to passers-by, and men settle to braid sennit cord or prepare fishing gear.

A great deal of Tokelau domestic life is thus wide open to the scrutiny of others. Yet for all that it is by no means completely public. Fellow villagers neither peer nor intrude unduly, and a delicate, clear sense of privacy is generally preserved. Neighbourliness is enhanced by casual exchanges of small quantities of cooked food, and whenever a household is dividing large quantities of fish for distribution to relatives, some is always sent to the adjacent households 'because they have been looking on'.

There are very few clearly marked sections or house lots within the vil-

Characteristically Atafu houses are open, with minimal walls or none at all. Blinds plaited of dried coconut fronds are lowered as siding during inclement weather. The foundation is retained by sections of kānava *timber embedded in the ground.* Photo: J. Huntsman

Nukunonu houses are set upon foundations retained by courses of coral slabs, and always have low or full side walls. Blinds are tucked under the eaves to be lowered over windows and doors as protection against wind and rain. Photo: J. Huntsman

Fakaofo houses characteristically have low walls and sometimes are perched directly on their stone foundations rather than having platforms around them. Here the blinds are raised, partly raised and lowered. Photo: Marti Friedlander

33

lages—except on Nukunonu, where a tight rectangular grid of paths sets off each domestic establishment from its neighbours. In Atafu and Fakaofo, land boundaries within the village are unmarked, and often not agreed upon. This gives scope for mild disquiet between neighbours, which erupts when somebody either plants a new tree or begins building in a space that others feel is rightly theirs. People do not, however, lightly contest the claims and actions of others. Village courts, following complicated and at times contestable evidence, are only too liable to come up with decisions which are agreeable to neither party, but which are in the interest of a completely different group. In these circumstances, accommodations and informal agreements between neighbours over boundaries generally prevail.

Public buildings

In addition to household dwellings, each village has a number of communal buildings and spaces, the most important of which is a meeting house, venue for all village-wide gatherings as well as for many smaller gatherings. Each village has a different sort of meeting house. Fakaofo, somewhat given to grandiloquent public buildings, has a large traditional thatched structure built along the lines of an ordinary dwelling but some 25 metres long and with massive posts and a steep roof soaring up among the surrounding breadfruit trees. Atafu's meeting house is rather smaller, with a low ironclad roof, while Nukunonu simply makes use of an open-sided cargo shed built by the New Zealand Administration. Visitors are formally received and farewelled in the meeting houses, and all communal feasts are held there. They are also the venues for dances, large church-based occasions, the meetings and work projects of various groups, wedding feasts and other festivities.

Communal village latrines, segregated by sex, allow for meetings of a different sort. These are squat rectangular structures supported by stout posts set out over the shoreline in the lagoon shallows, roofed and walled with coconut thatch and floored with wide, smoothly adzed boards set 100 mm or so apart. People may spend hours at a time in them, smoking and gossiping convivially. If the meeting houses are the prime site of village structure, where interactions tend to follow established and regular patterns and individuals and groups enact their formal roles, the latrines can be seen as the prime site of village communitas constantly being generated by random, slowly changing collections of individuals thrown together in intimate familiarity. The latrines are in fairly constant use at all hours of the day and night, and it is here that one can learn what is really going on, from the latest gossip and scandal to detailed news of just-completed fishing expeditions. In this setting a respected elder may be questioned closely about decisions made in the village council (a difficult thing to do in other contexts) and even, at times, told what others think about the decisions. Confidences may be exchanged and opinions casually tested.

Each village also has a cleared and open space where catches of fish and other produce or goods are brought for village-wide division and distribution. Then, there is an open space known everywhere as *te malae kilikiti* 'the cricket field' for Tokelau's favourite community sport. In both Atafu and Fakaofo the concrete pitch is simply set roughly in the centre of an open area right within the village with the field of play extending beyond obstructions like houses, churches and trees to the surrounding reef and lagoon waters. In the mid 1960s, Nukunonu created an open cricket field by filling in a brackish swamp on an islet connected by a concrete causeway to the village.

Other public buildings and places, built at the instigation of the Administration, are small hospitals, school rooms, copra sheds and shacks for radio transmitters. The schools, hospitals and 'radio shacks' are all well used, and their small local staffs—a doctor, a radio operator, teachers and nurses—are all fully involved in regular village activities.

The village churches, though, are by far the largest, most ornate and most loved structures in Tokelau. All are constructed of imported materials, bought with locally raised funds, and built with village labour. They are also intensively used, not only for three regular services and at least one other regular meeting every Sunday, but also for services and meetings and choir practices during the week. The local pastors, catechists and priests are provided with spacious and substantial housing, somewhat set apart from the rest of the village, yet heavily implicated in its socio-religious life.

The everyday world of Tokelau people is intensely centred on their villages, the places where everyone lives, from which people go out to harvest or fish and to which they return. The villages all have clear boundaries beyond which people should not go except for stated purposes and with the knowledge of others. A person walking along a path is continually asked: 'Where might you be going?' This is a standard sociable greeting but it is also an enquiry. Where a particular person is, or has gone, should be known, and if it is not, or the person does not reappear as anticipated, then something is awry—he or she is 'lost' and must be 'sought' and 'found'. In the villages people move to and fro, openly, their comings and goings unobtrusively monitored, their movements respecting the space of others. Here people are protected and safe among their fellow villagers. They, like their village, are bounded.

Given that atoll life centres on its village, and that the inhabitants of the atoll are so centred in the village, it is perhaps not surprising that atoll, village and people are all known by the same proper name. Atafu or Nukunonu or Fakaofo are both the places and the people who are of those places. Attributing character, words and behaviour to Atafu, Nukunonu or Fakaofo is to express things as Tokelau people express them.[7]

The Recent Past

The atolls, the villages and the people of Tokelau, thought by most people as remote and isolated, have sought, experienced and had thrust upon them contacts with the world beyond Tokelau waters during the past 150 years or so. The résumé that follows briefly charts those contacts.

The first reliable news of Tokelau reached the outside world in the 1840s.

Much daily activity centres on the cookhouses, where the meals for the day are accumulated and prepared, and people come and go. Women share cookhouses with their close kin, and neighbours will often be accommodated. Women casually request cooking space on an established fire if they have only a small amount to cook. Photo: Marti Friedlander

It reported that the islands were politically unified, and supported a population of around 1000.[8] Over the following generation or so, as the islands were steadily engulfed by the processes of European expansion, many people were forcibly removed, for the supposed good of their souls, or for the labour which they might provide. Five hundred people are reported to have been taken to Uvea by Marist missionaries in early 1852. In early 1863 slavers engaged in the Peruvian labour trade kidnapped a further 250 or so, most of

The interior of Fakaofo's spacious meeting house is spread with dried coconut frond mats. The view is from the front or lagoon end of the structure. Photo: Marti Friedlander

Latrines, separate for females and males, are set out over the lagoon: some extend out from reclamations, others are connected to shore by a plank walk. To the left, here, copra is laid out to sun-dry on a frame.
Photo: J. Huntsman

them men, and during the same month at least 64 others died of the dysentery brought by a Protestant mission ship. By mid 1863, the population was less than 300. The pre-European polity collapsed, and Tokelau became effectively three separate atoll villages.

In the years immediately before and after 1863 missions and traders moved in, bringing new ideas and institutions that reshaped the economic and belief systems of the remnant population. The group became a protectorate of Great Britain in 1889, and was in 1910 attached to the protectorate of the Gilbert and Ellice Islands for 'administrative convenience', and in 1916 was annexed to join the Gilbert and Ellice Islands as Britain's most remote colony. This arrangement lasted less than a decade, however. In 1925 Britain transferred its administrative responsibilities to the governor of New Zealand.

During all of this period Tokelau was left pretty much to itself, passing from protectorate to colony, from the remote hands of Great Britain to the scarcely less remote hands of New Zealand. Local officials were appointed and paid; laws and regulations were introduced, but were interpreted largely according to local canons of relevance; copra was made for sale, but the money obtained was not much, and it was in any case transacted according to the customary principles that governed rights to the coconuts from which it was made. Such formal education as there was remained the responsibility of Samoan-educated pastors and catechists. Each Tokelau village, linked only sporadically to the outside world and largely cut off from the other two villages, tended to its own concerns, evolving its own particular institutional structures to cope with the basic business of Tokelau life. Under New Zealand administration, very little changed. The people were generally healthy, peaceful and staunchly Christian. Each village took care of its own affairs. The official view was one of benevolent paternalism—Tokelau was regarded as an idyllic South Seas backwater, best left to its own devices.

It was not until well after the Second World War that New Zealand

Set on a reclamation adjacent to a canoe bay, this Fakaofo residential complex consists of the dwelling house (left), cookhouse, and latrine (right). Photo: A. Hooper

showed a concern for the development of social services. The group became formally 'part of New Zealand' in 1948, and Tokelauans became New Zealand citizens later in the same year. Secular education was introduced in the early 1950s. Schools and hospitals were built, and staffed by local people trained in Western Samoa and Fiji. Radio communications were improved, and, in the early 1960s, a few students were sent away for further education in New Zealand. The population had risen rapidly, reaching a peak of just over 1900 people in 1966, and concern over this increase led to the establishment of a government-sponsored plan for wholesale migration to New Zealand. In late 1967, when we first began our field research in Tokelau, this resettlement scheme was already well under way, and was regarded with enthusiasm by the people.

By 1971 some 356 people had gone as assisted migrants to New Zealand. Others had left under their own auspices, and the population was down to around 1600. Things were changing, though Tokelau life was still village life, caught within fixed and regular limits—the demands of subsistence, vagaries of weather and crops, social and institutional obligations, births, deaths, and the regular slow processes of seasonal change. Each island had a complement of between ten and fifteen salaried government employees—mainly teachers and hospital workers—as well as a group of ten men who worked for what were no more than token wages on construction projects. But there was really very little money around, and the annual per capita income was less than NZ$40. The subsistence economy prevailed. Houses were all made of local wood and thatch, and transport was by sailing canoes. An Administration-chartered ship from Western Samoa appeared only once every three months or so, staying a day or so off each island to transship mail, cargo and passengers. Then it was gone. Only a few households had radios. Urgent messages came and went by Morse, through the crackles and static of isolation. The villages really seemed oblivious, for long calm stretches of time, to the concerns of the outside world.

That was all to change very rapidly over the next decade, as Tokelau came under the scrutiny of the United Nations Committee on Decolonisation, and was thus linked very directly with the outside world. By 1980 or so, Tokelauans talked of the *poto fou* 'new understandings', which informed and motivated their collective lives, and would contrast them, at times wonderingly, with the older ones, which had prevailed only a decade before. That, however, is another long and complex story, and one better not attempted until its outlines become clear through the flurry and contradictions of the current aid-driven frenzy of 'Development'.

TWO
Te Nuku—*The Village*

Precepts of Village Life

Ulu ki loto o te fatu 'Enter into the rock'

This proverbial statement refers not to the hard, volcanic rocks of high Polynesian islands but to Tokelau's coral boulders, riddled with holes and crannies, which join and intersect, and where small fish seek safety from their predators. The village is the rock, physically *te kakai* 'place of residence' clearly set apart from surrounding sea and adjacent *vao* 'bush'. More to the point, the village is a constructed social order of institutions and organisations, as intricately linked as the coral passages, composed of *te nuku kātoa* 'the village whole'.[1]

Entering into the village involves more than just being present there, it means taking part, joining in, working and playing with compatriots, and submitting to the *pule* 'authority, control' of village life. Most people 'enter into' the village by birth; a few join it permanently by marriage or temporarily as visitors hosted by kinsmen. These who join are included within appropriate institutions and organisations, are expected to take part in village activities, and are automatically subject to the *pule*. Occasionally people of the village *tū kehe* 'stand apart' by not joining in village affairs, perhaps from shame over something they have done or disapproval of something others have done. Such withdrawal is never complete, and little is made of it, though most other people know the reason for it. After a time, efforts are made to draw such a recluse back 'into the village' and sooner or later they succeed.

Persons may be resident in the village who have neither been born there nor joined as spouses or visiting kin. They are outsiders referred to by euphemisms stressing their lack of attachment, helplessness and difference; they are accorded generous hospitality, but they are neither expected nor encouraged to enter fully into village life. Lacking the necessary skills and local resources, they can be accommodated but not fully included. Resident pastors are prototypical outsiders and the strategies devised to accommodate them are used as the model for dealing with others. The security which 'the rock' provides is extended to outsiders, their safety and wellbeing is a village preoccupation, but they can contribute little to that security—except as pastors may intercede with the Almighty.

What makes the village safe and secure is that it is ordered and controlled by precedents and institutions, regulations and practices, devised by ancestors and elders. The order emanating from the village extends to the whole atoll and the seas immediately around it, but beyond the village boundaries it is rather more tenuous, both because control is not so firmly established and because the unexpected may more often be encountered.

Only very rarely is anybody expelled from the village, partly because people tend to leave of their own volition when their situation becomes too tenuous. Repeated behaviour detrimental to the peace of the village is grounds for expulsion, which takes one of two forms. Banishment (*fakaaunukua* lit. 'caused to be without village') removes culprits socially and physically; they are ordered to go somewhere else at the earliest opportunity.[2] Constraint (*tūnoa* lit. 'stand bound or ignored') excludes the culprit socially: 'a person placed *tūnoa* is restrained in everything, is no longer free'. People so constrained are confined to their place of residence and socially isolated and ignored. Though remaining physically in the village, socially they are disconnected from it.

Te nuku māopoopo 'The village united'

Māopoopo is a pervasive theme of Tokelau rhetoric; rhetorical speeches are a prominent feature of all Tokelau gatherings; and purposeful gatherings are a routine part of village life. Those who have assembled, whether they represent the whole village or some recognised and organised group of villagers, can count on being praised for being *māopoopo* or faulted for not being *māopoopo*. Visibly a gathering is *māopoopo* if all who should be present are indeed present. They have set aside their other concerns and have committed themselves to those of the group; their physical presence is a statement of commitment and unity of spirit. Conversely, when a gathering is poorly attended it is apparent to all that those not present are not committed and not of like mind with those that are present. *Māopoopo* is a delicate essence. At its zenith all are caught up in an exuberant euphoria; at its nadir all are plunged into deep despair. It cannot be enforced for it ultimately resides in the feelings and judgements of many people, so it must be cultivated and nurtured, while at the same time it is rhetorically promoted as crucial to the wellbeing of all—'the village united' is where *feālofani* 'mutual compassion' and *filēmū* 'peace' prevail.

Māopoopo as a problematic ideal in action is of particular issue in two recurrent situations: *fono* 'meetings' and *fakamua* 'pre-emptive, communal' activities. Examples of both will be described in subsequent chapters; here these situations are discussed generally as they illustrate the dilemmas of *māopoopo. Fono* are a pervasive and indispensable feature of Tokelau social life. Any group larger than a nuclear family or household derives its legitimacy, organisation and continued existence from regular meetings. Here collective decisions are taken which are binding on all members, since they are party to them, and this applies to casual, transitory groups as much as to institutionalised, long-established ones.

A *fono* is fundamentally a meeting of the whole or its selected representatives, and its success in reaching agreement and the legitimacy of its decisions rest in large part on the proportion of the whole which is present and the consensus they achieve. On the one hand, a few zealous and active members do not constitute a *fono*, and on the other, the proportion of the whole required for the meeting to be deemed *māopoopo* is quite indeterminate. However, if a large portion of the whole is absent for whatever reason, then the *fono* simply does not take place, and this is dispiriting to those who have arranged the meeting and those who have attended. Rather than disband they are apt to sit around speculating about why others did not show up, examining their own and others' possible faults. Though some among them may attempt to lift their spirits, an atmosphere of *lotovāivai* 'discouragement' prevails. If a *fono* is begun by a small number of its constituent members, but in the hope that more of them will soon appear, the proceedings are lethargic, decisions are deferred, and the most spirited discussions may be about ways of inducing people to attend. Were the meeting to make any decision it would be severely compromised. It would not be considered binding on those absent and they may very properly challenge it later.

Thus the prerequisite of a successful *fono* is *māopoopo*, i.e. the physical presence of everyone. Whether the *fono* is a success depends on whether those present can achieve *māopoopo*, i.e. unity of spirit.

> *The chosen chairperson opens the* fono *with standard brief words of greeting, thanks and encouragement, addressed in part to God and otherwise to those attending, who are seated cross-legged at respectful attention in a roughly circular pattern. The chair announces the subject of the meeting, invites discussion and then retires into silence. A chair does not lead or direct the discussion nor intrude with his/her own views, except when urged to do so as a member of the meeting. Consequently, the discussion is wide-ranging, often diverging from the topic at issue and digressing to irrelevant concerns, until someone brings it back to the issue at hand.*
>
> *People are expected to speak frankly and directly, 'not concealing their thoughts'. Though this may mean that there is open disagreement, people are urged to speak out and unexpressed disagreement is disparaged since it cannot be countered or reconciled to achieve the intention of the meeting—consensus. Frank opinions contrary to those expressed by others are presented in a guise of humility and softened by apologies. The ways of doing this are standard oratorical techniques. One of the most prominent is to use the diminutive first person pronoun* kita *'my insignificant self'; another is to deprecate one's opinion by appending the modifier* tauanoa *'insignificant', as, for example,* he manatu tauanoa *'an insignificant thought'. Statements of opinion are prefaced by the phrase 'with respects to the meeting' or by reminding the listeners that 'this is an open meet-*

ing', implying that the speaker could not venture such a frank opinion in any other context, but that it is right and proper to do so here. Frank opinions humbly put are encouraged by listeners exclaiming 'well done' or 'view well taken'. Though all are urged to speak their minds, certain features of debate are absent. There are no interjections, there is no ridicule, and no one belittles the opinion of another (though at large gatherings unflattering comments may be murmured between congenial neighbours to relieve the boredom of a long, irrelevant speech). Fono etiquette and propriety demand that each person has a chance to express an opinion without interruption and thereby participate in the decision-making process. Accordingly, progress towards a decision is leisurely and indirect.

When, after all have had their say, there appears to be general agreement, the chair phrases the resolution as he or she understands the collective sentiment, and if there is no objection it is assumed that all present concur. Alternatively, if several distinct viewpoints have emerged during discussion, a show of hands is proposed. The separate propositions are voted upon and the number favouring each is announced. At this point, the chair calls for another show of hands and the proposition favoured by the majority is carried unanimously. All present have consented and are truly māopoopo.

Occasionally, when opinion is strongly divided and the issue a weighty one, the *fono* will be reluctant to press for a resolution and will *tolo* 'postpone' the subject for further discussion at some unspecified time in the future. To take a vote would endanger *māopoopo*. *Fono* etiquette would require one side to vote unanimously with the other despite strong feelings to the contrary, and this minority might only apparently consent. Preservation of precious *māopoopo* should not be jeopardised by pressing a resolution. Delay gives time for further thought, informal discussion and private negotiation. A *fono*, if it is to be successful, must conclude without rancour, for the feeling that one's heartfelt opinion has been dismissed or forcibly overridden prompts people to absent themselves from the next *fono*, which then, or course, cannot possibly be *māopoopo*. In short, a *fono* is not judged by the decisions it makes, but by the *māopoopo* it engenders. However, the decisions that are made usually entail collective activity—or *galuega fakamua*.

Lexically *fakamua* is a modifier composed of two morphemes, *faka-* 'cause' and *mua* 'first', which is contrasted with *fakamuli* 'cause last'. These literal glosses suggest one attribute of anything *fakamua*: it pre-empts or takes primacy over anything else. To do something *fakamua* is to do it instead of doing anything else; for example, a fishing expedition *fakamua* pre-empts any other kind of fishing. In the *Tokelau Dictionary*, *fakamua* is defined as 'communal, of the village' and *fakamuli* as 'remain at home, stay behind'; the opposition between the two words is not apparent unless it is recognised that to 'remain at home' implies not participating in communal activities, and therefore doing something on one's own. The most common synonym of *fakamua* is *fakatahi* 'as one, together' which is juxtaposed to *tautahi* 'alone, by oneself', or individually. In these contrasts is an implicit morality. When activities are *fakamua*, all relevant members of the village participate *fakatahi*, and in so doing embody village *māopoopo* 'unity'. People are expected to put aside all other activities or plans, things that they might do alone and at home or for their own benefit and welfare rather than that of the village as a whole.

Most often *fakamua* tasks involve only all able-bodied males, but women may on occasion be included in this village workforce or undertake some complementary or supportive task. Women also have their own *fakamua* enterprises, most often mat-plaiting projects, for which *māopoopo* is less strictly dictated in recognition that some women's tasks, e.g. infant care, cannot be set aside. Thus, *fakamua* activity as pre-emptive and communal is in fact interpreted to include everyone who should be present and is applied to some designated section of the village polity. If, for example, one 'side' (roughly half) of the village decides to fish *fakamua* and the other 'side' decides not to, the former may say that they, as a 'side', are *fakamua*, while the other 'side' is not, which carries the implication that they are *māopoopo* and morally superior. For *fakamua* activity is morally justified as better than *fakamuli* activity and this is why it comes first. Its morality is expounded as contributing to the welfare of the whole village and making everyone equal, since every single person of the village derives equal benefit from what is done. Assertions such as these are manifestly true and unquestioned.

Another more pragmatic rationale asserts that by working together tasks that for a few would be onerous and difficult—even impossible—are easily and quickly done. Both the pooled strength and skill of the village and the good fellowship that comes from being together contribute to the success of the venture. People are said to work with boundless enthusiasm. Often this is true, but not always. Again, it comes down to the delicate business of generating and maintaining *māopoopo*.

Sometimes lethargy can be attributed to the nature of the task itself. Understandably, a *fakamua* fishing party which catches only a few fish is dispirited. The fishermen may grumble that the enterprise was misdirected, or that if they had gone their separate ways there would at least have been fish for their immediate families. Tasks that drag on day after day, preventing people from attending to their own concerns, or tasks that seem minor or inconsequential and not worthy of *fakamua* status, provoke antipathy. Yet people are prone to attribute the prevailing discontent not to the circumstances but to the absence of *māopoopo* among the participants, even when all who should be present are present. What is missing is the spirit.

> *Its absence is marked by dilatory assembly, the non-appearance of necessary equipment, which has to be sought while everyone sits around grumbling about the delay, by people disappearing once the task is finally underway or only half-heartedly contributing to it. Muted recriminations are directed at those not doing their part by those that feel they are doing more than their share. The atmosphere is the very opposite of that which is supposed to prevail when people work together; it is one of bitterness and discontent, and attempts to raise spirits fall flat. When the task is finished, everyone quickly departs only to gather in twos and threes elsewhere and gripe.*

Such a state of melancholy does not last long since everyone is aware of it, and concerted efforts are made to overcome it and restore the spirit of *māopoopo*. The strategies are numerous: exhortation and recrimination are perhaps the least effective; modified work procedures and organisation may help; food is surely the most effective. Often when *fakamua* activities are being planned, the first matter decided is the menu and arrangements for feeding the workers. Food draws people together in getting it, preparing it and consuming it, and in eating together conviviality flourishes and *māopoopo* is generated.

Fakamua enterprises, even when enthusiastically joined, seem to an un-initiated observer unorganised and undirected, even chaotic. Actually, the workforce is finely organised and tasks closely supervised though there are no directors in evidence and little in the way of explicit direction. Having worked together for years, the participants know the routines and the strengths, weaknesses, abilities and ineptitudes of their co-workers. Tasks are taken or assigned on the basis of physical ability and skill. The young and strong labour under the watchful eye of an older experienced person; a task requiring particular expertise is undertaken by someone with that skill; the aged and weak do what they can and applaud the efforts of the more active.

A diffuse din punctuated with guffaws accompanies the activity as jokes and stories are told among groups of workers, and banter and taunts hurled between them. This dispersed jollity inevitably is suddenly broken by a louder than usual remark which rivets the attention of all. Someone, or perhaps a pair, are taking centre stage. An exchange of witty taunts, a bit of horseplay, a mocking parody has begun. Older people are the usual actors and performances erupt in slack periods of the day's routine, but performers may act up at any time and everyone will stop whatever they are doing to become their audience. The act may be planned or impromptu, a set piece or topically new. The dialogue or monologue is based on locally shared longstanding jokes, foibles of ancestors, idiosyncrasies of those present or absent, and well-known, usually absurd, events.[3] Action tends to be exaggerated and repeated, particularly if it gets a laugh, but a slight and telling gesture may get an uproarious response. Foul language laces the perform-ance and obscenity is sometimes its very core. That the performers, with some notable exceptions, are normally restrained and dignified older people only in-creases the effect. When the act ends and the laughter subsides, everyone returns to the task at hand still chuckling and full of good spirits.

Such comic diversions not only provide a welcome respite from hard work but also contribute to the feelings of *māopoopo* of the occasion, as everyone attends to the performance and shares their intensely local jokes. Everyone knows they will happen, since they are part of working together, but only the actors know what will happen and when. Anticipation heightens the general mood of the occasion and a striking turn may raise it to a state of euphoria. When this is achieved people will linger after the task or work of the day is done, reluctant to leave the atmosphere of *māopoopo* that the day's activities have produced.

Clearly, the ambience of *fono* and *fakamua* gatherings is utterly different, yet both occasions aim to achieve *māopoopo*. At a *fono* people are restrained and cautious, meticulously considerate and respectful of others. *Fono* should be dignified, and are the very antithesis of the derisive banter, teasing and horseplay which is so characteristic of boisterous *fakamua* gatherings. Between these two types of gatherings there is a mercurial change in atmosphere and behaviour, yet the two are linked in a continual alternation: *fono* resolving what is to be done followed by *fakamua* pre-emptive doing of it, then another *fono* and so on. The one is the necessary complement of the other and when both are successful *māopoopo* prevails, and the village *is* united.

He toeaina ke i te mulivaka 'An elder to be in the canoe's stern'

A Tokelau village, however united, contains within itself a clearly differentiated polity, and this proverb conveys the most pervasive basis of differentiation—age. A canoe's stern is the place of precedence, occupied by the person responsible for the welfare and safety of the crew. Its occupant should be experienced and knowledgeable, should be aware of all possible dangers and know immediately what should be done in any situation. He steers the canoe and commands his crew. Here there is no negotiation, no compromise, simply command and compliance. The canoe in the proverb is the village, and those entrusted with its safety, those who direct and control it, are those recognised as *toeaina* 'elders/(old men)'. (The gloss 'elder' is preferred because it conveys the respect denoted by the term *toeaina*. Elderly women are referred to by a term of like respect as *lōmatua*, pl. *lōmātutua* glossed 'matron'.[4] When referring to older people of both sexes, elder is used.)

The hierarchy of authority in a Tokelau village is clear and pervasive. Anyone older is entitled to command anyone younger, and the younger person is expected to comply. Between people of nearly equivalent age a younger person will usually defer to one slightly older, but the older will rarely issue commands. However, as the age gap between younger and older widens, the more likely it is that interaction will be characterised by command and compliance, and when a person reaches the status of elder or matron, roughly sixty years of age, he or she is accorded respect and may have a commanding position within the village.

In a sense this hierarchy is an egalitarian one, not because everyone has an equal say, but because anyone can look forward to having a greater say as the years go by. People are not unequal, they are older and younger, and, in the Tokelau view of human nature, experience and knowledge, judgement and wisdom increase with age.

An elder should be 'in the canoe's stern' because long experience has given him knowledge, made him far-seeing, with the ability to weigh all the implications of any decision rather than seeing only its immediate effects. His developed judgement and wisdom lead him to be considerate of others, rather than impatient and determined to have his own way, to be open to compromise and to seek to reconcile the opposing views of others.

In daily interaction people do show respect and defer to their elders in both word and action. An elder, if present, is the spokesperson in even the most casual gathering. For example, it is almost impossible to elicit any information about any aspect of Tokelau life (or anything else for that matter) from a younger person if older ones are present. All questions are simply referred to them. If their answer is equivocal, or even obviously irrelevant or wrong, no one younger will correct them. At the very most someone may prompt an elder with a question, as though asking for information, in the hope the answer given will correspond with that which the questioner already knows. The etiquette of respect requires a person entering an elder's presence to approach quietly, to sit formally, with crossed legs, and to remain silent until spoken to. Elders are served food first at any domestic or public gathering, and people await their word before commencing any task or activity. Elders are continually being consulted, asked permission, appraised of intentions by others, who are seeking approval and sanction for their plans. By courtesy they should be kept informed; by right they authorise action.

Male·elders are always at the forefront at formal gatherings, seated somewhat apart in places they habitually occupy and surrounded by empty space. They are always called upon to open and close the event with appropriate remarks, and if decisions are to be announced, reprimands given, or strictures laid down, an elder makes the pronouncements, even though he may have had no part in their framing. It is frequently said that the elders are the *leo* 'voice' of the village.

The ultimate elder status of senior elder (*taumatua*) may devolve upon a man when he is past his years of effective action and thought. Nonetheless, he receives formal homage and is celebrated for his achievement of longevity, even though his words may carry no weight. A man who reaches this exalted status while retaining some of his vigour and all of his mental faculties is consulted and deferred to in all matters of village concern. He is sought out, informed and gives his approval to tentative decisions reached in his absence, and when he is present he is the final spokesman.

Despite the veneration Tokelau people pay to their elders, they are realistic about the actual capabilities of individual ones. It is privately acknowledged that certain elders have never been particularly wise, knowledgeable or selfless, and that elderly people are sometimes senile. These individual exceptions are not cited to fault the basic premise, and there are numerous strategies to circumvent the entitlement to command. An opinion may be acceded to, but not acted upon; a dictate may be respectfully listened to, but ignored. And, because elders act in concert, the responsible among them make use of these strategies as much, if not more, than others.

While the premise of elderly wisdom and capability might possibly be questioned on the evidence of the living, it is unquestioned when people reminisce about the elders of former generations. Older people recall the elders of their youthful years as awesome figures and strict disciplinarians, who had great stores of knowledge and were revered by all, and furthermore achieved great age yet retained their youthful vigour. A photo of Fakaofo elders in 1924 captures some of their formidable qualities: their white tobacco-stained beards (beards are now regarded as disgusting, an aberration of rebellious youth), their well-worn walking sticks, their sombre garments tucked up in a distinctive way, their stern, even dour expressions. Whenever

47

*Elders of Fakaofo 1924.
Left front (with walking
stick) is Solomona/Teuku
who was Magistrate in
the 1910s and 1920s.
Front centre is Kauai
who returned from Uvea
in mid 1863, and was
probably the oldest elder
at this time.* Photo taken
by and courtesy of
E.H. Bryan jr

elders gathered, nobody, it is said, would dare to walk nearby or make a noise
which might disturb them. Yet people recall that hoots of raucous laughter
would issue from these restricted precincts, testifying that in the company of
their peers they were not solemn and stern. When they wanted anything
brought to them, they would shout a command to anyone within earshot to
fetch it. And woe to the child who wandered too near or was tardy in carrying
out a command, for he or she would be grabbed up by an elder and hugged
against his beard or—most horrible to recall—have rubbed under its nose an
elder's well-used toothpick. The recollections are endless. The following recounts the elders' daily routine:

> They would all normally waken before the cock's crow in the morning, going
> down to the lagoon's edge and there converse while gazing at the stars, because
> it was their responsibility to direct the people in what should be done—whether
> the spawning places were to be visited or the crossing places watched. . . . These
> fishing ventures were led by the elders accompanied by adult men, and they were
> undertaken for the village. Most fishing in those times was communal. This was
> because the elders were most concerned to provide for the young and helpless of
> the land. That is the true 'tradition' of the Tokelau way: those who rule and direct
> look to the welfare of all, and not to their own welfare. The following day the
> elders again awaken and go to the shore and converse there. . . . If an elder
> overslept others would say to him: 'You've slept as a child by sleeping soundly, for
> an elder sleeps with one eye while the other eye is awake.' When the discussion
> finished they would leave the shore and go to the Falepā [a men's house where
> fishing equipment was made and stored], where they stayed the whole day, and
> after darkness fell they put down their work of preparing sennit, twisting and
> plaiting line, or making fishing gear. . . . On every single day these are the things
> they did. (Perez n.d.2:11–12)

What is emphasised in this account, and in many others, is the elders'
diligence and concern for the wellbeing of all, and their pervasive control and

48

direction of community activities. Early this century, when the village populations were much smaller, such tight control was possible. For example, people tell of how harvesting trips to the outer plantations were regimented so that all canoes left the village together for the same designated islet, and how, when they arrived there, all would wait at the lagoon shore for the command of an elder to enter the groves, where each would go to his own section and harvest. The canoes did not have to wait to return together, but on arrival at the village the cargo of each was inspected to make sure the pre-announced limit of items had not been exceeded. These were 'the good old days', when elders were truly elders and everything was as it should be; and they affirm the rightness of a social order that in actuality must necessarily depart from the ideal. Furthermore, younger people today still affirm it; when they are faced with a difficult situation and are unsure what to do, they may lament *hagā ko lava he toeaina* 'if only an elder were here (to guide us)'.

E nofo te fafine i loto, ka ko te tagata e fano i te auala
'The woman stays inside, while the man goes in the path'

Most specifically, this oft-voiced phrase refers to the sister who remains in her natal home at marriage and her brother who departs that home at marriage to live elsewhere. More generally, the 'paths' of men take them into the public arena and out upon the sea, while women regularly 'stay' within their home and village. In this scheme of things, women are properly inside and men outside, but this is a relative matter and reflects Tokelau ideas about women and men rather than actual social restrictions.

The general Tokelau view is that women and men are different and complementary by their very nature. Women are regarded as valuable and at the same time vulnerable: valuable because they embody the life and continuity of their families and community; vulnerable because they are more apt to attract and are less able to withstand external dangers and difficulties than men are. Women should be cherished and protected *i loto o te kāiga* 'inside their family' and village where dangers are few and protectors are many. Men too are valued by their families and community specifically for their strength, which enables them to protect and provide for others. This strength allows them to withstand hardship and danger, but a man's strength is itself dangerous both to himself and others if it is not tempered by inculcated qualities of caution and self-restraint. The young are foolhardy; elders are judicious.

These ideas about the nature of women and men go some way towards explaining why men are prominent in doing, planning and directing for the village, and why women often appear to be at the peripheries of village activity. However, women are neither excluded from public affairs nor inconsequential as members of the village united. They have an essential complementary role to play whether in concert with their menfolk or as the 'women of the village'.

When working together with the men their activities are directed by the male elders, who pointedly applaud the women's efforts and tolerate (or are resigned to) the high-jinks at which some are so accomplished. However, when 'women of the village' gather, the matrons instruct, admonish and direct their juniors as do their male counterparts among the 'men of the village'. The matrons are the repositories of knowledge and expertise in particular domains, which not even the most knowledgeable elderly man would presume to possess, and therefore have their own sphere of control and authority. Yet, as 'women of the village', they insist that they abide by the authority of the elders. The point is that authority in relationships of complementarity is quite different than in relationships of hierarchy: complementarity entails some degree of autonomy. The elders of the village make requests to the 'women of the village' and the women decide how the request will be fulfilled. The elders may counsel but they rarely command. The older women for their part keep the elders—their husbands—informed and seek their endorsement of their own plans. In short, mutual deference and utmost consideration characterise the formal interaction of the 'elders of the village' and the 'women of the village'.

The underlying precepts of village life, while manifest in diverse situations and expressed in many ways, are fundamentally two: *māopoopo*, a communal, egalitarian ethic which speaks to selfless commitment and the equality of all; and *pule*, the moral necessity of authority and control exercised by the elderly. In the abstract, these two precepts may be counterposed, one positing uniformity and equality, the other differentiation and dominance. Yet Tokelau people take the two together as essential prerequisites for their order, well-being and safety. What links them is a notion of consent and judicious cultivation of it in a continual round of *fono* and less formal negotiations. Just as authority is vested in an assembly of elders who must agree among themselves in order to exercise it, so consent is not individual preference but the will of a group. It is in the multifarious and crosscutting institutionalised groupings within the village that the interplay of precepts and the achievement of consent may be appreciated in practice. The number of recognised bodies, committees, 'sides', sections and clubs that are regularly or occasionally active in a Tokelau village is astounding, particularly considering the number of people available to be members. Each village has a like repertoire of groups but each gives prominence to certain groups, and there are variations too in their organisational features, activities and the way they articulate one with another. In the sections which follow, the various types of groups are described, taking note of their distinctive features in the separate villages. These variations both reflect and mark the uniqueness of each atoll.

Te Nuku Pulea *'The Governed Village'*

Fono a Toeaina 'Council of Elders'

The pre-eminent institution in every Tokelau village is the Council of Elders.[5] This is the central governing body, and it has ultimate responsibility for everything that takes place within the village, and in the atoll and its immediate environs; it is charged as well with managing relations with the outside world. Much of what routinely happens in the village is under the direct control and supervision of the Council, and no other organisation can undertake any concerted action without first obtaining the Council's approval. Though the Council may allocate some set time each week for the activities of a particular organisation, it may decide from time to time that something else should take precedence. The Council, too, may ask or direct other organisations to undertake activities on its behalf, and such activities take precedence over any others. Any instructions or requests received from the Administration or any other source outside the atoll are transmitted to the Council for its information and discussion. From among the Council's membership two elected officials serve as the formal channels of communication for internal and external matters. They are elected for three-year terms by universal adult suffrage from a slate nominated by the Council, and are paid a small monthly stipend by the Administration.

The incumbent in the office of *pulenuku* 'mayor' is charged with oversight of internal affairs. He may act as chairman of the Council when it is discussing issues of village regulation and activity, but more often he is simply called upon to report requests, derelictions and problems, and given instructions about what to do. Though he is the proper conduit for the flow of information between the village and Council, other members may be as informed or informative as he is. Some kinds of permission he can give without consulting his peers, such as requests to visit plantations at other than appointed days for some particular purpose, since such requests are really to inform should some question arise subsequently. In some respects the *pulenuku* is the lackey of the Council. He is the caretaker of the village water tanks, holding the keys to their taps, opening them at announced times and supervising the rationing of water from them; he is collector of mats or other items that have been levied by the Council; he is inspector of the village, making sure that decrees of the Council have been followed and collecting the fines imposed for non-compliance; and he is properly always among the elderly leaders of any village enterprise, and may be responsible for organising and implementing it on the Council's behalf. Some of these duties may be parcelled out to other Council members, but whatever the case, a diligent *pulenuku* is a busy man, though his official responsibilities are ill-defined.

The duties of the *faipule* 'administrative officer' are more clearly defined in official terms because he is the local representative of the New Zealand Administration, and also the magistrate (see *mālo* discussion below).

The division of duties between the offices of *pulenuku* and *faipule* accords with Tokelau ideas about the separation of domains of authority. Put loosely, the former's sphere of responsibility is internal, daily, routine matters, while the latter's is external and things out of the ordinary. Yet neither of these officials will take any decisive action or make any but the most routine decision without first consulting the Council, and there is no reported instance in which an official acted contrary to the expressed opinion of the Council. Even in court sessions the *faipule* as magistrate sits together with all or some

Six members of the Fakaofo Council of Elders are seated outside with their backs to the meeting house awaiting the commencement of an event over which they will preside. Photo: Marti Friedlander

Council members, who hear the cases and question those brought before the court just as he does, and, though he pronounces the judgment of the court, it is a judgment reached by consensus, to which his associates usually add their own words of reprimand and forgiveness. The court in fact resembles a *fono* with the magistrate in the role of chairman. Certainly, the offices of *faipule* and *pulenuku* confer a certain eminence upon their incumbents—after all, they have been elected by popular vote—but they were also elected from among nominees of the Council and, though they may be considered otherwise by outsiders and administrators, the Council members view them as their functionaries, as their officers who carry out their wishes. Though their titles imply that they hold authority (*pule*), authority in truth rests with the Council of Elders.

How then does a person come to be a member of the Council of Elders? The obvious answer is: by becoming old. As a generality this is true, but the answer is not quite so simple because the criteria for membership are not uniform throughout Tokelau. Fakaofo practice conforms most closely to the simple answer. Any man over about sixty years of age may expect to join the Council at the invitation of those who are already members. The rationale of this procedure is unexceptional: the existing Council is best qualified to select its associates because its membership is made up of all the wisest, most knowledgeable men of the village. There is no particular formality attached to the procedure. Some day when the Council is meeting, the elders present will simply send an envoy to ask a certain man to join them. The envoy will likely as not return with the message that the man asks humbly to be excused for some reason, and it may take several requests before he will appear and take his place in the Council. The invitation is never rescinded in light of excuses, since it is very proper to show reticence at the undoubted honour which it carries. A man's status as an elder is fully recognised in being asked to join this select body of a dozen or so 'wise men'. But for all that, the selection of new members is by and large dictated by relative age (though a person's year of birth may be uncertain, who is younger and who older is well remembered). Occasionally, a not very intelligent or inarticulate man may be passed over for a younger man, but only for a few years; none of sound mind are passed over altogether and never attain membership. Retirement from the Council is a gradual process and a matter of choice. As members become enfeebled by age and illness they attend fewer and fewer meetings, and lose touch with the issues which their fellow elders are pondering. By necessity, or a disinclination to attend, they simply stay home, appearing perhaps only on ceremonial occasions to take their place with the other elders. Their retirement is not marked; a new member is simply invited to take their place. Thus, the Elders' Council in Fakaofo is just that and its membership is limited and a matter of its own choice.

Not so in Nukunonu and Atafu, because their ruling bodies are composed of the men who have been selected as heads (*ulu*) of extended families (*kāiga*).[6] Ideally, therefore, the Council's membership is representative of all the 'families' recognised as corporate groups within the village, each man representing one 'family' and each 'family' represented by one man. The councils could be more accurately called a Council of Family Heads, but they are not: Atafu and Nukunonu people refer to their governing bodies as the Council of Elders. Though the name may not exactly reflect membership of the Council, it accurately expresses the locus of authority within the Council. Furthermore, most members are indeed elders, and, in Nukunonu, elders who have relinquished their duties as *kāiga* heads (or may never have held such duties) may be Council members simply because they are elderly.

The ideal of one-for-one representation is never actualised. Though elders may lament that some Council members represent two *kāiga* and that some *kāiga* are not represented, there is little they can do since it is not they who invite their associates. Each *kāiga* selects its own head, who thereby becomes a member of the Council, ostensibly representing the interests of that *kāiga*. If that man already represents another family, so be it. If an incumbent has become feeble or incapacitated and nobody has been designated to replace him, or if the person selected chooses for one reason or another not to attend Council meetings, that's how it is. A person cannot be forced to attend, and younger, or 'not yet elder' men may be particularly reluctant to do so. These younger men are apt to excuse themselves on the grounds that they are still strong and able, and that their proper place is with their peers working for the village rather than sitting 'to little purpose' with their senior kinsmen (implying that it would be unseemly for them to take an active role in Council deliberations). They may add that their senior kinsmen (representing other *kāiga*) may be trusted to look after their interests. Little exception can be taken to excuses phrased in such acceptable terms. Others of the younger family heads have ostensibly joined the Council but attend meetings infrequently, excusing themselves because they are engaged in subsistence or other activities. Such excuses are not wholly acceptable, for village responsibilities take precedence over all others. Nevertheless, many of the younger men who are Council members are diligent in fulfilling this responsibility (a higher proportion perhaps in Nukunonu where the division between 'village authority' and 'the strength of the village' is less strict—see below).

Since the Nukunonu and Atafu Councils do not select their members, they cannot control the number of men who sit on their Councils. Were each to operate with its full complement, i.e. one member for each *kāiga*, the Nukunonu Council would number over thirty and the Atafu Council over forty members. As things work out, they each have about thirty members, a number of whom only rarely appear at meetings.

On the face of it, the Fakaofo Council could be characterised as 'gerontocratic' and the Nukunonu and Atafu Councils as 'representative'. But granted that there is indeed a difference in emphasis, which villagers themselves are prone to emphasise in support of their particular village's way of doing things, the contrast in practice is not so great.

In Fakaofo there are occasional meetings of heads of families called by the Council to discuss issues on which the elders feel wider discussion is advisable. If all those eligible did attend such meetings, over eighty men would be present, including of course the Council members who are all 'family' heads anyway. Such a meeting might in fact draw thirty men, Council members plus about an equal number of older men. Others will excuse themselves on the grounds that the issues have already been thoroughly talked out and resolved by the elders; that it would be presumptuous, even embarrassing, for them to voice an opinion contrary to that of their elders; and again that they trust their elders—many of whom are kinsmen—to look after their interests. They echo the excuses offered by their counterparts in Nukunonu and Atafu for not exercising their right to join the Council. Thus there is in Fakaofo a 'representative' body, though it is not concerned with routine governance of the village, whose potential membership of eighty men would make it a most unwieldy decision-making body. Furthermore, should eighty men be called upon to spend the time the Council does in its deliberations, the welfare of the village would be seriously jeopardised. While these pragmatic concerns may be recognised, Fakaofo people righteously stress that their village is truly and properly under 'the rule of elders'.

The Atafu and Nukunonu Councils include in their membership all the elders who would be invited to join the Council if they were in Fakaofo. The comparable elders are members because, like their Fakaofo counterparts, they are 'family' heads (in Nukunonu this is further assured by the inclusion of any elder). The difference is that the Councils include some younger men as well, but this difference in principle is abrogated in practice, for at meetings of the Council these younger members rarely speak. They may ask a question, provide requested information, even venture a non-controversial opinion when asked, but most of the time—if they are present—they listen to the voices of their elders. In Nukunonu, and to a lesser extent in Atafu, people point out that their Council rightly and properly represents in its membership the interests of all, that each 'family' has a spokesman. Actually, both Councils are dominated by twelve or so able and articulate elders whose words and opinions carry the greatest weight. In this regard they are little different from the Fakaofo Council.

Why then do people from the separate islands make so much of the difference, even to the point of arguing that the composition of their Council reflects the 'true Tokelau way'? The answer rests on the linked notions of sanction and consent. For any decision on any matter which affects the village to be considered valid, it must be sanctioned by the Council. The Council's sanction can be given only by consensus resolution in a *fono*. The question then is: on whose behalf does a Council member consent? Atafu and Nukunonu Council members consent on behalf of the groups they represent, and by that consent the 'families' they represent are obliged to undertake or abide by whatever has been decided. The argument is that if a 'family' is not represented, its members are not necessarily 'affected' (*lavea*) by the decision. Fakaofo Council members consent on behalf of the 'village united' as together they represent the village. No one is exempt from their decision—in Fakaofo phraseology, 'the elders' authority reaches into *kāiga*' and all people and their property are under 'the rule of the elders'. For stark contrast, Fakaofo consent is given by a select few at the apex of a hierarchy on behalf of all, while Atafu and Nukunonu consent is reached by representatives of diverse but overlapping groups and applies to all. In terms of perceived social order, governance by an elderly elite contrasts with governance by coalition. But contrasts may be phrased to seem more extreme than they are, for in actuality the consensus resolutions of any Council apply to everybody.

The routine concerns and procedures of Council meetings can best be described by illustrative example (from Atafu), bearing in mind that the tone and intricacies of the occasion are difficult to portray (and procedural details vary). They take place once a week, at a specified time, and additional meetings are arranged if there are pressing matters to be deliberated, so that at times the Elders' Council may seem to be in constant session.

It takes some time for a meeting to assemble, the participants enter the meeting house silently and unobtrusively taking their accustomed sitting places. There are no stated rules about where each should sit, but the more elderly have their accustomed posts and the more youthful position themselves at the gaps between posts, and even younger members cluster somewhere in the middle of the building, thereby closing the roughly circular assembly. When a person is settled in his place, an earlier arrival addresses him with the simple Tokelau greeting form 'you have come' to which he gives the equally brief reply 'I have indeed come'. Though the phrases are ones of polite formality, they are uttered in a casual, conversational tone, sometimes hardly above a whisper. An interchange of informal remarks, subdued conversation, a bit of banter and a continual transfer of tobacco tins, bits or rolls of pandanus cigarette paper, and lighters occupy those waiting for still others to gather. Following an almost imperceptible exchange of nods and raised eyebrows, someone intones 'Let us pray' and the meeting has opened. The prayer, long or short depending on the speaker and the weight of the matters to be discussed, is followed by a brief exhortatory speech by another speaker. (The communication by nods and eyebrows establishes who the two speakers will be.) Looking around, an elder comments upon the absence of certain members, which may draw remarks from others or be left at that.

With these preliminaries over, members raise various subjects for discussion, not always resolving one before another is raised and sometimes conflating two. Rather than trying to thread through the texture of what was said in sequential order, the topics discussed and the resolutions reached are presented separately, though arranged in more or less sequential order. By unravelling the text, at least its content is clear.

1. Was it now appropriate to recommence a village project which had been set aside so that men could attend to routine repairs of houses and canoes? Several people observe that repairs are nowhere near complete. Agreed that village work would be put off a while longer.

2. Supplies of pandanus leaves for thatch and mats are depleted in the plantations regularly harvested. Would it not be possible to open the restricted plantations for a day or so to enable people to cut pandanus there? Both the timing and control of opening the restricted plantations are discussed at some length. The meeting resolves to open the plantations early the following week, allowing people to harvest for their immediate needs while there, but forbidding them to bring anything but pandanus leaves back to the village.

3. An elder observes that a younger Council member has brought young palm shoots [used as plaiting material] from his plantations though there has been no announcement allowing this. The accused admits and explains his error, and states his willingness to pay the customary fine. He is thanked.

4. The Pulenuku announces that fines incurred during a recent village inspection have not been paid, and he will be going from house to house to collect them. He proposes doubling the fines that remain unpaid after this effort. This is deemed appropriate.

5. The Faipule reminds the fono that they have agreed to make a wooden box [a large one though he refers to it as 'tiny'] for a forthcoming inter-atoll gathering, remarking that a craftsman has not yet been assigned the task. An elder, with apparent reluctance, accepts the work pressed upon him by others.

6. The Faipule announces the incipient arrival of some official visitors and asks what is to be done about their accommodation and the customary gifts. Accommodation already offered is agreed to be suitable and the Faipule is instructed to approach the matrons about gifts.

7. An elder reports that two boys have maliciously stoned chickens. A younger member of the Council is sent to fetch them and in the meantime others decry youthful, unthinking irresponsibility. The boys appear sheepishly and are ordered to sit on a mat directly in the centre of the elders' circle. The glowering elders fire abrupt questions at them; they do not respond. Led by their grandfathers, the elders chastise them for their cruel, inconsiderate, mindless act. When their disciplinarians are done they are thoroughly shaken, and when ordered to depart they creep away in shame.

8. An elder observes that there are five sacks of flour in the cooperative store which will be consumed by weevils if not used soon, suggesting that the elders might acquire them at a reduced price on credit in the name of the village for distribution to 'the children'. After some discussion of the number of sacks of flour that should be acquired, the suggestion is approved.

9. Another elder notes that some of the older schoolboys have been picking drinking nuts from palms adjacent to the school. He is delegated to speak to the teachers about this violation of regulations.

The secretary is asked if there are any matters tabled from an earlier meeting that should be discussed again. After consulting his very cryptic minutes, he says that there appear to be none. The Faipule and Pulenuku are asked if they have any further subjects for discussion, and reply likewise. The meeting ends without ceremony.

The meeting recorded above was a routine one in all respects. Matters discussed had to do with village management and control, and all had been raised in one guise or another many times before. The Pulenuku sought approval for an action he proposed to take and the Faipule posed minor problems which the Council helped him solve. The Councils concern themselves with the minutiae of village life and are firm and assured in doing so. The same assurance does not prevail when they are required to discuss policies or programmes initiated outside the village.

These are usually proposed by the Administration and conveyed through the *faipule* to the Council for deliberation and approval. The communication radioed to the *faipule* is either in English or a very literal Tokelau translation of English, and is invariably cryptic. There is no detailed spelling out of the intentions or implications of the proposal, and aside from the *faipule* who holds the brief message and knows no more about it than anyone else, there is no representative of the Administration present to answer the many questions that invariably arise. When faced with uncertainty, the easiest thing to do is table the matter, but then another message will be received by the *faipule* asking for an answer. Another strategy is to call a special meeting, including all men, in hopes that someone may be able to shed some light on the matter, but this only adds more voices to the confused debate, more opinions about what it is all about, and more speculation. Though the communication problem with the Administration afar is a very real problem, it is not the only problem. The Councils are being asked to consider matters about which they have no background, no experience, no precedent, when they are after all local bodies concerned with local programmes, arrangements and regulations for the welfare and protection of all.

Their mission is clearly revealed at the beginning of each year when they set the village on course for the year to come. Each year in January the Councils devote several days to a lengthy consideration of the state of the village and the status of village regulations. Although there is nothing to prevent changes and revisions of regulations at other times, at the year's beginning all are thoroughly reviewed one by one and altered, discarded, or retained as they are. New regulations are considered to deal with matters that have arisen and require control. Once everything has been reviewed and resolved, the Council plans the agenda for the annual 'grand meeting'—who will speak about what and in what order.

> *In the morning a* kalaga *'announcement' summons the village whole to the Nukunonu meeting house, where the Council members are already seated at one end. The women sit in rows on one side, the men in rows on the other, and the children sit directly under the elders' gaze. They arrange themselves as they do in church, as if the elders occupied the 'pulpit'. The opening prayer and following oration are longer than usual, thanking God for His benevolent protection in the past and asking Him for future guidance, extolling the virtues of unity, peace, compassion, obedience and respect. Thereupon follows a series of addresses by Council members charged with particular responsibilities, asking to be forgiven for their possible errors of commission and omission, commending the villagers for their patience and cooperation, and admonishing them for their errors. Each inserts in his report exhortations to all to 'obey' and to 'rule with compassion'. A series of stern speeches remind people of various rules and regulations, particularly those that are apt to be disregarded. Finally, one or two venerable elders, acting as spokesmen for them all, announce whatever new regulations have been decreed by the Council and the penalties which will be incurred for their transgression. After a few closing remarks, the meeting disbands. No one responds; there is no discussion or dialogue.*

The intention is to 'again bring to mind the laws' of a *fenua pulea* 'governed land'.

Te kautagata: 'the body of men'

Counterpoised to the elders as the 'rulers of the village' is the *kautagata* 'body of men', referred to as the 'strength of the village'. The designation *tagata* 'men', as well as distinguishing men from elders, separates the men from the *tama* 'boys'.[7] Males are 'boys' until they marry, except in the rare situation of a man remaining unmarried well into his thirties. What is seen to separate men from boys is not age or strength but a sense of responsibility which marriage gives, and indeed the transformation from youthful frivolity to solid citizenship with marriage and, more specifically, parenthood, is often striking. The rhetoric and formalities of village life clearly distinguish the three categories of males, both in what is said and what each is expected to do. Categorically, boys are unskilled and irresponsible, in need of constant supervision and discipline; men are skilled and responsible, but still lack the acquired wisdom and judgement of elders. This tripartite categorisation permeates Tokelau life in principle.

In practice the lines are not drawn so sharply, for in doing the things that keep the village going everyone is expected to contribute as they are able and ideas about capabilities are phrased in terms of a gradual and variable transition. Using a tidal analogy, it is said that a man's strength gradually rises to a peak and then slowly ebbs, that a person has twenty to thirty years of real vigour and thereafter may compensate for his ebbing strength by his acquired experience and skills, but inevitably he becomes so weak that he himself cannot use his acquired experience and skills except to advise and instruct others. Thus, older boys whose strength is rising, and may even have

Members of the Fakaofo Āumāga are seated facing the meeting house and their elders. Photo: Marti Friedlander

reached full vigour, take their place with the men as the 'strength of the village', thereby gaining experience and acquiring skill. They are required to give their all and urged to extend themselves, yet are cautioned not to attempt to exceed their capabilities. They tend to be assigned the heavy but unskilled tasks. Although obviously past their years of full vigour, some elders retain a modicum of strength, and they too are expected to do their part. A few retain considerable vigour and are proud to work every bit as hard as younger men; they are admired. Those less strong do whatever they can and their efforts are praised. Those whose weakness precludes their active participation, but who are neither sick nor infirm, are expected to be present at the place where the work is being done. Sometimes they may offer or be asked for advice, but usually they just watch and periodically voice a stylised phrase of encouragement: *Mālō te galue* 'Work well done' and the like, which draws the reply: *Mālō te tapuaki* 'Encouragement well given'. To *tapuaki* is to show sympathy and support for the workers and their work by one's presence. Such support and the active involvement of able elders while expected cannot, in the nature of things, be required. Nonetheless it is wholly unacceptable for elders to set a task and then go off to tend to their own concerns leaving the men to do it. No one is exempt from the obligation to do his part by contributing by his presence and spirit to the occasion's *māopoopo*. Even an elder does not escape, for if he is not present people will know what he has done with his day. If he has done anything of consequence, he is open to barbed comment in private and oblique censure in public. A common ploy is to note with exaggerated praise the contribution of another who is patently less able. It is appreciated that only exceptionally able elders can take part in communal fishing expeditions, which call for fortitude, endurance and alertness. On a fishing canoe a passive observer, no matter how supportive, is an encumbrance. However, those that are left behind should be at the beach when the canoes return to hear accounts of the expedition, praise the efforts of the fishermen and comment upon their catch.

When the Āumāga has been engaged in a communal task at the instruction of the elders, the elders are expected to show their support by their presence. It would be impractical for the elders to be present during communal fishing, but they should be present to greet the Āumāga fishermen on their return and to laud their accomplishments.
Photo: Marti Friedlander

When it comes to doing things on behalf of the village, people are judged by what they do, and are expected to do as much as they are able. A communal and egalitarian ethic prevails, and nobody escapes censure for shirking. Yet in the formal organisation of the village there is a categorical discrimination of elders, men, and boys, and the explicit hierarchical ranking of them. At the top the elder decide and decree, regulate and discipline, and enjoy deference and respect. Men work, assisted by older boys.

Both elders and men are keenly aware that their categorical relationship is a delicate one, prone to resentment and exasperation, and both labour to minimise and counter the friction. When the men are aggrieved, they do not make a formal protest, but their displeasure is expressed to be overheard by their elders in the household, in the canoe-slips, in the latrines, and wherever else men and elders informally congregate. The elders take note but are not apt to argue the point. Elderly displeasure is formally expressed, but always in measured tones if directed at the men. If resentment is mutual, a formal elder protest may be followed by a respectful protest from the men.

The specific tensions between elders and men, and the manner in which they are handled, are partly conditioned by the organisation and operation of village institutions, by how the men are organised in relation to the Council. Central to any understanding of this is the role and structure of āumāga, a formal organisation of able-bodied males brought to Tokelau in the 1930s by Tokelau men who had been resident in Samoa. The institution as it variously developed in Tokelau is quite different from 'aumāga in Samoa. Put most simply, Atafu has a relatively autonomous Āumāga which takes a dominant role in village activities; Fakaofo's Āumāga is closely linked to the Council as its workforce; Nukunonu has no separate āumāga organisation. The closer examination that follows highlights these differences.

Atafu: From the time they leave school until such time as they take a place in the Council, Atafu males are part of the Āumāga and are required to respond whenever the Āumāga bugle summons them. Excepted from the strict requirements of membership are schoolteachers and the doctor on the grounds that their professional services to the community take precedence. Nevertheless, it is expected, if not required, that when they are not on duty they will join their peers, and they are not exempted from open and sharp criticism should they take advantage of their special status. Men who become members of the Council of Elders while still relatively young and strong, though not formally members of the Āumāga, are likewise expected to participate in Āumāga activities. The rule that no member of the Council may hold formal membership in the Āumāga serves to separate the two bodies by preventing Council members from holding elected Āumāga leadership positions. Consequently, men who are active leaders of the Āumāga tend to avoid joining the Council, even when they might be members, in order to retain their offices in the Āumāga. They assert that they wish to actively serve their village as long as they are able—a rather specious excuse, since it is expected that they will do so despite Council membership. What they are reluctant to lose is leadership status, conferred upon them by their peers. A junior place in the Council is unattractive in comparison.

The roll of the Āumāga contains the names of all full members, all of whom are eligible to vote and hold office in the organisation. Each year the membership selects its twenty officers by secret ballot: a president, four executive officers, two secretary/treasurers, a *satini* 'sergeant', and twelve *leoleo* 'guards/watchmen'. There are no nominations; each member simply writes down his choices on a piece of paper and a second round of voting takes place only if there are ties. The office of president is inevitably filled by an older member in recognition of his exemplary record of selfless commitment and service. The four executives effectively run the organisation; they decide, arbitrate, and organise. The other officers are functionaries with specific duties and are responsible to the executive. The secretary/treasurers keep numerous rolls and records of contributions, fines, meetings, regulations, and finances; the *leoleo*, overseen by the sergeant, carry messages, conduct inspections, clean up, check up, and so forth. The Āumāga is tightly and efficiently run, and its members, past and present, take pride in their organisation, as does all Atafu.

A measure of this regard is that the Āumāga has long had its own day each week, which is planned and programmed by its officers. Village improvement and maintenance projects and village provisioning are undertaken in the morning; the afternoon is devoted to cricket; and an evening of entertainment completes the normal programme. Plans for the weekly day on Thursday are made at the Tuesday evening meeting of officers and announced at the Wednesday afternoon meeting of the full membership. These meetings, as well as Thursday events, provide ample opportunity to proclaim the ethic of Āumāga *māopoopo*.

As well as its weekly day, the Atafu Āumāga has its Anniversary Day (which lasts at least four days) at mid year, commemorating the organisation's founding. The yearly Day is the weekly day writ large.

Preparations begin months in advance and the programme is planned in fine detail. It commences with a church service to which all members arrive in an ordered procession dressed in white. Immediately thereafter, all assemble to elect officers for the coming year. After the results are announced, food is served and numerous speeches follow, praising retiring officers, encouraging and advising new officers, recalling Āumāga history, and always proclaiming Āumāga unity and integrity. Cricket teams do not just gather, they arrive in regimented procession singing and beating their newly fashioned bats on the ground to confront one another across the pitch. The negotiations and oratory before the game are elaborate and intricate, and virtually the whole village takes part in the cricket spectacular of drumming, dancing, chanting, singing and playing the game [see below]. Many of the dance-songs performed during evening entertainments are newly composed and all have been carefully rehearsed. On the second and third days, cricket continues morning and afternoon, and entertainment fills the evenings. The last day begins with a massive village feast, followed by a final cricket match and an entertainment finale.

The details of the programme are varied and elaborated from year to year, but the outline remains the same. Thus, once a year the Atafu populace exuberantly celebrate their Āumāga in which they all take pride.

As a village institution the Āumāga is semi-autonomous. Certainly as the 'strength of the village' it is at the command of the Council and ultimately all its activities are under the Council's jurisdiction, but its membership, leadership and internal organisation are strictly separate. Furthermore, the Āumāga has its own rules and regulations, its own disciplinary measures, dues and levies, and stages its own village events to mark weddings, arrivals and departures. Of most marked significance is that its officers have been granted the responsibility of organising whatever it does, whether the doing is initiated by them or is at the behest of the Council. This responsibility is viewed as a privilege bestowed upon the Āumāga in recognition of its trustworthiness and effectiveness, a reputation that all its members are expected to uphold.

The Council indeed has great respect for the Āumāga. All of its members have spent years within its ranks and many have been its leaders in the past. Peers of older Council members have remained in the Āumāga as elderly advisers and spokesmen if not leaders, and younger Council members are continually involved with their contemporaries in Āumāga activities and in their everyday routines. The categorical distinction between elders and men is mediated by elders within the Āumāga and men within the Council even while the two bodies are counterposed as 'workers' and 'rulers'.

For its part, the Council is cautious about overburdening or imposing too heavily on the 'workers' and is careful to respect Āumāga integrity. Āumāga leaders in turn are punctilious in their relations with the Council, avoiding words or acts that might be interpreted as challenging their 'rulers'. A stated Āumāga policy is: Whatever instructions the Council gives are followed without question—the Āumāga does as it is told. However, having followed instructions, its leaders may subsequently suggest to an appropriate representative of the Council that the instructions and arrangement proved to be inappropriate or inadequate in some respects. Interaction between the two bodies is highly circumspect. Communications are transmitted via representatives of each, and, though both meet at least once a week, they rarely meet together. When they do, it is because the Council has summoned the men to meet with them. (The summons is issued to 'men' as a collectivity, rather than the Āumāga as a group, but the Āumāga bugle is used to summon them.) The impetus for such a meeting is invariably a matter which the Council judges warrants wider discussion, but wider discussion is rarely forthcoming. Either everyone readily agrees and the rhetoric of *māopoopo* flows, or people are of differing opinion but only elders say anything and the decision is left to them.

Fakaofo: Fakaofo males simply take their place in their Āumāga upon completing their schooling and leave its ranks when they have been invited as elders to take their place in the Council. However, an interlude between school and full involvement in men's activities is thought desirable, for it allows immature youth to gain strength and experience and keeps them away from convivial men's gatherings where their immediate elders' foibles are mocked and foul language flourishes. Schoolteachers and other professionals take their place in the Āumāga when not engaged in their regular duties. To take one's place aptly expresses being in the Fakaofo Āumāga:

> *Virtually every male in the village responds to the Council's crier*, Toeaina, taulelea ma tama! Māopoopo atu ki te fale fono! *'Elders, men and boys! Gather at the meeting house!', by taking a seat in the meeting house. Boys and young men crowd shoulder to shoulder in rows at one end facing the elders at the other, and mature men sit in single rows at the long sides of the meeting house half-turned towards the elders—the older of the mature men closest to the elders. Though there is no visible demarcation, it is clear where the Āumāga ends and the Council begins. Here the age hierarchy is all set out in the places taken.*

Nobody is formally entered on a membership roll, though the Council's scribe keeps a list of men which is updated from time to time and is sporadically used to monitor attendance. Nevertheless, every man and boy, once having taken his place, is expected to respond to the summons, if he is not legitimately indisposed. These frequent gatherings at the meeting house identify the Āumāga as a body subservient to the co-present Council, which initiates its activities and claims its allegiance. The two bodies, Council and Āumāga, are discrete—they occupy different places, but as rulers and workers they gather in the same structure at the same time to state and negotiate their continuing relationship of mutual dependence.

Despite its subordination to the Council, the Āumāga has its own officers, an executive of eight men elected by secret ballot for a two-year term. These eight elected men decide among themselves who shall hold the offices of president and vice-president; there are no other officers. The officers are middle-aged men, usually over fifty, who are still active and able. They are admired for their skills and their willingness to take on the most arduous tasks, for they lead both by competence and example. They also have a

reputation for 'straight talk'. Their election is a matter of considerable pres-
tige, even though the authority associated with their positions is limited. The
additional quality sought in selecting the president and vice-president is ability
to speak effectively, since these officers are the spokesmen for the Āumāga
at gatherings with the Council and should be adept in using the conventional
forms of respect and deference, while clearly and persuasively presenting the
wishes of the assembled men and boys.

These leaders do not meet regularly; they have little to meet about.
Rather, they consult one another informally as the need arises and, in fact,
a great deal of their consultation is hasty, held in the midst of gatherings with
the Council. Having not been forewarned of what the Council has decided
or planned, they must reach agreement on the spot about the details that
have been left to them. Their leadership is in doing rather than planning.
They are expected to direct the work, assign tasks, instruct the less competent, and see that jobs are done carefully and safely. The Fakaofo Āumāga
responds, but does not initiate, except as its spokesmen might persuade the
Council to accept its wishes.

The morning meeting of elders, men and boys begins any day that by
decree of the Council is to be devoted to village work, and captures the
nature of the relationship between Fakaofo's Āumāga and Council in their
ongoing face-to-face interaction. Most often this is just a meeting to get the
day's activities underway, for announcing and organising what is to be done;
but from time to time it is a forum for subtle though intense negotiation
between the men as 'workers' and the elders as 'rulers'. These are times with
the relations between Āumāga men and Council elders have become strained
and this tension noticeably affects the tenor of these morning gatherings. The
elders are acutely aware of the undercurrent of dissatisfaction and yet whatever they do seems to exacerbate rather than alleviate the criticism they
overhear. If they are strict and demanding, they are faulted as dictatorial and
insensitive; if they are lax and conciliatory, they are accused of not giving firm
direction. The men are uncomfortable too. They recognise that they are not
all without fault, but there is little they can do to discipline their ranks. They
cannot pin down their disquiet to any specific issue and are not disposed to
challenge their elders openly.

After weeks of tense and gloomy meetings and dispirited work days, what
finally brings matters to a head is the issue of presence. Most men have
continued to gather when summoned out of a sense of duty, but an increasing number beg off with weak excuses or simply do not appear. In the end,
the crisis is overcome, not because anything has really changed, but because
the problem has been brought into the open and the whole consensual system reaffirmed. Nobody has challenged the Council's authority or questioned
the Āumāga obligations. There has been no argument and both sides have
acknowledged their faults. Many things have been left unsaid, but the message is clear—the survival of the village depends on the preservation of the
system. So the Council's scribe updates the list of men, roll is taken at
morning meetings and absentees are scolded. The Āumāga accept the 'heavy

words' of their elders and grumblings diminish. The mood of the morning meetings returns to relaxed conviviality and the rules are strictly followed— for a while. Ultimately, the men do not want to be held accountable for decisions made—only an elder can brave having made a wrong one.

Atafu and Fakaofo have moulded and institutionalised the imported *'aumāga* organisation in characteristic ways. The differences may be pinpointed by what the two Āumāga do and their relations to their respective elders.

Both Āumāga are most usually referred to as 'the strength of the village', but each is also referred to by other phrases that are specifically apt. In Fakaofo it is said that the Āumāga 'helps the elders' take care of the village, while in Atafu the Āumāga is referred to as the *ivitū* 'backbone' of the vil- lage. Correspondingly, the Fakaofo Āumāga is viewed as an arm of the elders and under their jurisdiction, while the Atafu Āumāga is seen as a central and semi-autonomous village body. The way the two Āumāga are run and what they do, or do not do, reflects these perspectives. The Atafu organisation with its many officers and functionaries, its weekly meetings, its summoning bu- gle, its roll and regulations, its disciplinary procedures, fines and levies, its planned events and initiated activities, and, most particularly, its weekly day and Anniversary Day, is counterposed to the Council. Many of these func- tions duplicate those of the Council; however the Council's authority is wider, encompassing Āumāga members as well as everyone else, whereas Āumāga authority is restricted to its members. Fakaofo's Āumāga does not summon, monitor attendance, discipline, initiate, plan or have any kind of day, and consequently has no need to meet or have secretary/treasurers, ser- geants and guards. It does nothing that duplicates or compromises the func- tions of the Council. What the men themselves emphasise as crucial is the weekly day of the Atafu Āumāga, which the Fakaofo Āumāga does not have.

The sense of autonomy the Atafu body enjoys is derived from its day, but extends beyond it. The procedures of planning and running that day are applied to other days when the Council calls upon the Āumāga to act or when some situation calls the Āumāga into action. In any emergency—a sudden storm, a missing canoe—immediately, and without elder consultation, the bugle sounds with unmistakable urgency and the men are mobilised under the direction of Āumāga leaders. Without a day, the Fakaofo body remains always subordinate to the Council, and its activities and scope for action are constrained. Even when the advantages of doing something are obvious to all, such as intercepting fish crossing the reef, the Āumāga leaders are unwill- ing to initiate action unless so directed by the elders. Emergencies do not mobilise the Āumāga as such, but call forth a long-established club, whose leaders need not consult the Council and who can direct all who respond to the summons of the club's bugle, whether they are club members or not (see below p.92). In emergencies, the meeting that precedes any Āumāga activity is precluded, so the Āumāga cannot act.

What Atafu does not have is the regular meeting of 'elders, men and boys'. It might be said that what is sacrificed in the interest of efficiency and autonomy is the opportunity to interact directly with the Council. While it is indeed true that the age overlap between the two Atafu bodies mitigates their isolation from one another, nonetheless at times the tensions between the two bodies, especially between Council elders and all others, become palpable. (Younger Council members in sympathy with their peers have been known to boycott Council meetings.) Without the forum of regular meetings antagonisms tend to fester and backbiting thrives. Once relations take a bad turn, amelioration takes a long time, because there is no established formula for interaction that allows issues to be aired and commitments reaffirmed. At joint assemblies, the elders vacillate between authoritative and cajoling stances, and the men dissimulate. Those few, beside the elder Council members, who are apt to speak out are those with a foot on both sides, the elders of the Āumāga and men in the Council. But, as one of the latter remarked: 'It is impossible to argue when there is no argument.' For the men punctiliously do not criticise or state opinions, so only the elders can argue, and for them to publicly argue among themselves is considered unseemly. The men later either grumble about their elders' indecisiveness in not reaching a firm decision, or accuse them of having held a purposeless meeting, after having already arrived at their own unalterable decision. Clearly, the situation cannot be changed by a meeting; only time and a gradual mellowing of moods can alter it.

Much of the annoyance that Fakaofo men express might be avoided if the Āumāga were given responsibility for its own organisation and discipline, but this is not how things are done in Fakaofo where the hierarchy of authority— 'the rule of the elders'—is paramount. Likewise, regular meetings of the Atafu Āumāga and Council might be expected to lead to controlled public airing of difficulties between them, but this would compromise the Āumāga's cherished integrity. So 'elders, men and boys' continue to take their places together in the Fakaofo meeting house, affirming the age hierarchy, while the Atafu Council and Āumāga assemble in the same meeting house at different times, affirming that they are indeed separate.

A recurrent activity that Fakaofo and Atafu Āumāga carry out in like manner is stevedoring. In Fakaofo, as in Atafu, the work of cargo handling, both aboard and ashore, and of ferrying freight and passengers between ship and shore in whaleboats through frequently hazardous passes and surf, is programmed and directed by Āumāga officers without any consultation with the elders. The two Āumāga are paid for this job by the Administration, and use the money to buy food to feed the workers on this and other days. However, Nukunonu is different.

Nukunonu: Nukunonu elders have effectively resisted the establishment of any 'aumāga-like organisation, declaring it antithetical to 'Tokelau custom'. This conservative stance is persuasive in Nukunonu, which takes pride in maintaining selected 'ancient practices' and resisting foreign, most particularly Samoan, ways. More concretely the elders and others argue that any separate organisation of men would create a second locus of authority, which would be divisive and compromise the elders' authority and the *pulenuku* role. Not everyone concurs with this point of view, however. Some men have suggested that village work would be more efficiently performed if the workers organised and supervised themselves, and attempts have been made to found men's organisations dedicated to working for the welfare of the village and to 'assisting the weaker brother'. These attempts have been thwarted by the elders' refusal to recognise or call upon the incipient organisation. Unable to act in accordance with their stated purpose, these organisations cannot justify themselves.

Nukunonu village work is undertaken either *fakatahi* 'communally' or *fakafaitū* 'by sides', and either way role distinctions between elders and men are downplayed (just as they are in the composition of the Council). A task to be done communally is planned as necessary by the Council and implemented by the *pulenuku*, who may consult with selected elders. A work day is announced by a Council member designated as village crier at least a day before, and all males—elders and men alike—assemble accordingly to receive directions from the *pulenuku*, or go directly to the tasks that the *pulenuku* has personally assigned them. Elders are part of the workforce, and direct or supervise their juniors. They are expected to set the example and see that things are done properly—encouraging, cautioning, reprimanding as required. At one time there was a roll of this workforce, which had no apparent ordering of names. The only adult males missing from the list were incapacitated elders, the doctor, and schoolteachers.

When work is undertaken by the two *faitū* 'sides' of the village, the tasks decided by the Council are presented to each, and the organisation and implementation left to their respective officers. (A fuller discussion of *faitū* organisations and their place in the separate villages appears below. Some remarks about the Nukunonu 'sides' is necessary here, however, since their activities parallel those of Āumāga elsewhere.) Every member of the village is at least nominally associated with one 'side' or the other, so that each 'side' has its elders, who take decisive roles in its affairs though they do not hold named offices. When a 'side' meets to discuss how an assigned task will be carried out, elders are present to guide and advise; when it comes to doing, the elders are there working and supervising. Village work is delegated to the 'sides' when there are two separate, but roughly equivalent, jobs to be done (e.g. building a boatshed and a schoolhouse) or when a single task is easily and conveniently divisible (e.g. collecting and processing copra from the two village-owned islets). The spirit that loyalty to a 'side' engenders and the continual competition between them motivate the work teams. The work indeed takes on the quality of a game as each 'side' endeavours to complete its task before the other, and then publicises its accomplishment by dispatching some workers to assist the other 'side'. Whichever strategy is used for village work, the categorical distinction between elders and other men is minimised, while at the same time the elders are always in control. Whether organised as a single body of workers or divided into two equivalent and competitive 'sides', those who are senior take the leadership roles. A village regulation about the disposal of refuse is unequivocal about this: 'The refuse at lagoon and ocean shores is to be completely removed by elders and men.' It goes on to specify that each 'side' is responsible for one half of the shore and that excuses for absence from work are to be made to specified elders of each 'side'. Every Nukunonu able-bodied adult male is explicitly a village worker, and whenever they assemble to work the elders are in charge. The categorical distinction may be downplayed in terms of participation, but the locus of authority is clear.

Giving prominence to 'sides' as working groups in competition and delegating planning and organising to them effectively displaces the tensions that might arise between the generations. The 'sides', continually pitted against one another, are expected to display conventionalised antagonism; it is part of the unending game of one-upmanship in which they are engaged. All join in: elders, men, women, youths and even children. Elders are certainly in charge, but not as a separate institutionalised body at which grievances can be directed.

All Tokelau communities are confronted with a social dilemma arising from the ideological conflict between the principles of hierarchy and equality. This dilemma is most apparent in the relationship between men and elders, specifically in the organisational arrangements of the village. It is perhaps for this reason that in this area there are the greatest organisational differences between the villages—each grapples in different ways with the same social dilemma. Atafu's solution is to formally separate the men and the elders organisationally; Fakaofo's solution is to formally bring them together continually; Nukunonu's solution is to deny a separate men's organisation. Each strategy has its pitfalls and virtues. But there is more than social problem-solving involved here. Each community maintains that its organisational mode is most in keeping with the 'true Tokelau way' and therefore better, and, though there is quite general agreement about what the 'true Tokelau way' is, there are differing emphases. The strategies reflect the cultural precepts (or preoccupations) given precedence by one village or another even though they share them all. Atafu prides itself on its *māopoopo*, despite the strict separateness of elders and men. Fakaofo glorifies the rule of its elders even as some complain and view it as less than effective at times. Nukunonu celebrates its easygoing cohesiveness even if sometimes it is difficult to get things done.

These preoccupations are expressed in other organisations and practices, but nowhere are they as apparent as in the ways in which elders and men come together or stay apart.

Komiti a Fafine 'Women's Committee'

How women fit into the organisational structure of the village and their position *vis-à-vis* their male counterparts appears equivocal. On the one hand, 'our mothers' or 'the ladies' are seen as a peripheral or subordinate section of the polity, activated only at the bidding of the elders and utterly submissive to elder authority, or, on the other hand, the *lōmātutua* 'matrons', *fafine* 'women' and *teine matua* 'mature girls' are counterposed to the elders, men and older boys as a complementary half of the polity with distinctive spheres of activity, domains of concern and a separate authority structure. These rather different expressions of women's place in the village are not wholly contradictory; or, at least, Tokelau persons, both male and female, express differing views at different times, and much depends on circumstances, both personal and contextual. Rather than argue one way or the other, it is advantageous to entertain both perspectives.

In each village a *Komiti a Fafine* 'Women's Committee' was formed in the latter half of the 1920s at the instigation of the New Zealand Administration as an adjunct of the local health services. Committees of each village were to promote and monitor child and maternal welfare, cleanliness and sanitation, and to help maintain hospitals and dispensaries under the direction of the medical staff. The local committees still engage in these activities, though they have been overshadowed by other activities and undertakings.

All the villages also have women's groups within their churches, usually overseen by the wife of the pastor or catechist. Spoken of as 'the ladies' or 'our mothers', they are asked from time to time to prepare food and plait mats on behalf of the congregation, and they regularly clean the church and its surroundings. (The women's church organisations are discussed in more detail below.)

In Atafu and Nukunonu 'the ladies' of the congregation and 'the women' of the Committee are exactly the same people, so it is not always clear when the village women meet together which organisation they are gathered as, at least in terms of what their meeting is about. Furthermore, they may assemble simply as 'the mothers' or 'the women' of the village at the behest of the elders, and the village 'sides' may be implicated in the organisation of their activities under whatever name they are meeting. Consequently, the Committees may appear either to be more pervasive than they are, involved in a wide range of women's affairs and activities, or to be moribund as the communal pursuits of women are phrased in terms of other organisational sets. But it is usually possible to identify one set from another when women are gathered in a meeting by the structure of the meeting if not by the matters under discussion.

When the Committee meets, the wives of the *faipule* and *pulenuku*, as president and vice-president respectively, preside, and one or more appointed secretaries keep records. The membership is usually divided into named sections or companies, who take on various duties in rotation. This is the formal structure as it was constituted decades ago, which is overlaid by a decidedly Tokelau form of organisation, with the matrons, or elders among the women, firmly in charge. The presiding officers, unless they themselves are matrons, are not the leader of a Committees but its lackeys, whom the matrons instruct, direct and admonish just as they do other younger women. The hierarchy of age prevails over the externally constituted organisational structure.

Married (or ever-married) women are automatically Committee members, and unmarried women of thirty years or more are also members, but the membership status of unmarried older 'girls' is a matter of debate. It is useful to include them in regular membership, since they can be assigned the arduous and tedious tasks, and it is argued that they are being prepared for their future roles as wives and mothers; but then, it is asked, should 'innocent' girls be privy to the outspoken discussions and lewd antics of mature women, and would it not be easier for their mothers if they were to stay home and look after the younger children? So the debate goes on, but even if the 'girls' are considered members, theirs is a peripheral role. Attendance at Committee meetings and activities is in principle required of all members, but women's responsibilities being what they are, presence is not very strictly defined. Apologies are accepted for many reasons, including cooking fish (which would otherwise spoil), and putting in an appearance at some time during the day may count as presence. Village-oriented activities are what women do as well as their regular duties within their families, and there is some question as to what takes precedence in principle as well as in practice.

The original charter of the Committees as an auxiliary of the health services placed them under the guidance and direction of the local medical staff. In actuality, however, how much direction the medical staff gives, and how a Committee responds to direction, depends upon the medical staff involved. A long-serving, mature staff nurse may firmly direct certain Committee programmes and projects; a newly arrived young doctor will make tentative proposals and deferentially request assistance. Most doctors (invariably men) prefer to liaise with the Committee through the staff nurses, and if the doctor does appear at meetings the proceedings have an air of cautious formality. When the medical staff meet with the Committee they come as visitors; the officers are forewarned and the staff attend in professional dress with clear purpose, perhaps to inform the women of some new programme, or to seek their assistance for a public health campaign, or to ask them to provide new blinds for the wards. Their business concluded, they depart, though the nurses may later return, out of uniform, to join the other village women as Committee members.

Periodically, the Committee conducts village 'inspections' for the express purpose of promoting and monitoring village and household cleanliness. These are not casual events.

> An 'inspection' is announced for a particular day and time, and for weeks and days before the women and men prepare for it, repairing and refurbishing their houses and cookhouses. Since virtually every square foot of village ground is owned, the clean-up is truly of the whole village. In the final hours before the 'inspection' every inch of the village is swept. The women gather more or less at the appointed time and proceed on a prearranged route of 'inspection'. The occasion is a festive one, a celebration of civic pride and good housekeeping, but deficiencies are noted as 'not very good' and those responsible urged to 'try harder'.

Committees, now well established as village institutions, are much more than adjuncts of the health services; they have their own agendas and their

Women gather at the meeting house to plait several mats cooperatively. Three women may work simultaneously on the same mat, each laying down one length of plaiting. When one finishes her length, there should be space for another to begin another length at the other end. Having completed a length, a woman may turn to a small plaiting project of her own—a basket or hat—or may join with others in a game of dominoes.
Photo: J. Huntsman

own perceived roles in relation to other village organisations, and these have developed somewhat differently in each village.

The example of Nukunonu is apt here. The women in all the villages are asked by the elders from time to time to provide plaited mats to carpet the meeting house or to gift to visitors, and the women view this task as their responsibility on behalf of their village. Yet in Nukunonu, gathering and processing of plaiting materials and production of mats is an ongoing activity of the women. On the face of it, this might be because the control of the grove of valued fine pandanus adjacent to the village is vested in the women and they therefore regulate access to the resource rather than just handling materials brought back to them from the outer islets. But this does not really explain why Nukunonu women spend days and days assembled together plait-

Nukunonu women gather to process dried kie *pandanus leaves after gathering them from their separate stands in the grove. Collecting the fallen leaves, or cutting green leaves for plaiting materials, is undertaken only when the* lōmātutua *'matrons' so decree. The women are removing the prickles from the central spine of the leaves, having already removed those at the margins. Then they will straighten the leaves and roll them into reel bundles.*
Photo: J. Huntsman

71

In the shade of a stand of pandanus, Atafu women begin their day of play with a card game. Photo: J. Huntsman

ing mats, especially when the plaiting materials are levied from the stored supplies of each woman, and their way of working is by their own admission not particularly efficient. The explanation is not a 'practical' one; their special pandanus and the mats produced from it are valued throughout Tokelau and are distinctive to Nukunonu. Though the stands of pandanus are women's distinctive goods, they are a communal valuable, as both commodity and symbol. Nukunonu women together must produce the finest display of Nukunonu's worth.

The Committee also has a disciplinary and mediating role; the matrons admonish and chastise younger members, and disagreements are aired and at

The day of play is in full swing. Most women have shifted from the village to their playground next to the burial ground. Foursomes play cards, dominoes, and the Tokelau game tiuga, *involving the backhand throwing of cowrie shells onto a rolled-up mat, which is scored something like bowls.* Photo: J. Huntsman least temporarily resolved. Yet in Atafu this activity is pursued with notable vigour. Any dereliction, any disagreement invariably comes to the attention of the matrons, and women are urged to air their differences within the confines of the Committee rather than carrying them outside, lest the *māopoopo* of women, and therefore of the village, be compromised.

Women play as well as work under the auspices of their Committee. At the conclusion of meetings foursomes form to play raucous games of dominoes and cards, and cricket matches are often scheduled in the afternoon. When summoned to plait mats together, women arrive with dominoes and cards to begin play as soon as they have completed a turn at the task, and these gatherings are invariably enlivened by the antics of well-known clowns, performing singly or in company.

The occasions when women's play is most sustained and intense is when they arrange a *tāfaoga* 'holiday' at some location outside the village. A delegation of women clears the plan with the elders, who may be asked to arrange transport and provisions, and who invariably accede to the request.

> On the appointed day the women gather up mats, lengths of brightly coloured cloth, huge pots and other cooking gear, and of course their dominoes and packs of cards, and depart from the village. Once they are gathered and settled, there is nothing to do but play. Teams of two replace one another at the domino and card games, as losers retire to be replaced by new challengers, but attention is drawn away from these games when the antics begin. A trio of normally sedentary matrons begin a mock cricket match, roaring and stumbling about. Set comic turns—duels, wrestling matches, lewd dances—are performed, joined, repeated with ever greater abandon as the audience eggs the performers on. The audience anticipates the characteristic gesture and the accustomed phrase, and greets it with a responsive roar of laughter. The play continues, embellished and elaborated, until the *fāluma* 'clowns' are spent and the audience exhausted with laughter. The women return to quieter games, but others are plotting new routines, often inspired by recent happenings in the village.

Here is the stage and practice hall for established and aspiring performers where they can perform without embarrassment or restraint. Out of the confines of the village, away from men and children, there are, they say, 'no limits'.

> Young men assigned to take provisions to the women do not stay to watch lest they become the butt of their comedies; infants and young children may accompany their mothers, but they do not comprehend the comedy; older daughters have been brought along to help with the cooking, but they are occupied some distance away and form their own gathering further down the beach when night falls. The games are abandoned at darkness and the women begin to regale one another with stories of their past adventures and indiscretions. These are interrupted by comedy performances as the clowns again take the stage and in the moonlight cavort even more obscenely, to everyone's delight. In the morning, exhausted and dishevelled, they reluctantly gather up their belongings and return to again take up their duties within the confines of the village.

This is the 'private' play of women outside the village. Some days later the

73

Fakaofo fāluma *'clowns',*
dressed in purloined
men's clothing,
performing to an
audience of slightly
disconcerted children.
Photos: A. Hooper

women meet again in the village and the same matrons who regaled others with their past indiscretions and laughed and performed with such abandon are passing judgement on the inappropriate or immoral behaviour of younger women, but no one is admonished for what they said or did on the women's 'holiday', the highlights of which will be recounted and savoured.

It is not what women do that is at issue, it is where they do it. Within the village, behaving in their roles as mothers, daughters, sisters and wives, women should be restrained. Still, on occasion the accomplished 'clowns' will perform at public gatherings, but then they monitor themselves lest they be criticised for 'transgressing the limits' of propriety.

There are many subtle, though pervasive, differences in the tone and preoccupations of the separate atoll women's groups: the Nukunonu obsession with communal mat-making and the preoccupation with self-discipline in Atafu. What appears to be at the base of the more elusive differences is how women conceive of themselves as groups in relation to the village grouping of men. Their views are rarely stated explicitly, rather they emerge in their formal discussions and in private conversations, and, even in one village, not all women agree. Nonetheless, there appear to be local prevailing views which elucidate why they are different.

Atafu women organised as the Committee see themselves as the women's counterpart of the men's Āumāga. Like the Āumāga they have their weekly day of activities—Tuesday—and their competitive sides to which their husbands affiliate as they affiliate to their husbands' Āumāga side (see below). Their relationship with the Council also parallels that of the Āumāga. They are semi-autonomous, initiating the activities of their own day, responding to directives and requests of the elders, and keeping the elders more or less informed about their plans. Though the Committee is not as tightly organised as the Āumāga, the women's village activities are predominantly undertaken

in the name of the Committee. The women also have their annual Anniversary Day, but this they hold, with elaborations exceeding those of the Āumāga on their Day, not as women of the Committee, but as 'mothers' in the church.

Nukunonu women speak of themselves as *te itūpā o fafine* 'the women's section/side (of the village)', juxtaposing themselves to 'the side of men' including the elders. They conduct their meetings and run their activities much as men do—the matrons are omnipresent and in charge. The matrons too have jurisdiction over the special pandanus grove, which is seen as comparable to the elders' jurisdiction over the outlying plantations, and the women harvest the grove as the men harvest the plantations. In this regard, women and men of the village are juxtaposed as women and men are in *kāiga* (see chapter 3), with complementary spheres of authority and responsibility. And, despite the matrons' assertion that they defer to the elders, they in fact have considerable autonomy in their own domain and are wont to say that a matter at issue is 'not any business of the elders'. Here the Committee as an organisation takes second place to the women as a distinct constituency within the village mobilised by the matrons for yet another day of mat-plaiting and play.

The prevailing view in Fakaofo is that the women are responsive to the requests and directives of men, specifically the elders, that they support and implement men's initiatives, contributing in their own way to village enterprises, but that they rarely initiate their own projects. They are constrained in the same way that the Āumāga is by the pervasive authority of the Council. Yet their deference does not prevent the matrons from tendering advice to the assembled elders or even gently admonishing them.

Committee organisation was introduced into villages that already had well established concepts, and somewhat different ideas, of how women were placed in their particular scheme of things. How the separate Committees developed over the years reflects in large part these pre-existing ideas.

75

Whatever the differences, however, these organisations are not exactly as they were originally constituted; each has been transformed into a Tokelau village institution. An apt example is one memorable meeting in Nukunonu, when a matron, irritated at the insistence of the nurses that an 'inspection' be held, asked the assembled women: 'Who controls the Committee?' Nobody answered; it was a rhetorical question, for no one doubted that she and the other matrons were in charge, not the younger nurses.

Inati 'institutionalised sharing'

From canoes at the lagoon shore baskets of fish are being transferred to the village laulau *'defined space/platform', where several older men stand surveying the catch and commenting on the visible success of the early morning's net-fishing. They estimate that the fish number* tai afe *'nearly a thousand' as the last basket is emptied upon the heap and four men commence sorting the varicoloured reef-fish into several piles of like species. Soon all that remains of the heap are some odd fish, and around them are four uni-coloured piles. The preliminaries over, seven rows of ten fish each are laid out on the* laulau, *ending with a short eighth row of four. Then each man retrieves one of the discarded baskets and fills it with fish from one of the piles. Each walks the rows, laying a predetermined number of fish in each place, and periodically returning to replenish his basket. When the piles have disappeared, the odd fish are judiciously added to the seventy-four piles, the layout surveyed, a few changes made, and the* inati *pronounced satisfactory. Varicoloured fish neatly laid out in seventy-four piles have replaced the original heap. One man holding a list in hand, begins calling out names, and as each name is called, a child darts forward, basket in hand, to gather up a pile. Shortly thereafter all those 'nearly a thousand' fish are roasting on the hot coral of the village cookhouses.* Inati *have been made in the name of the village; in less than an hour, the morning's catch has been shared out absolutely equally to the whole village.*

Tauvāega *'village divider' laying out* inati *of skipjack—note that his work is being scrutinised.* Photo: Marti Friedlander

Tauvãega *allocating a pile of drinking coconuts harvested from village lands by the* Āumãga— *note the list of* inati *in the hand of the 'divider' (right).* Photo: J. Huntsman

The most eloquent expression of the Tokelau ethic of equality is the system of *inati*, whereby every member of the village—man, woman, child and infant—is allotted an exactly equal portion of something. 'No person receives more', everything is 'divided absolutely equally', for 'all people are equal' are the phrases people use in talking about *inati*. To Tokelau people it is a simple and logical system, a strictly regulated way of equally apportioning things among everyone. This is in principle; as practised, however, the system has its own complications. But before unravelling the complications it is advisable to understand the rules.

The word *inati* refers to a named group of people who receive a joint share from, and are levied joint contributions to, either the village as a whole or some recognised village body; and also to their share or contribution. It is both what is apportioned and the groups apportioned to.

Let us start with what is apportioned. The things most marked that are divided as *inati* are *ika hā* 'sacred fish'. The category includes turtles, swordfish and marlin, skipjack and *ō*, a tiny, silver-pink baitfish upon which skipjack specifically feed. These fish must be 'taken to the village' by their captors. No one can give a definitive answer as to why these particular fish and no others are called 'sacred'. In addition and rather more problematic is the rule that any large catch should be 'taken to the village'; but how large is a matter for the fishermen concerned to decide. If they do take their catch 'to the village' they will be publicly celebrated; if they do not they may be privately chided— there is no definitive rule. It is a rule, however, that the catch must be 'taken to the village' if village equipment is used or if communal fishing has been decreed, for the venture has used village resources, whether owned or pre-

77

The 'grand gesture' for a great communal catch: each inati, regardless of size, is allocated one whole fish, by the decree of the elder.
Photo: J. Huntsman

empted. Likewise, any other produce from communal resources, such as plantations and water tanks, must be distributed as *inati*. Goods or produce presented as gifts to the village or purchased with village funds, if they can be shared, are shared as *inati*. A major feast, whether planned by the village or by some of its families, should provide ample food so that *inati* can be allotted. For all village celebrations, the *inati* system is used to provide the feast food and often to distribute it. Each *inati* group is levied an assigned number of baskets of food, the exact contents unspecified. When the *inati* baskets have been amassed, all like items are put together and then each *inati* group gets a share of each kind of food. In effect, the massed food is thoroughly reshuffled giving everyone a bit of everything.

The directors and implementers of *inati* allocations are men who have been selected by the elders to hold the positions of *tauvāega* 'dividers'. Though one among them is the principal divider, they are all responsible to the elders, specifically the elders who have allocated *inati* before them. These particular men are chosen because they are trustworthy, but they should also be selected from among the descendants of specified nineteenth-century forebears. The genealogical precondition or prerogative is phrased in different ways. For example, in Atafu they are among the descendants of either or both of the two female offspring of the population's founding ancestors.

Some *inati* allocations are simple and straightforward, such as apportion-

Inati Name	a x b = c[1]
Fatia	12 x 1 = 12
Ahelemo	
Poseko	11 x 2 = 22
Vaha	
Lusiano	10 x 2 = 20
Tasesio	
Silao	
Amosa	
Pologa	9 x 4 = 36
Fitele	
Vanikai	8 x 2 = 16
Pale	
Ioane Tino	
Leone	
Vitale	7 x 4 = 28
Alapati	
Kele	
Tutu	
Tamiano	
Melesio	
Sanele	
Sosimo	
Fapiano	
Tuilave	6 x 9 = 54
Sioli	
Telima	
Tefou	
Malaki	5 x 4 = 20
Sani	
Ioane Leo	
Kamilo	
Fati	4 x 4 = 16
Maima	
Mase	3 x 2 = 6
Samu	2 x 1 = 2

35	*Inati*
232:	*Tagata* (persons):
116-1/2	*Tau tokalua* (2-person count)
58-1/4	*Tau tokafaa* (4-person count)
77-1/3	*Tau tokatolu* (3-person count)
46-1/5	*Tau tokalima* (5-person count)

1 a: the value of the *inati* derived from the number of its members
   b: the number of units of similar value
   c: the number of people in *inati* of the same value
   The number of persons included in the system is calculated by adding all the c numerals together. The number of *inati* is calculated by adding all the b numbers together.

Inati *list: A copy of an* inati *list for exactly half the Nukunonu village, with explanatory notes.* From Huntsman 1969b

Two small girls together shoulder their burden of the fish for their inati, *having received some help from a 'divider' in positioning it.* Photo: J. Huntsman

ing six sacks of rice, or a heap of coconuts, or a catch of reef-fish. All adults know how it should be done and for the dividers these are routine tasks. More complicated allocations, such as butchering and dividing a swordfish or apportioning the flesh, fat, eggs and blood of a pair of turtles, require expertise, and dividers will consult experienced elders before they begin their task and ask for their approval after the *inati* are arranged. Conversely, these same elders may instruct the dividers about how a particular distribution should be made. For example, when one hundred yellowfin tuna were landed one day at Atafu, the senior retired divider decreed: 'Make *inati* of one fish each'—that is, each *inati* group regardless of the number of people comprising it, was to have a whole fish. This was a grand gesture, a celebration of plenty, and also a good deal easier for the actual dividers who otherwise would have butchered and punctiliously apportioned all one hundred fish. They, however, could not have made this decision themselves, for it abrogated the primary rule of absolutely equal shares for all.

Dividers in fact do meticulously obey this rule—expediency must not compromise it. They must be seen to be fair, but at the same time do their job efficiently. To this end, they keep lists of the named *inati* groups of the village. What each of these groups receives (or contributes) must correspond to the number of people in it, so each group has a numerical value to insure that each will receive (or contribute) its fair share. This is all relatively simple on paper, but it can get rather difficult on the ground when the dividers are creating seventy-five or so equitably weighted portions. Fine discriminations are made between shares valued at ten versus nine, and a share valued at ten must be twice as large in all respects as one valued at five.

Dividers in each village have devised a number of strategies for arranging their lists and laying out portions to expedite their tasks. All the *inati* groups may be divided into two or four lists, each representing an equal number of people, and whatever is being divided likewise initially equally divided, allowing two or four separate distributions to be made. *Inati* of like value are always grouped together and they are all arranged in descending order of value so comparative quantities can be easily judged. Fractional counts may be established for each value and even an upper and lower limit of *inati* value set, e.g. not less than three or more than twelve. The procedures and judgements are always under public scrutiny. Though no one else is allowed into the designated area where the dividers are operating until the named portions are called, among the children waiting around the peripheries to be summoned are interested adult onlookers—many of them if the division is a major and complex one.

Besides their counting, calculating and allocating duties, dividers are charged with keeping their *inati* lists updated so that they correspond with the actual assignment of villagers to *inati* groups and include every resident member of the village. As new villagers are born, as old villagers die,. as people arrive and depart, even for short periods, *inati* values change and the lists must be adjusted accordingly. However, keeping updated lists is not just a simple business of adding one here and subtracting one there. People may decide to regroup, to transfer from one *inati* to another, to divide one *inati* into two or combine two *inati* into one. What *inati* group any person is to be a part of is determined not by the dividers but by the persons concerned. The dividers are simply expected to make the requested adjustments and to make sure that no one person is claimed by more than one *inati* group.

This right of people to assign themselves and their children a place within the system is what gives the system its own special complications. Consider a village population allocated among exclusive *inati* groups, and ask on what bases these groups are composed and why a person is in one group rather than another. To begin with, they rarely correspond to households, and are almost always composed of persons linked by bonds of kinship and marriage. But the combination of links between the persons included is so diverse that no rules governing their composition can be identified. The only way to understand the composition of *inati* groups is to identify the focal person or couple of the group, and then to determine why the other members have placed themselves or been placed in the *inati* with them. In the simplest, though uncommon, case, children are in an *inati* because the focal couple are their parents. More likely, a collection of grandchildren have been placed by their parents as the parents' replacements in an *inati* which focuses on their grandparents. And many groups are more complex in membership because parents or grandparents have placed children in *inati* groups that focus on their own siblings. Then again married people may elect to remain in the *inati* groups of their own parents or even of their own parents' siblings. As members are added, removed and substituted over time *inati* composition changes, usually becoming increasingly complex, and an elderly focal couple may have placed in their *inati* people both young and adult who are related to one of them (as siblings' children and grandchildren) or to them both (as children and grandchildren).

As dividers adjust and readjust their lists and try to determine just what

An inati *of turtle blood, in a coconut
shell, and eggs, in a tin cup, valued at
four is collected by the boy in whose
name the share is called.*
Photo: J. Huntsman

the composition of a particular *inati* group is, they might well think, and
indeed have been known to mutter, that their job might be made a good deal
easier if there were some established principles regarding the composition of
inati groups. But they do not say so outright, for people would surely object
with righteous indignation: they are only showing *alofa* 'concern and compassion' for others, specifically their kin, by placing their children in others'
inati. What they are doing as donors is forgoing a value to their *inati* and
transferring it to another. Children are 'counters' in the system, placed here
and there as evidence of the donor's *alofa*. The 'beloved' person's *inati* in-
creases in value and an extra share of an 'absolutely equal' division is received. When infants are given, one group benefits but no other group really
loses, since infants do not consume any share, and even young children do
not consume their fair portion. Yet some people remain in *inati* to which they
were placed as children when they are adults, and when they may be truly
forgoing their share for the benefit of others. Then it is proper, if not expected, for the beneficiary to recognise this by sending a portion of the
received *inati* share to the person in whose name it was received. Punctilious
recipients, showing their reciprocal *alofa*, may in fact do this for all people
placed in their *inati*, adding to the density of food transfers in the village.

It may seem somewhat ironic that the produce distributed as *inati* is
frequently referred to as 'food for the children' when children so often do not
partake of the shares assigned to them. But this phrase really refers to the
dependency of everyone on the village (personified by the elders) for their
livelihood. Children are indeed central to the operation and ideology of the
system. The call 'children of the village go to the *inati*' announces an *inati*

distribution and children are dispatched with baskets in hand to collect the named portions. Woe betide the child who dawdles or is inattentive, who is not there to respond or does not hear the name called. The child is sure to be rebuked by the dividers and, if particularly unfortunate, may be pummelled by their smelly, fish-bloodied hands. Literally, *inati* are given to children, and this is reinforced symbolically in the way *inati* are named. They are named after male children, though not necessarily a male child within them, or after a person who in other contexts would be considered a child. Most *inati* are designated by the name of a child or grandchild of the focal person or couple. The name may, however, be that of a married man who has remained in his parents' or grandparents' *inati* and therefore is still a child of it, or it may be the name of a mature son who has gone away or died, whom the *inati* name commemorates. People say that it gives them joy and comfort to hear the name called out. The name too is frequently one of a deceased forebear conferred upon a child. Again, people are reminded of that forebear even though the name is now borne by a child, and as often as not infrequently used for him. A very few *inati* are named for male adults who are focal persons in their *inati*. But these exceptions only illuminate the principle; they are all men who have married into the villages and, consequently, have no village forebears, property or resources. They are, in a sense, dependants of the village. In short, *inati* are named for the young, the absent, the landless, for those the village must provide for because they are helpless, for those that people wish to recall because they are 'gone'.

The *inati* system as a village institution is governed by well-known principles which are rigidly adhered to, and formally instantiates an ethic of absolute equality. Yet as people operate within the system—move themselves as they wish within it—they do not really all receive equally. However, this is of their own choice. Tokelau people claim the *inati* system is a central institution of their unique heritage—something that has 'always been'. It is an institutionalised statement of the equality they celebrate which they manipulate so that by consent some are more equal than others.

Faitū 'sides' and *kalapu* 'clubs'

Undeniably Tokelau people are very organised; they have a penchant for creating organisations for themselves. Within their various village bodies they establish companies or sections, and village occasions and enterprises spur the formation of new dyadic or triadic sets, or the resurrection of old ones, shelved years before, which will persist for a while and then lapse. All these groupings have officers or leaders, meetings, and often distinctive uniforms and banners, but they have different places in the village structure. Subgroupings within village bodies have been touched on above, and those within the churches will be discussed later. Here, two types of groupings are described: *faitū* 'sides', which are pervasive and include everyone, and *kalapu* 'clubs', which are transitory and exclusive.

Each Tokelau village is divided into two opposed *faitū*. The word used to designate these dual divisions is probably a Samoan borrowing (Samoan *feitū*) suggesting that this mode of organisation, at least in its present form, was modelled on a Samoan prototype. The founding of *faitū* is clearly linked with the introduction of *kilikiti* 'cricket' to the atolls—probably sometime around the turn of the century. It is impossible to be more precise about these recent historical innovations; no visitor records seeing cricket played in years when Tokelau elders recall that they were holding inter-atoll competitions,[8] but they are decidedly vague about when and in what context the game was introduced. Elderly people, even those born before the turn of the century, are unable to recall a pre-cricket era or a time when there were no *faitū*. It may be that both appeared gradually, introduced into the separate communities by young men who had been in Samoa, and after some time, perhaps quite suddenly, were taken up by everyone with enthusiasm. But there may be other explanations for this apparent historical amnesia.[9] Nobody, of course, asserts that *kilikiti* was an indigenous creation, yet as the Tokelau national sport its local beginnings are conveniently 'unknown': no person brought it, no village began it, it simply arose and flourished. As for the *faitū*, they may well have been a long-standing part of the Tokelau social repertoire, but otherwise named and constituted, and having other social purposes. From time to time other two-part divisions are invoked, such as *alatua* 'ocean path' and *alatai* 'lagoon-path', which are said to pre-date the 'sides'. Whatever their historical origins, the present sets of *faitū*, though primarily focused on perpetual cricket competition, are much more than just two competing teams.

Every person resident in the village, including the pastor and other visitors, is a member of one *faitū* or the other. The very old and the very young are nominal members, counted for the purpose of levies or distributions made in the name of *faitū*. Otherwise everyone, beginning in their mid teens, participates in their *faitū* activities, and most continue to be involved right into their sixties. *Faitū* loyalties are intense, generated by the ongoing competition between them, so that which one a person belongs to is a matter of real social concern.

When *faitū* were originally set up, they were territorially based. Those people residing in one half of the village were of one *faitū* opposed to those in the other—the dividing line was clear. These dividing lines are still recognised and people continue to refer to the halves of the villages by *faitū* names. However, their territorial distinctiveness has been compromised by residential shifts. When whole households, or sections of households, moved across the line, their members could hardly be forced to abandon their long-standing loyalties, so enclaves of one *faitū* came to be located within the territory of another. More commonly, people from opposed *faitū* marry, and one partner moves across the line to reside with the other. When this happens people agree that it is best that one partner change affiliation, since problems both practical and interpersonal are apt to arise if husband and wife have conflicting loyalties. But there is no rule concerning who should change, so the couple may be pressured by both *faitū* wishing to retain and gain members. It may be argued that the incoming spouse, who has moved across the line, should change. However, the incoming spouse is usually the husband, who already has played cricket for years with his *faitū* team and is as reluctant to abandon his team-mates as they are to lose him. The wife also is committed to her *faitū*, but anticipates that she will be too occupied with infants and small children to take much part in *faitū* activities for some years. Accordingly in most cases, though often not immediately, it is the wife who changes. Children automatically become members of their parents' *faitū* at birth, unless their parents specifically place them in the other as a replacement for the parent who has changed sides. In any case, a person may change sides when reaching sixteen years or so, at the time when he or she is beginning to be a fully active member. The times when it is accepted as quite legitimate for people to change affiliations are times when they are taking new roles and responsibilities; otherwise people should not change *faitū*. Very few do, and they are regarded as traitors by their abandoned *faitū*, and are somewhat suspect in their new one.

Faitū organisation is now an integral part of village life, essential to what Tokelau people refer to as their *olaga fiafia* 'joyous life', a central feature of which is usually good-natured competition. The *faitū* by their very nature are opposed in ongoing and diverse contests of one-upmanship, and this engenders elaborations and transformations of them. The case of Atafu best illustrates this. In the early 1960s Atafu's *faitū* were based on the standard territorial division of a village, but then the Āumāga created a new set of *faitū* based on a vote which had been held within that organisation. The members had been about evenly divided on the knotty question of exactly when to hold their annual commemorative day—at the usual time, which was before the next scheduled supply ship, or several weeks later after the ship departed. Translating this division of opinion into *faitū* they appropriately named them Fai 'Do (it now)' and Tolo 'Delay'. The women retained their old territorial alignments for their own purposes, while at the same time affiliating with their husbands or fathers in the men's Fai/Tolo division. Then in the early 1970s, the women too created a new set of *faitū*, to which the members of the Committee were arbitrarily assigned. These *faitū* were named Higano 'Pandanus blossom' and Oliana 'Oleander', and initially they were so popular that the men abandoned Fai and Tolo altogether and joined in the activities of their wife's or mother's *faitū*, even competing among themselves as Higano and Oliana. The Atafu *faitū* are admittedly unusually volatile,[10] and the reason given for this is the tendency for 'side' competition to escalate and thereby threaten village peace and *māopoopo*. However, there is another unstated and more positive reason for changing *faitū* names and makeup in this communally very committed village. New *faitū* are joined with tremendous enthusiasm and their creation corresponds with the initiation of a major village project. Competition between them in both work and play propels the unified village towards the completion of its projects. Furthermore, besides overcoming potential factionalism, the shifting alignments obviate the problem of spouses having different loyalties.

In Fakaofo and Nukunonu the original territorial *faitū* are still more or less in place, though they have undergone elaborations and changes. Over

On the annual celebratory day of the faitū Amelika, the President (left) and Vice-President (right) stand at attention on the platform of their 'White House' before their flag.
Photo: J. Huntsman

the years the Fakaofo *faitū* have been renamed: Poa 'Boer'/Egelani 'England' gave way to Hemani 'Germany'/Egelani, then to Hemani/Amelika 'America', and finally Hamoa 'Samoa'/Niu Hila 'New Zealand'. The name changes were inspired by distant conflicts, the final and most proximate being the Mau uprising against the New Zealand Administration in Western Samoa. The last name set has persisted for over fifty years and the sides they name have created internal divisions: Hamoa into Atua, A'ana and Tuamahaga, the major political districts of Upolu (Western Samoa); and Niu Hila into Maoli (Maori) and Pakeha ('European').

Nukunonu's divisions are not couched in the same inflated idiom of international conflict, though they are named for nations—Egelani and Amelika (earlier Niu Hila). Egelani appropriately occupies the old section of the village and Amelika the new. Even in this tiny village there is a traditional homeland which spawned a new nation. Egelani is consciously and proudly conservative; Amelika created internal divisions of Alami 'Army', Malini 'Marine' and Nekelo 'Negro'—this was in the late 1960s!

As independent, usually territorially based, organisations, often referred to in all seriousness as *mālō* 'nations, governments, empires', each *faitū* has its own internal organisation, and follows its own creative traditions and precedents. What they always have is some named offices, uniforms, a fund of money and an established meeting place. Amelika of Nukunonu calls its place of meeting (otherwise an ordinary family residence) the Fale Paepae 'White House'! Flags of the nations for which they are named, banners, stencilled shirts and scarves proclaim *faitū* identity. Uniforms for cricket and costumes for dance, which should not be worn for other purposes until replaced by new gear, visibly differentiate the two *faitū*. They also have their own fishing nets and, for distributing the fish caught in that net, their own *inati* groups, which are used as well to distribute other things and to levy goods and produce in the name of the *faitū*. Naturally, they have their own cricket bats and balls, and, since they also form competitive dance teams, they also 'own' the songs and dances they compose, in the sense that the opposing *faitū* should not perform them, except as a village dance team competing with another village. Fakaofo and Nukunonu *faitū* have commemorative days devoted to cricket and dance competitions, feasts and whatever other events have been created in their tradition, e.g. flag-raising ceremonies. The less durable Atafu sides understandably do not celebrate commemorative days, but the current set is omnipresent in the events of the annual days of the Āumāga and the Women.

Faitū cut across the village age/sex organisation by including people of all ages and both sexes, but then partially duplicate that organisation in their own. Younger men usually fill *faitū* offices, such as president, and leadership positions, such as cricket captain, but the elders of *faitū* are deferred to and voice the resolutions of any meeting. Men and women convene separate meetings about events or projects of their particular concern. General meetings in Atafu and Nukunonu are attended by men and women as couples; in Fakaofo, wives stay at home.

Though *faitū* initiate diverse activities and may be activated for village projects, their prime purpose is seen to be entertainment, and of Tokelau entertainments none is more celebrated than *kilikiti*. It is not altogether inappropriate that a cricket field is known in Tokelau as a *malae*—a word which was used for sacred precincts in pre-European times. A game of *kilikiti* is referred to as a *taua* 'battle, war' and a player is not 'out' but *mate* 'dead (as of animals)'. While hardly a battle, Tokelau *kilikiti* is a much more exuberant and direct sort of contest than its English ancestor. The essential features of cricket are there: two competing sides, the ball bowled from one end of a pitch and struck by a batsman at the other, runs scored and kept count of, and batsmen dismissed by being bowled, caught or run out. But the resemblance ends there.

A central feature of the transformation from staid traditional cricket into boisterous Tokelau *kilikiti* is that everybody is involved. True spectators are few because nearly everyone present participates, if only to take their turn at bat. While the number of 'outs' may be counted, a side is not retired until all who might be persuaded to bat have done so, and in major contests they may number over a hundred. The idea that there is a set number of players or an equal number on each side is rarely entertained. Fielders are always fewer than batters, but they still are numerous, stationed more or less as they choose.

Younger and more agile players choose positions close to the pitch where the action mostly is, and the older or less skilled select spots which will see little action and where there is some shade which they occasionally leave to chase an errant ball. But all are alert to what is going on at the pitch, even as they chat with people seated or passing nearby. Bowlers, stationed at both ends of the pitch, are replaced at any time and the ball is simply delivered from whichever end of the pitch it is returned to in the previous play. There are no 'overs'. On the pitch of worn and scarred concrete, using a small and very resilient gum-rubber ball, a practised bowler quickly bowls opponents out, and a batter has little chance of placing shots out of the reach of up to seventy fielders. Yet many younger men are stylishly batsmen, swinging away, much like a baseball batter, rather than judiciously defending their wicket. By lofting the ball high beyond the clustered in-

Below left: *A pause in play while a ball is retrieved or a batter replaced.* Photo: Marti Friedlander
Right: *A runner quickly calculates whether to 'go' or 'not' to go, while hearing perhaps conflicting shouts of advice on the matter, but should attend to his adviser on the right.* Photo: Marti Friedlander

A fast overarm bowl down the pitch. The men leaning on bats to the right and left of the bowler are the referees. Six fielders are visible. Photo: J. Huntsman

fielders and into the breadfruit trees where its trajectory is confused by branches, leaves and twigs, a batter is very unlikely to be caught out. In any case, the aim of the game is to make runs, and to this end a batter having hit the ball remains in the crease. Young, agile runners are stationed at each end of the pitch holding a light stick about the length of a cricket bat. As the ball is played, they crouch poised to run, their stick touching the ground adjacent to the crease. When the ball is hit, responding to the shouted commands of others, they hurtle headlong up and down the pitch, skidding and turning at each end just as their stick touches inside the crease, stopping only when instructed. Having separate runners not only results in more runs, but also makes it possible for older people to play and the young to play all the time. Except for the immediate environs of the pitch, the field of play is littered with trees and buildings. A boundary score is achieved only when the ball reaches the sea, so the village itself is the arena of play, and the many obstructions have engendered a host of local rules. Generally, a catch taken off a roof, building or tree is a fair one, dismissing the batter. A ball landing within an adjacent house may be an automatic two, simply to discourage fielders from barging in. Balls lodged firmly in specific coconut palms gain set scores and a hit that lands into the Fakaofo village well, some 15 yards from the pitch, gains a two.

Yet to just describe the game misses the sheer exuberance of *kilikiti*, for the game is not just played, it is orchestrated.

A gentle underarm is bowled to a female batter. Women are always bowled underarm; men only sometimes, to break the pace. Photo: J. Huntsman

On the sidelines the batting side drums and dances and sings to distract the fielders, and to entertain themselves. Photo: J. Huntsman

Rhythmic drumming on a large biscuit tin by one the fielders proclaims each fallen wicket—the batters are literally drummed out—and the fielders in concert perform set routines to the drum beat—shouting, clapping, stamping, jumping. The biscuit tin of the batting side sounds from behind a row of dancers, singing and dancing to encourage their batters and distract the fielders, while among them clowns cavort. Added to the din is a chorus of shouts to the young runners to fano fano fano *'go go go' or* aua aua *'don't don't (go)'. A well-hit ball brings clamour from the outfield as fielders shout to one another where the ball is:* i luga *'above'* i tua *'seaward', and direct its passage as it is thrown around familiar obstacles through a chain of fielders back to the pitch. Only the referees stationed at each end of pitch evince the decorum of English cricket, but then they get embroiled too when a call is questioned.*

The play does not end with the conclusion of the contest.

This fielder has a second role. As each batter is out (or mate 'dead') he picks up his drumsticks and literally drums the batter out with a sharp rhythm on the biscuit tin. Photo: J. Huntsman

The two faitū, *sitting at their accustomed, shaded places and facing one another across the now empty pitch, plot and plan. The winners may summon the losers to the centre of the field and berate and ridicule them, this is their punishment for losing. Or, the leaders of each side may take turns haranguing and challenging the other. The winners may decide to parade their victory, setting out on a circuit of the village, singing as they go along, and being stopped from time to time by their supporters who rush from their houses to anoint them with perfume and oil. Whatever the immediate celebration, after a brief respite, the two* faitū *will face one another in the meeting house, vying to out-dance and one-up each other in the subtle repartee of song and speech. Mockery, taunt and challenge laced with humour characterise the interchanges, and the upshot may well be another cricket contest on the morrow.*

No *faitū* is ever definitively victorious, since there is always another match to be played, song to be sung, and dance to be danced.

Whether the village is engaged in a major communal enterprise or people are simply going about their accustomed, everyday tasks, the *faitū* are in evidence—meeting, plotting and planning, and even in casual games of dominoes or cards, the paired opponents may well represent opposing *faitū*. At certain times *faitū* virtually take possession of the village for weeks at a time, daily competing in *kilikiti* and nightly competing in dance. Routine tasks are put aside, and everybody is provisioned by their respective *faitū*, the men fishing together, the women cooking together. There is excitement, display,

The Takiala/*'Guidance' Club devoted to home improvement posed in their club uniforms for a group portrait.*
Photo: J. Huntsman

and a euphoria of *māopoopo* generated by this prolonged carnival. But eventually it comes to an end, either because people have become tired of it and concerned about other things that need to be done; or occasionally because the carnival threatens to get out of control; good-natured competition becomes increasingly hostile and village *māopoopo* and peace are in jeopardy. Almost everyone is quietly relieved when the elders decree the carnival over.

Structurally *faitū* divide the villages, but without compromising their cherished *māopoopo*. Each replicates, with idiosyncratic elaborations, the principles of village organisations, and promotes the precepts of village life with an intensity engendered by competition. Here cooperation and competition are not antithetical; they operate as a duet. Devoted primarily to play, entertainment and enjoyment, the *faitū* unify the village in controlled opposition.

Clubs or *kalapu* are quite different; they are voluntary associations of like-minded people created for and devoted to a specific purpose. They are not organisations of the village though they are organisations within the village and subject to village authority. Clubs are vulnerable to community censure, but are by and large tolerated because they are generally seen to be benefiting the community in some way. For their part, clubs take pains to appear to be serving others, rather than just their own members, lest they be suspected of self-interest. But despite the fellowship and sense of purpose that clubs are supposed to engender, they rarely last very long. Typically, a club is founded, flourishes for a while and then disbands. This instability may be the outcome of their voluntary form; people can simply opt out, and in small communities lines of cleavage are in flux, shifting in response to events. Tokelau village institutions deny such cleavages, while Tokelau kin loyalties produce the most stable ones. Clubs, given their exclusive character, may produce cleavages within the village and thereby they fall into disrepute, and may even be ordered to disband. What usually precipitates a club's demise, however, is money. Members initially agree to pay dues to establish and maintain a treasury, and they raise funds in other ways to augment it. But then, predictably, something untoward happens: members are delinquent in their dues payments, or find the dues excessive, or disagree about how monies

A fāili *'band'* club posed
for a group portrait in
their uniforms and with
their instruments.
Photo: A. Hooper

should be spent. Some decide to resign and demand their share of the treasury, which complicates matters further. Animosity defeats fellowship and the club dissolves. But this does not discourage people from forming clubs and devoting a lot of time, energy and a bit of scarce money to them.

Clubs are founded for a variety of purposes. Entertainment clubs are formed to play pop music; their treasury is used to buy musical instruments and they meet to practise their repertoire. Their membership is relatively large and not restricted to those with musical talent, and, once equipped and practised, they play at parties and feasts, sometimes for a small fee. Homemaker clubs are founded to collectively upgrade the amenities of their members' homes; their treasury is used to purchase housewares, and they set themselves goals, such as plaiting new floor mats for their homes. Cooperative work clubs are formed to assist members with major tasks, such as housebuilding, building up their treasury by hiring themselves out to work for others and then using their treasury to buy materials for themselves.[11]

At times there is a profusion, and rapid turnover, of clubs devoted to entrepreneurial endeavours. While clubs with other stated purposes often take on entrepreneurial activities to enrich their treasuries, entrepreneurial clubs aim to import goods and dispose of them at a profit. Their modes of operating are diverse. At one extreme are relatively large clubs that import a limited range of goods, selling items to club members at cost and to others at a small profit. They always find plenty of buyers, but their enterprise is constrained by limited capital. At the other extreme are clubs of two or three persons engaged in real profitmaking ventures. One person runs the venture; the others provide a bit of capital in return for small profits and give what is really a business legitimacy as a club. Village regulations prohibiting private businesses are evaded by forming a club, and a club can avoid extending credit to kin and friends, whereas an independent storekeeper would be heavily pressured to do so. The entrepreneurial instigator has established sources of supply for goods and ample capital. The goods are sold easily and at reasonable profit.

The formation of one type of club often stimulates the establishment of others with like purpose, which adds an element of competition. At times it seems as if the whole active adult population of a village is engaged in club enterprises, though this does not last long. Clubs, with their apt names, elected officers, regular meetings, planned occasions and uniforms seem superficially similar to *faitū*, and as in *faitū*, affiliation is by married couples, though they are usually initiated by several men or women. However, unlike *faitū*, no particular club has a permanent place in the village structure. The exception to this statement in fact supports it, at the same time indicating what clubs are all about.

> *The Piula club was founded in Fakaofo some 50 years ago, and sons have succeeded their fathers as members. It has the usual elected officers, regular meetings, uniforms, a flag and a fishing net. What makes it unique is its purpose which is to support fellow villagers in times of distress. Its primary mission is to provide services when there is a death in the village. Members dig the grave where the family wish the deceased to be buried and make the coffin from a supply of timber they have on hand. They enter the house of mourning at the appropriate time to place the body in the coffin, close the lid and carry the coffin to the church. After the service they transport the deceased and mourners to the islet where the grave has been dug, solemnly carry the coffin to the grave and place it therein. After the graveside service, they fill the grave and then go fishing on behalf of the bereaved family. Piula members are summoned by the conch shell, and anytime the conch shell sounds they assemble immediately. It may be that a canoe or person is overdue and may be lost. The Piula strikes a tone of Christian high moral seriousness in all its activities. Members must attend meetings in white shirts and ties; are disciplined for any moral lapses, and urged always to defer to their elders and respect one another.*

What is it that makes the Piula, unlike any other club, a village institution, to the extent that the club is granted an annual day of commemoration and celebration? First, it is unquestionably devoted to the service of others and can in no way be seen as self-serving or divisive. Second, the specific tasks it performs, especially at times of death, are not or cannot be performed by any other village organisation. The Piula persists because it is valued by the community it serves.

Lotu 'churches'

To be a Tokelau person is to be a Christian person. Christian rituals are part of everyday life: morning and evening devotions are held at home or in church, grace precedes any meal, meetings always open and usually close with prayer, Christian homilies lard speech, and biblical passages inspire song. On the Sabbath virtually everyone congregates in the churches morning and afternoon to worship. In accordance with the command of the Almighty, after six days of labour all Tokelau rests.

Over 130 years ago Christianity was introduced into the fabric of Tokelau life. It has assuredly transformed the society and culture, but as Christianity is propounded and practised in Tokelau, it manifests what Tokelau people consider to be their ancient and shared heritage. Two Christian denominations were established in the 1860s: Atafu readily accepted the Lotu Taiti or

The women's side of the Fakaofo church: the normal, if not prescribed, women's attire for Sunday morning service is a white dress and saucer-like hat skewered to pinned-up hair. Photo: Marti Friedlander

London Missionary Society Protestantism, Nukunonu eagerly embraced the Lotu Pope or Roman Catholicism, and Fakaofo somewhat reluctantly allowed the presence of both and most of the people eventually became Protestants. This situation has not changed, for each village enacted local regulations which prohibited proselytism or public worship by any other denomination. The regulations are retained not so much out of denominational intolerance, for people of both churches espouse Christian harmony and fellowship, but in the firm belief that should other churches be allowed, factionalism would inevitably follow and destroy the precious *māopoopo* of village life.

Tokelau people are acutely aware of how their denominational traditions

Before the service begins: inside the Atafu church that was demolished at the beginning of 1970. Photo: J. Huntsman

93

differ. Protestant women must wear hats to church but Catholic women must not, Protestants sit to pray and Catholics kneel, Protestants diligently read their Bibles and Catholics diligently say their rosaries, Protestants must rest on the Sabbath while Catholics may play, and so on. These differences are visible to all and may even be the subject of good-natured banter. Doctrinal divergences are not debated, though they are well known, and no one today attempts to persuade another to leave his or her church to join the other. What a person believes is not the business of another, unless they are members of the same church. What does matter very much is that the two churches live in Christian harmony, and to this end they are meticulously accorded equal respect and precedence when Catholics and Protestants are together. Yet however much doctrinal divergences are played down and differing practices respected and accommodated, there are significant differences in the institutional structures of the two churches, which are reflected in the ongoing life of the villages. These are most apparent of course in Atafu and Nukunonu, where village polity and congregation are synonymous, while in Fakaofo, where two congregations are accommodated, the differences pale. It is tempting, as numerous commentators have done, to attribute the distinctiveness of the atoll communities to their religious affiliations, but such explanations are simplistic. Differences indeed there are, but they cannot necessarily be attributed to religion, for the local organisation of the congregations, whether Protestant or Catholic, mirrors the organisational structure of the village polities, and these polities confront the same issues in dealing with their church institutions. Nonetheless, two contrasts seem salient and are best dealt with before discussing the parallels between local organisation of the churches and their polities. These are (i) the structure of church authority, and (ii) the mode of moral discipline exercised by the church.

In the Catholic Church, where a ranking of sanctity underlies a hierarchy of authority, a priest is sent by his bishop to shepherd a Tokelau flock. A priest is the religious authority in the parish and the link between his flock and a worldwide hierarchy with its apex in Rome. He directs the religious life of the village in which he is placed, is answerable to his distant superior for his conduct, and responsive to the dictates from above in what he does. Whether he stays or leaves is a matter decided from afar. In keeping with his vows, he is something of a social isolate, however much he may welcome the controlled companionship of select members of his flock and enjoy the awed attentiveness of the community. He is their Patele or Father, a man of another order.

A Protestant pastor and his wife are invited by a Tokelau congregation to serve them, as both 'servants of God' and servants of a congregation with which a pastor has a *feagaiga* 'contract/covenant' for a predetermined number of years. The deacons of the local church, on behalf of the congregation, invite, dismiss, counsel and direct the pastor. In the performance of his duties and for his and his family's general conduct, he is responsible to them, and they are responsible for the welfare of the pastor and his family. The Tokelau Protestant parishes are part of the Christian Congregational Church of Sa-

A Protestant congregation departs after the Sunday morning service to change into more casual garments, to eat the big Sunday dinner (prepared overnight) and then to be quiet— preferably to sleep— until the bell for the afternoon service tolls and they change back into church-going garments. Following the afternoon service, the restrictions on activity are lifted a bit, so that groups may meet and plans be laid for the coming day and week. Photo: Marti Friedlander

moa, and their pastors have their place in that institutional structure, but this body cannot dictate what happens in the local congregation, it can only advise. No pastor stays if the congregation decides he will go, and though he may ultimately be answerable to God, he is immediately answerable to the congregation he serves.

A Protestant congregation is composed of communicants, who have a voice in church affairs, and non-communicants, who do not. A person who has a voice is expected to be morally above reproach and so communicants are answerable to their fellow communicants if they stray from the dictates of the puritanical moral code of the church. Communicants who are suspected of sin must appear before their fellows and be publicly examined. They may confess their moral lapses, or may profess innocence but be found guilty in light of other testimony. Those found to have sinned are removed from communicant status—they have 'fallen'. They may be reinstated later after some scrutiny of their subsequent behaviour, for after all to 'fall' is human and 'this is earth' not heaven. Nonetheless, to 'fall' is shameful and to avoid 'falling' some people, particularly young men, delay becoming communicants. This does not mean that their sins will be overlooked, for they will be judged and disciplined in other venues, but then they have not professed to be morally upstanding.

Catholics privately confess their sins, personally repent and ask for forgiveness. A person's moral status is not a matter of public scrutiny and a person's sins are not a matter of public record, though they are the subject of gossip and may be raised in village meetings if they threaten village harmony. Furthermore, the Catholic moral code is not so puritanical. It follows the Ten Commandments, but has never counted dancing, singing, or strong drink sinful.

These differences between the Protestant and Catholic Churches are surely important, and they have had their influence on the character of the villages. Yet what is so striking on closer examination is how alike the local religious organisations are; whether Protestant or Catholic, they have been moulded into institutions of the Tokelau social order. Not only do the church organisations parallel in their arrangement the structure of the village polities, but also in the confined spaces of the village churches the social order of the village is neatly laid out: males on one side and females on the other from front, the youngest, to back, the eldest. Practical considerations, such as easy egress for women with infants or assigned duties, only minimally modify the overall pattern. The choir is positioned between the adults at their back and the children, who are themselves arranged in rows by age. Thus children begin their disciplined Christian life, having left the laps or sides of their parents, right before the pulpit where they receive a sharp rap from a deacon if they are inattentive and are dismissed from the service under the gaze of everyone if they are disruptive. As they mature and can discipline themselves, they move backwards row by row, with fewer people watching over them and more people to watch over. Invariably at least some elders are seated at the very back where they can oversee everybody. The only other people who have such an overview are the ones conducting the service, but then they can be seen by everyone else.

The village elders are in charge of the church buildings and the congregations gathered within them. The amount of control or direction they exercise over the weekly and yearly round of religious activities depends on their established relations with the pastor, priest, catechist or acting pastor in residence. They must be informed, they should be consulted, and a prudent pastor seeks their advice. Oversight of the Protestant churches is vested in the *kaufaigaluega* 'working party' made up of deacons and lay preachers who meet together once a month. (The work here referred to is the *Galuega o te Atua* 'Work of God'.) Given Tokelau assumptions about how people acquire the attributes required of those elected to be deacons and lay preachers, it follows that they tend to be the same people that have been selected as members of the Elders' Council. So though the two bodies are not identical, there is considerable overlap between them. That others are in the *kaufaigaluega* is testimony of their good character and they will presumably join the Council in due course. In Catholic Nukunonu the two bodies are synonymous since the devotional group (*mistelio*) under the patronage of the Sacred Heart, to whom the church is dedicated, are in charge of the church, and this devotional group is composed exclusively of the heads of extended families who make up the Council. So these, mostly elderly, men, whether meeting as a devotional group after the Sabbath Benediction or as the Council on Monday, are the group with whom the priest or catechist confers on

A deacon reprimands inattentive children in the front pews with a rap of his fan. Photo: Marti Friedlander

church matters, just as the Protestant pastor confers with the *kaufaigaluega*. Certainly the Protestant body normally has wider statutory duties in running the parish and more direct control than its Catholic counterpart, but irrespective of degree, the two bodies fill the same structural position.

Men as a group do not have a place in the organisational structure of either church, though they are marked as a separate category within the congregation. Following the Protestant Sabbath afternoon service, the Christian Endeavour Group, known as the Au Taumafai, regularly meets. Subdivisions within this assembly are assigned biblical texts and are called upon in turn to explicate them. One of these divisions is composed of men not yet elected to the *kaufaigaluega*. Catholic men who are not members of the Council are divided among several devotional groups under the patronage of male saints and meet after the Sabbath Benediction to perform their devotions. Within both church congregations men are not juxtaposed to their elders; they are awaiting to become elders. This exactly reflects their structural position in the Nukunonu polity and probably reflects their position in the pre-Āumāga polities of Atafu and Fakaofo. They are a category of persons who will, given time and longevity, become one of the marked group of elderly wise rulers.

Every Catholic woman is a member of one of several devotional groups, naturally under the patronage of female saints, and all are members of the encompassing 'Women of the Church', headed by the eldest active woman among them and dominated by the matrons of the village. Protestant women are together members of the 'Mothers' Fellowship' under the direction of the wife of the pastor and wives of the *kaufaigaluega*, and are also members of named companies within it. These Catholic and Protestant women's groups serve their churches in the same ways. They clean the church and its environs weekly, the devotional groups or companies undertaking the task in rotation. Periodically they tidy the graveyards and thoroughly scrub the church interior. They regularly produce mats to furnish the residences of priests or pastors, to adorn and carpet the church, and to be given on behalf of the congregation to church visitors and departing pastors and priests. By collecting dues, or imposing fines, or staging festivals, they contribute to church coffers. At their meetings they plan their activities and also discipline their members, admonishing them for inappropriate behaviour within and outside the confines of the church, absence from meetings or neglect of assigned duties. The matrons, however, reserve their most severe reprimands for women whose words or actions might in any way disturb the relationship between the village and its spiritual leader, and give the women a bad reputation in the eyes of these eminent outsiders. Strict decorum of women is required if they are to, as the matrons say, 'protect the village [reputation]'.

Children are a well-defined and clearly placed category of persons, socially grouped by age grades in the village school five days a week, and in Sunday School on the Sabbath under the direction and tutelage of adult teachers.[12] Infants are appendages of their parents carried or escorted beyond their homes and under constant supervision within and around their homes. However, young people when they leave school at the age of fifteen or sixteen are betwixt and between. They are no longer children but are not yet competent adults either. They are in the village but have no defined place in the village structure; socially they are in limbo. Older people recall how in their youth they remained in school or otherwise attached to the mission establishment, where they were closely supervised until they married or were otherwise considered adults. People are ambivalent about such arrangements. Misconduct, only to be expected from youth, can put strains on the relationship between pastor and village, and while serving the mission these able youths are not helping their families or the village. Though youth are socially devalued as irresponsible they are nonetheless strong and able, and in practical terms valuable. Recently, reflecting the past attachment of youth to the missions, youth clubs, brigades or fellowships were formed under the aegis of the churches, modelled on similar organisations overseas. They are organised for the youth of the village by a responsible adult, ideally their spiritual leader, who supervises and directs their activities. The idea that they might be established by the youth would simply not be entertained, since youth are considered incapable of organising anything. Nonetheless, some of the older youth are given leadership roles and these groups appear to be replicas of adult groups, holding regular meetings, having uniforms and flags, and so forth. They divide into teams for sports and work together on community service projects. But if youth in the village are in social limbo, so are their organisations, for they cannot be sustained by the youth. The priest or pastor leaves and, in the absence of adult direction, the youth cannot legitimately plan or do anything; they can only await new adult initiatives. A new pastor or priest may get around to reviving the dormant club or brigade or fellow-ship, but it will be for a new generation of youth.

It is not surprising that the local organisational structures of the Tokelau churches mirror the structures of their polities given the precepts of Tokelau social order. But then one might ask why the two structures are maintained side by side and not simply integrated, especially in Atafu and Nukunonu where the polity and congregation are synonymous. The phenomenon might be explained in terms of imported models, for there is the same kind of arrangement in Samoan villages, or in terms of historical causality, for colo-nial administrators insisted that church be separate from state, yet Tokelau people take it as essential to their social order. Using Samoan-derived terms they distinguish in principle between *fālelotu* 'church concerns' and *fālenuku* 'village concerns', even if this distinction is not always strictly kept in prac-tice. This explicit statement of the separation of *lotu* and *nuku* is not appar-ent in records of the nineteenth century, but once introduced it was seized upon to deal with some real dilemmas that the polities had encountered in having foreign spiritual leaders in their midst (these difficulties are discussed in chapter 7).

Christianity is right inside every village, symbolised by imposing churches erected at great cost and labour, testimonies of Christian devotion and sources of village pride. Tokelau congregations have also designed spacious com-pounds and built substantial residences for their spiritual leaders who have come from afar to shepherd and serve them, but these are all located at the peripheries of the villages and are not considered part of it. They are the bounded domains of the resident spiritual leader who remains for all his presence outside the village.

On the village side, rules and regulations specify who may enter these bounded compounds, at what times and for what purposes, and the pastor or priest is expected to remain within the privacy of his compound unless his duties require him to move out into the village.

In physical terms, a priest or pastor has much more privacy than anyone else. His residence is set well back from public paths and screened from public view by walls and plantings. Exterior walls hide the inside from the outside, and partitions may divide the inside into separate rooms. People passing on the path can catch only a fleeting glimpse of what is going on inside and visitors can only surmise what is happening behind a partition. But in a Tokelau village physical privacy, for all the regulations and screens, is not social privacy. People are understandably curious about what these outsiders are doing and saying, even in the privacy of their domains. People do not stand and stare into the compound, but the many passers-by do cast furtive glances within and report to others what they see. Less socialised children may loiter and stare, until someone comes along and reprimands them for disturbing, at the same time taking a good look to see if the people within are indeed disturbed. This discreet surveillance contributes to the ongoing conversations about what the pastor has or might have done, what he is doing or might do, what he said or would say. He is a stranger whose past is not intimately known, whose reactions may be unpredictable, whose intentions may be obscure, placed in the midst of people who know one another intimately. He is the focus of interest as people try to interpret him.

Some pastors and priests enjoy the apparent privacy they are given, others accept it as appropriate to their station, and a few attempt to break through the physical and social boundaries to make themselves known and join the village. But this they simply cannot do because the village does not want them to. They are leaders in *fālelotu* and they meet with the organisations of *fālelotu* and interact with people in their *fālelotu* roles; all this is in line with their duties. But they are excluded from *fālenuku*, except by invitation. Were the organisational structures of the church and polity integrated, the exclusion could not be maintained.

When a spiritual leader encounters members of his congregation, whether individually or in groups, whether casually or in some structured setting, their interaction is constrained, formal and reserved. That their verbal interaction is frequently in Samoan, and 'proper' Samoan at that, not only marks this formality but also produces it. If an interchange is ostensibly in Tokelauan, the speech is larded with Samoan phrases. People do not engage in banter with their spiritual leader or direct a casual remark to him. If the occasion is festive and some jest appropriate, the jokes are bland and tried, though everyone will make a point of laughing.

As the pastor perambulates the village on his accustomed round of visitations his progress is surrounded by an unusual hush. He must walk slowly so people can prepare for his appearance, of which they are forewarned by the words that precede him: 'The pastor is coming'. Children stop their boisterous play in the paths as he approaches. Women halt their casual chatter, the retort to some remark hovers half-said in midair. Men working lay their tools aside and men lounging sit erect until he has passed. If it is anticipated that he may pay a call, there is a brief flurry as people put themselves and their surroundings in order as best they can on short notice. Should he enter a house and take a seat on the rarely used chair, neighbours surreptitiously spy on what is transpiring and whisper reports of what seems to be happening to those in less advantageous positions for viewing the scene.

A pastor is expected to be in the village only at certain times and for particular purposes. It is inappropriate for a person in his position to just stroll around and it is not convenient to the members of his congregation that he do so. They want their privacy from him in exchange for the apparent privacy they give him. If they wish him to be present at a village gathering, they will invite him. If he is not invited, he should not show up. They will not have prepared for him and what they are doing is 'not his business'.

The regulations enacted by the village, the established protocol of deference and formality, the lifestyle and privacy provided, and the strict separation of *fālelotu* and *fālenuku*, all are designed to 'protect (or shield) the village', as they say. What though is the village being protected and shielded from? On the one hand, it is shielding itself from the intrusions of an outsider and, on the other hand, it is protecting its own relationship with that outsider, by keeping him uninformed and unaware of certain things that happened and are happening in the village. The people want to be well regarded by their spiritual leaders; they hope they will depart with high opinions of the village. To this end they keep them at a distance.

When a Tokelau catechist or acting pastor is serving a congregation, as is frequently the case, the relationship between the village and its spiritual leader is markedly different. These spiritual leaders are neither treated so formally nor so strictly segregated, and this is not just because they have lesser religious status. People freely pass through the mission compound and children play within it. Visitors enter the mission residence with little show of formality. No one is terribly concerned about their own or the village's relationship with them, and they stroll around the village as they wish creating no stir as they pass. They casually join groups of men to pass the time of day and joke, and may even engage in banter with women. There is no reason for constraint, for everyone knows all about them and they know about everyone. They, after all, are also in the village, and caught up in its network of kin.

Tokelau people have absorbed Christianity into their lives, have made it an integral part of Tokelau culture, have placed it inside their villages, but they have kept their outside spiritual mentors at a distance, remote and removed from the ebb and flow of ordinary village life. They may phrase this as respect for men of God, but it does also serve to 'protect the village'.

Mālō 'government'

The common gloss for the Tokelau word *mālō* is 'government', though it is not used with reference to their local councils but for national governments located abroad, including kingdoms and empires. For Tokelau the *mālō* is New Zealand, most immediately the *ofiha* 'office' located in Western Samoa and most distantly the *Tupu Peletania* 'British Sovereign'. The New Zealand Government calls the 'office', located at the back of the New Zealand High Commission on the main street of Apia, the Tokelau Administration. It is in charge of a district officer who is immediately responsible to the high commissioner in the front office of the building, but ultimately responsible to the Department of Maori and Island Affairs in Wellington, which is the New Zealand government department responsible to the New Zealand Parliament for the administration of Tokelau. The district officer is well known to Tokelau people and called by his surname only, but beyond him the *mālō* is peopled by shadowy figures called 'governors' or 'commissioners', whose rare appearances are marked by ceremony. This then is the *mālō* abroad, which is physically present in the villages four times or so each year when a supply ship chartered by the Administration brings the district officer to each village for a day or two.

The ship is anticipated weeks in advance, though there is some uncertainty about the actual arrival day. For at least a fortnight before, rumours are rampant about when the ship will leave Apia and what its circuit will be. It is usually delayed and its schedule may be adjusted just before departure or even once it has arrived at Tokelau. People prepare for its arrival: cutting and bagging copra, finishing handicrafts they hope to sell, planning what staples they will buy and holding farewell feasts for whoever may be departing. The radio shack is busier than usual as people converse by radio-telephone with kin in Apia who may send them goods or to place special orders with trading firms there. There is wide speculation about who might return or visit on the ship. The following is the scenario of a 1970 'boat day' in Fakaofo.

The ship's actual appearance offshore is heralded by a chorus of children's shouts—Ahoy!—if it appears in daylight. More often it is somewhere offshore as day breaks, to be greeted by a few men out fishing. But there is no official communication between ship and shore until the village has prepared itself. Men gather at the landing place to assess the state of the channel, to plan how the ship will be worked, and to receive assigned stevedoring tasks. Women prepare food for anticipated returnees and visitors. In due course the first vessel goes out to the ship, conveying village officials to greet the visitors and discuss the day's schedule with the District Officer, the Doctor to receive special medical supplies, the Radio Operator to collect the mail, and the men who will work on board. As lighters come ashore people gather at the landing: elders to formally greet some official visitors and others to peer curiously at strangers. Tokelau arrivals are warmly greeted by their kinfolk and led away to bathe and eat. In the course of the day as the lighters ply between ship and shore bringing in sacks of flour, rice and sugar, tins of kerosene and beef dripping, cartons of soap and a trade box full of cloth and small goods, and taking out sacks of copra, many matters are attended to on shore. Local officials and mālō employees collect and sign for their pay packets, remittances from New Zealand are distributed and signed for, mail is passed out and letters and parcels posted, copra is weighed and paid for, bulk staples are bought and other purchases made from the trade box, special orders are checked and signed for. The District Officer confers with mālō employees and perhaps meets with the elders to pass on information from the Administration and hear their requests. Much gets done but no one is hurried. There is a lot to observe and hear, and later to be reported and discussed. Strangers are shadowed; their actions and words noted. They are curiosities: who are they, why have they come, what are they doing? These questions are not immediately answered but they will be speculated about, and those who have been able to speak with them will later tell others about them. Tokelau arrivals coming ashore, whether to stay or again depart, bring stories and gossip from the other atolls, from Samoa or even New Zealand, and are subjects of interest in their own right.

If there is a distinguished visitor—a 'governor'—the village is forewarned and has prepared a reception: a special vessel to bring him ashore with official escorts, a line of elderly greeters at the landing, perhaps a decorated entryway to the village at which he pauses while children sing an appropriate anthem and then passes through to inspect an honour guard, and invariably a feast during which there is an exchange of greetings and compliments.

A delegation of visitors from another atoll is honoured and feted in quite other ways, and when the village is hosting several parties of visitors for some special occasion, such as a church dedication or cricket match, the ambience is one of carnival with gift presentations, speeches, feasts and dancing.

The day of the ship begins to end when passengers are called to assemble at the landing to be ferried out to the ship. This announcement has been preceded by

Left: *All day the ship stands in and drifts out—there is no place to anchor. Commodious and cumbersome lighters ferry cargo and people between ship and shore through passages that have been blasted in the reef. Crossing the reef— whether surfing in on the crest of a wave or passing out through the breakers—can be tense, and there is an almost audible sigh of relief when the boat comes to rest in the calm of the pass or bobbing upon the ocean swells.* Photo: Marti Friedlander

an encounter between local officials and the District Officer. The issue is whether the ship will stay the night or depart this evening. The Tokelau side argues that the business of the day has not been concluded and furthermore the tide is falling or the sea is high so that it is dangerous to transport passengers out to the ship; the District Officer counters that essential business has been done and the channel is perfectly safe, and furthermore the schedule must be followed lest the expense of another day's charter is incurred.

Below: *A lighter bearing passengers departs from the Fakaofo landing through the pass. The structure at the back is the copra shed.* Photo: Marti Friedlander

Leaving aside the question of the safety or otherwise of the channel, about which Tokelau leaders have better knowledge but may be being overly cautious, and which in any case will be becoming more hazardous as the argument continues and darkness falls, the real issue is who controls the ship under charter, and what the voyage is all about. From the Tokelau perspective, the ship has come primarily to bring them goods which they buy with money they receive from the sale of copra and from salaries and remittances. Before they can begin to buy, their copra must be weighed and paid for, their salaries and remittances collected, and this all takes time. Since a market is only present in the village every three months or so, the decisions about what to buy are not inconsequential and involve negotiations within families. Indeed, a day is rarely long enough for their business. By contrast, the *mālō* sees the ship's visit as an opportunity to conduct administrative business as quickly as possible with the aim of getting back to Apia as soon as possible. In addition, the village and its Tokelau visitors would like to spend the evening eating together and talking together ashore, while the *mālō* wants to spend the evening and night aboard ship and be at the next village on the morrow. While the confrontation may be seen to arise from different ideas of what the day of the ship is all about—trade or administration—it is also about control. The Tokelau community would seem to hold the upper hand, since they man the lighters and therefore control movement from shore to ship. But the *mālō* controls the charter, and may simply decree that the ship will leave, threatening to strand its passengers in the village for three months unless they are conveyed out to the ship that very evening. Usually the *mālō* prevails.

> *The landing place is crowded with people departing and people farewelling them; the lighters leave the landing heavily loaded with passengers and their parcels, including members of the village leaving for Samoa or New Zealand; and finally the last lighter returns to shore with all those who have been aboard the ship working, saying final farewells or conducting last minute business. Gradually the landing is deserted as people turn their backs to the ocean and return to the normal routines of village life which will be enlivened with accounts of the events of the day and information acquired from afar during that day.*

The *mālō* outside is only briefly present in the villages; to conduct administrative business and very occasionally to consider matters of government with visiting 'governors', phrased as pan-Tokelau meetings to discuss 'The Future of Tokelau'. However, the *mālō* is represented in the village in two ways: by villagers who are employed by the *mālō* to provide services for the village, and by the locally elected *faipule* and his appointed aides, who are the local officials of the *mālō*.

The usual complement of *mālō* employees in a village is one doctor, two staff nurses, eight teachers and a radio operator. These people are all professionally trained, their training having been received outside Tokelau and arranged and paid for by the *mālō*, and they receive small salaries. In the 1960s to their number were added people without any qualifications. They are selected by the elders (who can also dismiss them) for employment as nurse aides, teacher aides, and wage labourers. The aides receive a very small salary indeed, and the wages of the labourers are between eight and eleven cents an hour. The professionals have a special place within the communities, not so much because of the salaries they earn, but because of the qualifications they hold, their wider experience and the services they provide. But they are not set apart from the village, since they are of it and take part in village activities and events whenever their professional duties allow. The others are simply considered fortunate in having monetary employment that provides a bit of cash for themselves and their families. In fact, the elders' principal criteria for selecting them is to spread such employment among the families of the village. Though the monetary gains are paltry, people are eager for such employment. After all, their unemployed fellows are working just as hard for the village and their families for nothing, and they may gain on-the-job training and have future prospects.

The elected *faipule* is the local representative of the *mālō* and the village magistrate. Both roles, while ostensibly clearcut, are somewhat equivocal, though in different ways. As local representative of the *mālō*, he is supposed to be the recipient of all communications from the *mālō* afar to the village and the spokesman for the village to the *mālō*, and he is in principle responsible for the *mālō* employees within the village. The problems are that virtually all communications from the *mālō* to the village arrive in English and are therefore incomprehensible on arrival to the *faipule*, that virtually all face-to-face communication between the outside *mālō* representatives and this local representative has to be mediated through interpreters, and that though the *faipule* is responsible for local employees he does not employ them. On the one hand, he cannot really be an effective conduit for communicating between *mālō* and village because whatever he receives or sends has to be translated and is more often than not garbled in the process, owing as much to cultural misinterpretation as to linguistic mistranslation. On the other hand, his fellow elders and the village perceive his role rather differently than the *mālō* does; not as the representative of the *mālō* but as their spokesman to the *mālō* advocating their interests. From the village point of view, an effective *faipule* is one who confronts the *mālō* rather than serving the *mālō*. Consequently, a *faipule* is apt to be accused of misrepresentation and disloyalty by either the *mālō* or the village, though this is rarely his intention.

Thus the role of the *faipule* as the representative of the *mālō* in the village is compromised in many ways, but if he is to retain his office he must fulfil the expectations of the village, for it is the village that will re-elect him. The few who are re-elected are forceful spokesmen for the interests of their constituents.

The other role of the *faipule*, that of magistrate, empowers him to preside in a local court, pass judgments on infractions of laws or regulations and impose fines or prison terms. To assist him in these duties there are two or three policemen and a scribe. Though their responsibilities are officially defined, what they actually do and the duties they are seen to have are defined by the elders of each village. The same applies to the laws and regulations of the *mālō*, and the stated penalties for their infraction, which the *faipule* and his aides are charged to uphold. In short, there is an official version of how the *mālō* operates set down in statement and statute, and rather different local versions which are simply known and accepted. The operation of the local judicial system, encapsulated in the court, is seen to be the essence of the *mālō*.

Occasionally, when a number of cases have been brought to his attention, the *faipule*, in consultation with the elders, decides to hold a court session. The policemen are despatched to collect whatever evidence seems to be required and to notify those people who will be called to testify or attend.

> *On the appointed morning the Atafu court assembles, the policemen in their freshly laundered, starched and ironed uniforms, the scribe with his weighty Court Record Book and perhaps a copy of a 'Law Book', the Faipule and the elders he has selected to act as his advisors. Aside from the uniformed policemen, all are attired in white shirts and most wear ties. The court sits with the Faipule flanked by his scribe at the front, his elderly advisors to one side, and the police-men somewhat apart ready to summon plaintiffs, defendants, and witnesses. The Faipule informs his court of the order of the cases to be heard; they are already aware of the issues involved and the circumstances if not the details surrounding them. This is not an uninformed, impartial jury but a group of judicious elderly advisors assembled to witness and give weight to the Faipule's judgments. A prayer is said asking for God's guidance in their deliberations and the business of the court begins. They hear requests for the return of objects lost which have been discovered to be in the possession of others and complaints of slanderous assertions made. Both entail detailed investigation to establish the facts, which serve to show that the object that was lost is indeed the same as the object that was found, and that the assertions considered slanderous were unwarranted. No one is found guilty; in fact people are officially cleared of any guilt that might otherwise be presumed.*

The Atafu court considers charges of theft, physical abuse and sexual derelictions[13] which have come to the attention of the *faipule* and policemen. In these cases there need be no plaintiff; the abuses of the law have been seen or suspected in the village and therefore must be brought to court.

> *The suspects are questioned, witnesses are heard if innocence is asserted, and the Faipule hands down his judgment and the prescribed penalty after consultation with his advisors. The penalty is mitigated as often as not after those found guilty have been verbally admonished by the court. Finally, and last on the court agenda, are the complaints over real property—boundary disputes and assertions of un-acknowledged rights, many of which have been heard before. The reason they are scheduled last is because they are so often unresolvable and because the testimony is apt to be very lengthy and very contentious. As the afternoon draws on, the Faipule defers consideration on the grounds that the court has been in session long enough and it is getting on to night. What has been at issue has been aired again, and the parties concerned have gained further knowledge of each other's argument to which they can devise counter arguments. The court hesitates to judge these cases, lest its members be charged with favouritism, which indeed may be the case. Instead, the court counsels the contestants to return to the village and talk the matter over further between themselves and seek a peaceful compro-*

mise. On the issue of a boundary between adjacent plots of land, the court goes to inspect the situation, hear testimony on the spot and decree where the boundary will run, marking it with an upright slab.

This, however, is not necessarily a final resolution of the dispute. After some time, the boundary may be transgressed, the dispute again raised, and upon inspection it may be found that the marker has disappeared or it may be asserted that it has been shifted. Thus the court may be seen more as a place to air property disputes than as a venue to resolve them.

The laws of the *mālō* and the procedures for enforcing them were introduced into villages which had long had rules and ways of punishing infractions of them which had come from their forebears and had subsequently been modified by laws associated with Christianity. When speaking about *tūlāfono* 'laws/rules' Tokelau people will distinguish between 'laws of the village', 'laws of the church' and 'laws of the *mālō* (government)'. That the three are distinguished, however, does not mean that they do not interact, and since the 'laws of the *mālō*' are the latest addition, they have been interpreted in light of the other two. Furthermore, having been imposed from outside and designed for societies quite different from Tokelau, they do not always suit Tokelau social arrangements. Though Tokelau people have not been consulted about *mālō* laws, they have accepted them while at the same time not exactly following them. They have ignored, elaborated and reinterpreted them somewhat differently in the three villages, so that though many of the formalities are the same, law enforcement and court procedure are not uniform. For example, any person appearing before the Atafu court swears a promise to tell the truth upon the Bible and receives a warning from the magistrate about the consequence of false testimony—'the wrath of the Almighty will be visited upon your parents and children, your brothers and sisters and their children'. This is not a feature of court procedure in Nukunonu and Fakaofo.

The documents known as the *tūlāfono o te mālō* 'laws of the *mālō*' are presumed to be in the care of the *faipule* and to have been transferred from a retiring *faipule* to his successor. Be that as it may, few people have seen, much less read, these documents. All adults, however, know what the laws, procedures and punishments of the *mālō* are by hearsay and precedent. They agree that murder, assault, fighting, theft, fornication, adultery, abusive language, slander and insubordination are prohibited, and that if they transgress these prohibitions they will be brought before the magistrate and punished. This is enough to make the 'laws of the *mālō*' a reality and the judicial mechanism of the *mālō* legitimate, for the people consent to the way the local officials operate, though they may not always feel that their judgments are correct.

Certain 'laws of the *mālō*' are totally irrelevant to Tokelau, and these can easily be ignored. Others are considered unsuitable—'not appropriate to life here'—and they have come to be ignored. For example, the punishment of flogging (in the Gilbert and Ellice Islands Colony No.2 of 1917) is one that no magistrate has ever been able to carry through. In some instances laws have been more broadly interpreted than their written form would warrant, and frequently stated penalties are reduced or annulled or otherwise modified.

There are no 'laws of the *mālō*' which apply to hearing and considering disputes over property; these are supposed to be arbitrated or resolved 'according to their customs' (*AJHR* 1971). Since there are no relevant statutes, why should such issues come before the *faipule* charged to enforce 'laws of the *mālō*'? The answer is that people think they should and so they do. Indeed the practice may be justified on the grounds that the magistrate was authorised back in the 1910s to '. . . hear and advise in all native land disputes'; but then why do people press the *faipule* for a judgment?

Court proceedings are outwardly the most striking presence of outside imposed *mālō* in Tokelau: the uniformed policemen, the court reporter with his weighty record book, the white shirts and ties, the formal and solemn set procedures. On a small scale it seems to be a British court following the procedures of British jurisprudence. Yet apart from these superficial resemblances it is a thoroughly Tokelau institution. It is a gathering of elderly men attending to the complaints and derelictions of their fellow villagers, intent on smoothing over disagreements and maintaining peace and order in their village. They may not be doing exactly what *mālō* laws instruct them to do, but they are upholding Tokelau morality and preserving the peace.

Whatever presence the *mālō* has in Tokelau villages, it is a presence 'under the authority of the elders'. The elders govern the villages, not the *mālō*. What then is the role of the *mālō* if it is not to govern; or put somewhat differently, how do Tokelau people conceive of the *mālō*? They say that New Zealand, their *mālō*, 'looks after and takes care of' them. Their word is *tauhi* or *taukikila*, which is what parents do for their children, and they elaborate this analogy in their formal speeches to visiting governors, referring to him as their 'father' and themselves as his 'children'. This, of course, is the same rhetoric used in village meetings where the elders are 'our father', but the intention is not the same. The governor 'father' is being persuaded to provide more for his 'children', whereas 'father' elders are being acknowledged as having authority over their 'children'. As an eminent representative of the *mālō*, a governor is seen to be able to grant Tokelau requests if he can be persuaded to do so. This persuasion does not take the form of arguing the merits of the requests, but of appealing to the compassion, the *alofa*, of the governor. Flattery and gifts are given to make a governor amenable, to instil in him an *alofa* for Tokelau, which will be realised by providing more. As Tokelau people see it, the authority of the *mālō* is manifest in decisions to accede to or reject their requests, not in deciding what Tokelau will do—that is the responsibility of their own elders.

THREE

Kāiga—*The Kinship Order*

Counterpoised to the *nuku*, and not uncommonly competing with it for time and attention, is the order of *kāiga* or kinship—no less explicit or elaborated than the village order, and even more pervasive in its significance, but less obviously and openly declared. Kin relationships are known and understood rather than pronounced. Kin groups are simply there, operating for the most part without formal meetings of any kind.

The contrast between the domains of village and kinship, *nuku* and *kāiga*, is clearly recognised and frankly discussed. *Nuku* matters are *fakamua*, and always take precedence over both *kāiga* and individual concerns, because they are communal and for the welfare of all. People who are particularly exemplary in their commitment to the *nuku* are praised for their *lotonuku* 'village loyalty', but so too are people commended for their *lotokāiga* 'devotion to *kāiga*'. Nevertheless, if these are in competition, *lotonuku* is morally superior. *Kāiga* loyalties, after all, are ongoing and fundamental, part of a person's very being, involving rights to land, to produce, to food and shelter, and embedded in relations of kinship and marriage. In short, *kāiga* are the basis of the production and reproduction of the whole Tokelau world.[1]

Kāiga *in Principle*

Like its cognates in other Polynesian languages, the Tokelau term *kāiga* has a number of distinct, though closely interrelated meanings. In one commonly used sense a *kāiga* is a cognatic descent unit or 'stock' (Radcliffe-Brown 1950:22, Freeman 1961), which may or may not be a corporate unit, comprising all the descendants of an ancestral couple. Here, to enhance the precision and clarity of the exposition, the term *kāiga* is used only for corporate units, that is, for *kāiga* as cognatic descent groups with exclusive rights to an estate, which is jointly exploited by its members, and its produce distributed among them.[2] In what follows, the five elementary features of *kāiga* are stated in turn, much in the way they are regularly articulated by Tokelau people. A diagrammatic account follows.

1 Kāiga *are resolutely cognatic, including all persons who can trace any path of ancestry to their founders.* Consequently, people have rights in as many *kāiga* as they have recognised forbears who were founders of *kāiga*, and *kāiga* are non-exclusive, virtually all their members having commitments and loyalties elsewhere. Commonly, people express this as a person being within four *kāiga*, via their four grandparents, though many people (particularly older ones) have fewer affiliations and many others (particularly children) have more—this is because *kāiga* are disbanded and reconstituted (see below).

2 *Each* kāiga *is divided into complementary halves known as* tamatāne *'children of males' and* tamafafine *'children of females'.* This division is based upon the first generation or the generation of the children of the founders. All the descendants, both female and male, of the founders' sons are *tamatāne*; correspondingly, all of the male and female descendants of the founders' daughters make up the *tamafafine* division. Each division has distinct rights and duties within the *kāiga*. *Tamatāne* have *pule* or 'authority' over all members and work the estate for the benefit of the whole *kāiga*; *tamafafine* reside in the *kāiga* village homestead and divide and distribute to all members the produce brought to them by *tamatāne*. However, given that *kāiga* membership is non-exclusive, it follows that a person is *tamatāne* in some *kāiga* and *tamafafine* in others.

3 *Post-marital residence is uxorilocal.* This is in line with the rights of *tamafafine* to reside in the *kāiga* homestead and the Tokelau adage: *Ko te tuafafine ē nofo; ko te tuagāne ē fano i te auala* 'The sister stays (in the natal home); the brother goes on the path (to his wife's home)'. Consequently, related women tend to reside in the same house—as mothers and daughters and sisters—and households are commonly continuously occupied by lines of women—grandmother, daughter, granddaughter—along with their husbands and minor children.

4 Kāiga *are strictly exogamous.* Though Tokelau commentators often express marriage proscriptions in terms of degrees of relationship, the basic Tokelau view of the matter is that no two people who share common rights to land may marry. If they should do so, the principle is upheld by the simple expedient of dissolving the *kāiga* of which they are both members at the time of the marriage, making the couple thereby 'no longer related'. In point of fact it is often marriages between kin which precipitate the break-up of *kāiga*. The 'expedient', however, has wide ramifications, affecting not only the couple but others in the *kāiga* concerned, several of whom will be elderly and very closely related.[3]

5 *New* kāiga *come into being with the dissolution of old ones and the division of their estates.* For all the immediate agitation *kāiga* dissolution brings, people readily admit that the corporate unity and identity which *kāiga* may develop over the generations cannot go on forever. When *kāiga* span four or five generations they are likely to be made up of a fairly large number of people widely dispersed in households throughout the village. It becomes increasingly difficult to manage cooperative use of resources and equitable

division of produce to the satisfaction of all. In the event, at some time after the death of founders, and usually after their offspring are dead as well, lands are divided, in more or less equal fashion, in the name of founders' children who then become founders of separate estates and *kāiga* of their own descendants. After property has been divided former *kāiga* cease to exist, and their members are even held to be 'no longer related' to one another—at least for the calculations of kin relationships between those who might wish to marry. By this process of *kāiga* dissolution, rights to land are shuffled and reshuffled, rather than fragmented, as generations pass. For when *kāiga* split and lands are divided in the name of the founders' children, the lands are immediately or eventually combined with any which their spouses may have to form the estates of new *kāiga*.

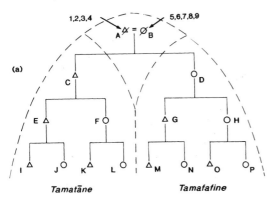

The story of a *kāiga*

(a) A kāiga is composed of all those who can trace ancestry to its founders. This four-generation kāiga 'cognatic descent group' was founded by A and B, now deceased, and all its members share in the A/B estate consisting of properties 1–4 from A and 5–9 from B. The kāiga is internally divided into tamatāne or founders' sons and their issue, i.e. C and his issue, and tamafafine or founders' daughters and their issue, i.e. D and her issue.

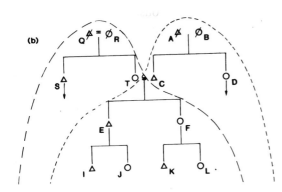

(b) People are usually members of more than one kāiga. C, of the A/B kāiga, is married to T, and consequently their children (E and F) and grandchildren (I, J, K, L) are members of the kāiga founded by T's parents (Q and R) as well as the kāiga founded by C's parents (A and B). In addition, I and J are members of kāiga of their mother (the wife of E), and K and L are members of kāiga of their father (the husband of F).

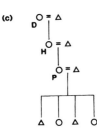

(c) Lines of women reside in kāiga homesteads. The people living in the A/B homestead are D, A and B's daughter, and her husband, her daughter H with her husband, her granddaughter P with her husband and children. This household is the centre of the A/B kāiga where the tamafafine reside and where produce from the kāiga estate is deposited and allocated to its members.

111

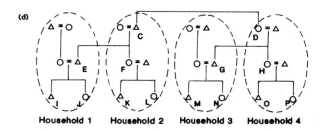

(d)

Household 1   Household 2   Household 3   Household 4

d) Members of kāiga *reside in several different households. The three generations of A/B* kāiga *members reside in four households because when its members have married the males have gone to reside with their wives and the females have remained in their natal homes. Thus (from right to left) D, H, and P have all remained in their natal home, the A/B* kāiga *homestead (see above); G went to his wife's household at marriage and his daughter, N, remains there when she marries; C joined his wife's household at marriage and his married daughter, F, remains there with her husband and children; while C's son E went to the household of his wife at marriage. When the next generation marries, the members of the A/B* kāiga *will be more widely dispersed among village households.*

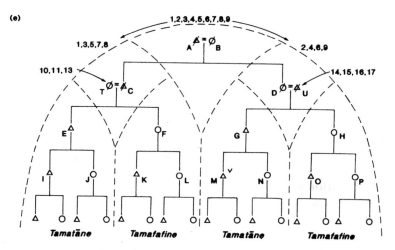

(e)

Tamatāne   Tamafafine   Tamatāne   Tamafafine

(e) Kāiga *must at some time divide. A generation later the A/B* kāiga *is of five generations' depth, and the founders' children, C and D, have died. The* kāiga *has become too dispersed and unwieldy to cooperate effectively and share the A/B estate (and perhaps members of the youngest generation are proposing to marry). The senior members (E, F, G, and H) agree to divide the* kāiga *estate (properties 1–9) into two parts in the names of their deceased parents (C and D). In both instances, these properties will be combined with those of C's wife (T) and D's husband (U) to become the estates of two new* kāiga, *and these* kāiga *will again be internally divided as* tamatāne *and* tamafafine. *The old A/B* kāiga *no longer exists, but some of its people and property remain in the new C/T and D/U* kāiga.

Kāiga *in Practice*

The land area of each atoll is divided into named islets or parts of islets. Most of these named *fenua* 'lands' are further subdivided into marked sections which are the property of specific *kāiga*;[4] a few small islets are held by a single *kāiga*. Typically, a *kāiga* owns a variable number of sections (or islets) dispersed around the atoll.

The number of people counted as members of a *kāiga* varies widely, as does the extent of its land holdings. Some have fewer than ten members and a few have over a hundred. In general, the size of a *kāiga* relates to its generational span; those which have large land holdings tend to have both greater generational depth and larger memberships, while small *kāiga* are usually of shallower generational depth and have fewer land resources. But these are tendencies only. There are many other contingent factors which lead to there being *kāiga* with a few members and extensive resources or with a lot of members who share meagre resources.

These variations do not necessarily mean that there are large differences in people's access to productive resources, however, since almost every person has rights in several *kāiga*. Not only does a person receive shares of produce from several sources, but a household will receive shares also from all *kāiga* in which any one of its residents has rights.

But it is not just the system that promotes equality; it is also how people operate and work within the system. *Kāiga* in fact manage their affairs somewhat differently, taking into account contingencies and circumstances, and people who manage *kāiga* affairs explain quite frankly why they do things as they do. They feel constrained to justify their practice because people have very explicit notions of how *kāiga* should ideally operate. All follow the principle that men provide while women divide, but exactly which men are providing and which women dividing varies. Every *kāiga* should have as part of its joint property one or more canoes which are used by organised parties of men from the *kāiga* to bring back produce (coconuts are the staple item) from the jointly owned lands to the village, and that produce should be taken directly to the *kāiga* homestead where the senior resident female member should divide and distribute it to all members of the *kāiga*. The shares should be allotted to branches of the *kāiga* at a certain generational level, and should be received by designated women who may apportion them again. In large *kāiga* there may be yet another division before the ultimate shares of produce reach their final destination. All this may seen cumbersome, but this is the way it should be done, and the sight of children carrying portions here and there is an intrinsic part of village life.

All men and older boys of the *kāiga*, whether of the *tamatāne* or *tamafafine* division, may be active providers, without contravening any deeply held principles as to how such practical day-to-day affairs should be conducted. Even men who have married in are major providers for some *kāiga*. Which men actually do the providing is taken into account by women making the distributions. Women divide produce equitably rather than equally, making adjustments to acknowledge who has worked to provide what is being shared. Consequently, harvesters and fishermen allocate more of their labour to *kāiga* from which they will get the best return. Men work where the productive resources are, as well as where their efforts are most needed, and in this way the imbalances of labour and resources generally get evened out.

Just who should divide the produce is not subject to quite the same degree of negotiation and choice, and most *kāiga* adhere to the principle that

113

Top left: *A young man brings down a bunch of green coconuts from a palm in the village. Older boys and younger men, and even agile elders, casually harvest from palms close to hand, but of course by right or with permission.* Photo: Marti Friedlander

Right: *Women prepare welcome refreshment for fishermen returning sunburnt and parched from sea. A favourite is* vaihū tāmoko, *made with scrapings from the moist husk of a green coconut, together with its sweet liquid and jelly-like meat combined with some gratings of coconut.* Photo: J. Huntsman

it should be done by a senior woman of the *tamafafine* who is resident in the *kāiga* homestead. Hers is the highly marked role of *fatupaepae* 'foundation stone' in the *kāiga*. The image is exact and powerful, drawing attention to both the unity of the *kāiga* over time, and the stable base upon which all else rests and depends. The *fatupaepae* role, more than anything else, is the central Tokelau symbol of *kāiga*, and, in a very direct way, the smooth day-to-day operation and solidarity of the whole group depends upon the fairness and moral authority of the woman in that position. Her decisions and actions are virtually unquestioned, particularly by her brothers and their children, for she is respectively their sister and father's sister. Furthermore, the *kāiga* homestead is her domestic domain. This is important because all formal discussions of *kāiga* affairs should take place there. People may of course talk about *kāiga* concerns at any time, but a proper assembly, with authority to take binding decisions, must have a proper setting.

The *fatupaepae* position is normally passed from mother to daughter, since the woman holding it must be resident in the *kāiga* homestead, and daughters, in principle, remain in their natal home after marriage. Just which of a woman's daughters shall succeed her is more problematic. Oldest daughters are more likely to, particularly if they have remained in their mother's home. If, however, the eldest has moved elsewhere, it is likely that the role will devolve upon another daughter who has remained. In fact, there is really no moment of transfer, since a co-resident daughter will gradually take on the role, under her mother's direction and guidance, as her mother ages. A *fatupaepae*'s task can be a strenuous one both physically and mentally, and the younger woman may lift and carry, count and arrange for many years at her mother's instruction, so by the time a *fatupaepae* retires or dies it is well established who her successor is.

The corresponding male leadership of *kāiga* is also flexible, at least in matters to do with day-to-day life. Ideally, the senior male of the *tamatāne* should be the one who directs all *kāiga* affairs and also represents the group's interest in the village. However, there is no distinctive Tokelau term for this position that has the force and salience of the corresponding *fatupaepae*. *Pule* 'authority' or *ulu* 'head' or *toeaina* 'elder' are used interchangeably, and some refer to the role as that of *tamana* 'father'.[5] The flexibility of the system is such, however, that the men who fill this role are not necessarily drawn from *tamatāne* divisions of those *kāiga* which they represent. It is largely a matter of choice and negotiation. Some *kāiga* may have no particularly suitable men among their *tamatāne*, while others may have no suitable males at all, and so select an affine to represent them. In Atafu and Nukunonu, where the chosen male is automatically a member of the Council representing the *kāiga* in the village, it is of considerable moment who is selected. In Fakaofo, where the Council is differently constituted, it is not as crucial, and the internal direction of the *kāiga* is a matter of ongoing negotiation among its senior men.

At this juncture it is prudent to emphasise that, despite the division of *kāiga* into the *tamatāne* and *tamafafine* and the two distinct male and female offices, which gives the superficial appearance of a system of double descent, the Tokelau system is unequivocally cognatic. The *tamatāne* and *tamafafine* divisions give the system a special twist, but they are not in any sense independent descent units; each exists only in relation to its complement.

The general Tokelau ideological precepts that underpin the principles of village organisation apply also to *kāiga*, but with weightier moral overtones arising from that essential quality of kinship—*alofa*, variously glossed 'concern, compassion, affection, sympathy', but certainly not 'romantic love'.[6] *Alofa* is something that kinfolk should naturally have for one another, and should demonstrate in their acts and deeds. *Māopoopo* 'unity' is absolutely basic, and it could not be otherwise. *Kāiga* members have common interests and common being from their forebears, so naturally they have common purpose and do things together; they should 'eat as one; live as one'. Again, deference to elders and compliance with their direction is intensified in *kāiga* because elders are collectively parents, who have demonstrated their *alofa* by

Bottom left: *Wading through the lagoon shallows, a young man balances two bound-up bunches of* uto *'sprouted coconuts' across his shoulder on the paddle of his canoe that is moored in deeper water. Other harvesters float their burdens. When harvesting, it is wise to calculate the tides so the canoe, which will accept the burden, need not be moored too far off the lagoon shore.* Photo: Marti Friedlander

Right: *A fully laden canoe sailing back to the village with a harvest from* kāiga *lands across the lagoon. The villages are sited on the leeward margin of the atoll so that the loaded canoes can sail back.* Photo: Marti Friedlander

Top left: *Prepared for fishing, the fisherman awaits his canoe at the shore. He has already dipped into his provisions and is gnawing a pandanus section from the fruit below. His tuluma 'round fishing box' holds his gear.* Photo: Marti Friedlander

Right: *Sharing a harvest within a kāiga requires care and discernment, and is a woman's duty and right. Here a woman makes six portions of husked drinking and sprouted coconuts destined for the six branches of the kāiga. In the background, copra is drying.* Photo: J. Huntsman

Below: *A boy summoned or sent to the kāiga homestead to collect a portion of husked drinking coconuts. The unhusked bunches of green coconuts in the background may be collected later.* Photo: J. Huntsman

providing for their children, who in turn provide for them. When parents castigate their children, they are, in Tokelau parlance, speaking 'words of *alofa*'. The complementarity and mutual deference between women and men in the village is predicated on the relations of women and men as kin, and particularly on the complementary rights and obligations of *tamatāne* and *tamafafine*. Within *kāiga*, these ways of behaving should come naturally, whereas they need to be carefully nurtured and continually monitored in the village.

So it is no wonder that dissension within *kāiga* makes people very aggrieved. When friction surfaces within *kāiga* it is between its branches—members of which are more closely related because their common ancestor is one of the founders' offspring. The disagreement is about sharing and providing; one side asserting that they are not receiving the share to which they are entitled, and the other countering that it is they who are doing all the work and should receive more. Where there is strong leadership and relations are generally good, acceptable compromises can be arranged about working and sharing, or a decision is amicably reached about how to divide the land. But when disagreement is precipitated by unauthorised harvesting, bypassing the *fatupaepae*, or when dissolution is forced or thought unfair, *alofa* is thoroughly compromised. Whatever the specifics of the case, the dissolution of one *kāiga* only brings into being other *kāiga* which will more closely exemplify the ideal because their members are closer kin.

Relations of Kinship

Like many other Polynesians, Tokelau people use the notion of kinship in a wide variety of contexts to convey a sense of common identity, purpose and destiny. In the most expansive register, it is sometimes said that 'all Tokelau people are kin'. At the same time, in less rhetorical contexts, kinship calls for precise knowledge and calculation, since the whole system depends for its successful operation on information about the nature of all the links involved. Individuals differ in the extent of their knowledge of pedigree relationships: grandparents usually do know them (in the sense of being able to recite from

Top left: *Returned from the sea, the fisherman deposits his catch adjacent to the* kāiga *homestead where it will be divided by the* fatupaepae *among the* kāiga *and any crew that are not* kāiga. Photo: Marti Friedlander

Right: *A fatupaepae butchers a yellowfin tuna before apportioning it to the* kāiga. Photo: J. Huntsman

memory a pedigree that connects any two people within their own village), parents should know them, and children should learn them.

Calculating kinship

Pedigree relationships are expressed in terms of *ala* (or *auala*) 'paths'. These are spelled out something like: 'The father of the mother of the mother of X, and the mother of the mother of the father of Y, were brother and sister.' Such 'paths' are traced to a pair of siblings rather than an ancestral couple— except when the points of linkage are half-siblings, and which parent those siblings had in common is of moment. By tracing to siblings, it is established *how* two people are related; that they *are* related is assumed. In fact, in many instances, people may be linked by two or even more 'paths' of this kind, relating them in different ways and increasing the closeness of their relationship. Kinship relations are spoken of as being either *mamao* 'distant', or *pili* 'close', the same terms as are used to express a spatial relationship between concrete objects. Also people speak of the *vā* between kin—*vā* meaning 'to be separated, apart', or 'gap' or 'relationship' between people or things. Within a kinship context the extent of the *vā* between people is calculated in terms of *tupulaga* 'generations', with siblings being taken as the first generation (after the common ancestor).

Below: *A fatupaepae directs the harvest of a breadfruit tree. She directs the harvester above from her vantage point below, and repeatedly cautions him to 'hold on tight'—some say so the 'spirits' are assured that he is up there under her guidance.* Photo: J. Huntsman

While the idioms of 'paths' and generational distances are the direct and common ways in which kinship links between individuals are expressed in practical, everyday contexts, they are not really the way in which information about such matters is systematically ordered and taught. More important to knowledge of Tokelau kinship are *gafa*—genealogies beginning with either a single individual or an ancestral couple and going on to trace the lines of descendants in a more or less set and orderly form.[7] It is through the knowledge of a body of *gafa*, in fact, that the 'paths' between individuals can be readily established.

Learning *gafa*, memorising and keeping records of them, is said to be the duty of the senior males of any sibling group, but they are not necessarily the best informed. There is no restriction on anyone, male or female, acquiring

Shouldering a 45 kg (100 lb) sack of copra. Shortly before the trading/administration vessel is scheduled to appear, copra production intensifies. The credit or cash payment for these 45 kg sacks of copra will go to buy flour, rice, sugar, dripping and kerosene for the kāiga, *all of which will be apportioned by the* fatupaepae. Photo: J. Huntsman

what information they can from parents or others; a few people make a speciality of this, partly for the intellectual pleasure of being able to fit the pieces together and partly perhaps for the potential power which the information brings. For example, land rights are often argued in village courts on the grounds of genealogical connections and, in most cases, decided on the basis of the fullness and internal consistencies of the records put forward. Those directly involved rarely admit to any doubt about their evidence, while others, aware perhaps of variant records, wearily acknowledge the equivocal, if not manipulated, nature of such genealogical evidence.

In keeping genealogical records, people are concerned that the connections should reflect 'real biological' parentage (something which accounts for variant versions). For recent generations there is seldom any dispute over such matters since questions of paternity have, for years now, been pursued with some fervour. When unmarried women become pregnant or adulterous unions are revealed, both village councils and the churches take up the issues—not, so it is maintained, out of any prurient interest but simply for the sake of the children concerned. A 'real' father is expected to provide for the material support of his child, this support extending to inheritance of property rights in all of the relevant *kāiga*. Furthermore, decent social order in succeeding generations can only be guaranteed if parentage is established, lest a person unwittingly marry some close relative.

Speaking of kin and behaving as kin

In speaking about the 'paths' by which people are connected to one another Tokelau speakers use a set of relationship terms which, in this context, refer to primary kin types and are unambiguous. The terms, together with their appropriate English glosses, are as follows:

> *tamana* 'father'
> *mātua* 'mother'
> *taina* or *uho* 'sibling of the same sex'
> *tuafafine* 'sister of a brother'
> *tuagāne* 'brother of a sister'
> *tama* 'child', to which may be appended *teine* 'girl' or *tama* 'boy' (usually, and more properly, 'child of a woman' or 'child of a couple').

ātaliki 'son of a man'
āfafine 'daughter of a man'.

Outside of the 'paths' context, however, each of the terms has a wider seman-
tic range, following the 'generation' mode of other Polynesian (or 'Hawaiian')
systems.[8] This usage has many appropriate Tokelau social and cultural corre-
lates, emphasising as it does inclusiveness and only the distinctions of sex and
generation within a wide and otherwise undifferentiated body of kin. At the
same time, though, it completely elides the importance attached to the
Tokelau brother–sister relationship. When this is relevant two pairs of complementary terms are used—*tuātina/ilāmutu* 'mother's-brother/sister's-child',
and *mātua tauaitu* (or *mātua hā*)/*tama hā* 'father's-sister/brother's-child'.
These sets focus upon the cross-sibling relationship involved.

The meanings of many relationship terms thus shift according to these
two common contexts of speaking about kinship. In what might be called the
'generational' mode, *tamana* may be used to designate either father's brother
or mother's brother, but where the cross-sex linkages are emphasised the
appropriate term for mother's brother is *tuātina* and *tamana* may be appropriately used only for father and father's brother. In the same way, *mātua*
comes to have the more restricted meaning of mother and mother's sister,
with *mātua tauaitu* being used for father's sister.

The basis of these cross-generational pairs and of their behavioural corre-
lates is the highly marked *tuafafine/tuagāne* 'sister/brother' pair, the relational pair which is most heavily weighted with explicit formalities,
prohibitions and observances.[9] Children are taught the importance of their
opposite-sex siblings from a very early age, and from adolescence onwards
patterns of respect and deference are followed, and from then on until the
end of their lives they are observed. The relationship is spoken of as a
feagaiga, the word used to translate the concept of 'covenant' in the Samoan
Bible. Otherwise, Tokelau people variously describe the relationship as one
entailing *alofa* 'compassion, affection', *hā* 'restrictions', *fakaaloalo* 'deference,
courtesy', *mamalu* 'respect, honour', and *mā* 'shame, disquiet'. How particular brother/sister pairs manifest these qualities in their behaviour differs.
Some avoid direct speech altogether, others speak but avoid eye contact, still
others converse quite freely but avoid any joking or banter, even with a third
party, in the other's presence. The differences very often have to do with the
relative ages of the pair; those of comparable age are more restrained than
those more widely separated, and older sisters and younger brothers are
often quite open and relaxed with one another. However, though degrees of
restraint and avoidance are variable, obligations are more definitive and uniform. Sisters and brothers as a matter of course provide for one another, and
for one another's children, giving both material and moral support. Brothers
are their sisters' guardians and protectors, sisters are their brothers' refuge
and defenders. Each honours the requests of the other, no matter how onerous or inconvenient, and in times of distress or need gives absolute, un-
questioning support.

But for all the social and moral import of the sister/brother relationship, it is not altogether beyond the scope of the powerful Tokelau sense of comic absurdity which may break out at almost any communal gathering. Well-known brother/sister comics may perform, for instance, haranguing each other from opposite ends of the meeting house, to the delight of all. They do not even have to say or do anything particularly clever or remarkable; that they should shout at one another, or carry on at all, is what is so comical.[10]

The expected behaviours of mother's-brother/sister's-child and of father's-sister/brother's-child logically follow from those of brother/sister, and are somewhat different in content because they are cross-generational. The senior member is respected and deferred to as an elder, but again because of the 'covenant' the senior member cherishes the junior.

The most specific obligation of these relationships is the one of a sister's son to his mother's brother, which is called *mate*, calling upon the younger man to accompany and support the older in potentially dangerous enterprises (cited are overseas journeys and battle) as his 'companion in death'.[11] The sister's-daughter role in relation to her mother's brother is less defined. She is primarily a surrogate of her mother, doing for her mother's brother what her mother is constrained from doing for her own brother.

The marked term for father's-sister is *mātua tauaitu*, lit. 'spirit-keeping mother', which speaks to her attribute of mystical powers, in particular the power to bless or curse her brother's children. It is this woman who in principle resides in the *kāiga* homestead of one's father, and who as the *fatupaepae* is at the core of that *kāiga*. She is the person to whom all goods and produce should be delivered and from whom shares of it are received. Her position within the *kāiga* may be linked with the 'spirit-keeping' attributed to father's-sisters. On the one hand, brothers'-children are constrained to obey her, and specifically to take *kāiga* property to her, lest they provoke her ire. On the other hand, a father's sister is expected to particularly cherish her brother's children, and to bless them when they marry and have children.

The relations between affines are also implicated in the sister/brother 'covenant'. Spouses in Tokelau are truly partners, usually united for life, and relations between spouses are typically easy, open and free of restraint—the antithesis of those between sister and brother. However, husbands have sisters and wives have brothers, and the unity (or equivalence) of spouses results in an inverse relationship to that between siblings among same-generation affines. Put simply, women are constrained with their husbands' sisters but interact easily with their husbands' brothers, and men are constrained with their wives' brothers but relaxed with their wives' sisters. It is all very logical and moreover practical; sisters with their husbands and brothers with their wives are daily in situations where they cooperate and socialise. But the relations of constraint between in-laws of the same sex are 'accident prone' when the 'men of the village' or the 'women of the village' are gathered. Not uncommonly someone will say or do something in this communal context that is improper because it impinges upon a brother-in-law or sister-in-law relationship. For example, at a Women's Committee meeting when feelings are running high, a woman, without thinking, may speak sharply to her husband's sister. The tenor of the meeting is instantly transformed: the sister is embarrassed, the wife is shamed and everyone is uncomfortable. Or, men engaging in obscene banter while working together may forget exactly who is within earshot and make remarks about someone's sister's husband. Realising what has been said, all fall silent; there is no possible apology, since to speak further would only make matters worse.

Kāiga *and* Nuku

The relations of parents and children, of brothers with brothers and sisters with sisters closely parallel village roles. In fact, the elders are often spoken of as 'our fathers' and they may speak of the men as their 'sons'. The women of the village are referred to as 'our mothers' or 'our sisters' (though never as 'our wives') and among themselves they refer to each other as the occasion calls for as 'mothers', 'daughters' and 'sisters'. It might even be said that the village is organised as a *kāiga*, but it is not that simple. Though the village and things *fakamua* should be given primacy and *kāiga* and things *fakamuli* should be set aside when the community calls, the division cannot be absolute. Fellow villagers are kin and the proprieties of behaviour to kin cannot be set aside. They always colour and are continually implicated in the village context, from the most casual encounter to the most formal gathering. Most village interaction is not of the straightforward dyadic sort. Meetings involve people related to one another by diverse links, and they talk about other people who are related in different ways again to those present. The permutations of all the relationships in such situations are quite impossible to calculate, though people are certainly aware of them. This is one reason why formal meetings, and any less formal gatherings, appear so tentative and circumspect, why criticism is so oblique and admonishments so muted. In fact, when the young are publicly censured by their elders, not infrequently the strongest abuse is from a senior kinsperson of the culprit, and the 'heavy' words that are spoken are called *kupu alofa* 'words of compassion'.

Yet for all the caution and propriety, it is just these relationships which are the primary wellspring of Tokelau humour. Though an elder should not be slighted, especially in the hearing of a grandchild, a source of great mirth are the well-known foibles of old people—living and dead. But while parents and grandparents, and sometimes children, may be targeted to the slight discomfort of their kin, it is different with sisters and brothers and those relations that they implicate. Only they themselves can make public mirth of their own relationship.

INTERLUDE

Telling of Tokelau Pasts

> . . . we must be prepared to analyze not one tradition and one past, but many
> traditions and many pasts. . . .
>
> —Cohn 1961:248

When in 1980 our direction changed and we made past structures and their transformations central to our interpretation of Tokelau culture, we found ourselves engaged in a lively, emerging new direction in Polynesian studies— a rapprochement of anthropology and history as 'historical anthropology'. Our involvement in the Tokelau book project gave us immediate experience of the complications of representing the past—'the anthropology of history'. The new directions of anthropology and the complications of history impinged as we set about writing of Tokelau pasts.

Telling a story of the Tokelau past presented new problems, not unrelated to earlier ones. The first was the same heterogeneity which we had encountered in the present; the pasts of Tokelau, while indeed linked, were three. The second was the diffuse nature of the records and documents, stories and anecdotes, most particularly the very different worlds of 'outsiders' writing about Tokelau and 'insiders' telling their own stories. The third, related to the second, was how to combine the anthropological notion of cultural orders within a chronological narrative of past events (Silverman 1992:32–34).

Three places—three pasts

Certainly the same cyclones, the same sorts of foreigners, and like events impacted upon the atolls, yet they were not experienced alike. They were encountered from differing viewpoints, manipulated by diverse individual and group projects, and modified and incorporated by different existing structures. Of these happenings and others, each atoll has different stories to tell. They have experienced different pasts and represent their pasts differently. Yet the places are not unrelated; their pasts intersect and what happened in one atoll had impacts for the others. Tokelau stories telling of the same event are often contested in detail and significance; however, this contestation is constrained by the impropriety of a person from one atoll relating a story that is properly about another. Again, each atoll has its own repertoire, its own past.

Dealing with the sources

The records of foreigners document primarily their own projects, for example conversion, commercial gain, administrative efficiency, in which Tokelau figured peripherally and sometimes inconveniently. What understanding Tokelau people had of the interests and forces that motivated these projects was interpreted in terms of their own systems of meaning. In a comparable way, Tokelau stories and texts are testimonies of their own projects and relationships, of which foreigners had little comprehension, often attributing Tokelau action and reaction to the instigation of competing foreign interests.

Nonetheless, the two sets of sources often complement one another, filling gaps, adding details, and providing confirmation. Sometimes foreign and local accounts are conflated, as when enquiring visitors inscribed stories told them of the past that are now forgotten, or when visitors provided information or voiced speculations which have been incorporated by creative Tokelau raconteurs into their own narratives.

Representations and transformations

The local and foreign records of the Tokelau past include representations of how things were, that is, more or less static orders of being, and narratives of transformations, that is, more or less dramatic happenings and their consequences. This contrast echoes E.P. Thompson's 'being'—'past states of consciousness and the texturing of social and domestic relationships'—and 'becoming'—'the processes and logic of change' (1977:251). For Tokelau, there are records of eventful times when people came and went, and protagonists were highly visible; and then stretches of years during which nothing much is recorded to have happened. These 'hot' and 'cold' periods are partly an artefact of the historical record, or more aptly of the preserved fragments or snippets, since 'record' implies some continuity. Foreign accounts are characteristically sporadic and short; yet during some brief periods one or another atoll hosted considerable numbers of welcomed and unwelcomed interlopers. For these years, there are multiple sources to draw upon and an eventful narrative may be constructed. At other times, sometimes for years, there were no visitors, or at least none that recorded anything. Tokelau stories, taken together, provide a more continuous tale. They too are about things that happened—after all that is what stories are about—but the events they tell of are memorable for different reasons. Some indeed do have transformative significance; others impart moral lessons relating examples of propriety or impropriety. Many, however, are simply about odd and memorable events, which are amusing to tell and retell.

The long stretches of time when Tokelau people were left alone—times when they could sort things out among themselves according to their own lights—are particularly ill-documented, so perforce we draw upon local stories, reminiscences and anecdotes to help us imagine how things were. Our imaginings, however, are always constrained, grounded at a particular time in a particular place, and informed by our ethnographic understandings of Tokelau people and their lifeways.

Structuring a narrative of the Tokelau past

Balancing three separate histories, juggling diverse sources, and negotiating the space between event and structure have all contributed to how our story of the Tokelau past is constructed. In addition, our story takes a particular perspective and has an intricate plot to weave. The practical strategies devised for handling the nature of the situation and sources have come to serve that plot.

We use two modes of historical storytelling—two narrative voices—alternatively: the even-numbered chapters are episodic narratives of happenings externally and internally motivated, and the odd-numbered chapters are more or less impressionistic portraits of Tokelau at several different periods. In effect, we chart the transformations from 'the beginning' to the ethnographic present, and construct representations of them at particular points in time. This alternation divides the Tokelau past into eras or epochs, marked sometimes by dramatic, even catastrophic, events and at others by gradual redirection.

Throughout, Tokelau texts and foreign documents are treated as equally valid and complementary sources; neither is privileged in principle, though one or the other may be in a particular instance. Sometimes they are juxtaposed to provide a double vision; at other times one supplements or fleshes out the other. At some junctures, particular sources dominate. For example, foreign sources can have nothing to say directly about events in Tokelau before European contact, yet their descriptions of Tokelau at contact add information about which Tokelau narratives are silent. Conversely, when Tokelau people were moving or being moved around in the mid nineteenth century, these movements can be securely traced only from foreign records; in Tokelau they just come and go. The even chapters on historical transformations tend to be derived more from foreign records, while the odd chapters representing portraits of an era are, not unexpectedly, based primarily on Tokelau evidence.

There had to be three histories; this was essential to the plot. The even chapters relate an inclusive narrative of all Tokelau, of transformative episodes and events that impacted on all the atolls, and on the relations between them. The odd chapters focus on the separate atolls at particular periods, telling how they adapted the impositions and incorporated them to their own projects and preoccupations. These also involved relations between the atolls. So the odd chapters portray first the local ambience and concerns of each atoll, and then the relations and contrasts between them.

Structure and plot

Our original aim was to 'do' a history for Tokelau, that is, to construct a continuous narrative by making the most we could of the scattered and scant records. This was an exercise in detection and deduction. The story would unfold in Tokelau, portraying how events were perceived, experienced and manipulated there, which would entail some disciplined imagination. The partial and fragmentary documents could be made to tell a story 'if you worked them hard enough' (Sahlins 1992:9), framed them in the context of Tokelau places and people, and linked them with local accounts.

As our detective work and imagining proceeded, we came to see another plot, a story centred in Tokelau, focusing on three places and peoples interacting with one another. Our overarching or master narrative plot is how their relations were transformed by events of their own making; how they maintained and at times enhanced their differences, by embracing and manipulating inputs from without and pursuing courses of action within. The Tokelau past is indeed eventful, and its dynamic is essentially in Tokelau as three places and three people, but one place and one people too.

FOUR
Tokelau Formed

In the beginning, as Tokelau raconteurs tell it, people were just there in the atolls. Although there are several published accounts of how the original inhabitants of Fakaofo came from elsewhere—from the Ellice Islands [Tuvalu] (Powell 1971a), Samoa (Newell 1895) and Rarotonga (Burrows 1923)—nobody gives them any credence. They are incidental stories, made up, perhaps, to satisfy questioners who demanded factual answers to what they took to be sensible, scientific enquiries. Lister undoubtedly got it right with his blunt and categorical statement that 'There is no tradition that the Fakaofo people came from Samoa or elsewhere' (1892:53). The same may be said about the original people of Nukunonu and Atafu.[1]

Tokelau Narratives

Myths

Tokelau does, however, have origin stories that are cognate with several wide-spread Polynesian myths and legends. We have been told them, others have published versions that they have been told, and Tokelau manuscripts contain yet other versions. They do not comprise a connected saga, nor are they placed in any temporal order. Though referred to as *tala* (stories of happenings), they are not taken with great seriousness or claimed to be particularly unique. There is the story of Lū, the son of Tikitiki and Talaga, separating the earth and sky, placing the winds and acquiring fire (see Lister 1892:52, Burrows 1923:153–4, *Matagi Tokelau* 1981:14–16). Another tells of the atolls being fished up and named by voyagers all called Maui (see Turner 1861, Lister 1892, Smith 1922, Burrows 1923:153 which is repeated by Macgregor 1937:16). The story of the origin of the people of Fakaofo belongs perhaps in a slightly different category. Although it has a fabulous element—two brothers who grew from maggots that emerged from a fish or a stone pecked by a bird (Lister 1892:52, Burrows 1923:152, Macgregor 1937:17–18)—these brothers are unequivocally linked to the historical, social world as the founders of that island's chiefly genealogy.[2] Nukunonu has its own genealogy of autochthonous origin beginning with a founding couple, Pipi and Fekei, from which the paired *aliki* lines of that island sprang. No originator or genealogy is known of the original Atafu people who disappeared (see below). They are depicted as a particularly barbarous lot and in no way connected with the original people of Fakaofo or Nukunonu.

What the local stories of origins definitively posit are three separate peoples, different in the very beginning. Just as there are no accounts of migrations to the atolls, there are also none of settlement from one to the others. Each is distinct, unique, 'just there' at the very beginning of Tokelau's history.

The oft-told, apparently simple story of reciprocal theft by *aitu* 'spirits' rather than people places the 'treasures' of Fakaofo and Nukunonu. This is how Alosio Kave told the tale to start off an evening of storytelling in Nukunonu at his sister's house, pointedly introducing it as a *tala* to distinguish it from the *kakai* 'fictional tales' he more usually told.

> The story of two spirits: Hemoana, a Nukunonu spirit, and Fenū, a Fakaofo spirit[3]
>
> *Hemoana, the spirit of Nukunonu, lived at a place called the Kava of Hemoana. Even while staying right over there Hemoana still realised that the well off at Hā Toga was murky. Hemoana went over there to check and discovered the spirit of Fakaofo, Fenū, had come and stolen Nukunonu's water, filling up a coconut shell and racing off with it. So Hemoana set right off in pursuit of Fenū. Racing, racing, racing—their race ended at the Nukunonu islet called Motu Akea. Here Hemoana caught up with Fenū and here Hemoana struck the coconut shell of water so that some of the water spilled, but the shell remained grasped in Fenū's hand and Fenū raced off with the shell in hand to Fakaofo.*
>
> *To this very day there is still a well at Motu Akea. The village uses it only when there is a dearth of rain—a drought. Then people go there to draw water and bathe.*
>
> *Well. One day some time later, Hemoana was thinking about how the* kie *pandanus thrived in Fakaofo but did not grow in Nukunonu. Hemoana suddenly had the idea that he would go and steal this pandanus in Fakaofo for Nukunonu. Hemoana went there searching all around lest Fenū should see him. The Fakaofo spirit was not anywhere to be seen. The fine pandanus of Fakaofo was stolen straight away and brought to Nukunonu. When Hemoana raced off with those pandanus cuttings, Fenū never even knew it. The cuttings were brought here and planted.*
>
> *They have thrived to this very day in Nukunonu, where this pandanus is plaited into fine mats. Even in recent times, since the coming of Christianity, when Fakaofo people would come and take cuttings to replant them in Fakaofo, they would not live.*
>
> *Well, take note that* kie *pandanus thrives upon Nukunonu, and also that the well is still evident at Motu Akea—to this very day.*
>
> *Well, also note that Fakaofo got the well, that Fakaofo is blessed with fresh water because of Fenū, the Fakaofo spirit, who raced off with that shell full of water.*

This apparently simple just-so story of mutual theft explains why Fakaofo is blessed with a freshwater well in its village and sub-surface accumulations of fresh water on some other islets, while Nukunonu has only a small well inconveniently located on a tiny uninhabited islet, and also why the fine *kie* pandanus (*Freycinetia* sp.) flourishes only in Nukunonu. These two valuable resources have multiple significances and the story is emblematic for Tokelau history. Fakaofo's valuable resource of fresh water (*vai magalo*) is the source of life and productivity. Wells of fresh water in the village were carefully tended and used, but more important sub-surface accumulations permit intensive pit cultivation of root crops which cannot otherwise be grown. Nukunonu's grove of *kie* pandanus is tended and propagated by women, and processed and fashioned by them into fine mats that are women's valuables. In the past, these fine mats were expressly made to shroud and conceal stone images of gods, and *kie* was used to plait into men's loincloths or *malo*—again to conceal. Further significances of this 'simple story' will become apparent in due course.

Aho o na taua 'The days of battles'

Another phase of the distant Tokelau past is recounted in stories of intrepid voyagers and of the mighty deeds and feats of strength performed by named but shadowy warriors. Again many of them are variants of widespread Polynesian legends and the events they relate were of no lasting consequence in the atolls (see *Matagi Tokelau* 1991:19–27, as well as Lister 1892:56, Newell 1895:605, Burrows 1923:148). The stories portray a time of conflict when bold voyagers and warriors ventured afar to engage in contests of strength and daring, and when those from one atoll harassed the others. This local belligerence is ascribed, on the one hand, to the desire of one place to gain ascendancy and the unwillingness of any atoll to recognise the paramountcy of the *aliki* of another, and, on the other, to a raw demonstration of superior strength for no longterm gain. The original Atafu people exemplified the latter—they are said to have been a particularly ferocious lot, while to Fakaofo is attributed a determination to dominate its neighbours—in which it succeeded. Two of these stories compose the founding charter of Tokelau. They are widely known and frequently told, and what they relate had lasting consequences. Together they are called *tala o na taua a Tokelau* 'stories of Tokelau wars'; each records a Fakaofo conquest and the establishment of the sociopolitical order which linked the atolls in a single polity dominated by Fakaofo. Indeed, they tell how Tokelau came to be, for before that there was no Tokelau, only Atafu, Fakaofo and Nukunonu.

The two stories, referred to as 'The Defeat of Nukunonu' and 'The Flight of Atafu', though customarily related as discrete events, may be temporally sequenced by inference. Both are long and replete with references to named places and allusions to subsequent situations that may be hotly debated, yet the essential plots and incidents are the same in all renditions. Manuele Palehau, Nukunonu's master storyteller, in recounting Nukunonu's defeat didactically highlights significant characteristics of the two polities in conflict.

The defeat of Nukunonu[4]

This is a story of those times past (heathen times) when battles were fought between the islands of Tokelau. This particular story is about the battles of Fakaofo and Nukunonu. The situation between Fakaofo and Nukunonu had been that Nukunonu did not initiate battle, but just prevailed whenever Fakaofo's war canoes came. Well, the arrangements for Fakaofo's battles were as follows. There were two divisions at Fakaofo, the Youth corps and the Mature corps. The Youth corps first came to engage in the first battle. They came but did not prevail and returned in defeat. It happened again another time. The Youth corps came a second time and did not prevail. Well, at yet another time the arrangement of the Fakaofo forces was altered. The Mature corps came.

Upon their arrival, this is the way the Mature corps came. Entering at the reef passage, they took the formation of two sides (fakakauvaemagō) upon their approach to the shore and as they came upon Nukunonu's soil. (Doubtless you all understand the meaning of this word 'fakakauvaemagō'. It is a formation like the jaw of a shark.) Thus they entered the reef pass, coming nearer and nearer, coming ashore at the Ahaga.

Meanwhile in Nukunonu word of the impending battle was spread among the people, but they paid no heed. Well. The story of Nukunonu's response to the alarm of the impending battle is as follows. The leaders spread word of the impending battle to their fighters, but their response was this: 'Go away don't bother me, just let me alone to patch up the leaking roof of my house.' Well, that was the response of some. Or there was some other domestic or family chore in which the men of Nukunonu were engaged, and they were not inclined to bother themselves about war. Nukunonu's chief warrior at that time was Feuku.

Fakaofo launched upon their attack—a man was struck down from up in a house and, excuse my saying so, run right through with spears. A person lashing a canoe met the same fate. In this way the men of Nukunonu were quickly overwhelmed. The warrior chief of Nukunonu saw that his fighting force was depleted, so he went straight away to his house—his house was named Loiloifia—and pulled down a bundle of dried coconuts. Off he went with it . . . using it as his float he swam towards Tokelau [the islet at the northeast point of Nukunonu atoll]. Well, we'll leave Feuku there for the moment—swimming to Tokelau.

Here was the force of Fakaofo marching [through Vao] northwards to Te Alofi. As the Fakaofo troops marched along, spread out in a line from the ocean side to the lagoon shore, they called out to one another. They shouted like this, those at the lagoon shore calling to those at the seaside: 'There, there! Right over there! About to climb up.' Likewise, those at the seaside called to those at the lagoon shore: 'There, right over there! About to enter into that place.' But they really had not seen anything. They were just doing this to spread terror so that they could easily spot a person going to hide here or hide there. Well. The person who was climbing up the palm would think he had really been seen and so would slither down again. The person about to hide some place would just stand there exposed. Well. This is what is said about Fakaofo when they pursued their conquest. They never really saw anyone but nonetheless shouted out: 'There, there!'

Well, the force of Fakaofo, marched right along. Passing along the Alofi—going going along—reaching the Ahagaloa [northern margin of the atoll]. Marching along the Ahagaloa [eastward]—carrying carrying on—reaching the Pūoneone [the shore of Tokelau]. Going off from there, Fakaofo marched on towards Avaloa.

At Avaloa Feuku had laid himself out. Let me explain: at the very moment that Feuku came ashore, there was a child walking along the beach. He grabbed the child and split it in two bathing himself in its blood. Well, the Fakaofo march

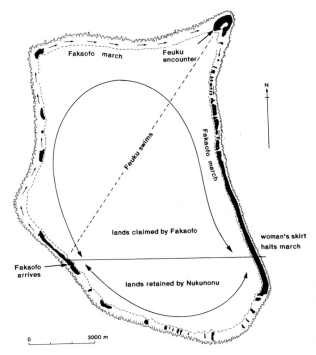

The geography of the
'Conquest of Nukunonu'
showing the clockwise
route of the Fakaofo
warriors, the location of
marked incidents, and the
division of the atoll.

reached there and Feuku was spread out face down. The men of the vanguard
approached him and spoke these words: 'What a waste of redness.' Well, that was
all and the march continued on. Going on and on and on and on until all the
troops had passed by. Then Feuku stood right up and shouted out this challenge:
'Fakaofo's "game" is war!' Well, now Feuku was safe, he had escaped and there
was nothing that they could do to him. This was because of our rule—a law of
the Tokelau isles: If a man escapes to the rear of the battle nobody can turn back
to kill him. Should anyone ever do so he will come to a dreadful end.

Well. The troops continued marching on and on, reaching Manukatele [on the
east margin], marching along while Feuku kept shouting out: 'Fakaofo's "game"
is war!', all the time passing right among with the troops, mingling together with
them. The warriors marched down along the lagoon shore of Fakanaitino. Marching on and on, they were just about to cross the boundary between Nataulaga and
Vaitupu [more than halfway down the eastern margin], when the vanguard commanded a halt to the march. Yes. There the advance ended, for there was something they saw there—a woman's skirt was suspended from an ironwood scrub.
The advance stopped for that reason. The vanguard knew that an unclothed
woman was bathing in the sea. Because to us still, we speak of women as manuhā
'sacred beings'. Well, that is why the advance was halted.

They stopped right there calling for Feuku to come forward, to come to the
place where the two of them were. Looking across to the village [on the other side
of the lagoon], those in the vanguard proceeded to divide Nukunonu. They were
Pule and Niko, these two leaders of the Fakaofo forces. There was this open space
where the Church now stands, which was very visible from across the lagoon.
This pair of leaders decreed as follows: 'Yours is that side there, ours is this side
here'—pointing from over there around and stopping at the place they were
standing.

You must appreciate that we are repeating what the elders have passed on to us: from Lalo going downwind to Vao and right to the Afagā [that is, counter-clockwise from the place they halted on the eastern margin to the open place in the village] was what was taken over by Fakaofo as a result of the decree of their leaders at this time. As for Nukunonu's land, it extended from Vaitupu [clockwise] to the same place, at the village side of the present Church as we know it now. That part was designated for Nukunonu.

Well, after some number of days had passed, Fakaofo went back to their own land. They departed with their victory, as was the way in those times. That then was the third of Fakaofo's attacks and they were victorious.

Well. The woman's skirt of the . . . as I said before this skirt was seen by the vanguard, a skirt like . . . whose skirt . . . of whom . . . of Matua, Matua a daughter of Talafau. That was what checked the Fakaofo forces. That is the story that has been passed on to us by word of mouth from our forebears.

The key episodes in this and other versions of the conquest story are the reluctance of Nukunonu warriors to join battle, the march around the atoll, Feuku's feigned death and the 'rule of war', the skirt that halted the Fakaofo advance and the division of the atoll at this point. This particular story attributes Fakaofo's success both to the maturity and discipline of the troops and the disinclination of Nukunonu's defenders to take up arms because they were preoccupied with domestic repairs. The characterisations are apt, reflecting particular features ascribed by Tokelau people to their separate communities. This master raconteur teaches his Nukunonu audience the lesson that uncompromising commitment to family concerns may jeopardise the welfare of all, by elaborating the epitomising phrase: 'Leave me alone to repair my leaking roof', and, though 'Fakaofo's game is war', he stresses that it was war according to the rules successfully pursued by a disciplined 'Mature corps'.

Had a Fakaofo audience been present there would have been disagreement about who the woman was whose skirt halted the advance. Our narrator asserts, with tantalising hesitation (there was a Fakaofo listener), that it belonged to Nukunonu's chiefly daughter and implies that by her agency a significant portion of the atoll remained under Nukunonu control, while a Fakaofo narrator would maintain that the leaders recognised the skirt as that of a Fakaofo woman living in Nukunonu and were showing appropriate deference to a woman of their own land by stopping!

Proper names ground and authenticate narratives of the Tokelau past. In the story above and the one to follow, actions happen at very specific named places and these places are testimony that they did happen. However, the named and genealogically recorded actors are few: here, only Feuku, the warrior who saves his own skin. The disciplined but callous Fakaofo leaders, Niko and Pule, are not genealogically known.

While 'The Defeat of Nukunonu' describes a one-sided battle, 'The Flight of Atafu' recounts a battle that did not happen. Kolo Tito's rendering of the story hints of the ambivalence that Atafu people have about those barbarous autochthons in whose land they now reside, and about their distant forebears who resided in Fakaofo.

The Flight of Atafu[5]

Nukunonu was completely overcome, Fakaofo too was completely overcome by the cruelty and might of the people who dwelt in Atafu. A fleet of warriors set off from here [Atafu], a fearsome fleet indeed, for they utterly overwhelmed Nukunonu, utterly overwhelmed Fakaofo. This party of warriors and their canoes remained there in Fakaofo which had been utterly defeated. The situation regarding food, even food like dried-up coconuts, was desperate. These people would simply snatch it away. It is difficult in these days to imagine the circumstances with such cruel people staying there [at Fakaofo]. Now the desperate strategy of the Fakaofo people was to go with their dried coconuts to the coral head between Nukumatau and Falē, which is called 'Te Puga Foavaka' [The Canoe-shaped Coral-head]. There people would dive down and crack open their dried coconuts. The place was at least two arm spans deep. All this was because should a coconut be cracked at the village, those terrifying people would hear and snatch it away. It was just the same in Nukunonu, because Nukunonu had been utterly defeated too.

Finally this party of Atafu men at Fakaofo set out to return to Atafu. As they departed a woman was fishing on the north side of Fenuafala. This woman was the daughter of the paramount chief, Kava-vahe-fenua. The leader of the Atafu party commanded: 'Steer the canoe towards shore. Let's go up there and grab that person fishing.' They brought her down and—in the manner of barbarous men— they held the woman down and bound her by her legs to a canoe, and then the canoes raced off at full speed—the canoes all being lashed together because of the strong wind. Perhaps she never came to the surface, certainly she soon was dead, this daughter of Kava-vahe-fenua.

On that very day Fakaofo assembled to deliberate. They would engage Atafu in battle because of what had been done to that woman, the daughter of the paramount chief, and the person in command would be Tevaka, a son of the paramount chief. Every single canoe of Fakaofo set out to sea—each with two aboard.

Well. These people who had done that outrageous deed to the daughter of the paramount chief had returned and were in Atafu. Well, as for the appearance of those canoes here [in Atafu], they approached here while the sun was still below the horizon, exactly like the mornings when the sun is just rising in a cloudless sky. Well. There were people on watch perched in the highest palms—remember that the islands were in a continual state of war, never at peace. The watchman made out a canoe approaching: 'Hail! One vessel.' The warrior chief of Atafu was sitting in the communal house where meetings were held. Lefotu was his name. 'Hail! Two vessels', called the watchman, and Lefotu stepped out. 'Alert!' Then the number was three vessels—on and on and on reaching ten and still continuing, reaching twenty—still going reaching thirty. The warrior chief of Atafu exclaimed: 'Alas, what is this now. They keep coming and coming. Now my innards are in turmoil.' This meant that he was afraid and once the chief warrior is gripped by fear, all other men become afraid. 'Alert!' They stopped counting the canoes appearing but the words of Lefotu were echoed: 'My innards are in turmoil.' He was afraid. There was no way to resist this force approaching in countless canoes.

Well, what was to be done? A meeting was convened. Malaelua was the person who chaired the meeting. It appeared that the opinion of every single Atafu person was the same as his. Malaelua spoke; this is the speech he made: 'There is absolutely no other option for us; what we must realise is that we cannot possibly prevail. This is the situation. The warrior chief is frightened, so Atafu shall flee upon the sea. Prepare at once, let not a person be careless. Take the whole fleet of canoes, take the children, take the entire population, take all upon the canoes. Not a single person shall remain.' So it was. All Atafu fled.

133

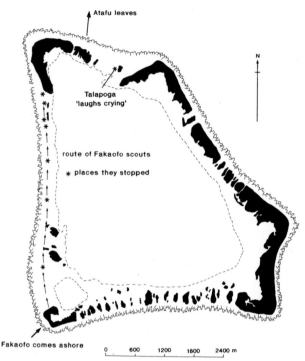

The geography of the 'Abandonment of Atafu' showing the route of the Fakaofo scouts, departure of the Atafu people, and Talapoga's predicament.

On the same night when this meeting was held, the Fakaofo war canoes hove to. They could be seen off Fenualoa. Well. When the depths of darkness came down in the night, scouts—or spies—set out to discover where the Atafu people might be. Three men came along [northward]. Coming, that they might know where Atafu was, where the warriors were. Coming, gaining the shore, coming to that reef-flat at the far side of Alofi. There was no sign that they could see— neither a fire nor a sound, nothing. One of them said: 'Let's go on. It's useless just sitting here.' Coming along, coming to the place called 'Pou's rock-pile' where there is a large, very wide rock. Coming, stopping there. Not a fire did they see, not a voice did they hear. 'Stand up. Let's go.' Coming, coming to the reef-flat of 'Tonuia's Fish-trap' where the reef again is wide. Again stopping—not a flicker of a fire, not a murmur of a voice. 'Are there any people there? Let's go.' Coming along, stopping at the tiny reef at the far side of the 'Ulugagie' that they might really know if there was any hint of voices murmuring or sign of fires alight. Nothing at all. Coming right up to the far end of the 'Ulugagie'. Stopping there. Still there was not a sign of a fire or a sound of a person. Coming over to the near side of the 'Ulugagie'. Again stopping. As before there was absolutely no hint of a human voice or a burning fire, not a single thing to show that there were people, nothing at all. 'Let's go.' Coming along coming to 'Fishermen's Reef'. Just as before and they did not stop long for again not a single thing, not a sound. 'Stand up. Let's go.' Coming straight along, coming to the shore, to the old shore where Amio's house is now. Sitting down. Not a single sign. 'Stand up. Let's go.' Coming, coming right into the village. Coming to nothing, not a person, Atafu was nothing. And then these men spoke the following words: 'What's this now— Atafu has fled. Instead of saying to us, let's just stop, stop fighting, they have fled from battle like startled wild pigeons.' They felt compassion for the true people of Atafu who had abandoned their homeland.

Well. Morning lightened and the men aboard the canoes came along. They searched suspecting that some people might be in the outlying islets. Going across the [northern] reef-flat they approached Fogalaki. There was a someone at Fogalaki. This someone was Talapoga. He had overslept and not left at the time it had been determined they would all put out to sea, when all the canoes could be launched at the Ahagaloa. Alas his canoe was stranded by the falling tide and there was nothing he could do when daylight came. So he just sat there on the reef at Fogalaki. The warriors approached and he laughed, he laughed at the warriors. Those warriors spoke these words: 'Talapoga laughs crying.' As soon as they reached Talapoga, they grabbed hold of him and bound his legs, dragging him through the sea. Alas, they were not satisfied to stop at that, but took him and dragged him upon the reef—unenlightened men. And so ended the life of Talapoga.

Well. The search continued. Going on and on and on, there was nothing, there was no Atafu. Atafu had fled from battle, from the trickery that Fakaofo played. Well. This is what truly happened. Not a single Atafu person was left here. All of us are Fakaofo people. This place was handed over to Tonuia.

The teller repeatedly comments upon the fierce and barbarous nature of the Atafu autochthons, implicitly contrasting them with the peaceful Christian Atafu people of today. He is both presenting the usual characterisation of the original Atafu people and distancing himself and his compatriots from them—yet with some ambivalence, for he and his fellows identify themselves with the lands of those that fled from battle. But then too, his Fakaofo ancestors of the time were on the one hand 'unenlightened', but on the other felt compassion for those who had abandoned their homeland.

Again the story is given veracity by the identification of places, particularly the places where the scouts stop and sit as they come towards the village, but none of the original Atafu people named are genealogically known, confirming that all of them disappeared and that they had no kinship links with Fakaofo or Nukunonu. The named Atafu actors are stereotypes: Lefotu, the ferocious warrior turned coward; Malaelua, the sensible civil authority who takes control; Talapoga, the foolish man who becomes the scapegoat, while the Fakaofo characters are genealogical—the *aliki* and his son (his violated daughter is anonymous).

Though this telling of the story is replete with detail, one important feature of the story is neglected (probably assuming that the listeners knew it, as they most certainly did). The many canoes of Fakaofo did not in fact represent a huge fighting force for they were peopled with dummies accompanying the 'two aboard' (the version in *Matagi Tokelau* elaborates this ploy). Therefore, the 'true' Atafu people fled before the apparent, though contrived, might of Fakaofo.

The three texts above compose the essential charter of the Tokelau ancient order. They are not stories of heroes and heroism, of nobility and glory, but of trickery and deception, self-interest and stupidity. *Aitu* spirits are sneak thieves, the Fakaofo forces trick people out of their hiding places, the Nukunonu warrior Feuku saves his own skin by bloody deceit, and the Atafu warrior Lefotu turns out to be a craven coward. Nukunonu warriors are too preoccupied to fight. The Atafu autochthons foil their opponents by disappearing, except for Talapoga who traps himself and absurdly 'laughs crying'. Tokelau storytelling, whether of past or present happenings or of imaginative fiction, is characteristically ironical, and their mythic charter is no different.

Tokelau united

Tokelau became a historic entity as a result of these conquests (that also included Olohega as substantiated by stories set after the conquests—*Matagi Tokelau* 1996:37–43); Fakaofo had created Tokelau and was its overlord. A few narratives tell of events during the decades, perhaps centuries, that followed before Europeans arrived on the scene, and sages relate genealogies and make pronouncements about the nature of the Tokelau ancient polity (see chapter 5).

Genealogies, in a different idiom, provide a parallel account of the relations between the atolls. To mark their conquest Fakaofo forces took a chiefly woman from Nukunonu to be a consort of their *aliki*, Kava-vahe-fenua. Who exactly she was, and what her status in Fakaofo was, are variably phrased. Nukunonu asserts that she became a beloved chiefly wife, and the union was a founding alliance between the two peoples, while Fakaofo speaks of her as a 'slave'. It is generally agreed that her Fakaofo name was Nau,[6] a name that does not appear in Nukunonu genealogies, and she is referred to as *te fafine o te halaga*, a phrase that has two plausible meanings. For those who depict her as a 'slave' it means 'the woman of the punishment' from *hala* 'to punish'; for those who celebrate her it means 'the woman of the foreshadowing' from *hala* 'the monthly appearance of a species of fish in small numbers foreshadowing their subsequent appearance in large numbers'. According to this latter interpretation, hers is the first of many unions between Nukunonu and Fakaofo, the foundation of an ongoing alliance between them. The differing perspectives on Nau's status are echoed in the status ascribed to her son, Pio Toevave. Pio, all agree, was fathered by Kava-vahe-fenua, but his status is disputed, particularly *vis-à-vis* his half-brother, Tevaka. Predictably those who accord Nau low status accord it also to Pio—he begins a line of inferior chiefs by virtue of being the son of a 'slave' woman; while those who celebrate Nau's chiefliness give pre-eminence to Pio too. Again, the issue of Pio are of no consequence for those who regard him as insignificant; however, the genealogy issuing from him is recited by those for whom he is a significant forebear. Predictably, Nukunonu acknowledges him both as a chiefly son and as the first of their categorical 'sisters' sons' in Fakaofo. Atafu acknowledges him too, but for different reasons (see below).

Fakaofo's pre-eminence is restated yet again in a spiritual idiom. In the accounts of the battles between the atolls there is absolutely no mention of gods or spirits; a few spirit familiars are invoked in the stories of voyagers and warriors; and the spirits in the story of mutual theft have no human counterparts. However, once Fakaofo achieved pre-eminence Tui Tokelau, the great god of all Tokelau, becomes a presence and appears instantiated in a huge stone erected in Fakaofo. In essence, Tui Tokelau is invoked with the establishment of the overarching polity of Tokelau itself, and is solidly positioned in Fakaofo where the paramount *aliki* was the god's principal supplicant and celebrant.

Fakaofo overlords exacted tribute from Nukunonu as annual offerings to Tui Tokelau. In the mid-year months, goods and produce were brought from Nukunonu for the annual rites of the god. Specifically, Nukunonu provided fine mats and *malo* 'loincloths' plaited from the fine *kie* pandanus, which flourished only on that atoll. Although Nukunonu had acquired a monopoly of this treasured resource by retaliatory theft, Fakaofo extracted the valuables manufactured from it by many hours of women's labour. The fine mats were the premier offering to Tui Tokelau—concealing the stone within a heavy shroud. All conch, cowrie and pearlshell collected in Nukunonu were appropriated by Fakaofo. Some of the shells ornamented the sanctuary of Tui Tokelau; others were fashioned into hooks for the use of Fakaofo fishermen and adorned Fakaofo canoes. Lines and nets made of hibiscus bark fibre (*fau*) and sennit (*kafa*), bowls (*kumete*), tackle boxes (*tuluma*), paddles and bailers adzed from the hardwood timber *kānava* (*Cordia subcordata*) by the men of Nukunonu were also levied, as were other women's plaited goods. Large quantities of fresh, dried and preserved foodstuffs were supplied from Nukunonu for the annual ceremony. Clearly, Nukunonu was not just making offerings to Tui Tokelau; the people of Fakaofo were benefiting from the extracted resources and labour of Nukunonu. Again, from that portion of Nukunonu which Fakaofo had claimed by conquest, all mature nuts were harvested and transported to Fakaofo.

Fakaofo exercised *pule* 'political control/authority' over Nukunonu. All 'laws and regulations' were decreed from Fakaofo, and Fakaofo made appointments to positions of authority within Nukunonu and assigned Fakaofo men—specifically male descendants of Pio, the son of Nau—as deputies of the Fakaofo *aliki* there. Though civil affairs continued to be administered by Nukunonu's elders, they were constrained by Fakaofo authority, which in turn was sanctioned by Fakaofo's privileged access to Tui Tokelau, the source of fecundity and prosperity.

The subordination of Nukunonu is particularly highlighted by the statement that many Nukunonu women, especially chiefly daughters, were taken to Fakaofo as wives, following in the path of Nau. Since all commentators accept that ideally couples in the past as in the present reside uxorilocally, they invariably remark that Fakaofo men brought their Nukunonu wives to Fakaofo, explaining that if the men remained in Nukunonu they would have been implicated in the servitude of Nukunonu (as well as being junior and therefore subordinate members of their wives' families). This marked exception to uxorilocal residence was in fact tribute in yet another form. Fakaofo appropriated the reproductive resources of Nukunonu—its women, which goes far in accounting for the tiny number of Nukunonu residents in the largest atoll of the group (see below).

By genealogical reckoning, many generations passed without recorded or memorable incident. Fakaofo's supremacy was unquestioned—it was *te fenua aliki* 'the land of chiefs'. Nukunonu, submissive and exploited, paid homage to these chiefs and to Tui Tokelau. Atafu was uninhabited though visited from time to time by Fakaofo emissaries—again descendants of Pio—to oversee the land and exploit its timber and fishing resources.

Another series of events—firmly linked with genealogies and related in a mode more historical than mythical (Cohn 1961)—begins with reference to another Pio, Pio Tanuvalevale, who was a descendant of the earlier Pio and therefore of Nau.[7] He married a Nukunonu woman named Tomo by whom he fathered many children and he was despatched to Nukunonu as deputy of the Fakaofo *aliki*. In his wife's homeland he found great favour among his categorical 'mother's brothers' as their categorical 'sister's son'. However, Pio could not remain; he was summoned back to the land of his birth when he was selected to succeed the Fakaofo *aliki*, and reluctantly returned.

The above story of Pio Tanuvalevale, as told in Nukunonu, is the prologue to a composite story that again relates events of lasting significance (see genealogy below). From Fakaofo, Pio Tanuvalevale assigned his younger son, Tepine, to go and reside in Nukunonu as his deputy and instructed his elder son, Hogā, to go on to Atafu. However, things did not work out exactly as Pio decreed. Hogā, like his father before him, became enamoured of a Nukunonu woman and preferred to tarry there rather than travel to remote and unpeopled Atafu. He proposed to Tepine that they switch assignments, and the younger brother properly acceded to his elder brother's words and went off to Atafu. He did not remain there but returned to Fakaofo, and some time later his son, Tonuia, was commissioned to colonise Atafu, which he did with his wife, Lagimaina, again a Nukunonu daughter of chiefly lineage. Their six children, to whom a seventh was added by Tonuia's subsequent union, founded the

The genealogy of Tokelau 'formed'. The union that 'founds' the relationship between Fakaofo and Nukunonu is that of Kava-vahe-fenua and Nau. How that relationship is interpreted—as appropriation by Fakaofo or as gift from Nukunonu—differs. The issue of that union is Pio, who is of Fakaofo on his father's side and of Nukunonu on his mother's. From Pio's line springs Tonuia, whose 'founding' union with a woman from Nukunonu initiates the new population of Atafu. Again, they are of Fakaofo on their father's side and of Nukunonu on their mother's.

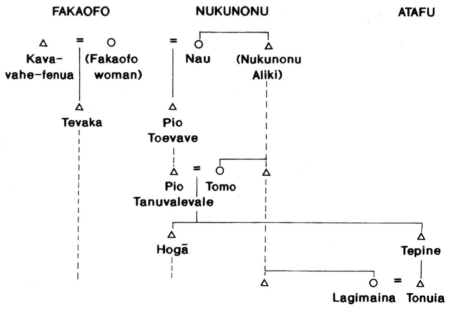

Falefitu or 'Seven Houses' of Atafu. Thus Atafu's new polity issued from the paternal line of Pio of Fakaofo (including Pio Toevave and ultimately Kava-vahe-fenua) and on the maternal side from Nukunonu (from Lagimaina but also Tomo and ultimately Nau). Atafu people are claimed as 'sister's children' by Nukunonu and Atafu agrees that Nukunonu people are their 'mother's brothers'. However, Atafu and Fakaofo do not agree about their categorical relationship, though they concur that in some way they are 'brothers', and this disagreement hinges on the status of Pio Toevave, the son of Nau.

With Hogā, the elder son of Pio Tanuvalevale who preferred to tarry at Nukunonu, there begins a patriline of Fakaofo men sent to Nukunonu as *aliki* (as Fakaofo asserts) or *kovana* 'governor/deputy' (in the Nukunonu view, as a governor-general is deputy of the Queen). While they too had Nukunonu consorts (though not of chiefly status), each in turn fathered his successor by a Fakaofo woman. Therefore, these men are not connected to Nukunonu by maternal links and Nukunonu is not categorically 'mother's brother' to them, except as their remote ancestress was Nau and a distant forebear was Tomo. The fourth in this line, Hogā's great-grandson, was known as the *aliki/*'king' of Nukunonu in the latter half of the nineteenth century.

The story of how Tokelau came into being from the beginning to the nineteenth century is concluded. The stories, or perhaps what are really several episodes of the one story, are discontinuous and contested, but no one would question that they relate how Tokelau was *anamua* 'in the past' or *aho pouliuli* 'dark days' (before Christian enlightenment) with Fakaofo ascendant, Tui Tokelau in place, and the three atolls linked politically and at the same time by network of kinship, based not just on the founding political unions of Fakaofo men and Nukunonu women. Although the earliest foreign visitors might not have realised it, their observations in fact confirm the basic outlines of Tokelau representations of this distant past.

Tokelau Observed: June 1765 to January 1841

The 'discovery' of Tokelau hardly figures in European annals of exploration. The early records of sightings and encounters are slight and problematic, and these events do not figure at all in Tokelau remembrances. Yet the voyager accounts resonate with Tokelau stories of the past, so they are worthy of some attention if only to back up the stories that Tokelau people have told.

Commander Byron of HMS *Dolphin* came upon Atafu in June 1765, and wrote of it: 'It is not inhabited and I believe that we are the first People that ever saw it', after he sailed around and explored the atoll (Gallagher 1964:109). He named his 'discovery' Duke of York's Island. His observation was correct but his belief erroneous.

Twenty-six years later, in June, Captain Edwards on HMS *Pandora* sought the *Bounty* mutineers on Byron's Duke of York's Island (Edwards and Hamilton 1915:45–48, Edwards n.d.). He too declared it uninhabited after 'a most minute and repeated search' failed to find anyone, despite undoubted evidence of human presence—houses, canoes, fishing gear and what Hamilton,

Documented Visitors

Ship, Captain etc.	Activity	Sources
1765 HMS *Dolphin* Cmd. Byron	Found Atafu uninhabited. Named 'Duke of York's Island'.	Gallagher 1964
1791 HMS *Pandora* Capt. Edwards Surg. Hamilton	Searched Atafu and declared uninhabited. Found Nukunonu but people disappeared. Named 'Duke of Clarence's Island'.	Edwards & Hamilton 1915 Edwards n.d.
1824 *Phoenix* British whaler Surg. Dalton	Offshore at Atafu (?) and men came aboard.	Dalton 1990
1825 Nantucket whaler Capt. Macy	Saw people on Atafu.	Reynolds 1835
1825 USS *Dolphin* Lt H. Paulding	Encounters at sea at Fakaofo and on land at Nukunonu (misidentified as Nukunonu and Atafu respectively).	Paulding 1970 *Dolphin* log 1825
1835 *General Jackson* Bristol whaler Capt. Smith	'Touched' at Atafu. 'Recruited' at Nukunonu. 'Chased' at Fakaofo. Fakaofo identified and named D'Wolf's Island.	YANKEE 1835 Ward (ed.) 1967
Jan 1837 *Admiral Cockburn* Surg. Broughton	Went ashore for wood. Fired on flotilla of canoes. Killed one or more people and sank canoes.	Broughton 1838 in Ward (ed.) 1967
April 1837 *Nautilus* New Bedford whaler	Traded at Fakaofo and Nukunonu. (Not at Nukunonu and Atafu, because thereafter saw a third island further north.)	*Nautilus* Log 1835–38
Jan 1839 *General Jackson* Capt. Crocker	Drew maps of three islands. Onshore at Fakaofo 'found the natives friendly'.	Crocker 1836–39
Jan 1841 USEE *Peacock* & *Flying Fish* Capt. Hudson *et al.*	Ashore at Atafu. Unable to make Nukunonu. 'Discovered' Fakaofo and went ashore. Named it 'Bowditch Island' and all three 'The Union Group'.	Wilkes 1845 Hale 1846 Hudson Reynolds Whittle etc.

the surgeon, described as a temple with white shells laid upon three altars. Accordingly, Edwards speculated that 'it was an occasional residence and fishery of the natives of some neighbouring islands', and in this he was correct. He then looked around for neighbouring islands and came upon Nukunonu, which was unquestionably inhabited though the inhabitants were elusive. From shipboard they '. . . saw several sailing canoes with stages in their middle, sailing across the lagoon for the opposite island. . .', and when a party got ashore they found the village deserted. Sailing around to the other side of the atoll, they found only '. . . marks of the bare feet of the natives in different parts, but more particularly about the cocoanut trees, most of which were stripped of their fruit, but not a single person or canoe . . .'. The people had apparently left the atoll altogether on their double canoes, probably bound for Fakaofo with an ample supply of coconuts. He named Nukunonu Duke of Clarence's Island.

There were no further records of sightings until the 1820s, and in that decade there are two recorded encounters: the first by the whaling ship *Phoenix* in 1824 (Dalton 1990:77) and the second in 1825 by the United States schooner *Dolphin* (Paulding 1970:76–93, *Dolphin* Logbook). Both reported that Atafu (Duke of York's) was inhabited.[8] Atafu was undoubtedly settled shortly after the visit of the *Pandora*, so in retrospect these reports are unremarkable. However, it is doubtful that all these observations were made at Atafu. Internal evidence persuades us that the whale ship *Phoenix*'s encounter was at Atafu,[9] but the *Dolphin*'s two encounters as reported are misplaced.[10] The island first encountered by the *Dolphin* was not Duke of Clarence's (Nukunonu) as Paulding reports, but Fakaofo, and the 'second island' was Nukunonu rather than Duke of York's (Atafu). This is an important issue, and one that has been verified with some care. Its significance is that the USS *Dolphin* was very likely the first European vessel to touch at Fakaofo, and the reception it received is particularly notable.

According to Paulding's account, 'nearly a hundred canoes were assembled', while on shore there was 'a numerous group of men, women and children, inviting our people to land' (1970:82). The men of the island came directly out to the ship. When thrown a rope, they motioned for more and when no more was forthcoming, gathered in as much as they could and cut it off. One powerful man came on board 'without seeming to fear us in the least' (1970:79) and began to throw into his canoe everything he could lay hands on. When he was forcibly dissuaded from this, other men came on board, while others threw onto the ship 'clubs, cocoa-nuts, or whatever they had in their canoes, that could be used as missiles . . . acompanied by loud shouting' (1970:81). When a boat was lowered it was soon surrounded by canoes and threatened, leading to retaliation with pistol fire which wounded one Fakaofo man in the hand. Later, however, when the boat had been hoisted aboard, the canoes again came up to the ship and the wounded man reappeared to have his hand dressed. Fakaofo proved to be as unwelcoming on land as it was at sea, since a party sent ashore from the *Dolphin* in the evening had to return empty-handed because of threats.

At the next island, Nukunonu according to this reconstruction, the *Dolphin* was met by only fifteen or so men, who were reported as resembling those seen in Fakaofo '. . . in dress, color and every thing, except they had a sickly look, and, in strength and activity, seemed much their inferiors' (1970:91). They were described as shy and timid, though rather sly in their dealing. At neither atoll did they meet any women, though they saw them from afar: at Fakaofo, a 'great many . . . assembled on the shore singing and amusing themselves' (1970:86–7), and at Nukunonu a small number removed to a 'large raft' in the lagoon.

These descriptions of men at the two islands are almost caricatures of dominance and subordination. Atafu men at roughly the same time (Dalton 1990) showed some of the same daring and acquisitiveness as those at Fakaofo.

Not until 1835 was it reported that there were three, rather than just two, atolls in the area. In hindsight, this was a recognition rather than a discovery, and the credit for it goes to Captain Smith of the American whaler *General Jackson*, though several others were to claim credit later. First reports of his 'discovery', which he had named D'Wolf's Island, added that he had been 'chased by about 30 canoes' when about three miles offshore (*New Bedford Mercury* 23 October 1835, in Ward (ed.) 1967). When doubt was cast about the existence of a third island, Smith, or his advocate, countered that he had 'touched at Duke of York's Island' and 'recruited at Duke of Clarence's Island' before making his 'new discovery' (YANKEE 1835). A later captain of the same ship, submitting cartographic evidence, confirmed Smith's account of there being three islands, adding his own observation that D'Wolf's Island

ATAFU

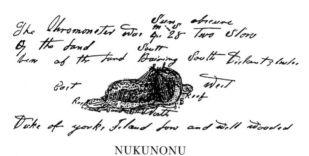

NUKUNONU

FAKAOFO

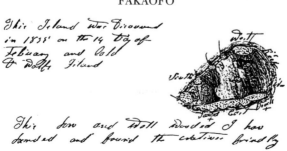

Captain Stephen Crocker's sketch maps of the three atolls. Crocker succeeded Smith as captain of the General Jackson *and undertook to verify Smith's 'discovery', which he had named D'Wolf's Island after the owners of the* General Jackson. *Note that the atolls, though differently oriented, are recognisable.* From S. Crocker MS. Journal, reproduced by courtesy of the Nicholson Collection, Providence Public Library, Providence, Rhode Island was 'low and well wooded' and that he had landed there 'and found the natives friendly' (Crocker n.d.). While this report resolved the doubts about how many atolls there were, it has other significances.

Smith's account that he 'touched' at Atafu and 'recruited' at Nukunonu implies that he was ashore at both these islands and had encountered no belligerence, but at Fakaofo thirty canoes chased the ship, suggesting that Smith would have the same sort of aggressive welcome as that given to the *Dolphin* ten years before, had he not sailed away. Yet only four years later, in 1839, the captain of the same ship reported of Fakaofo that he had 'found the Natives friendly' (Crocker n.d.). What, then, had happened to so radically moderate the bold manner of the Fakaofo men, and their strategy of direct confrontation?

The answer may lie in a brief and fatal burst of hostilities with the British whale ship *Admiral Cockburn* in 1837 (Broughton 1838). The captain sought to procure wood and a party went ashore at an island identified as Duke of Clarence's, but quickly retreated in the face of 'an old man' who intimated 'as plainly as he could, any further stay would be attended by danger'. Later, as the ship lay becalmed about four miles from land, a 'large fleet of canoes' appeared.

When they were about a fourth of a mile from us they formed into a line, approaching the ship very fast. We mustered out arms as quickly as possible, they were soon within musket shot and they divided into two parties, one approaching the bow and the other the quarter. We waved them off without effect and we were obliged to fire on them and killed the King. Their taste for battle was now altered, and after a little more firing, which sank some of their canoes, they made good their retreat.

There is no mention of this violent incident in Tokelau accounts, but a text of the time strongly suggests that the island was Fakaofo.[11] A young Tokelau man from Fakaofo told the Rev. Turner (1861:529) that: 'A party of them once went out to visit a ship, and when near the vessel, one of their number was shot dead, all the rest fled to the shore.' The reported claim that the King was killed is a familiar elaboration. Otherwise the two accounts agree that the episode was a rout, and the 'little more firing' evidently had the same effect as Wallis's 'little grape shot' had had upon Tahitians in 1767 (Pearson 1969). This bloody demonstration of the power of foreign ships seems to have persuaded Fakaofo men to adopt a different manner with foreigners, and to at least appear deferential and conciliatory—or so it would seem from the very brief report of an encounter at Fakaofo scarcely three months later. A whaler recorded '. . . at 11.30 a.m. had several canoes off from shore with coconuts we bought their coconuts from them and paid in iron hoop and whales teeth. NB. pearl shell very good trade at this Island . . .' (*Nautilus* Log, 25–28 April 1837). The final note is convincing evidence that the ship was at Fakaofo, for where else would there have been good supplies of pearlshell?[12]

These then are the records of Tokelau encounters with foreigners on ships through the 1830s. Once untangled and put in their proper place, the reports have a definite historical value, although all of them are little more than spare factual accounts of the 'incidents on board' variety. Were it not for the records of the visit of the United States Exploring Expedition in 1841 there would be practically no solid documentation of the Tokelau polity or the social system of the mid nineteenth century, before more intrusive European contacts wrought a radical transformation.

Two of the Expedition ships were in Tokelau waters for some ten days in early 1841. Those aboard included the Expedition's redoubtable ethnologist and philologist, Horatio Hale, a number of other 'scientific gentlemen', and several officers, all of whom kept detailed journals of their observations. Taken together, these make up a considerable record, despite the absence of any observations at Nukunonu, where they were unable to land owing to contrary weather.

At Atafu, after having taken the precaution of sending their women and children off in canoes to the middle of the lagoon (Reynolds n.d.), about forty men came directly out to the ships in three double canoes 'all united in song', with those not employed in paddling 'keeping time with the music and some holding up mats and other articles of trade' (Whittle n.d.). In one canoe 'the head man unrolled his wares and spread them out to view, with the dexterity of a practised auctioneer' (Hale 1846:150). A party that went ashore found that, '[t]heir deportment evinced a singular union of confiding warmth and respectful fear. Some were shy, and retreated as we approached; others, more bold, put their arms around our necks and urged us to accompany them to their village. None of them, however, could remain quiet, and their agitation was evinced frequently in their peculiar mode—by singing' (Hale 1846:151).

The village was at the lagoon shore and consisted of between twenty and thirty houses, all of rectangular shape, with steep roofs sloping to within a couple of feet of the ground.

From the number of houses and the forty or fifty men reported by the landing party, a total population of 120 was estimated (Wilkes 1845:8). There were no discernible signs of differences in rank among the men. 'When we asked for their chief, some pointed to an old, portly man, who appeared to have the most consideration among them; but others declared that there was none present, and that the great chief (*aliki*) lived on an island in a southeast

At Atafu, '. . . the two oldest of the men, seating themselves on the ground, with two short sticks, commenced chanting and drumming on a large stick, whilst another wrapped a net about his middle, and began to dance: the more they were interrupted, the more vigorous became their efforts, both in the song and dance' (Wilkes 1845:9). Etching by T. Agate

direction. . .' (Hale 1846:152).

Hale learned that the island where the great chief resided was called Fakaofo, and upon asking whether there was a god-house in the village the people 'pointed to some place in the distance'. Hale formed the opinion that the people believed 'that we came from the sky, and were divinities' (1846:153). This interpretation at least provided the members of the Expedition with some sort of explanation for the incessant singing and chanting. Hale wrote (1846:153): 'It is indeed natural to suppose that their constant singing arose merely from a desire to propitiate our favour, according to their simple mode of worship.'[13]

After their day at Atafu, and several days in the vicinity of Nukunonu, the ships headed for Olohega. During that night they unexpectedly came upon another island, not marked on any of their charts. Fakaofo was 'discovered' again.

They quickly realised that this island was inhabited by a people like those of Atafu, but the reception here was strikingly different. At dawn eighteen canoes, each carrying four men, put off from one of the islets and commenced fishing. They appeared to take but little account of the ships at all, and '. . . pursued their occupation without taking the least notice of us' (Hale 1846:154). The men managed to maintain their indifferent manner even when two ship's boats approached the fishing party, and only liberal gifts eventually enticed some to come alongside the ship, whereupon 'they sang for us and kept up a most vivacious chatter' (Reynolds n.d.:168). Hale was a member of the party which followed the men ashore. He quickly learned that the name of their chief was Taupe, who was at the village on another islet, and that the name of their god was Tui Tokelau, who resided in the skies (1846:156).

'Near the centre of the town was a large building, which they called the malae, and declared to be the house of their god, Tui-Tokelau. . . . The house was oblong, about forty feet by thirty, and at the ridge-pole about twenty feet in height. The roof, which curved inward somewhat like that of a Chinese pagoda, descended at the eaves to within three feet of the ground, below which the house was open all around. The circumference was supported by many short stanchions, small and roughly hewn, placed a few feet apart; but the ridge-pole rested upon three enormous posts, of which the largest was about three feet in diameter. . . . [I]n front of it was . . . the god himself,—the great Tui-Tokelau. Whatever may have been inside was so thickly covered that it appeared like a pillar of matting ten feet high and as many in circumference' (Hale 1846). That the god-house is here located 'near the centre' suggests that it stood in the vicinity of the present meeting house; no one is quite sure. The smaller mat-wrapped object is reported to have been another unidentified god. The figures in the foreground document the several reports that the 'natives' were startled by 'the emission of smoke from the mouths of those who were smoking cigars' (Wilkes 1845:18). Etching by T. Agate in Wilkes 1845: opp. p.14

The visitors were received at the village islet the following day by some twenty old men, the *aliki* or 'king' foremost among them, all seated on the ground behind a little pile of coconuts, while 'the rest of the crowd (above a hundred in number) stood in the near ground, all singing, shouting and gesticulating, in a state of the highest excitement' (Hale 1846:156). Captain Hudson recorded (1840–42:111) that upon their approach:

They pointed to the sun, and made motions for us to be seated, for which purpose they placed mats on the coral for us to sit on. . . .[I] found it a matter of some difficulty to pacify the King. He embraced me, rubbed noses with me, rubbed his nose on my chin, pointed to the sun, howled, hugged me again, and again, moaned, howled, pointed to the sun, put a mat around my waist, and secured it with a cord made of human hair, rubbed noses again, cried, howled etc etc, and in this way some fifteen or twenty minutes were passed during which time my utmost efforts seemed unavailing to pacify him. The King was much more agitated than any of his subjects, and set up a most piteous howl the moment I attempted to leave his side.

Not all the Fakaofo men present were as ingratiating or effusively welcoming as the 'king' appeared to be. Some of the younger men '. . .would frequently skulk out of the crowd and at a little distance take a view of matters and things. . .' (Stuart n.d.). This reception, both effusive and reserved, had none of the apparent open, welcoming conviviality that had been shown at Atafu.

After perhaps an hour the visitors were reluctantly allowed to move inland. There they found 'very numerous' houses similar to those seen at Atafu, and near the centre a god-house, 'oblong, about forty feet by thirty' with a ridgepole twenty feet above supported by three posts about a yard in diameter. The inside was decorated around the eaves with suspended mother-of-

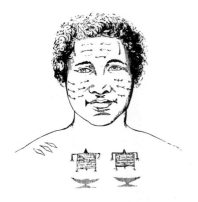

'. . . some of them had, besides, rude figures, representing tortoises, imprinted on the breast and sides' (Hale 1846:154). The natives had figures of turtles, paddles fishes &c, tattooed crudely on their bodies' (Whittle n.d). Agate etching from Wilkes 1845:12

pearl shells.[14] Outside was the monumental instantiation of Tui Tokelau (fourteen feet high, according to Hudson) thickly enveloped in mats, a smaller stone idol only partially covered in mats, and a 'table', similar to several within the god-house, cut out of solid wood. In deference to their hosts who insisted that they keep their distance, the visitors could not closely examine the mat-wrapped figures.

Also notable was the carefully maintained well near the centre of the village, and, along the lagoon shore, some fifty empty canoe houses, because all the canoes were out in the centre of the lagoon, and upon them the women and children. Again, the population had to be estimated; judging by the number of men seen (about 150), Hale proposed 500–600. More telling was his remark that the tiny village was 'very well peopled' indeed and his musings on how the balance between population and resources was maintained (1846:160).

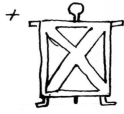

'Tatooing . . . somewhat peculiar in the figures. The most general one is a square body with the cross of St. George. These they have in a line across the breast, surmounted with fishes and crescents' (Reproduced from Poesche 1961:179). The square form again suggests a turtle.

For the Expedition members, Fakaofo was a new, exciting and wholly unexpected 'discovery'. Hudson gave Fakaofo the name of Bowditch Island, after a notable astronomer, and by calling the three islands together the Union Group he 'dovetailed the name of our republican countryman . . . with the Royal pair whose names the two other islands bear on the charts' (Hudson 1840–42:109, see also LMS Samoa District 1841).

From a historical point of view the outstanding feature of the accounts of the Tokelau past that we have brought together here is their remarkable consistency. The Tokelau narratives, whether in the form of myth, historical tales, genealogy or religious practice, depict a consistent set of structured relations between the atolls which were the foundation of Tokelau's *ancien régime*. Furthermore, it is just this structure that gives meaning and coherence to the diverse and often fragmentary accounts by early European visitors. Read together, the two separate kinds of sources allow us to see something more than the bare outline of the minuscule, though typically Polynesian, kingdom centred upon Fakaofo in the early nineteenth century as well as some of the strains and contradictions which were inherent in that order.

FIVE
The Ancient Orders

The United States Exploring Expedition members' perception of the pan-Tokelau sociopolitical order was by and large astute. They recognised that the three places were linked and something of the nature of their relationships. Hale correctly recorded that the people of Atafu 'belonged properly' to Fakaofo, but his further assumption that they were 'mere temporary residents' in the atoll was erroneous, at least by this time (Hale 1846:16). Hudson went further, drawing upon Hale's information. 'Bowditch Island [Fakaofo]', he declared, 'is the Capital of the . . . group and the residence of the king. His majesty gave to Mr Hale the names of the chiefs of the two other Islands. I presume they are not under much control and their visits to each other "must be few and far between"' (Hudson 1840–42:114). Certainly, the 'well-peopled' village, and the god-house and mat-shrouded god figures were testimony to the pre-eminence of Fakaofo, but Hudson probably underestimated the frequency of contacts between the islands, and the extent of Fakaofo's influence.

By this time, early 1841, Tokelau people had known of European ships and goods for two generations, the period of fifty years which had elapsed since the visit of the *Pandora* to Nukunonu and Atafu in 1791. Each of the islands, including Fakaofo, had had encounters with foreign ships and their crews, and stories of these contacts had doubtless spread throughout the group. Although they can hardly be said to have been familiar with such visitors, they probably knew more about them than their 1841 visitors knew about Tokelau; after all, the members of the US Exploring Expedition had thought to find Atafu uninhabited (relying on Edwards's account of 1791), and were of course ignorant of the existence of Fakaofo. They tended to equate their hosts' ignorance with their own, and this point has some bearing on how we might construe the records of their encounters.

Obviously the members of the Expedition found Tokelau behaviour bizarre and extraordinary. The Atafu men might have given the impression of being straightforward traders, anxious to please and complete a deal; but there were also what struck the visitors as 'ludicrous outbursts of song' and 'hearty laughter without the least apparent cause'. Again, on Fakaofo, there was the king's 'howling and lamentation', contrasting with the suspicious 'skulking' of younger men and a number of 'audacious thefts'. Hale (1846) and Hudson (1840–42), as well as several other reporters of the visit, all attribute these carryings-on to a Tokelau belief that the visitors were divinities rather than mortals—a view which was repeated in Wilkes's later official account (1845). On this point the crucial evidence comes from Hale, the only man on board who could communicate at all effectively with the people. As the Expedition's philologist, Hale was an experienced and accomplished linguist, with an 'admirable trait of understanding native dialects, as well as making himself understood' (Hudson 1840–42),[1] and he appears to have been in no doubt about the matter. 'Their decided belief', he wrote of Atafu, 'is that we came from the sky, and were divinities. This they repeated to us frequently, and we could not convince them to the contrary' (1846:153). The same views were repeated at Fakaofo, where once again the people 'could not be convinced that we were not deities, but men only (tangata lava)' (1846:156).

There is no reason to doubt the general accuracy of Hale's account. It does, however, invite speculation because he does not record the Tokelau word which he glosses as 'deities' or 'divinities'. His gloss for the Tokelauan (and common Polynesian) term *atua* is simply 'god', yet he does not state that the Expedition members were referred to as 'gods', only as 'divinities', a term which implies a somewhat lesser degree of spirituality. His statement about 'divinities' might in fact be based simply on the Tokelau declarations that the visitors had come from the sky or the sun (and should return there without further ado). Tokelau ideas about space corresponded with the general Polynesian idea of the *lagi* as not just a layer or space somewhere above, but a sphere that bounded the human world beyond the horizon as well as the sky above. In this sense, the strange visitors did indeed come 'from the sky' and therefore were not *tagata lava* 'just human'. Furthermore, like other pre-Christian Polynesians, Tokelau people of the time probably did not radically dichotomise 'gods' and 'men' (cf. Valeri 1994:125–6). Aspects of the divine could appear in human form, and humans could take on divine qualities—the *aliki* certainly did. That was why he treated with *atua*, and with his counterpart *aliki*, Captain Hudson.

Another feature of this encounter is the reported variability in the way the people comported themselves before the visitors. The striking differences in the Expedition's reception at Atafu and Fakaofo may be put down to the differing social, political and religious situations in the two islands; had the Expedition called at Nukunonu, things would almost certainly have been different again. But there were also obvious differences within each island—most noticeably at Fakaofo where the fear and abasement of the *aliki* were in marked contrast to the impression of menace given by the younger men 'skulking' on the outskirts of the formal proceedings. Behaviours also appeared to change suddenly. In Atafu, there was the 'singular union between confiding warmth and respectful fear'; and, in the initial contact with the fishing party at Fakaofo, the abrupt change from silent, disciplined restraint to 'vivacious chatter', singing and trade. What the Expedition had was a mixed reception; their hosts' experiences and perceptions differed, and this was reflected in their actions.

What these Tokelau people in 1841 thought about their strange visitors was obviously conditioned by their perceptions of their own gods and divinities and by their ideas about other beings, where they were to be found and what their powers were. The extant information is from Fakaofo, whether from local texts (Fakaofo n.d., Perez n.d. 1 & 2) or from brief enquiries into these matters by interested foreigners (Turner 1861 based on information gleaned a young Fakaofo convert in Samoa; Lister 1892 from information acquired via twice-translated answers to his twice-translated questions during ten days in Fakaofo; and Newell 1895 from 'two brief visits to the islands in 1885 and in 1894'), and all the accounts were written by committed Christians. Chance remarks and observations of unsuccessful early missionaries, and present-day Tokelau ideas about the ancient beliefs of remote forebears complement the explanatory texts. There is, however, no record by anyone who explicitly believed in the efficacy and powers of Tui Tokelau and other deities. The most consistent and full accounts and observations are about Tui Tokelau.

Tui Tokelau and other divinities

Tui Tokelau was an all-pervasive *atua*, a god whose being was beyond, in the sky or heavens. Newell (1895:606) wrote, 'The story of the remarkable man Tuitokelau, who was deified as a great god, is . . . forever lost.' More likely there never was a story, for no other source imagines Tui Tokelau as a man. The god was just there, instantiated in the huge stone enveloped in mats, standing outside the god-house in Fakaofo. When the London Missionary Society made their first unsuccessful attempt to install a teacher on the atoll they found it remarkable that 'None of the people . . . seemed to feel any surprise, or fear, or displeasure, when we told them that their gods were only stones, and that the only true God is in heaven' (Stallworthy and Gill 1859:5). Tokelau people unequivocally assert that their ancestors did not believe the stones were gods, and their supreme god did indeed dwell in the *lagi* 'sky' above.

Tui Tokelau was the ultimate cause and controller of good fortune and of the productivity and fruitfulness of the whole Tokelau world. The theme of life-giving productivity was central to the formulaic invocation of the god which was made on behalf of all Tokelau by the Fakaofo *aliki* (as set down in Fakaofo n.d.).

> It was the aliki *himself who said the prayer. The complete words of the prayer are not remembered, and only the words which it is certain that the* aliki *prayed are written down.*

Tulou! Tulou! Tulou lava!
Eat dirt, eat your shit.
Bring your piss that I might drink.
May you attend to your ocean:
A bounty of shark,
A bounty of fakaulu,
A bounty of ikapō. . . .

In this particular version there follow in order the names of ninety-eight fish, beginning with varieties of shark and other large pelagic fish, and ending with smaller varieties. According to elderly informants, repeating what they had been told by their elders before them, the words were intoned loudly, each name drawn out to emphasise the stressed syllable: for example, *He tai magoooo!* 'A bounty of shaaark!' Following the recitation of ocean fish, there is a new series of 134 named varieties of fish, echinoderms and shellfish of the reefs and lagoon. The final section looks towards the heavens, requesting abundant rainfall to sustain named products of the soil (see *Matagi Tokelau* 1991:48–49 for another version).

In addition to the prayer, offerings in appreciation of blessing and bounty were directed to Tui Tokelau when the god's blessings were realised, particularly when there were abundant catches of fish. 'All the different fishes and birds [were given]. If a large catch of fish were made, the chiefs chose one or two large fish or ten from the heap of fish. The biggest fish was then lifted up, and the prayer said' (Fakaofo n.d.). Lister (1892:50) reports much the same: 'If a good haul of fish was taken, part of it would be offered before the stone by the king, and afterwards it was distributed . . .'. This reported sharing of bounty is reflected in *inati* distributions today, as is the category of *ika hā* (sacred fish) which must be divided among everyone. These are the particular fish that are said to have been *hā* or sacred to Tui Tokelau (see below).

As well as regular offerings recognising the god's beneficence, there was an annual ceremony in honour of Tui Tokelau when offerings were conveyed to Fakaofo from Nukunonu and Atafu, at which appeals were made to the god for continuing prosperity (see below).

There is no record or local report of any instantiation of this 'great god of all Tokelau' at Nukunonu, but a smaller stone, likewise wrapped in mats, stood in Atafu (Thomson n.d.). These absences and presences are in accord with the relations of the two islands to Fakaofo: as conquered tributary and outpost respectively. Additionally, the smaller, less attended and partially shrouded stone next to that of Tui Tokelau may have figured in these arrangements. Several accounts refer to the god thus embodied as Hemoana, but there is less agreement about the god's attributes, powers, or relationship, if any, to Tui Tokelau. Possibly the neglected stone embodied the god of the conquered—a supposition not attested in the record but corresponding to appropriations of conquest elsewhere in Polynesia. This possibility is supported by the association of Hemoana with Nukunonu in myth (see chapter 4), in a Nukunonu song about voyaging to Fakaofo for the annual celebrations, and in the naming of an ancient blossoming tree that stood on the seaward side of Nukunonu village until it was felled by storm in 1914.

Several other gods, whose presence and specific attributes are associated with Fakaofo, are variously mentioned. Fakafotu, for example, is reported to have been 'the god of storms and hurricanes' whose anger was manifest by thunder (Lister 1892:51), though a local account relates that a being of the same name was an *aitu*, spirit, who held authority over all other *aitu* (Perez n.d.2). (The name survives on the island as that of the village meeting house, and now has no ghostly or spiritual connotations.) Just who 'all the other *aitu* of Fakaofo' were is nowhere recorded in any systematic way, and there are only fleeting references to *aitu* that resided in and about Atafu and Nukunonu. Today people tell stories of *aitu* encounters and associate them with strange, eerie events, but they are an undifferentiated and largely unnamed category of beings. Perhaps they were in the past too.

The issue, however, cannot be set aside so easily. As the previous paragraph intimates, there appear to have been different kinds of beings—gods (*atua*) and spirits/ghosts (*aitu*). The distinctions between the two are confounded in many texts, because *Atua* has come to refer to the Christian God, and consequently *aitu* is often used with reference to pre-Christian 'gods' and thus becomes a general term for all pre-Christian supernatural/divine beings.[2]

Another category of beings, referred to as *aitu* in both local and foreign texts, were associated with major descent or kin groups. These *aitu* were variously embodied or manifest as fish, plants, and so on. What was distinctive about these beings was that those people with whom they were associated were proscribed from eating their embodiments, and in this regard they were totemic in character. For Fakaofo it is written (Perez n.d.2) that if an associated person went and ate their *aitu*'s embodiment secretly, a curse would fall upon the whole group, but that other people not of that group could eat the spirit's corporeal form and nothing would happen. Again, in-house shrines were dedicated to these guardian spirits, where they were worshipped; the spirits responded to the wishes of their worshippers, protecting them from other *aitu* associated with other interests. The Fakaofo (n.d.) manuscript specifically associates the several Fakaofo *falepā* with one or two fishes of the sea which they worshipped and prayed to (see below).

These statements also accord quite closely with Lister's observations that: 'In Fakaofo the "Feki" (the octopus) was the "aitu" of certain families, who always abstained from catching or eating it. The *"Pusi"* (a species of *Murœna* which frequents the reef, much dreaded by the natives for its severe bites) was another family aitu' (1892:51).

A suggestive and simplified outline of the Tokelau pre-Christian ideas about the non-human beings beyond and among them may be drawn from these few sources. Tui Tokelau was the pre-eminent god who received offerings and prayers from all Tokelau and in turn gave plenty and wellbeing—in Tokelauan, *manuia*. The god resided above and beyond, in the sky or heavens, and the mat-shrouded stone in Fakaofo was the god's instantiation.

Hemoana, also represented by a stone, would seem to be of the same 'type' as Tui Tokelau, but an inferior or demoted god. Other god/spirits had more specific attributes and constituencies—Fakafotu, for example, had specified attributes or tasks, and was, at least by one account, located at Fakaofo. Other spirits, perhaps like present-day *aitu*, might be encountered as human-like beings in dark, unfrequented places, and guardian 'totemic' spirits associated with descent groups were manifest in non-human living things, particularly fish. Such *aitu* may still be suspected of animating birds or fish that are behaving in uncharacteristic ways, or are encountered in out-of-the-way places.

The separate places

Fakaofo, Nukunonu and Atafu were distinct places, each with its own internal social and historical order, aspects of which are asserted in the representations of each island's past. Both Nukunonu and Fakaofo had autochthonous origins, Nukunonu from people who were 'just there' and Fakaofo by way of a more complex generation from fish, bird and maggots. Although Fakaofo defeated Nukunonu, subjecting it to externally appointed authority and exacting tribute from the people, Nukunonu was not truly 'colonised' by Fakaofo settlers. Much of the original social order remained intact. Atafu, by contrast, was from its beginnings a colony—an outpost consciously founded by Fakaofo decree, by a man of that island's *aliki* line and a woman from the *aliki* stock of Nukunonu. It was thus, presumably, doubly and perpetually subject, to Fakaofo as a junior agnate (son or younger brother) and to Nukunonu as sister's son. As things turned out, this was an ambiguous situation which Atafu eventually solved only by seizing the opportunity to assert an independent identity.

Each of the islands has its own historical trope. Fakaofo represents itself as the *fenua aliki*, the 'land of chiefs', where all the Polynesian signs of paramountcy were brought together, thus naturalising the island's dominion and overall rule. Important events are calibrated on Fakaofo's *gafa aliki* 'chiefly genealogy', largely agnatic in form, as well as on several quite congruent lists of *aliki* in order of succession. Nukunonu is the *Falefā*, the 'Four houses', an enduring coalition of four autochthonous cognatic lines mapped onto the ownership of defined sections of the atoll and associated with the offices of *aliki*, *faipule* or 'civil ruler', *toa* or 'warrior', and *tautai* or 'master fisherman'. Atafu represents itself as the *Falefitu* 'Seven houses', in actuality a single stock from the founding couple and their seven children, without associated offices or original land divisions.

Beyond these various tropes, encapsulated most clearly in the different genealogical idioms, there is another difference—one that sets Fakaofo off from the others. Doubtless because of its position as the premier island during the first half of the nineteenth century, more has been written about the social order of pre-European Fakaofo than about that of the other two islands. In part this arises from the ethnological inquiries of visitors with ethnological interests such as Turner (1861), Lister (1892) and Newell (1895).

By comparison the Roman Catholic missionaries, who were the most frequent visitors to Nukunonu, seem to have concerned themselves very little with the traditional history of that island or its pre-Christian social order. And Atafu did not arouse the same curiosity among its mission visitors as Fakaofo did, perhaps because its social order was less hierarchical and complex.

The most important reason, though, is the existence of the local account which we have called simply Fakaofo (n.d.). Beyond its chauvinism and the rhetoric about *fenua aliki*, it gives an extraordinarily well organised, self-conscious, 'academic' description of the institutions of Fakaofo in the 'days of old', as well as accounts of later events. Nearly all the information it contains is congruent with the observations set down in outside historical sources. Much of it, however, is unique.

Fakaofo: Fenua Aliki *'Land of Chiefs'*

Brief as they are, the early nineteenth-century accounts of Fakaofo capture much of what was distinctive about the island at that time, setting it off from neighbouring Nukunonu and Atafu. Three features stand out: the confident, aggressive stance toward outsiders shown during the visit of the USS *Dolphin* in 1825—which was later tempered (probably by experience with the *Admiral Cockburn* in 1837) to the tightly controlled restraint shown by the fishing party as the ships of the US Exploring Expedition lay to off the atoll in early 1841 (these encounters stand in marked contrast to Atafu's effusive welcomes and Nukunonu's timid retreats); secondly, the formality and hierarchy manifest in the tense on-shore reception of Hudson and his party; and thirdly, the physical presence of the 'densely peopled' village itself, with the massive stone slab of Tui Tokelau and the commodious 'god-house'. Fakaofo was clearly something different—the foundation, in fact, of the Tokelau imperium, where power, sanctity and hierarchy were drawn together.

The following passage, which describes the island's polity at an undetermined time that falls logically between the 'days of war' and the mid nineteenth century, encapsulates the characteristic local view. Using the master trope of the 'land of chiefs' it invokes a whole Polynesian grammar of hierarchy, autochthonous origin, invocation of the supreme god through his earthly instantiation, agnatic descent, seniority, age, success in war, tribute, honorific and ritual display.

> *Fakaofo was the village of honour in the old days. It was known as the 'home of chiefs' since the ways of the people were noble and gentlemanly and their respect and concern for one another was unbounded. Thus nobody on the island acted without consideration; everything was ready and prepared to maintain the honour and majesty of the land. Everyone maintained good behaviour, with the families showing mutual concern—even though this was in the days of heathenism and foolishness. They did things together and nobody thought only of themselves. Children respected their parents and the men respected the chiefs and elders, neither answering back nor complaining. Noise was strictly prohibited, and nobody could call out within the village.*
>
> *Fakaofo set up the stone idol of the great god of Tokelau, namely the idol Tui*

Tokelau, which means the 'Supreme Ruler of Tokelau'. There could be no doubt about the dignity of the island . . . once Tui Tokelau existed to mark and embody it. Fakaofo was not an idle village, but one which was always ready and prepared for any disaster, and was closely guarded against enemies coming to wage war. The enemies of Fakaofo in the days of darkness were Tonga, Atafu and Nukunonu.[3]

Fakaofo's religious pre-eminence, which underpinned its *aliki*'s paramountcy and its chiefly authority, was annually confirmed by a gathering at that atoll to celebrate Tui Tokelau. This event evidently took place during the Tokelau month of *uluaki hiliga* (April/May) marked by the dawn rising of *taki-o-Mataliki* 'precursor of the Pleiades'. Lister (1892:50) gives a dramatic summary of the event.

A yearly feast was held in honour of Tui Tokelau, and the people of Nukunonu and Atafu came over with offerings of mats and pearl shells—the mats hung to the masts of the ships as they approached, to display them. When they landed the mats were wrapped round the stone, to remain until they rotted away, and the pearl shells were placed along the eaves of the house sacred to the god, close at hand. . . . The stone was anointed with coconut oil scented with flowers; then the king was carried in front of the stone, seated in his chair, with the coconut leaf emblem of royalty round his neck, and a black line of charcoal drawn over his forehead[4]—the people following in procession with shouts of 'Tu-tu' and general rejoicing.

This was also the occasion when the god was reclothed in new fine mats, with 'the chiefs' screening the stone while the old mats were stripped off and replaced with fresh ones (Fakaofo n.d.). It was a time of festival when there were nights of dancing, and fire lit up 'the temple all the night over during the month with what they call "light in honour of the god"' (Turner 1861:527).

Aliki

The office of *aliki* is intimately associated with both Fakaofo and Tui Tokelau. As the priest of the supreme god, the *aliki* was imbued with at least the temporal aspects of the same sanctity inherent in the god. The *ao* or title associated with the office was 'Kava', which was derived from the name of the elder of the two autochthonous 'spirit men' who are taken as the founders of the Fakaofo population (see chapter 4).

The *gafa aliki* or *aliki* genealogy, the premier genealogy of the island and the one upon which almost all important historical events turn, derives from this original Kava.[5] From Kava there issues a line of males, between two and four in the variant versions, also bearing the name of Kava; the last in this line is the first 'historical' chief, Kava-vahe-fenua, Kava 'divider-of-lands', who is the focal ancestor of all subsequent generations. Kava-vahe-fenua had two wives, the first being a woman of the *kāiga aliki*, and the second the aforementioned 'slave' woman from Nukunonu, called Nau. He had a son by each of these wives. Tevaka, his son by the first wife, had in turn two sons, from whom the body of the *kāiga aliki* are descended. Pio, his son by Nau, 'was not highly regarded by the people of Fakaofo, having no honour because

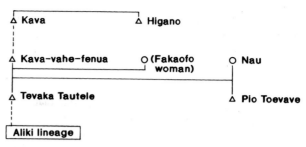

The origins of the Fakaofo aliki *lineage from the original*
Kava to the sons of Kava-vahe-fenua, Tevaka Tautele and
Pio Toevave.

his mother was a woman from Nukunonu' (Fakaofo n.d., cf. chapter 4), and
his issue do not appear in the Fakaofo *aliki* genealogy. In the five generations
following Kava-vahe-fenua only males are recorded. In the sixth generation
there are a few female names, but no record of their issue, and it is not until
the ninth generation from the original Kava that females are recorded with
their issue. Even in its most widely known and accepted version, the *aliki*
genealogy is clearly a selective record of a well-known kind which La Fontaine
distinguishes as 'descent' genealogies, which '. . . relate groups by reference
to a hierarchically ordered series of ancestors' (1973:45). The genealogy takes
in all but one of the *aliki* from Taupe onwards (whose names and order of
succession are well attested by independent historical records) but omits a
number of *aliki* prior to Taupe who are mentioned in the well-known '*aliki*
lists' that are given in other local manuscript sources (see *Matagi Tokelau*
1991:50). The one more recent *aliki* who cannot be unequivocally linked to

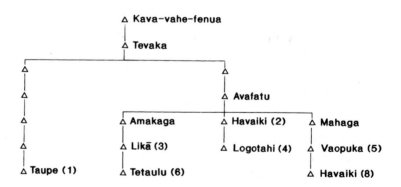

Genealogical links between historical aliki *(following* gafa aliki *in Fakaofo*
n.d. manuscript), and their order of succession:

1 *Taupe:* Aliki *in 1841 met by US Exploring Expedition*
2 *Havaiki:* Aliki *c.1846–c.1852 associated with famine (Lister 1892:60)*
3 *Likā:* Aliki *c.1858 (Stallworthy & Gill 1859)–c.1870 (Whitmee 1870)*
4 *Logotahi:* Aliki *1871 (Powell 1871b)–?*
5 *Vaopuka:* Aliki *?–May 1881 when shot*
6 *Tetaulu:* Aliki *1881–c.1890 (he was photographed by Lister in 1889)*
7 *Tefuli/Tavita:* Aliki *c.1892 (Cusack Smith 1892a)–c.1901(Hunter 1900)*
8 *Havaiki/Ielemia:* Aliki *1902–c.1915*

the genealogy is Tavita/Tefuli, who appears as the son of Poufau in a section of the genealogy labelled 'The descendants of Poufau'; Poufau is listed in the 'aliki lists' as being aliki immediately before Taupe, but none of his antecedents is genealogically recorded.

Membership of the kāiga aliki, and thus eligibility for the office of aliki, was exclusively through agnatic links. Lister recorded that 'If a man of the royal family married a woman of another family, his sons were eligible for the kingship [i.e. aliki]. But the sons of a woman who married out of the royal family were not eligible' (1892:54). Although the exact process of selection is not known, it is clear from all sources that the aliki were chosen from among the mature or elderly men. Turner records that, 'There are three families from which the king is selected, and they always select an aged man. They say that a young man is a bad ruler, and that mature age is essential to the office' (1861:526). This is echoed by Lister in his statement that 'The king was chosen by the whole body of the people—a middle-aged or old man belonging to the royal family' (1892:53), and Newell's later account differs only slightly: 'The "ariki" [sic] is always the oldest male member of the four principal families of Fakaofo, all of whom trace their descent from two brothers . . . Kava and Pio. . . . When the "ariki" dies the oldest man then living among these four families becomes "ariki". No others possess this title, and there are no clan names or titles outside this circle' (1895:605).

The 'families' of Turner's and Newell's accounts were probably divisions of the aliki lineage, which by the mid nineteenth century had branched into a number of agnatic lines, as shown in the second figure on page 156. Whether there was a single 'royal family', as Lister has it, or three, or four, depends on the particular point of reference taken. Including Taupe, aliki in 1841, there are four 'families'; thereafter the office appears to have dominated by the three lines issuing from Avafatu.

Descent lines within the aliki lineage were evidently ranked relative to one another according to which line a particular aliki belonged to. The line of the aliki was spoken of as the lātūpou, as distinct from the other lines, known as the lāfalala. Lā is the term for the branch of a tree; the lātūpou was thus the main branch or trunk, and the lāfalala the side branches.[6] It is not known, however, whether the distinction implied any great measure of material privilege or precedence.

There appears to have been no special residence for the aliki; however, he controlled the gathering and distribution of a number of valued foods which were regarded as 'sacred' to Tui Tokelau (see above). Among those mentioned are tridachna and ō, a valued baitfish. Pandanus fruits were also sacred to the god and kept in the house of the aliki (Lister 1892:50). The lifespans of aliki also regulated the planting of coconuts. Lister mentions that, 'The death of the king was the occasion for the planting of coconuts. If anyone planted them at other times he would die' (1892:54), and this is echoed by a local text (Perez n.d.2) stating that, 'When a king died only then could new coconuts be planted in the lands across the lagoon . . . [and] the coconuts were then called the "Selection of the new king". On Fakaofo a person could please himself about the piece of land on which to plant at the selection of the new king.' Since the planting of coconuts gave harvesting rights, and thus, in effect, land rights, the custom of periodic and widespread planting allowed all people to establish rights and prevented any from monopolising the land. It also probably served to commemorate and stress an *aliki's* identification with land and productivity. (Over the period of seventy-five years or so between Taupe and Havaiki II, there were eight *aliki*, or one every nine or ten years. If we can assume that this interval also prevailed before Taupe's time, the times allowed between plantings seem reasonable.)

'Priests'

It is clear from most sources that the *aliki* was the sole priest of the god Tui Tokelau. Turner (1861:526) states that '. . . the government is monarchical, and the king, Tui Tokelau is high priest as well'. This confuses the god with the *aliki* (perhaps understandably) but it does correctly describe the religious nature of the *aliki* office. This was certainly also the impression given to Stallworthy and Gill on their 1858 visit, when 'Lita [Likā], who is styled ariki [sic], or chief, . . . was described as *le polo o le Atua*, or priest of god.'[7] Furthermore, there is the unequivocal local statement: 'There were no *taulāitu* of the idol, so it was only *aliki* who directed the refurbishing of the idol.'

In modern Tokelauan, as in Samoan, *taula-aitu* is commonly glossed as 'priest', the etymology of the term suggesting the notion of a connection (conveyed by *taula*, a rope or anchor line) with an *aitu* or spirit being. Although the Fakaofo manuscript makes no other reference to *taula-aitu*, Lister (1892:50) makes a clear distinction between the *aliki* and *taula-aitu*, whom he called 'priests', and who, he wrote, were 'chosen by the king and formed an upper class in society'. Presumably (Lister is not explicit on this point) these 'priests' were concerned with the other, lesser gods to which he makes reference, but what their 'upper class' status might have been remains obscure in his account.

Newell's statement that '. . . the son of the "ariki" became king, but the son of his sister became priest' (1895:606) offers a possible explanation, particularly as he also gives 'the exact words of the statement . . .: *O tamafafine na fai ma vakatua, o tamatane na fai ma ariki.*' (*Vaka-atua* can be glossed as 'priest' in modern Tokelauan, though the term also carries the connotation of the individual as a vessel, or *vaka*, of the *atua*, or god.)[8] Newell glosses this phrase, 'Daughters became priestesses; sons became chiefs.' This is ambiguous, a much more likely gloss being 'The female [sororal] line supplied priests; the male [fraternal] line the *aliki*.' If this were the case, the statement can be taken to mean that *vaka-atua* were chosen from among those who stood in a *tamafafine* relationship to the *aliki*. Newell's confusion derives from the term *tamafafine*, which can mean both 'daughter' and 'a male or female in the female line'.

These 'priests' (either *taula-aitu* or *vaka-atua*) might possibly have been associated with the *aliki* in performance of his duties to Tui Tokelau. Alter-

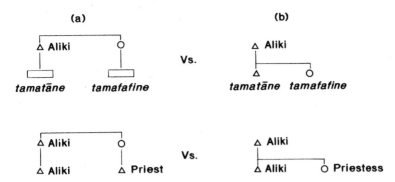

(a)   **(b)**

△ Aliki   ○   △ Aliki

Vs.

tamatāne   *tamafafine*   *tamatāne* *tamafafine*

△ Aliki   ○   △ Aliki

Vs.

△ Aliki   △ Priest   △ Aliki   ○ Priestess

Newell's confusion is not unusual. With reference to a set of siblings, daughters are tamafafine/tamateine *and sons are* tamatāne *(b), but within* kāiga *the designation is applied to the issue of founders' daughters and sons respectively (a). What Newell quoted was intended to have the (a) meaning, but he glosses it with the (b) meaning.*

natively, their duties may have been to one or more of the lesser gods or spirit beings which are recorded.

Governance and *faipule*

It is clear from all the accounts of the US Exploring Expedition's brief visit that Taupe, the *aliki* of the time, was the central figure in the island's reception for Captain Hudson and his party. Taupe was 'seated forward' of the others (presumed to be 'minor chiefs'); he offered the island's gifts and it was he who took charge of Hudson, after reluctantly allowing the foreigners to tour the village. He appears to have deferred to nobody else, and it was only he who is reported to have spoken. Much the same scene was reenacted some twelve years later, in 1853, for a party from a visiting ship that was received by 'His Majesty . . . seated on a mat near the spot of our landing, surrounded by his counsellors—dignified old men . . .'. On this occasion, though, the visitors 'were conducted through the village by one of the dignitaries, very likely the Prime Minister, the others the meanwhile retaining their place on the shore' (*Nautical Magazine* 1861:474).

From that time on all of the visitors to the island perceived, and commented upon, a distinction between two offices—that of *aliki* or 'king', and another which is variously described as that of 'prime minister' or 'chief counsellor' or 'civil chief'. These two offices were distinguished from that of 'counsellors' or 'minor chiefs', who were much more numerous. Protestant missionary visitors in 1858 were confronted with the same sort of division of authority. They record that: 'When we reached the people, we found sitting in their midst Litā [Likā], who is styled *ariki* [sic], or chief . . . Pisanga [Pihaga], who appears to be the civil chief, but inferior to Litā; and Foringa [Foliga], who appears to be acting magistrate, as it was said to belong to him to punish theft and the like; and we were directed by Litā to address ourselves to him as chief speaker . . .' (Stallworthy and Gill 1859:4).

Likā on this occasion could express nothing but humility and abasement before the missionaries (for their having brought back a man of the island from Samoa), but it was quite otherwise with Foliga, whose rejection of Stallworthy and Gill's proposition to land a Samoan teacher was direct and confident to the point of aggressiveness. This same Foliga appeared again as the island's spokesman on the occasion of Ella's 1861 visit, when he 'peremptorily ordered away the teachers' who had been brought. It was this encounter that led Ella to speculate that, 'Evidently Foringa was the man having authority there and Leua [Likā] was merely chief in name' (Ella 1861a).

Ella oversimplified the authority structure of Fakaofo. All these accounts testify to a division of roles on the island between Likā the *aliki*, who doubtless continued as the supreme sacred authority but did not speak on matters of civic concern, and Foliga, who was the magistrate and the main spokesman on civil matters. The antiquity of this role division is problematic, particularly in light of Taupe's singular role in relation to Fakaofo's 1841 visitors.

If Taupe and his contemporaries did believe that the US Exploring Expedition had come from the sky, as Hale and others asserted, and were divinities of some sort, the *aliki* was the only proper person to confront them. Twelve years later, after all sorts of foreign incursions (see chapter 6), people would certainly have understood that such visitors were mere mortals, and the *aliki* could be left to concentrate on his spiritual business while some civil authority dealt with them. While this separation of sacred and civil spheres might have been an innovation, it seems more likely that it was an old and established division of authority which visitors, expecting a singular 'king', found remarkable. Or Foliga might have had some charisma which gave him prominence, and which led Likā to call upon him to speak for the island as a whole. (Foliga was a son of the 1841 *aliki* Taupe, and therefore of the other major line of *aliki*, which might have had something to do with his prominent position.)[9]

Whatever the explanation for Foliga's considerable authority, there is other evidence indicating that there were fundamental changes made in the political structure of Fakaofo around the time of Taupe, which involved some diminution of what had presumably been more absolute *aliki* authority. (This transformation is related in Perez 1977.) Taupe himself, as the (presumably unwitting) 'instrument of God's profound and serious purpose', instituted a council of '*aliki* and *faipule*', thus giving some degree of conjoint authority in political affairs to those who were not of the *aliki* lineage. From that point on, the governance of Fakaofo was carried out in the following manner:

> First of all, the Aliki (king) met with aliki of the Latupou and aliki of the Lafalala, and they decided what was to be done before they invited the group called Faipule to talk about the things agreed upon by the high aliki. At the end of their meeting they decided the day for a meeting of the whole village. The meeting of Aliki and Faipule was usually held at Hakavā.
>
> Meeting of the whole village. This meeting was usually held at the Malae of Fakafotu, the place for village meetings, where it was revealed what the Aliki of Fakaofo had decided should be done. Nobody of the village made any reply, or stated their opinion, but obeyed directly.

This account makes no direct reference to a particular office embodying civil as distinct from religious authority. It is, however, plausible to assume that it was one of the 'Faipule group' who 'revealed what the Aliki . . . had decided should be done' at village meetings, since that would conform with what was definitely the situation in the later nineteenth century when there were two distinct offices, *aliki* or 'king' and *faipule* or 'lawmaker', whose incumbents spoke for Fakaofo, and who on occasion signed their names as the joint authorities of the island government (see chapter 7).

Falepā and *puikāiga*

Falepā were houses of a special kind, which occupied an important place in the pre-Christian social order of Fakaofo. They are known only through Tokelau accounts, and it is commonly agreed that there were nine of them. (Some accounts give ten, together with an explanation of how one of them came to be abandoned.) Their names are still widely known, and most of the sites where they stood are also known, and in some cases still used. It is also generally thought that the *falepā* were used only by men, who may or may not have slept in them. The Fakaofo manuscript gives the fullest account:

> There were houses set up all round the village. These houses were called falepā, and only men dwelt in these houses. Each puikāiga dwelt in its own falepā, and could not live mixed up with others. These houses were somewhat like work camps. Each house had a name. Also each individual falepā had its aitu [spirit] which was worshipped and which protected them from aitu from other villages who came to raise conflict. Certain fishes of the sea (but not stones) were worshipped as aitu. Each individual falepā had one or two fishes of the sea which they worshipped and prayed to.

This manuscript says the *falepā* were eleven in number,[10] but describes only three of them—Hāfiti, Tolugafale and Logopehe, each of which had a specialised function. Hāfiti stood at the southwestern corner of the village islet adjacent to the pass from the open sea, and its men (renowned for their bravery and alertness) had the task of guarding the village from attack; their associated spirit was the sea eel. Tolugafale, on the northwestern side of the village islet, is distinguished as the house associated with political control, where only elderly men stayed. Logopehe stood on the northeastern sector and was associated with the storage (and perhaps also the manufacture and maintenance) of the ropes used on communal expeditions to catch birds.

Two lands on the eastern side of the atoll, known as Fenuatapu and Palea, were at this time divided among the *falepā*. 'Fenuatapu and Palea were all divided among these groups. And when they went to work there, each group went directly to its own portion. Each portion was known as a "Tefākiga"' (Fakaofo n.d.). Perez (n.d.2) gives a variant list of the names of the *falepā* (with substantial overlaps) and makes the same associations with men and some of the specialised functions of the various houses.

The discrepancy between the two manuscript lists of names is perhaps not surprising, for a number of reasons. As male-dominated organisations associated with various spirits, they became defunct in the 1860s (see chapter 6), and their specialised functions and control of the two lands across the lagoon were carried out by men of the village as a whole. Moreover, the *falepā* organisation was by its very nature a fluid one, associated with demographic and other changes. An indication of this is the strong association between *falepā* and *puikāiga*, the term used to refer to descent units of the greatest generational depth and span. The Fakaofo manuscript makes this association most clearly, to the point of stating that 'each *puikāiga* lived in their own *falepā*' (meaning presumably only the men of each *puikāiga*). Perez (n.d.1:25– 26) depicts the *puikāiga* as the basic unit of local organisation, as follows:

> They lived strictly by puikāiga, and each puikāiga had its aitu/spirit (tupua/guardian) to worship and tell of the things that were desired. Their atua/gods were various. Some had as gods fish, plants, dead people, spirits, white things like unopened terminal buds of coconut palms, buds, white clouds in the sky, anything at all that was white was a god to them. . . .
>
> It was only the members of the puikāiga who were forbidden to go and eat their god (spirit). If they went and ate it secretly a curse would fall upon the whole of that puikāiga. But members of other puikāiga could eat the spirits of other puikāiga and nothing would happen.

The internal structure of the *puikāiga* is nowhere explained in any detail. The Tokelau manuscript sources, and indeed all present-day Tokelau informants, assume that they were organised much the same way that contemporary *kāiga* are—and they are probably correct, despite all the dramatic changes of the past hundred years. *Puikāiga* it appears were the basic corporate units of Fakaofo. They were descent units whose members held rights in common to an estate consisting of plantation land, dwelling houses, house sites, sections of reef and perhaps also the lagoon, *falepā* and the propitiation of their associated totemic spirits. Each was under the control of senior male members, and was very likely divided (as present-day *kāiga* are) into *tamatāne* and *tamafafine*, with complementary rights associated with each of these divisions; dwelling houses were probably occupied by females of the *tamafafine* while *falepā* were associated with males of the *tamatāne*, with the totemic observances and prohibitions associated with the *falepā* falling upon both the men and women of this division. It is also likely that marriage was uxorilocal; although Lister is the only nineteenth-century source to mention the practice, his comment is clear: 'I was told that a man went to live with his wife's people; I suppose in the case of the first wife only' (1892:54). If this were indeed the case, it would follow that the male goods of a *puikāiga*—fishing gear (such as *pā*) and gear associated with canoes and economic, exploitative activities, and perhaps warfare—were stored together in a special house associated with the men of the *puikāiga*, and perhaps more exclusively with those men who were affiliated through a succession of agnatic links.[11]

Rights to plantation land were probably the property of the *puikāiga* as a whole, with control vested in males of the *tamatāne*. What made the lands of Fenuatapu and Palea distinctive was that they were used only for provisioning communal activities of the *falepā* rather than the various domestic commensal units—an interpretation which is in accord with the way in which the lands are exploited today, for undertakings sanctioned and directed by the village council.

The Falefā 'Four Houses' of Nukunonu

The accounts of explorers and voyagers say virtually nothing of Nukunonu. The people shied away from encounters early on and did not welcome visitors later. Repeatedly, although the atoll was sighted, people did not go ashore, and if they did, the people retreated. Fortunately Nukunonu has a relatively rich recalled past which compensates for the virtual absence of foreign records. Until very recently the ways and events of the past were recounted only orally, aside from some inscribed genealogies that in essence duplicate oral accounts. Episodes in the story of Nukunonu's founding and history were related to us by numerous people there, but it was during the extended 'conversations' with two renowned 'wise elders' in 1981 that the most detailed and coherent story was pieced together (see p.12). It is impossible to specifically attribute the material drawn upon here, and in any case those two 'wise elders' attributed their knowledge of the past to their own elders who told it all to them. Thus, the following account may be read as Nukunonu's collective representation of the atoll's past.

A genealogical and geographical constitution

The founding social order of Nukunonu comprises four distinct genealogical lines and is recited or written thus in *tala gafa* 'genealogical accounts'. No mythical accounts relate how the founders of these genealogies came into being; they were just there at the very beginning. All accounts grant primacy to a couple, Pipi and Fekei, who began the genealogy known as Talafau or Uluga-Talafau (Paired Talafau), the latter alluding to the two lines distinguished as Talafau-Alo and Talafau-Nonu by appending the names of the senior and junior brother respectively. The issue of both lines together become, as they proliferate, the stock of Talafau whose entitlement is the social position of *aliki*, with the senior line providing the incumbent in that position within the autochthonous polity of Nukunonu.[12]

Juxtaposed to the Talafau genealogy is another, commencing with a single male, Lehiho, followed by a line of four names. The last, Letele, names the ensuing stock, whose entitlement is the social position of *faipule* 'ruler'.

In this genealogical idiom, an original, complementary duality of the Nukunonu social order is expressed: two completely separate descent lines, each associated with a *tofi* 'social position/office'—Talafau with the *tofi aliki* 'paramount office' and Letele with the *tofi faipule* 'ruler office'.[13]

Two other distinct lines, both originating from single males, complete the original constitution of the 'Four Houses' of Nukunonu, although their appearance and positions are secondary to those of Talafau and Letele. From Pule issues a line of *toa* 'warriors' and/or *leoleo* 'wardens', which, as a stock, is known as Tuipagai. (Feuku, Nukunonu's chief warrior in the story of conquest, figures in this line.) Lua or Lua-atua begins another line, which becomes a stock of the same name, with entitlement to the position of *tautai* 'master fisherman' and/or *tauvaega* 'distributor of produce'.

These four genealogies, recited in the initial generations as a list of names, are emphatically discrete lines. Only in the premier Talafau genealogy are siblings recorded, creating senior and junior lines. But then after some six

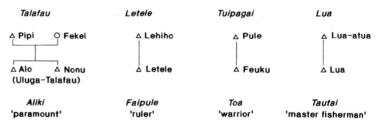

The Nukunonu originating genealogy of four separate ancestral lines, from whom issue the four stocks or 'Four Houses', each associated with a particular tofi *'status' within the polity. Talafau is originally distinctive by having a founding couple and by quickly bifurcating into senior and junior lines.*

generations a sibling set appears in the Letele line, and the lines of Lua and Tuipagai are linked with Letele by unions with Letele daughters. On the one hand, by this linkage, the primary duality is maintained and the three lines together may be spoken of as Letele juxtaposed to Talafau. The three social positions with which they are associated have to do with the affairs of living people (*tagata*) in contrast to the sanctified position of Talafau as mediator between the people and their gods. On the other hand, the lines of Tuipagai and Lua remain distinct with reference to their male forebears and 'Four Houses' are constituted.

These two ways of reading and referring to the basic order of Nukunonu society are only apparently contradictory. One formulation expresses an essential duality between cosmic relations, or intercession with powers beyond

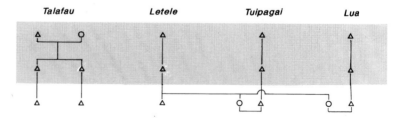

Tuipagai and Lua are linked to the Letele line by unions with Letele sisters, thus creating a subset and a duality of the aliki *stock and the rest.*

society, and social relations, or the maintenance of society. In the other formulation, cosmological relations remain the exclusively responsibility of Talafau/*aliki*, but responsibilities for societal order and wellbeing are differentiated: Letele/*faipule* ordering relations within the polity, Tuipagai protecting the social order from human disorder (as *toa* from aggression from without and as *leoleo* 'warden' from anti-social acts within), and Lua provisioning the society as *tautai* 'fisherman' and *tauvaega* 'distributor of produce'.

These genealogical statements are reiterated spatially in the entitlements of the four lines to sections of the atoll. The initial division of the atoll is between Talafau and Letele: the southern half under the jurisdiction of Talafau, the northern under Letele. The genealogical duality is repeated, with pre-eminent Talafau assigned the greater area of land and more accessible half of the atoll (from the village counter-clockwise to the opposite side of the lagoon). Subsequently, just as Tuipagai and Lua are linked into Letele genealogically, they are allocated areas within the Letele northern half of the

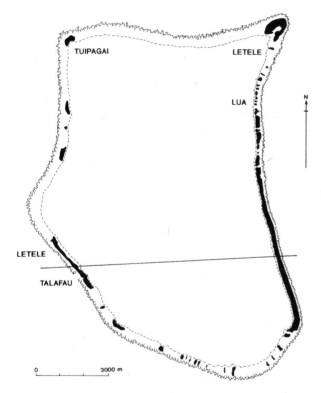

The 'Four Houses' are located in the division of the atoll. The initial two-part division is between Talafau and Letele. Then Letele allocated particular places to the lines of Tuipagai and Lua. Thus, geographic placement neatly parallels genealogical relationships.

atoll: Tuipagai is given jurisdiction over the northwestern islet of Te Fakanava, a place where voyagers may enter and leave the atoll; Lua is given jurisdiction over the islet-dotted northern reef area of the western margin, where there are particularly rich fishing grounds; while Letele retains the large northeastern islet of Tokelau.

The genealogical and geographical statements parallel one another with satisfying redundancy, stating unequivocally that this is how Nukunonu was constituted. Originally, everything was beautifully ordered. However, this order was compromised by external impositions following the Fakaofo conquest and by its own inevitable internal processes.

After conquest

By conquest Fakaofo gained control of half of the atoll—the half assigned to Letele (or Letele/Lua/Tuipagai). Recall that in the Nukunonu story of the conquest (see chapter 4) the *titi* 'skirt' that halted the circuit of Fakaofo forces around the atoll was the 'skirt' of a Talafau woman, and so it was through her agency that half of the atoll was retained for Nukunonu (this theme of intercession will recur). What is not explicitly stated in the story of conquest, but nevertheless known to those who listen to it, is that the 'skirt' marked the boundary where the lands of Talafau and the lands of Letele meet on the eastern side of the atoll opposite the village. Thus the lands that remained under Nukunonu control were the entitlement of its *aliki* stock; all other lands were forfeited to the conquerors.

The Fakaofo victors demanded tribute from Nukunonu and prohibited replanting of its lands; they further decreed that henceforth the Nukunonu *aliki* would be appointed from Fakaofo, that *pule* 'rule' would emanate from Fakaofo, and that only Fakaofo's *aliki* was the supplicant and intermediary to the pre-eminent god, Tui Tokelau. The latter decree undermined the position of the Nukunonu *aliki*, assuming that he had been the intermediary to

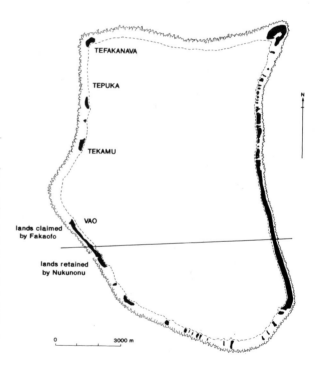

In the division of the atoll as a result of the Fakaofo conquest, the Talafau portion is still controlled by Nukunonu, while the Letele portion is surrendered to Fakaofo control. Islets on the western margin are attributed to the 'Four Houses': from south to north to names associated with Talafau, Letele, Lua, and Tuipagai.

the local god(s). Yet, within Nukunonu, Talafau remained the pre-eminent stock, despite these controls and strictures on the *aliki* position. No god-house or god-stone was located in Nukunonu (and none is mentioned in any

European accounts), yet Talafau still looked after the welfare of the lands and people, controlled the exploitation of resources and in turn received a special portion of any catch of 'sacred' fish. Others might be appointed by the Fakaofo *aliki*, but a Talafau *aliki* remained a symbol of Nukunonu's separate identity, still having exclusive entitlement to local lands, above and beyond Fakaofo's jurisdiction.[14]

The Talafau senior stock, Talafau-Alo, retained its local distinctiveness too: the women established alliances with prominent Fakaofo men, and the men joined with Talafau women whose kinship to them was rather distant.[15]

The other Nukunonu genealogies intertwine, with repeated unions between their members, continuing the process that began with the unions of Lua and Tuipagai men and Letele women mentioned earlier. The Lua and Tuipagai stocks virtually merge, creating what is called the Gafalua or 'Dual Genealogy', and the junior Talafau-Nonu segment comes to be multiply coupled with Letele. Yet whenever segments of the Nukunonu polity are recited in any connection, the number is always three plus Talafau. For example, in reciting the redistribution of four areas along the northwestern margin of the atoll at some undetermined time, the formulaic recitation is:

> *Tuku te vao o Vao kia Telima*
> The bush of Vao went to Telima [Talafau]
> *Tuku te vao o Te Kamu kia Letele*
> The bush of Te Kamu went to Letele
> *Tuku te vao o Te Puka ki te Gafalua*
> The bush of Te Puka went to the Gafalua [Lua?]
> *Tuku te vao o Te Fakanava kia Pule*
> The bush of Te Fakanava went to Pule [Tuipagai]

The ordering moves from south to north, and again the associations of the islets concerned are apt for the social positions originally assigned to each.

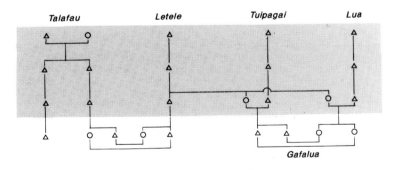

The stocks associated with the 'Four Houses' become intertwined by subsequent unions between their sons and daughters, so that, as some commentators say, 'everyone is aliki', *or has some Talafau ancestry. (This genealogy, in particular, is drastically abridged in this schematic representation, as well as in the text.)*

Happenings and their consequences

When recalling the consequences of their defeat, Nukunonu raconteurs customarily list the one thousand of every sort of valued item that Fakaofo demanded in tribute. This poetic exaggeration prefaces the account of how their burden of tribute was lightened by the intercession of the *aliki* of Olohega and how he too took a woman of Nukunonu as his consort (*Matagi Tokelau* 1991:37–38). This event has many significances, which need not be unpacked here; that it has a Nukunonu woman connected with intercession on Nukunonu's behalf is sufficient.

The story of Pio Tanuvalevale (see chapter 4) is elaborated in its Nukunonu telling, tracing his ancestry from Pio Toevave, son of Nau, and telling of his union with another woman of Nukunonu, thus accounting for his compassion and his reluctance to leave Nukunonu when summoned to be the *aliki* in Fakaofo. Pio's son, Hogā, is reputed to have had eight wives, and his reluctance to leave Nukunonu for Atafu is attributed to his infatuation with a Nukunonu woman, or more accurately Nukunonu women since he took four of them to wife (all of the Talafau stock), as well as four Fakaofo women. Hogā begins a patriline of men, deputised by the Fakaofo *aliki* to Nukunonu. In each generation the mother of this deputy was a Fakaofo woman, though

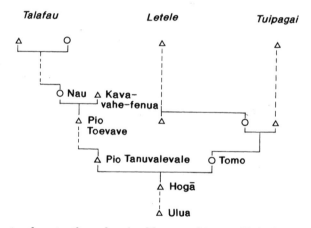

Another significant line (and later stock) is established in Nukunonu by the union of Pio Tanuvalevale (whose ancestress was Nau via Pio Toevave) and Tomo (of the Tuipagai and Letele stocks). From them issue a line of aliki/kovana *deputised by Fakaofo to Nukunonu, who have close or more distant maternal ties here.*

none but Hogā acquired such a great number of wives. His grandson too espoused a woman of Talafau, although again his successor was the son of his Fakaofo wife. That successor was Ulua, the historic nineteenth-century *aliki/* 'king' of Nukunonu, about whom there are numerous stories and of whom assessments differ. Those who are related to him and therefore hold land from him are apt to celebrate him; those who are not connected to him by ancestry and property tend to disparage him, telling how he appropriated lands of others, how he installed himself as a paramount, and how he invoked spirit familiars to gain his ends. All this changed, but that is the beginning of another story. What is important here is that the patriline from Hogā, doubly allied with Nukunonu by their ancestresses Nau and the consort of Pio Tanuvalevale, established another stock in Nukunonu which had to be accommodated within the 'Four Houses', for Ulua and his son founded their own 'house' with yet other Nukunonu women (though not of Talafau).

The constituted social order of Nukunonu was compromised not only by Fakaofo decrees and intrusions, but also by internal processes. Predictably, unions over many generations produced people attached to every genealogy. Take, for example, Pule, whose ancestral genealogy shows how the original formulation of four had become a complex network of overlapping stocks; he was of them all.[16] In light of such multiple affiliations, which are explicitly stated in recounted and recorded genealogies, how could a constituted social order of 'Four Houses' be retained? Again, the case of Pule is instructive. Pule was a significant ancestor, and his most significant ancestry is within the Tuipagai stock (from which his own name is taken), but his other connections are neither ignored nor dismissed. He thus became the more recent apical ancestor of a stock identified primarily with the ancient line of Tuipagai, but to which people belong because Pule is their ancestor. The contemporary *puikāiga* is called Pualuku after the name of the house site where Pule resided.

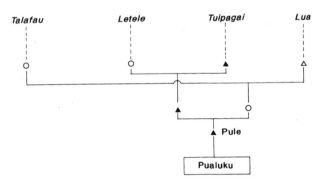

The connections of Pule to all of the 'Four Houses' and his specific ties to one of them, illustrate the simultaneous inclusiveness and exclusiveness of the 'Four Houses'. He was of them all, but a focal ancestor of one—recently named Pualuku linked by him to Tuipagai.

Indeed, the most singular aspect of Nukunonu's social order is the emphatic and persistent four-part segmentation of their society on a genealogical basis, despite the inevitable and acknowledged linkages and mergings related in their genealogical accounts. Repeatedly, as the genealogies of the past are further entangled, they are resorted, so the major conceptual segments of the polity are always four. This insistent four-part division has to do with Nukunonu perceptions of a past social order, which is reiterated right

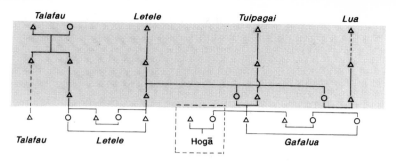

The stock founded by Pio Tanuvalevale and Tomo, and their son, Hogā, is accommodated in the Nukunonu social order of 'Four Houses' by coalescing the intertwined stocks of Tuipagai and Lua as the Gafalua, a name which may be glossed 'Doubled genealogy'.

to the present, even though less inclusive kinship groups figure far more in Nukunonu's ongoing social, economic and political life.

The transformations of the Nukunonu polity since contact will be documented and discussed in the chapters that follow. Here, to round off this chronicle, it should be noted that a man of most appropriate Talafau ancestry was installed in the *aliki* position before the nineteenth century ended. One Nukunonu commentator explained that, though he was long regarded as their *aliki* in Nukunonu, he was finally confirmed in that position by a Fakaofo *aliki* who was his father's sister's son. As one 'sister' of Talafau long ago interceded and saved Talafau lands for the Nukunonu polity, and other Talafau 'sisters' were taken to wife by *aliki* and other men of note (see below for Atafu), so another 'sister' of Talafau was instrumental in returning a 'true' autochthon of proper ancestry to the position of Nukunonu *aliki*, a man whose ancestry may be traced through a line of males to Pipi and Fekei, the founding couple of the Talafau genealogical stock.

The Falefitu 'Seven Houses' of Atafu

Essentially, all that is really known about the social order of Atafu's ancient autochthons is related in the story of the atoll's abandonment. As fierce and barbarous warriors they were led by Lefotu; as assembled villagers they were directed by Malaelua. This paucity of information has encouraged speculation about them by Tokelau people and others. Macgregor (1937:12) suggested that the original people were related to the 'Handsome People' whom Quiros allegedly encountered in 1606 at Gente Hermosa (misidentified as Olohega) and described in such glowing terms (Markham 1904 v.II:424). Some Tokelau savants have elaborated Macgregor's suggestion—or, perhaps, they learned of the Quiros account before Macgregor's visit and suggested the association to him. In any case, the association may be dismissed.[17]

Setting aside the Quiros account, and combining bits of information from stories of past eras (chapter 4), from Gordon Macgregor's field reconnaissance and statements of contemporary Atafu people to Macgregor (1932),

Andrew Thomson (1928) and us, it seems certain that the Atafu autochthons differed in no remarkable way in their looks or lives from the ancient inhabitants of Nukunonu and Fakaofo. They processed sennit (on the evidence of stone-lined soak pits); their village hugged the lagoon shore which was lined with breakwaters; they constructed a sanctuary for their stone idols adjacent to the reef pass of their time; named men were socially recognised as war leaders and civil authorities, and they assembled in a meeting house. They were, however, noted for their barbarous behaviour, and were not the progenitors of Atafu's 'Seven Houses'. Since none of them remained to pass on genealogies and accounts of their particular past we know virtually nothing of what else might have been distinctive about their social order.

Of the era that began with the resettling of Atafu under the guidance of Tonuia a great deal more is known, both because the era began about 200 years ago and because it is firmly linked to the present by genealogy, patterns of land-holding, and remembrances transmitted by as few as two generations, as in the case of Macgregor's principal informant. Virtually anyone in Atafu can relate stories about Tonuia and his progeny, and the stories are consistent from person to person. The social order that they depict is a monolithic stock founded by Tonuia and Lagimaina (and Matua, mother of the last of Tonuia's progeny) that expands generation by generation, and is subdivided into the 'houses' or *puikāiga* of their seven children.

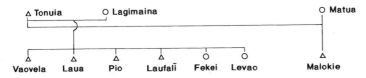

The Atafu social order of 'Seven Houses' is based upon the seven children of Tonuia. The order in which his children are named is uniform, except for the first two (Laua and Vaovela) who are alternated as first and second: (i) the four sons of Tonuia and Lagimaina, (ii) the two daughters of Tonuia and Lagimaina, and (iii) the last child (male) of Tonuia by another Nukunonu woman.

The village of Tonuia's time

Tonuia, his family and companions, did not occupy the ancient village site but instead created a new village at the end of the southern arm of the same islet. Most of the area they settled was probably not dry land in the days of Lefotu and Malaelua, but had been built up during storms and become stabilised in the intervening years. One statement of the pattern of settlement explains: *Ko Folahaga na leoleo te Ahaga, ko Togia na leoleo te Ava, ka ko Tonuia nae moe i lototonu* 'Folahaga guarded the Inlet, Togia guarded the Pass, while Tonuia slept in the centre'. Macgregor's reconstruction of Tonuia's village (1937:55) bears out this statement. Folahaga and Togia[18] are referred to as Tonuia's companions, and their dwellings and those of Folahaga's descendants were indeed located on either side of the site identified as that of Tonuia's house—Togia's to the south where a pass from the sea skirted the southern

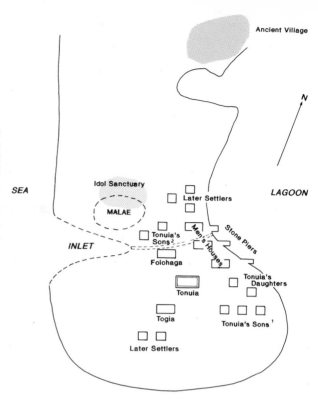

Tonuia's village as it might have been. The reconstruction is derived from Macgregor's field notes and a sketch map drawn by him (1932), supplemented by more recent ethnographic information and earlier historical records. The suggested tidal channel linking the inlet and lagoon probably corresponds to a southern reef shoreline before Tonuia's time. The southern shoreline as it is mapped here was extended by storm deposition this century.

end of the islet, and Folahaga's to the north where there was a tidal inlet. This inlet was probably the residue of a pass at the south end of the islet in earlier times, and now is a low-lying area known as Lotomalae. Tonuia's house was secure at the centre, and on the evidence of Macgregor's reconstruction and contemporary house locations, the houses of his two daughters were directly *gātai* 'towards the lagoon' from his, while three of his sons dwelt *gātai* of where Togia stayed guarding the pass. Tonuia's other and younger sons resided just north of the place where Folahaga guarded the inlet; their establishments were probably of later date. Subsequent colonists from Fakaofo located themselves further to the south and north of the guardians, Togia and Folahaga. Though Tonuia is said to have 'slept' peacefully in the centre, his daughters were even more thoroughly protected, surrounded by their father, brothers and guardians, their 'houses' were set at the shore of the tranquil lagoon. Three *falepā* 'men's houses' and three reclamations, from which latrines projected over the water, were built along the lagoon shore just north of the daughters' houses. A new idol sanctuary was not built; the stone images were placed at the site of the ancient sanctuary (probably that described by Hamilton in Edwards and Hamilton 1915:127–29), still removed from the village, but to the north near the inlet rather to the south at the pass, with an open *malae* towards the village from it.

Something resembling this village was the village visited by members of the US Exploring Expedition in 1841: twenty houses or so, three 'stone piers' (reclamations) with small houses at the end (see Figure p.145), a population of about 120 including about forty adult males, and a 'god house' not seen but indicated to be 'some place in the distance' beyond the open *malae*.

By 1841 Tonuia had disappeared, otherwise he would surely have been pointed out to the visitors. He had met his death (or disappeared) at sea in divine retribution for violating a *tapu* decreed by the Fakaofo *aliki* over the felling of *kānava* timber (*Matagi Tokelau* 1991:44; see chapter 6, p.200). For the pioneer settlers Tonuia had been the *aliki*, who performed the priestly duties as intermediary to the god Tui Tokelau. It is said that his house was also the *fale atua* 'god-house', suggesting that the ancient sanctuary was not used until after his death. No one immediately succeeded Tonuia as Atafu's *aliki*. None of his sons was given or claimed this position, which perhaps explains why the Expedition party could not clearly identify anyone as pre-eminent. The 'old, portly man' who appeared to exercise some kind of authority, as old men invariably do in Tokelau, denied that he was the *aliki*, but very probably he was one of Tonuia's sons.

The little community appeared to the Expedition observers to be egalitarian, and it probably was. It was little more than an extended family into which all other settlers had married and become incorporated, and was led in concert by its elder members, none of whom claimed any formal pre-eminent position. Later, grandsons and great-grandsons of Tonuia would be called *aliki*. Perhaps as the population increased and the bonds of kinship among members of the polity became attenuated, an *aliki* was installed as the embodiment of the united polity. (This, in fact, was Macgregor's explanation.) Alternatively, one might surmise that *aliki* were named in order to fulfil European expectations. Foli, Tonuia's grandson, is the first one named by a foreign record-keeper (Ella 1861) and Macgregor was told that he was the second *aliki* of Atafu (1932). The *aliki* who succeeded him were accorded little reverence: one was 'dethroned', in European parlance, and another was threatened with banishment (see chapter 7). The Atafu pioneer colony had little tolerance of paramountcy.

The genealogical charter

Atafu's social order is founded on a single family, expressed as the *Falefitu* or 'Seven Houses' of Tonuia's seven offspring: his sons Vaovela, Laua, Pio, Laufali and Malokie, and his daughters Fekei and Levao (see *Matagi Tokelau* 1991:42–45 for details). Seven genealogies comprise the *Falefitu*, and forebears with other origins are simply linked in via their spouse, so that even though many forebears are recognised to have other ancestries elsewhere, the Atafu people present themselves as a single stock issuing from Tonuia. For several generations the 'Seven Houses' retained their discreteness, the issue of Tonuia marrying the issue of other colonisers or new arrivals, but by the generation of Tonuia's great-grandchildren the issue of the 'Seven Houses' began to marry one another and their issue consequently came to be affiliated with more than one of the 'Seven Houses'. In recounting their own forebears, people will recite one and then another and another of the lines which connect them to several of the seven offspring.

About the birth order of Tonuia's children there is some ambiguity in the foreign records and the recall of Atafu people, particularly about which of the sons was the oldest.[19] But the prerogatives attached to seniority of birth were apparently few; descendants of at least three sons were titled *aliki* in later years (Macgregor 1937:25). Some significance, however, was attached to being linked to Tonuia through a son or a daughter, i.e. being a *tamatāne* or a *tamafafine* within the Atafu stock and polity. The prerogative of allocating food or produce in the name of the village rested with (and continues to be exercised by) men with entitlements of *tamafafine* because their ancestors were Fekei or Levao, hence their duties for the village as those of female *tamafafine* for less inclusive *kāiga*. That all named *aliki* were issue of Tonuia's sons suggests that a complementary prerogative of *pule* 'authority' rested with *tamatāne*.

It is related that Tonuia did not formally divide the islets of Atafu among his children and companions, but told them and their spouses to go and clear and plant the outer islets to provide for their offspring. Thus entitlement to productive land is traced ultimately to Tonuia's children or their spouses, and to Folahaga (Togia having no issue). The cleared and planted islets were subsequently divided and recombined, but when people defend or assert rights to a particular area they begin stating their case by calling upon Laua or Pio or Fekei, and so on.

An Atoll Kingdom

What we, in this chapter, have called the 'ancient orders' is the period which Tokelau raconteurs refer to as *na aho anamua* 'the days past' before the *malamalama* 'enlightenment' of Christianity. When people in Nukunonu talk about *na aho anamua*, they speak about passing generations, about events linked to genealogical persons and events which impinged upon the subordinate position of Nukunonu as a conquered tributary. The underlying message is that the oppression their forebears suffered became less onerous over time, because of the support from others such as the Olohega *aliki* (*Matagi Tokelau* 1991:37–39), and the influential presence of Nukunonu women and their children in Fakaofo and later in Atafu. The recurring motif is of Nukunonu women being sought by or given to eminent others as wives.

Likewise for Atafu there is the unfolding of the genealogy of the Falefitu and the well-known story of the retribution visited upon their ancestral father for his rebellion against Fakaofo authority, but this short chronology (probably less than fifty years) is overwhelmed by later events of greater local significance. About those days long past Nukunonu tells a long story and Atafu a short one.

Fakaofo accounts indeed record *aliki* lists and genealogy, but the story told is not of events but of stable and persistent order, of a situation that is ideal and constant. (The exceptional Perez 1977 account of change in Fakaofo is actually embedded in a later chronological text.) This contrast between the different 'pasts' of dominant or hegemonic and subordinate or subaltern groups has been discussed elsewhere (Huntsman 1994, see also Cohn 1961). It is sufficient to remark here that Fakaofo's account celebrates a past state, while Nukunonu (and to a lesser extent Atafu) record a narrative of change.

There are other contrasts too between the social orders, which have been implied or alluded to above, that warrant some comparative discussion to draw out the significant differences.

'Houses' and *puikāiga* and *falepā*

Sets of *fale* 'houses' figure in descriptions of each atoll's ancient order and in the oratory of pan-Tokelau gatherings today when Fakaofo is addressed as the *Faleiva* 'Nine Houses', Nukunonu as the *Falefā* 'Four Houses', and Atafu as the *Falefitu* 'Seven Houses'. However, what 'house' connotes in each instance, whether of the past or in the present, is not exactly the same.

Fale in one respect connotes place, a location in the village (itself referred to everywhere as Falē). Fakaofo's 'Nine Houses' refer specifically to named and placed *falepā* 'men's house' structures of the past, to which agnatically related men (or male *tamatāne*) were affiliated. Each had communally defined privileges and duties having to do with men's activities, for example warfare, bird-snatching, special kinds of fishing, and each had rights to designated sections of plantation and associated totemic spirits. The three structures referred to 'men's houses' in Atafu may have been *falepā* too, perhaps, by analogy with Fakaofo *falepā*, occupied by sons and grandsons of the founding couple, Tonuia and Lagimaina. There are fleeting references in Nukunonu to two places where *falepā* stood and 'warriors' are said to have assembled there, but their linkage with the 'Four Houses' is unstated.[20] Fakaofo's 'well-peopled' village may have had something to do with its complex *falepā* organisation and its chiefly hierarchy is consonant with their distinctive agnatic character. The intimations of some kind of 'men's house' places and organisations in Atafu and Nukunonu may be considered reflections of the more elaborated Fakaofo institution in much less populous places. Instead, Atafu and Nukunonu 'houses' were associated with named residential homesteads or compounds within their villages, whose natal members held rights to designated lands outside the villages. These names and places are still invoked when rights to land are challenged and defended.

What Nukunonu's 'Four Houses' and Atafu's 'Seven Houses' connote are encompassing cognatic stocks arising from significant forebears. Nukunonu's 'Houses' are of ancient origin and repeatedly re-formed to maintain a coalition of four, each associated with particular positions or offices within the polity; or, put the other way round, each holding an office which was assigned to one of its members, such as *faipule* 'ruler' or *toa* 'warrior'. Atafu's 'Houses' are stocks too, but of far more recent origin and each with a distinct ancestral founder who was a son or daughter of Tonuia. No specialised activities (as for Fakaofo) or offices (as for Nukunonu) are associated with them, though certain character traits of their apical or later ancestors may be attributed to their members, and men of the 'houses' of the two apical daughters (e.g.

tamafafine) are designated *tauvāega* 'distributors of *inati*', and only men from the 'houses' of the apical sons (e.g. *tamatāne*) were designated *aliki* in the nineteenth century.

Despite these differences in the referents of the 'house' designations for the three atolls, they are all linked with *puikāiga*. In fact, in Nukunonu and Atafu they are synonymous with *puikāiga*, and retain at least an occasional and symbolic presence in the social order. People speak of belonging to them, and sporadically align themselves with one or another of them. In Fakaofo, where the named 'houses' refer primarily to 'men's houses' (*falepā*), they are still associated with *puikāiga*, in that agnates of specific *puikāiga* were affiliated with the named 'men's houses'. However, these *puikāiga*, like the *falepā*, are no longer part of the social order. The ancient apical ancestors that founded them are vague, if not forgotten—given that remembered ancient genealogy is concerned almost exclusively with the agnatic line of the *aliki* genealogy, and the *puikāiga* of the present day have different beginnings (see chapter 7).

Notably, guardian or totemic spirits figure explicitly only in the accounts of Fakaofo *falepā* and *puikāiga*. It seems unlikely that such beliefs and practices were exclusive to Fakaofo, especially since *aitu* are referred to in Nukunonu and Atafu oral accounts, and the author of one of the Fakaofo local texts (Perez n.d. 1 and 2), in orally recounting the past, generalised these beliefs. This suggests that beliefs and practices of a totemic nature were pan-Tokelau even if the specifics are now uncertain.

The 'Houses' and associated *puikāiga* are configurations or refigurations of remembered ancient orders. They were in some ways comparable institutions, linked to places, ancestries and activities, yet they were not exactly alike because they are situated within the different histories and genealogies of the atolls where they were constituted.

Genealogies, metaphor and metonymy

'Histories', in Greg Dening's words (1991:349), 'are metaphors of the past: they translate sets of events into sets of symbols. But histories are also metonymies of the present: the present has existence in and through their expression.'

Among the many forms that 'history' may take in Dening's generous usage (which includes reminiscence, parable, tradition, myth . . .) genealogy is perhaps the idiom which shows most clearly the ways in which present-day social realities are connected to those of the past, simply because the linking chains are made up of biological 'facts' of ancestry and generation which are basic, ongoing parts of the general human and social condition. Genealogies, however, are seldom if ever complete records of ancestries; they are partial and selective constructs, 'metaphors' of the past, and thus as contestable as any other form of history. They are also subject to reinterpretation and change with the alteration of the social and political contexts to which they refer.

In most, if not all Polynesian cultures, genealogy is one of the prime idioms of historical discourse, providing a basic conceptual framework for the construction of cosmological, religious, political and social orders, as well as of depicting the relationships between them. Tokelau genealogies make few statements of cosmological import. None of the important gods, including Tui Tokelau, are ancestral figures, and the only hint of a kinship between humans and the natural world is given in the brief Fakaofo story of the growth of men from maggots generated by a fish and enlivened by a bird. They do, however, depict the fundamental structures of the Tokelau religious, political and social orders—both at the level of the individual islands and, more tenuously perhaps, at the 'national level'.

One of the striking points about the three 'political' island genealogies is the fundamental structural difference between them. It is not simply that each relates the separate past of the island concerned through a distinctive cast of named characters. Those casts are brought together in very different ways, following distinctive plots which may themselves also be seen as metonymns of other local historical forms.

As we have seen, the premier genealogy of Fakaofo is founded upon a single agnatic line of *aliki*, continuing through nine generations before account is taken of females and their issue, and the form changes to that of a single comprehensive stock. Fakaofo is *fenua aliki* 'chiefly land' in a wider sense because the generation of the entire population is hinged upon connections to the chiefly line; other characters may appear who are apparently not of chiefly descent, but without records of their antecedents, so that they become of significance only through their connections to the chiefly line. What this structure connotes is unity, genealogical stratification, male authority, centralisation and power. It conforms to a social order well tuned for warfare and predatory expansion of the sort depicted in other historical forms telling of the conquest of the other two islands and the appropriation of Nukunonu's fertility in the form of both fresh water and women. It can also plausibly be related to the centralised nature of village authority in the present day, but this depends upon the story (related below) of the historical transfer of authority from *aliki* to 'grey-headed men', the direct antecedents of today's local council of elders.

Nukunonu's history, as we have also seen, is largely a genealogical account, but with a radically different structure from that of Fakaofo. Instead of a single line, the Nukunonu 'island' genealogy is founded upon four initially unrelated and quite distinct lines, each associated with a distinct sphere of authority and having land rights in different sections of the atoll. After some six generations there are intermarriages between the lines, which continue as stocks, becoming more and more complexly interrelated through the generations. In the Nukunonu telling, however, these complexities are recurrently resorted in such a way that the polity can always be presented as four conceptually distinct stocks. What such a structure connotes is coalition rather than overriding centralised authority, and the complementarity of male and female spheres as it appears in *kāiga* rather than village contexts.

Since the intertwined *kāiga* of Nukunonu are the focus of the village polity, and the founding 'Four Houses' are reiterated in the formation and

177

reformation of *puikāiga* 'encompassing stocks', the acts of women and connections through women are of some importance. The salience, indeed 'glorification' of 'sisters', beginning with the Talafau woman whose *titi* it was in the account of conquest (chapter 4), reflects the value attached to its women. In local Fakaofo and Atafu accounts there are no such significant women. Nukunonu's preoccupation with everyday family or *kāiga* matters finds exquisite expression in the story of conquest in which the Nukunonu warriors, called to defend their land, respond: 'Don't bother me, just leave me alone to patch up the leaking roof of my house.' Though reluctant to mobilise themselves under a single overriding authority, Nukunonu people have repeatedly ordered themselves into multiple groups differentiated in the idiom of kinship, but more inclusive than the *kāiga* of day-to-day village life.

Atafu's island genealogy is a more or less straightforward account of population increase through the issue of the seven children of the founding couple. It is by reference to these children that Atafu is known as the 'Seven Houses', although there is no particular social or cultural significance attached to that number in the way that four has such salience in Nukunonu.

The basic structure of a stock genealogy such as this is given by biology: it is a record of generation, reflecting few if any 'cultural' imperatives such as rank or canonical divisions of rights and authority among major social units, apart from those based on age and gender. It is a historical record which also has clear metonymical relationships to both past and present-day social realities, connoting a fundamental unity as well as egalitarianism.[20]

The different forms that the local *gafa* take reflect their distinctive constituted orders. In the case of Fakaofo, everyone at the end (in the last several generations) is included, but in a highly selective way by virtue of everyone's connection to the one ramifying *aliki* genealogy. None of the multitudinous genealogical links between these ancestors or the ancestry of their mates or consorts are recorded in the *aliki* genealogy, although these are known and recorded in other contexts. This is the *fenua aliki* because everyone is linked to the *gafa aliki* somehow—though some more so than others, and the outcome is a statement of hierarchy. Nukunonu genealogical accounts have four starting points and systematically follow through the generations from each. When put together, they interweave in complex and repetitive ways, reflecting a structure of communal coalition and repetitive ongoing alliances. The Atafu genealogical records are probably the most comprehensive and straightforward, given their relatively short generational span. Essentially this is a single stock, subdivided into seven substocks. Atafu genealogies note little of the ancestry of those that became united with the issue of Tonuia by marriage. They are named, but their ancestry is irrelevant, at least from the Atafu perspective. Comparatively, Fakaofo is genealogically a ramifying chiefly, and largely agnatic, stock; Nukunonu is genealogically four intertwined, even involuted, stocks; while Atafu is one expansive family. The genealogies reflect their polities as well as specifying ancestry.

Tokelau's overarching genealogy is another kind of statement. For one thing it is of our design, based upon the separate local constructions and abbreviated to highlight the armature of the Tokelau ancient order as clearly as possible. Only a few genealogical personages, that is, people genealogically identified, are actors in accounts of that order's establishment and history, but these are the people that tie the separate local genealogies together, and thereby establish relations between the atolls which continue to be differently interpreted (see chapter 4). The key persons are Kava-vahe-fenua, Nau and Pio, though others join them in the separate accounts. By putting these three accounts together, and without prejudice to any version, the three atolls

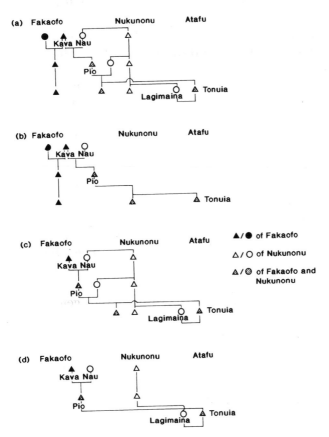

Genealogy expresses the unity and relationships of the atolls via their aliki lineages. The differences between the representations are what is left out, rather than what is put in. The genealogies are radically abridged, deleting generations and replications, to make the same points that are made in narratives. (Adapted from Huntsman and Hooper 1985.)

(a) An overarching genealogy constructed by combining the separate atoll representations in order to highlight their differences (below).

(b) The Fakaofo representation focuses on Kava and the patrilines issuing from him, and emphasises the 'pure' Fakaofo line of aliki.

(c) The Nukunonu representation focuses on the unions of Nukunonu women with significant men from elsewhere, or, put another way, upon the sororal linkages of the Talafau aliki with aliki elsewhere.

(d) The Atafu representation focuses on the Fakaofo aliki ancestry of Tonuia and the Nukunonu aliki ancestry of Lagimaina.

are united as Tokelau. Yet how this unity is interpreted is contentious, for it has to do with precedence and loyalty. Fakaofo claims precedence because the *aliki gafa* issues from the unnamed senior, superior Fakaofo wife of Kava-vahe-fenua, contending that Nau was a secondary, inferior Nukunonu wife whose issue, while loyal to the land of their father, are inferior. By implication, all the unnamed Nukunonu women taken as wives in Fakaofo were likewise inferior, but produced loyal sons. Nukunonu reads the genealogy as an enduring union whereby children of Nukunonu women retain strong attachments and loyalties to the homeland and to the brothers of their named mothers. Matrilateral links and sororal/fraternal loyalties, manifest in the obligations of children to their mothers' brothers, are highlighted (see Huntsman and Hooper 1985). Atafu people agree that indeed they, the issue of Lagimaina, have special links with Nukunonu, the homeland of their mother, but they do not concur with Fakaofo about the position of Nau's son Pio. In speech and song they have asserted that he was the first and most cherished son of Kava-vahe-fenua, and contrary to the long genealogies of Nukunonu and Fakaofo which name two Pios, Atafu collapses them into one, so that only two generations separate Kava-vahe-fenua and their founding father, Tonuia (Kava —>Pio—>Tepine—>Tonuia).

Greater Tokelau

For an unknown number of generations Fakaofo held sway over Nukunonu, appropriating valuables, produce and women. Over time Fakaofo's tyranny was mitigated by the bonds of kinship established between the two atolls, though clearly Fakaofo remained dominant and continued to exploit Nukunonu's resources. This worldly dominance made manifest by *pule* 'rule' and appropriation was sanctified by the instantiation of Tui Tokelau in Fakaofo and the role of the Fakaofo *aliki* as supplicant to the god. Nukunonu, with no manifestation of the god, was dependent upon Fakaofo for the god's blessings of abundance and fertility. Thus Nukunonu's servitude was divinely sanctioned and its people acquiescent. Atafu, beyond being a fishery and source of timber, did not become a part of this atoll empire until about the end of the nineteenth century. Its people were pioneer colonisers, resettling an abandoned land and making it their own. The wilfulness of the designated founder of the polity suggests that servitude and acquiescence were not characteristic of these pioneers, who also had a (less imposing) instantiation of Tui Tokelau in their midst.

We glimpse the character of the polities of this atoll empire in the earliest European accounts: Fakaofo controlled and assertive, Nukunonu tentative and wary, Atafu spontaneous and audacious. The story continues and, despite dramatic changes and catastrophic occurrences, these qualities marked in the earliest encounters with Europeans persist, and much of what is distinctive of the separate social orders is retained in their transformations.

SIX
Tokelau Transformed

If the reports of the US Exploring Expedition are to be believed, Tokelau people in 1841 were not only dazzled by their strange visitors but also ignorant of other Polynesian places and peoples. This might have been a misinterpretation or an exaggeration. Nonetheless, Tokelau people had not yet journeyed afar and returned with enthralling accounts of *papālagi* people and their exotic behaviours and beliefs. In this regard things changed markedly in the middle decades of the nineteenth century; Tokelau people departed and returned, the atolls received many more visitors with differing agendas and embraced or rejected those agendas in pursuit of their own interests; and the atoll people became unwitting objects of foreign plans.

Outsider perceptions of Tokelau also changed. Although the three atolls were all in some sense 'known' to the outside world, nobody paid much attention. Fakaofo was 'discovered' on three more occasions,[1] and whalers continued to frequent the seas around the islands, drily recording their sightings in their logs, but rarely much more.[2] The atolls were not attractive watering places; they offered little more than a few coconuts for barter offshore. Whalers occasionally picked up people from one island and took them to another, or came across canoeloads of people at sea and took them where they thought they wanted to go.

No stories are told in Tokelau of these incidents, doubtless because they were not particularly dramatic and did little to change the circumstances of Tokelau life. There are, however, also many Tokelau accounts of what happened during the nineteenth century which have survived, telling of events that did change life and the relationships between the atolls. Many are not recorded in any other contexts, and provide clear indication of Tokelau perceptions and motivations; and where they can be linked with foreign records of the same events (as they frequently can be), they often amplify the bare historical records in interesting and significant ways, as the following example shows.

The first memorable event that is both recorded outside and recounted inside took place in 1844. The following story of 'The Ship Burned at Atafu' was told by Vagi, an elderly Atafu woman in 1971 (for another version, see *Matagi Tokelau* 1991:77–78).

> *A single-masted vessel came ashore at Atafu captained by a huge and mighty Frenchman. He terrified people and wanted women. The elders pretended to let him have his ways, but bided their time and ambushed him when he was absorbed in amorous abandon—lying across a woman's legs as she searched his hair for lice. The men crept up to him and noosed him around the neck with a stout rope. Unable to restrain him, they tied the ends of the rope to two coconut palms, which he nearly brought down in his attempts to free himself. When he had been killed, they dragged the foreign vessel upon the reef and burned it so that no outsider would know that the vessel had been at Atafu. Nonetheless, the incident became known and a French man-of-war sailed to Atafu to fire upon the village in retaliation. Atafu was spared however by the intercession of the French Catholic Bishop in Samoa who argued that they had acted in heathen ignorance, and, though the man-of-war did loom off Atafu shores and they feared the worst, it only showed its might and then sailed away.*

There are a number of European records bearing on this same event. The French Captain Morvan reported in 1845 that the *Angeline*, a French whaler, had 'put in here [Atafu] from the Mulgrave Islands, with the loss of the surgeon, second officer and ten men. It seems they were tempted to land, and were immediately seized by the natives and carried off, whether to be massacred or kept as prisoners, is not known. The *Angeline* laid by eight days, with hope of removing them, but in vain, and bore away from here—' (Ward ed. 1967, v.2: 314–15; 'here' refers to the atoll where the reported event occurred).

This third-hand report bears little resemblance to the Tokelau story, yet it is about the same incident, for in June 1844 the *Adolphe*, under the command of Captain Morvan, conveyed Monseigneur Bataillon, Bishop of the Marist Mission in Western Polynesia, from Apia to Uvea (*Journal de la Société des Océanistes* 1962:18). This suggests that Morvan, while in either Samoa or Uvea, learned of the *Angeline* incident and went to Tokelau, but was dissuaded from avenging his countrymen, perhaps by the bishop. By his own report Morvan was in Tokelau waters in September 1844 and his vessel was a man-of-war. Such a vessel would have been remarkable, and it was remarked upon to a Catholic father in Apia some seven years later: 'These islanders do not recall having seen in living memory more than six ships of which one was French and had 44 guns' (Padel n.d.:16 August). The first discrepancy between the Morvan and Tokelau accounts is where the incident took place. Morvan apparently places it in Fakaofo, which he claimed to have discovered (see note 1). But he could not have been planning to bombard an island he did not know the existence of, so the incident had to have occurred elsewhere at a known island.

That the incident did take place in Atafu, as the Tokelau story tells, is confirmed by the report of a later visitor, who had heard from '. . . one who

Monseigneur Pierre Bataillon, Titular Bishop of Enosi, periodically sought to include Tokelau within the realms of the Catholic faith. He arranged two significant mission voyages to Fakaofo (which he referred to as Clarence, perhaps through some misunderstanding of the reports from Hula Tirel). Most dramatic was his scheme to save the whole Fakaofo population by uplifting them to Uvea—in which he largely succeeded. He apparently arranged for Takua from Nukunonu and Lua from Fakaofo to be trained as teachers at Clydesdale (in Sydney), and then returned to their atolls to convert their fellows. That scheme only half succeeded; Nukunonu converted, Fakaofo did not. The Nukunonu converts then appealed for his intervention in 1863, for which he is given undeserved credit (see below). Reproduced from Rieu 1936:18.

had some means of knowing that such was the truth', that some years before his own 1860 visit to Atafu '. . . the islanders had put to death a boat's crew of sailors, who had landed from a whale-ship, and given offence by unwelcome familiarity with the women' (Hague 1868:40). He was told of how the Atafu men had tricked their offending visitors by leading them below a stand of tall coconut palms where 'men aloft threw down cocoanuts upon them with so great and such well-directed force, that they were at once overcome, and then finished by those on the ground' (ibid.).

This memorable incident had no longterm repercussions. Its notability lies in its narratives—both for being the first for which there are complementary local and foreign stories, and for succinctly illustrating the problems and benefits of multiple representations of past events. There can be no doubt that something memorable happened, but the narratives of it are the products of different cultural imaginations.[3] Nonetheless, the Tokelau stories of the event, the outcome of nearly a century and a half of telling, are undoubtedly fuller and more coherent than any of the preserved records of the event made not long thereafter.

With these considerations in mind, we have formed our narrative of events from the stories and records, notes and anecdotes in both Tokelau and European annals,[4] and proceed to tell a saga of Tokelau diaspora and European intrusion that wrought a transformation of the Tokelau social and cultural order.

Escape from Famine: 1846–52

Tokelau accounts assert, and European documents record, that Fakaofo was a very well populated place, and Tokelau historians recall that after the reign of Taupe (the *aliki* encountered by the US Exploring Expedition in 1841), an

Cast of Characters

Atone (aka Antonio Pereira/ Antonio Perera Vitorino de Barres): A Cape Verdean Portuguese, who arrived in Fakaofo to trade for A. Unshelm/the German Firm in mid 1863. He travelled between Fakaofo and Samoa, where he also had interests, until sometime in the 1870s when he left his affairs in Fakaofo in the hands of his son, to whom he willed his Fakaofo assets.

Faivalua: Voyaged from Fakaofo to Olohega, probably in the late 1840s, and then to Upolu, where he became an LMS convert. In or about 1858 he returned to Fakaofo on his own to convert his compatriots, but without success. So he went on to Atafu, where he was regarded as the original bearer of the 'Good News'. He conveyed a request from Atafu for a 'teacher' to the Samoan LMS mission in 1861 and died shortly thereafter.

Falekie (aka Tavite): A Nukunonu man castaway to Uvea in 1846 after precipitously joining the (unsuccessful) Fakaofo voyage to Atafu. He returned to Nukunonu mid 1863 with his companion Telakau (see below). Upon his return he became the senior person of the Letele stock and a leader of the polity.

Foli: Atafu *aliki* who welcomed LMS missionaries in 1861. He was taken by the slavers in 1863.

Foliga: A son of Taupe, the *aliki* encountered in 1841 by the US Exploring Expedition. He, as spokesman on behalf of the *aliki*, forthrightly rejected Christian overtures. His brother's son, Lua, was probably one of the returnees from Uvea in 1861, thus accounting for his negotiations with the bishop which allowed the converts to remain. He was taken by the slavers, and it is said that he coined the phrase: *Tenaka ka ko Tenaka* 'Tenaka is just Tenaka' referring to self-serving duplicity, which was passed to another captive who returned to Fakaofo.

Hoifua: Father of Takua and senior of the Talafau *aliki* stock in Nukunonu—'second in rank to the "King"' (Gill and Bird 1863). He survived the slavers and directed those few people that remained in hiding after his son, the 'King' and others voyaged in Samoa.

Hula (aka Jules/Sula Tyrell/Tirel): A Frenchman and one of the oil-making beachcombers at Olohega in 1848–49 who terrorised the Tokelau people there. Subsequently in 1851, he was engaged to salvage a wreck at Nukunonu, but finding it unsalvageable turned again to making oil from local resources with local labour. Upon his departure, he took Takua and others with him. In Apia, he concocted with the bishop a scheme for removing all the people of Fakaofo, and was the 'first lieutenant' in carrying out the scheme—'The Exodus of Hula'. Some years later he was killed at Suwarrow in the northern Cook Islands (Sterndale 1890, see also Hooper 1975).

Ilai (aka Eli Jennings): Appeared at Olohega in 1856 and claimed that it was not permanently inhabited, thereby establishing his ownership which has been periodically contested. He was probably involved with one of the slave ships which stopped at Olohega on its way to Tokelau and on its way back.

Lea: Genealogically not of *aliki* stock, he was an early LMS Christian convert in Samoa and was allowed to remain in Fakaofo in 1858. Though he appears as the local leader of the LMS and the associate of Peni and the 'teachers' in the 1860s, in the 1880s his daughter converted to Catholicism and married Peleila.

Lik : Became Fakaofo *aliki* c.1857 and persisted in rejecting Christian overtures until 1863, when he accepted Protestant 'teachers'. He did not himself accept their teaching and following the return of his son, Tefono, from Uvea, was baptised a Catholic.

Lua: Grandson of Taupe (the 1841 *aliki*) who was among those taken to Uvea in 1852. He was sent to Clydesdale (in Sydney) for training as a Catholic teacher and was one of 'two well-tried young men, sons of influential chiefs' was left in Fakaofo in 1861 and designated to be the Catholic teacher there by the bishop. He apparently had little success and in 1863 fell victim to the slavers.

Mafal : A Samoan LMS 'teacher', with Maka at Atafu in 1861, who attempted to establish himself in Fakaofo in 1862. His voyaging party was castaway to Samoa, and upon their return he was accepted as a 'teacher' at Fakaofo. He left soon after the slavers, but returned as Fakaofo's first pastor in 1868.

Maka: A Rarotongan LMS 'teacher' who established the first church and school in Atafu and interceded to save some of the people from the 'slavers'.

Peleila (aka José Pereira): Son of Atone who handled and inherited his father's assets in Fakaofo. He married Moiki, the daughter of Lea, by whom he fathered many children. He also had offspring by two other unions. Note: When people in Tokelau refer to Peleila, they mean José.

Peni (aka Ben/Benjamin Hughes): An American who arrived in Fakaofo via Olohega in early 1863 (before, during or after the slavers) as a semi-independent trader. Whether he had any role in the slaver depredations is uncertain. Unable to buy coconuts for oil or to employ local labour, he forced the sale of Fenuafala and brought in workers from afar to make oil. Locally harassed, he finally sold his interest in Fenuafala to the German Firm in Apia in 1866, and disappeared.

Sakaio: A Samoan 'teacher' who joined Mafalā in introducing Protestantism to Fakaofo. He arrived in early 1863, departed for Atafu and got castaway to Fiji at mid year, returned in August, and a year or so later voyaged away again owing to his un-Christian behaviour.

Takua (aka Susitino/Justin): Son of Hoifua, senior of the Nukunonu *aliki* stock. He was taken to Samoa and Uvea by Hula, and became a Catholic convert in 1852. It seems he was well regarded by the fathers and sent to Clydesdale (in Sydney) for religious training in the mid 1850s. He was returned to Fakaofo in 1961 and soon thereafter moved to Nukunonu where he quickly persuaded all to become Catholics. He shepherded the parish polity for decades and succeeded Ulua as *aliki* in the 1890s. He died in 1914.

Tenaka: Sometime, probably in the 1850s, he had gone to work at Olohega, where he married Tautele, who according to one account was with child by Hula. He and his wife were Protestant converts at Olohega at the time of the 'slavers' and returned to Fakaofo soon after to support Lea in the cause of Protestantism.

Taupe: Fakaofo *aliki* when US Exploring Expedition visited in 1841. He probably died shortly thereafter. This reign is regarded as prosperous, but thereafter famine came (at least by 1846).

Tefono (aka Oto): Son of Likā, probably taken to Uvea in 1852. He returned to Fakaofo in May 1863, was the primary opponent of Peni and the local leader of the Catholics there. He did not succeed his father and never became *aliki*.

Telakau (aka Paulo): From Nukunonu was a castaway to Uvea in 1846, when he precipitously joined a Fakaofo voyaging party. In Uvea, he converted to Catholicism and returned to his homeland in mid 1863. He became the 'elder' of the Tuipagai/Luà stock or 'Gafalua'.

Ulua: 'King', or deputy of the Fakaofo *aliki*, in Nukunonu from the early 1850s. When he acceded to Nukunonu's Catholic conversion, his power was compromised—he was '*King only in name*' (Gill & Bird 1863; emphasis in the original). He died sometime in the 1890s.

ogefenua (lit. 'land famine') arose in Fakaofo, and, as was their usual practice in such circumstances, people from Fakaofo went to Atafu, Nukunonu and Olohega to live until such time as their homeland again became bountiful. So it was that in 1846 a voyaging party set out from Fakaofo to stay for a while in Atafu. They stopped as usual at Nukunonu where they spent the night and harvested coconuts as a provision for the rest of their journey. When their canoes were being launched through the breakers, two young men of Nukunonu, Telakau and Falekie, precipitously leapt aboard one of the vessels. On their way to Atafu the canoe fleet encountered contrary winds under storm-obscured skies and were *lēlea* 'blown off course'. Only three of the twenty or so canoes are reported to have eventually reached land.

Two of the canoes (with fifteen people aboard, including the two Nukunonu men) reached Uvea on 31 October 1846 after being at sea for a month and a half. They were enthusiastically welcomed and extravagantly entertained by Uvea people and the Marist fathers, and were often over-whelmed and sometimes terrified by the attentions they received. A special Mass was celebrated in praise of the mercy and guidance of the Heavenly Father, during which a canon salvo was fired at 'the moment of elevation', to impress the 'poor infidels'. Far from being merely impressed, they were thrown into panic. Bishop Bataillon decreed that they be taught and baptised, and only then returned to their island as apostles to begin the conversion of their countrymen (Verne 1895). The two Nukunonu men did return, and figure prominently in that atoll's later history as Paulo Telakau and Tavite Falekie. Some of the Fakaofo people must also have returned, but exactly who they were is uncertain.

The third canoe was picked up on the high seas by a whaler and reached Samoa on 21 November 1846. The castaways immediately became objects in the rivalry for converts between the Marist fathers and LMS missionaries abetted by their respective Samoan converts (Padel n.d.: 27 November, 7, 10, 12, 15 December 1846 & 3 March 1847; Harbutt 1847). Each side tried to hold on to the castaways in order to teach them and return them to Tokelau as harbingers of their particular Christian faith. They were enticed here and taken there, but all these efforts were in vain. Within three months or so, eight of the eleven castaways had died, and nothing is reported of the fate of the other three. These unfortunates were the first recorded Tokelau sojourners in Samoa; others followed shortly by other routes.

In June 1848, twenty-two Tokelau people arrived in Samoa, conveyed to Apia from Olohega aboard a schooner that had gone there to pick up casks of coconut oil. These people could have been longtime residents of Olohega, or they may have taken up residence there because of the Fakaofo famine. In any case, Tokelau people were settled in Olohega when three beachcomb-ers—two Frenchmen and one American—arrived to make oil, and they had abandoned Olohega at the first opportunity because, according to their report at the time and to narratives in Tokelau annals, one of the beachcombers had killed their chief (Padel n.d.: 30 June 1848, Hooper 1975). They explained that they had come to Samoa to seek a passage back to Fakaofo, but

Date & Ships	Missions	Entrepreneurs	In Tokelau (see chapter 4)
1841 USEE Capt. Hudson	LMS mission urged to visit FF	At AT[1] seeking women and wood	Intruders killed and vessel burned
1844 Angeline Fr. whaler			Warship appears but does not attack
Adolphe Fr. warship	Conveys Bishop Bataillon from Samoa to Uvea		
1846			Famine in FF[2]
Oct/Nov	Tokelau castaways to Samoa and Uvea		Voyage castaway, including Telakau and Falekie of NN[3]
1848	22 Tokelauans from Olohega to Samoa because of killing	Two Frenchman and one Englishman making oil at Olohega	Faivalua and Timoteo etc from FF to Olohega then to Samoa
1849 Dec	Hula appears at Catholic mission	Frenchmen leave Olohega. Englishman ??	
1851 Wreck of Novelty at NN		Pritchard buys salvage and sends Hula to NN as his agent. Unsalvageable so Hula makes oil.	Passengers of wrecked ship hosted at NN. Hula comes, makes oil, and departs taking Takua and Poufou
1852 Jan–Feb Kate from Apia to Uvea to FF to Uvea	Hula arrives at Apia with Tokelau companions, reports famine in FF to bishop, who arranges 'rescue' of bodies and souls to Uvea		Takua and Poufou to Uvea. 500 people removed from FF and god-house burned
1853 Anon voyage			Notes Novelty wreck and burned god-house. Estimates 250 people in FF
1856	Takua and another at Clydesdale training as 'teachers'		
Oct	Ilai Jennings establishes himself at Olohega		

Date & Ships	Missions	Entrepreneurs	In Tokelau
1858 *John Williams* at FF	1st mission voyage rejected at FF but leaves Lea, a convert		Faivalua brings 'good news' to AT, and Lea joins him there
1860 Anon. ship	Visitor notes man with a Bible at AT		
1861 Sept Ship from Uvea brings Bishop to FF	Catholic converts from Uvea left at FF		Takua returns to NN and all convert to Catholic faith
Oct *John Williams* to FF and AT	2nd LMS mission voyage—rejected at FF and welcomed at AT		Maka and Mafala begin teaching at AT
1862 mid year	LMS receives letters from Maka at AT reporting success but that 'heathenism' persists in FF		AT party reports Christians persecuted at FF
Dec		American named William at AT	Mafala rejected at FF and all wishing to be taught go to AT and are castaway People in FF sick and dying of dysentery
1863 Jan *J. Williams* at FF	Castaways from FF and AF arrive at Apia, and return to FF on 3rd mission voyage. Teachers accepted at FF.	Peni arrives at FF	
Feb Slave ships		Half the Tokelau people removed by 'slave ships'	'Slavers' terrorise all Tokelau. NN party voyages to Apia to inform the Bishop
c. May:	NN voyagers land at Samoa and proceed to Apia Mafala leaves FF for Samoa		
May Ship returns other castaways			
Augustita at NN & FF	Elloy visits NN & FF, bringing back Uvean converts, and thinks NN deserted	A. Pereira arrives at FF. Peni 'buys' Fenuafala and leaves to seek labourers	Telakau and Falekie return to NN. Tefono and others return to FF. Vaopuka etc. return

Date				
June Ship at FF	Priest baptises *aliki* and others at FF	Peni arrives and departs again. A. Pereira remains		Teacher Sakaio leaves FF for AT and is castaway
Aug Ship	Teacher Sakaio returns to FF	Peni returns with labourers to work Fenuafala		
? Ship	Sept: Voyagers from NN baptised in Samoa			
1864 May		Peni & Lea in Samoa laying complaint with Consul Williams; Sese Perez arrives to trade at NN		Letter from Williams read at FF
1865/6 *Ophelia* wrecked at AT		June: Peni in Samoa laying complaint with Consul Coe		Sept: Coe's letter read by Sakaio in FF and rejected by Tefono; *Ophelia* wrecked upon Atafu's western reef; captain and crew there for 6–9 months and construct vessel from wreckage in which they voyage to Samoa with two Atafu escorts
1866		Peni sells Fenuafala to the German Firm and disappears		
1868 Jan *Samoa* visits en route to Uvea	Bataillon visits FF & NN			Samoan catechist, Matulino, installed at FF.
Aug Visit of *J Williams*	Murray visits FF & AT, and establishes congregations			Pastor Mafala installed at FF and Pastor Fataiki at AT

1 AT = Atafu
2 FF = Fakaofo
3 NN = Nukunonu

that five of their compatriots had remained at Olohega despite the beach-combers. Who these twenty-two people were and what became of them is not reported. It is probable that some came under the influence of LMS missionaries, judging from later reports of Tokelau converts in Samoa (see the story of Faivalua below).[5]

The two French beachcombers returned to Apia at the end of 1849, after a year and a half at Olohega, with plans 'to seek fortune elsewhere' and one of them, known as Hula in Tokelau annals, paid a friendly call at the Marist mission (Padel n.d.:17–18 November 1849). He appeared there again on New Year's Day 1852, after having spent five months at Nukunonu, where he had indeed been seeking his fortune.

An event six months before explains how and why he came to be there, so a brief digression is required. San Francisco newspapers reported in September 1851 that

> The English bark *Novelty*, hence for Sydney, was wrecked on Duke of Clarence Island [Nukunonu] on the 6th of July [1851], . . . and is a total loss. The Captain and three of the crew reached Upolu on the 30th of July, after being three days in a long boat. One of the men perished while attempting a passage through the surf. The vessel was sold at auction and the proceeds of the sale appropriated in defraying the expenses of the passengers to their destination. The consul despatched a vessel to the rescue of the passengers. (in Ward ed. 1967, 5:273–4)

Nukunonu stories recalling the event are more fulsome (see *Matagi Tokelau* 1991:79–80), telling of how the ship and its crew and passengers were discovered, how they were hosted and fêted, how one person drowned when he fell out of a canoe (to their astonishment he could not swim), how they helped to construct the vessel that carried the captain to Samoa, and how rusted iron from the vessel was used decades later to nourish newly planted coconut palms.

Linked to this story is another, telling of Hula's stay in Nukunonu. He made coconut oil by squeezing the oil from gratings with a huge, fine mesh net—or rather he got Nukunonu people to do it for him. He exploited Nukunonu resources and labour, promising the people a share of the proceeds when the casks of oil were sold in Samoa. However, Nukunonu people never saw him again, nor did they receive a cent for their labour and resources. What is most memorable, however, is that he took two young men, Takua and Poufou, with him to Samoa. Takua returned permanently ten years later and Poufou also came back, though only briefly.

Recall that the wrecked vessel had been sold for salvage and another vessel despatched to rescue the passengers. George Pritchard, who had bought the wreckage, engaged Hula to go to Nukunonu (probably because he was familiar with the people and their language from his months in Olohega) on his behalf aboard the rescue vessel to negotiate salvage of the ship. Little could be salvaged, but Hula nevertheless spent a profitable time in Nukunonu and returned to Samoa with not only two young Tokelau men but also some further intelligence about Tokelau. What happened thereafter is reported more fully by a Marist father (Padel n.d.:1 January to 10 February 1852) than in Tokelau annals or in later more tempered published mission accounts (Monfat 1890:304–10).

Immediately upon his return from Nukunonu on the first day of 1852, Hula was closeted with Bishop Bataillon for three hours, during which time they concocted a plot 'for transporting all the inhabitants of the Tokelau Islands who are dying from famine to Futuna where they may be taught and where they will have an abundant livelihood'. Hula's intelligence concerned a 'famine' at Fakaofo; the Nukunonu people whose resources he had plundered and who had provided generously for the stranded Europeans were certainly not 'dying of famine'. In any case, the Bishop was persuaded to pursue a plan to save the famished bodies and souls in Fakaofo, enlisting the services of Hula and undertaking to charter a vessel. Less than two weeks later, he had concluded a deal with the captain of the English barque *Kate*, whereby the vessel would first go to Uvea to take on supplies of coconuts and other victuals (to be levied from the Uveans) and then proceed to Fakaofo, in return for 500 piastres, which would be augmented if more than 500 persons were transported to Uvea at the rate of one piastre per head.[6]

The *Kate* left Apia on 15 January 1852 with Father Padel in charge of the expedition and Hula as deputy. The young Tokelau men, Takua and Poufou, whom Hula had brought to Samoa, joined the voyage to Uvea and stayed there, while four Tokelau men who had been at Uvea for some time (after landing there in 1846) joined the ship at Uvea as crew for the voyage to Tokelau. All went to plan until the ship reached Fakaofo on 9 February 1852. Father Padel stated his 'humanitarian' intention to the 'chiefs' and they replied 'that they would discuss the matter among themselves'. Their response was 'that they were not at all prepared to come aboard' the ship. The father and 'his sailor', Hula, could not accept this reply; the Bishop clearly intended that all the people should be shipped to Uvea. Therefore, 'it was necessary to employ some cunning to accomplish their final salvation'. First, some 'chiefs' were persuaded to go out to the ship, and when aboard were invited below deck to take refreshment, along with others who had gone out to the ship of their own accord. Once they were below the hatches were closed and the 'birds were trapped'. Then, Hula went ashore with members of the crew armed with weapons and 'a packet of phosphorus matches to set fire to their devil's houses . . . the final objective of the expedition'.

Ashore Hula directed a campaign of persuasion and intimidation, and set fire to the god-house and the mat wrappings around the stone in front of the god-house. The following morning, those ashore were rounded up, pushed and shoved aboard lighters and canoes, and transported out to the ship. The Fakaofo people did not leave their homeland willingly, and despite all their efforts, Padel and Hula had to leave ninety behind: 'old people who would not budge and a few young people to look after them.' But nearly 500 people did leave Fakaofo in the *Kate*. Tokelau chronicles refer to this event as *te umaga a Hula* 'the exodus of Hula' (Fakaofo n.d.) and identify Hula as 'the Frenchman who burnt the house of Tui Tokelau'.

The names of those taken away appear in the baptismal, marriage and death records of the Uvean parishes, but not many of them can be identified as the forebears of subsequent generations in Tokelau.[7] A few did return to Fakaofo, but most were buried sooner or later in Uvea and their part-Tokelau descendants are living there today (pers. comm. Th. B. Cook SM).

An anonymous visitor to Fakaofo in 1853 (*Nautical Magazine* 1861: 470–4) penned an account that is remarkable in light of the previous year's events. Internal evidence dates the account and its overall acuity testifies to its veracity. The writer noted that Fakaofo was the most populated atoll of the group, having 'fully one-half' of the estimated total Tokelau population of 500, and inferred that Fakaofo was the 'superior state and authority', citing the aloofness of the *aliki* 'surrounded by his counsellors—dignified old men'. Further, though the 'temple' of Tui Tokelau had been burnt, 'the presiding deity is so covered with votive offerings as to be quite obscure in form and feature'. Fakaofo still had the largest population, the principal *aliki* and 'the god of the group'. If indeed only ninety had been left behind the year before, as Padel reported, others obviously had returned or come to stay from other islands.

The actual length and severity of the Fakaofo famine are nowhere recorded. Hula and the Catholic missionaries made much of it, using it to justify another agenda. Undoubtedly Fakaofo had been suffering scarcity of land products for a number of years and so people in want went elsewhere.[8] Some of their voyages took people to Samoa and Uvea—the 1846 castaways certainly, the people who left Olohega in 1848 perhaps, and most certainly the reputed 500 people who were 'persuaded' to leave Fakaofo by Father Padel and Hula in 1852. Despite the recorded dispersal of the Fakaofo populace only a year later the atoll was well peopled, if not as fully as before.

The observations of this 1853 visitor are notable in another respect. He explicitly contrasts his reception and the general ambience of Atafu and Fakaofo, a contrast that replicates what is implied by the accounts of the US Exploring Expedition. The Atafu men were avid traders, gregarious, curious and expansive, and their *aliki* was hardly distinguishable from others and 'handled a paddle with the commonest, and was as eager to trade'. At Fakaofo, the *aliki* was clearly 'His Majesty' seated at the shore to receive his visitors, and the atmosphere was one of controlled formality. There was no hubbub of trade, only a silent exchange of gifts.

In 1860, another literate visitor (Hague 1868) described Atafu in much the same terms, but unfortunately his report ends: 'We visited the other islands of the group . . .; but our experience there was so much like that already related, that a detailed account would involve too much repetition'. However, he made a noteworthy observation at Atafu: a man there had a copy of the Bible in Samoan and claimed he had been sent as a missionary, though 'it did not appear that he had gained much, if any, influence among the people'. The visitor perhaps misjudged the situation, since accounts from other perspectives tell the story differently.

Arrival of the 'Good News'

When Captain Hudson of the US Exploring Expedition reached Apia after his Tokelau adventures in February 1841, he reported his Fakaofo 'discovery' to the members of the London Missionary Society, and urged them to visit the atoll (Hudson 1840–42, Mills 1841, LMS Samoan District 1841). Hudson argued that because Bowditch (Fakaofo) was the principal island and where the 'heathen idol' was located, the missionaries should direct their efforts there. Not until 1858, however, did the LMS missionaries visit Fakaofo, and they were rebuffed precisely because Fakaofo was the pre-eminent polity and sanctified place of Tui Tokelau. Hudson's advice and the mission's efforts were misdirected. Statements of Fakaofo's *aliki* and his spokesman, as reported by the missionaries, clearly indicate why (see below). But the missionaries persisted in their belief that it was from the 'principal island' of Fakaofo that the 'Good News' would spread to the other atolls. In the event, a Tokelau man is credited with introducing the 'Good News' to the atolls in both Tokelau and mission accounts (Murray 1868). His name was Faivalua and it was in Atafu that his message was received.

Faivalua's message: Faivalua was a young Fakaofo man who went to Olohega with several companions, having heard that the atoll was 'well stocked with provisions'. Upon their arrival they found 'white men' making coconut oil there. Some of their party remained at Olohega in the employ of the 'white men' and others went to Samoa. In Samoa, two of them learned the 'truths of the gospel, learned to read, and came . . . under the strong influence of the truth they had been taught'.[9] These two young men were Timoteo, who was later unsuccessful as a missionary teacher in Nanumanga and returned to Tokelau in the 1870s (Powell 1871a, Pratt 1872, Gill 1872), and Faivalua, who was 'the son of the principal chief of Fakaofo', and who returned to his homeland to 'introduce the Gospel'. At Fakaofo his message was not welcomed, so he went on to Atafu where the 'chief and people welcomed him, renounced heathenism and embraced Christianity. . . '. This is the mission version (Murray 1868).

According to Atafu stories, Faivalua 'brought the Good News' in 1858. The accounts do not say that his message was immediately embraced by all; however, his message was listened to, he held services with his wife's family, and in time his message prevailed and he later went to Samoa with a request from the Atafu *aliki* for a teacher. This was in 1861, so Faivalua was possibly the man with the Samoan Bible whom the 1860 visitor noted. It is not of great moment how quickly the Atafu people embraced the 'Good News', but it is significant that it was first preached in Atafu and people did listen.

The 'First Missionary Voyage' was to Fakaofo also in 1858, and was reported by the missionaries (Stallworthy 1858, Stallworthy and Gill 1859) and recorded in Fakaofo annals (Fakaofo n.d.). The missionaries included in their party a Samoan teacher and his wife, whom they hoped to establish in Fakaofo, and two young Tokelau men: Lea, who 'had been for some time a member of the church, and enjoyed the benefit of Malua Institution', and another deemed of 'less satisfactory character' (LMS Samoa District 1858). The missionaries were greeted as was usual by 'the king and his counsellors' seated near the landing place. They refused to accept the Samoan teacher, expressing 'fears that he will not find food; and they appear to have an apprehension that their *pule* [authority] may be interfered with' (Stallworthy 1858). A Fakaofo story (Fakaofo n.d.) relates that the rebuffed Samoan teacher reacted by flinging most of his belongings into the sea. An apt Samoan scripture is added: *Ia outou tutu atu le eleele na i outou vae* 'Shake off the dust under your feet' (Mark 6:11 'And whosoever shall not receive you, nor hear you, when ye depart thence, shake off the dust under your feet for a testimony against them'—King James Version).

The mission ship departed, taking the Samoan teacher, but leaving Lea and his compatriot who had been welcomed by the 'king and his counsellors'. They held Christian services at the shore, but attracted no audience, and soon left Fakaofo for Atafu.

The 'Second Missionary Voyage' to Tokelau was launched in 1861 in response to 'the urgent request of the chief and people of Oatafu [Atafu] . . . for a teacher', conveyed to Samoa by Faivalua (Gee 1861), but the missionaries still regarded Fakaofo to be their prime target—'being the most populous island, it was desirable to commence work here' (Ella 1861). The mission ship reached Fakaofo in November 1861 and aboard it were Maka, a Rarotongan teacher, Mafalā, a Samoan student at Malua, and 'three natives of Fakaofo, who had lived some eight years or more in Samoa'. The mission was rebuffed again; the returning Fakaofo people were welcomed, but not the outsiders—'Foringa [Foliga, the spokesman for the *aliki*, Likā] peremptorily ordered away the teachers'.

At Atafu the missionaries and teachers were welcomed. Foli, the 'chief', and many others immediately came out to the ship to greet them, Foli gave the teachers a house and promised to protect them and 'treat them kindly'. The situation was very promising, even though a large party (some 200) from Fakaofo were at Atafu building canoes, and they were less welcoming. The *aliki*'s son was among the Fakaofo party, and when urged to receive the teachers' message replied that 'he could not make any decision without his father'. The Atafu people had requested the teachers, but the Fakaofo people refused them. Nonetheless, the teachers were instructed to proceed to Fakaofo should they 'have intelligence that one of their number would be received . . .' (Ella 1861).

Maka's letters: Subsequent events are related in letters from Maka, the Rarotongan, to his missionary mentors in Samoa (Gee 1862) and in reports by Mafalā (Williams, J.C. 1863, Gill and Bird 1863, Bird 1863a). Maka first wrote 'that they had been prevented [from] building a chapel on account of the king's son from Fakaofo being there in order to cut trees for boat-building', but that the Atafu people met morning and afternoon with the teachers. About a month later he reported that some of the Fakaofo people 'were desirous of becoming acquainted with the good news of salvation but they feared the king of Fakaofo would be angry with them if they did so', and that the Atafu people had built houses for the teachers and had burned their idols. A few months passed and he reported that 'they had built their Chapel' and 'no less than 176 persons . . . come to them daily for instruction'. By now the Fakaofo party had returned to Fakaofo, and a letter dated the following month relates events in Fakaofo reported to Maka by Atafu people who had gone there with the Fakaofo party and returned. According to Maka's intelligence, the king of Fakaofo was very angry with the Atafu visitors for changing their religion and forbade them to pray in the village. Christians in Fakaofo were 'daily reviled' and people 'threatened to cut them to pieces with axes and then burn them asking if the god in whom they trust would be able to deliver them then'. Finally, it was rumoured that 'the King of Fakaofo intended to make war on Atafu because they have given up their idols, & received the Teachers'. The final sally was that the people of Fakaofo had said that 'from what they have seen of the Roman Catholic religion they like it better than ours because they do not condemn their old customs . . .'.

Mafalā's voyage: Though the threats of the Fakaofo *aliki* and people were not carried out, there was no evidence of any softening of their opposition to the mission. Nonetheless, Mafalā, accompanied by twenty-two Atafu men, including Foli, and an American named William, departed Atafu in early December 1862 to carry the 'Good News' to Nukunonu and Fakaofo.[10] At Nukunonu they discovered that the people had all accepted the Catholic faith (see below). The Atafu party stayed there a week, and apparently denominational differences were not a problem. Not so at Fakaofo. Likā at first seemed conciliatory, responding to Mafalā's question about his religion: 'I worship my land which yields me food', and thereby evading Mafalā's requests. Shortly thereafter, however, he 'issued a proclamation that whosoever embraced the Lotu of Jehovah *would get no food*' (emphasis in the original). Mafalā erroneously inferred from this statement that Likā controlled the distribution of all food. Some days later, two Atafu young men, in defiance or ignorance, collected clams (*fāhua*) and ate them. When this was discovered, they were summoned to the meeting house and beaten, and when Mafalā objected, he was told that clams are 'a fish sacred to Tui Tokelau the great god of the group' and the Fakaofo people were outraged that the Atafu youths had violated what was sacred to Tui Tokelau. This incident thoroughly compromised Mafalā's mission, and, as the Atafu party was preparing to depart, a further Fakaofo proclamation was made: '. . . all who wished to follow Jehovah must leave Fakaofo . . . all who wished to follow Jehovah were at liberty to go off to Atafu . . . all who live on Fakaofo must worship Tui Tokelau'.

Forty-six Fakaofo people joined Mafalā, the twenty-two Atafu converts, and one American on their return to Atafu. They sailed away in eight double canoes and reached Nukunonu easily. But between Nukunonu and Atafu they lost their bearing and became '"castaways" upon the wide waste of waters'. Two canoes separated from the rest, and Mafalā guided the six that stayed together, firm in his faith that God would preserve them. The others with him were not so certain and even Foli despaired: '"Mafalā *e*, I fear if we are lost, the heathen will rejoice and say their aitu (gods) destroyed us. They will say that their gods have triumphed over us and our Teacher, where was Jehovah to protect them? It was all lies about Jehovah. Tui Tokelau is the great & true god."' Mafalā's faith was sustained and Foli's fears were stilled, for after nine days at sea they arrived at Apia. (It was not known until some weeks later that the two other canoes had fetched up at Tutuila and Savai'i respectively; consequently these other castaways did not return to Tokelau immediately.)

The 'Third Missionary Voyage': Less than a week after their arrival in Apia, the Tokelau castaways were on their way back to Fakaofo in the company of two missionaries and two Samoan teachers, Mafalā and Sakaio, after having been exuberantly celebrated and handsomely gifted in Apia. From the missionary perspective, the voyage was a Christian victory; viewed from Fakaofo it was a disaster. On the fourth day at sea, 'a little boy died of dysentery' and five days later many were 'suffering from dysentery', but the mission vessel did not turn back. Even as the ship was in sight of Fakaofo, an elderly man died, at least the fourth victim of virulent bacillary dysentery. We cannot tell whether the missionaries had any qualms at the time or even considered Likā's request 'to tell the Fakaofo people we had brought back "To be sure to leave any disease they might have behind them on the mission vessel"'.[11] The missionaries of course knew that their passengers could not leave behind the infection, but nonetheless they landed them, for had they not done so they would have had to abort their mission of salvation. Bird, at least, did have second thoughts. Some months later he wrote that dysentery had 'raged with deadly violence' in Fakaofo, killing sixty-four people in three weeks, and that he had 'dreaded this from the moment we landed the diseased Fakaofoans . . .' (Bird 1863c).

After the castaways had 'told the thrilling story of their adventures' and the missionaries had attributed their good fortune to the goodness of God and the Protestant mission, the *aliki* and his advisers relented, and accepted the Samoan teacher, and so the way had been opened 'for the conversion of these poor heathens!' Again, the *aliki*'s spokesman, Foliga, had the last word: '"We wish to commence the new religion at once. But we have no lavalava (cloth). Now would you give us a lavalava apiece to start the new faith with?"'

Having finally succeeded at Fakaofo, the missionaries called at Atafu and Nukunonu. Atafu was portrayed as a model Christian community: all had embraced Christianity; the teacher was brimming with health, and was well housed and provided for; a fine wooden church had been built to hold 'the entire population who never failed to assemble at the sound of the gong'; the people were 'neatly and modestly attired' and most had learned to read.

Nukunonu, however, was labelled a 'dark island'—not heathen but Catholic—where no other Christian faith was tolerated. There was no church building, no books and no instruction in reading. The teacher was Takua who 'had been trained in Popish tactics in Wallis Island'.

The return of Takua: The story of how Nukunonu had come to embrace Catholicism has its beginnings in the escapades of Hula. Recall that when Hula left Nukunonu at the end of 1851, one of the young men he took with him was Takua, who then went with Hula and Father Padel to Uvea in the *Kate* but did not join the voyage to Fakaofo. He was baptised Justinum in the parish of Matautu, Uvea (Diocese of Wallis and Futuna) and trained as a catechist. Though not named, he was in fact one of two 'natives of Tokelau' being trained at Clydesdale (Sydney) in 1856 (Rocher 1856). Nukunonu people state unequivocally that Takua went to Australia and he was described by Father Poupinel as one of 'two well-tried young men, sons of influential chiefs of their country' (1882:167). Both of these young men—the other from Fakaofo—were taken by Bishop Bataillon to Fakaofo in 1861 to be catechists in their homeland, together with 'two good families of Tokelau origin'. The chronicler of this voyage (Poupinel 1882) wrote that the Bishop initiated the voyage in response to prayers of Tokelau converts in Uvea that their kinfolk left behind in Fakaofo should not 'die unbelievers'. As it turned out, those left behind had no intention of becoming believers. The people 'fed and fattened on coconuts' like pigs were 'of a stoutness such as I have not seen anywhere', wrote Poupinel, and further, they 'looked in a compassionate and pitying way at their compatriots who had come from Wallis . . . and asked them why they had been left to die of hunger'. The abundance those at Fakaofo now enjoyed was testimony of the beneficence of their god, Tui Tokelau, whose 'sacred stone [was] covered from top to bottom with the most beautiful mats in the land', whereas those arriving from Uvea who appealed to and believed in another god in a foreign land were obviously undernourished.

The *aliki* Likā, after deliberation with the chiefs, announced that those returning could stay 'on condition that they abandon the strangers' religion and live according to the customs of the land'. The Bishop would not accept this condition, though the converts pleaded to stay. The impasse was overcome when the *aliki* was persuaded to relent by the 'civil chief', whose 'son' was one of the converts, and, in turn, the Bishop allowed 'his Christians' to go ashore 'entrusted to divine Providence' upon the promise that they would not be required to abandon their faith.[12]

Tokelau stories and anecdotes tell of how these Catholic converts fared. They were indeed permitted to practise their faith in Fakaofo, but not within the village; they worshipped together on the *papa*, the reef-flat just north of the village. Perhaps they were the Christians who were being 'reviled and threatened', or maybe their behaviour prompted the Fakaofo people to state that they preferred the Roman Catholic religion 'because they do not condemn their old customs', as Maka wrote in 1862 (Gee 1862). In any case, they were a beleaguered minority.

Nukunonu's story of Takua's return is one of understated drama, marking the turning point of their history.

In 1861 Takua and others were sent from Uvea to bring the faith to Tokelau. Takua was assigned to be Nukunonu's teacher. Initially all of them were in Fakaofo. The Fakaofo converts in the dark of night gathered up discarded rubbish around the village and heaped it at the side of Tui Tokelau. In the morning it was suspected that they were the culprits and they were summoned for judgement. Their leader was Lua. They were severely scolded but not otherwise punished for their disrespect to Tui Tokelau.

Shortly thereafter, Takua came here. The very day of his arrival he said to his father: 'Hoifua, I have brought a religion with me.' Hoifua replied: 'What?' 'I have brought a religion that worships God from Uvea.' Hoifua quickly replied: 'That's fine. When evening comes we will gather the elders to make your thoughts known to them.' So that night Hoifua made his son's thoughts known to the elders. The elders' response was one of agreement and acceptance. Hoifua spoke again: 'When it is daylight let us go to the aliki's place.' So the elders rose in the morning and left for the aliki's *place, going directly there, they addressed the subject straight away: 'Hoifua's son has brought a religion to be set upon Nukunonu, a religion that worships God, not like the religion we practise now in heathen worship of Tui Tokelau.' The* aliki *too was agreeable to this. Ulua said: 'Fine, I will worship thus and so too will the whole village.' So that is the story of Nukunonu's commitment to the religion brought by Takua. From that time offerings to Tui Tokelau ceased. . . .*

Everyone in Nukunonu forthwith became Catholic and Takua was their teacher, and henceforth Nukunonu was closed to any other mission.

The politics of conversion

The foregoing story of the arrival and acceptance of Christianity has been presented as a relatively straightforward narrative based on Tokelau stories and annals, and European records. Both explain these events in terms of belief or faith, using the trope of 'the light' overcoming 'the darkness'. The missionaries speak of 'introducing the light of Christian truth' to 'poor benighted natives' (Stallworthy and Gill 1859), leading them 'from darkness to light' (Ella 1861), and following 'the light of divine teachings' (Monfat 1890). Tokelau people commonly speak of their conversion as the beginning of a new era, when they left *te pouliuli* 'the darkness' and entered *te malamalama* 'the light'. They do not explain their conversion in terms of politics, but they are not unaware of its political dimension, and these are readily apparent from other texts.

Conversion provided Nukunonu with a chance to reassert an old identity, and Atafu with a means of designing a separate one. Fakaofo rejected Christian overtures, aware that conversion would undermine the very basis of the Tokelau order they had created. Christian conversion began to 'undo' the overarching Tokelau polity.

By the mid 1850s a considerable number of Tokelau people abroad had been converted to Christian faiths, but probably none of them were residing in the atolls. In Uvea were the castaways of 1846 and those removed there in 1852, most of whom had become Catholic converts. A smaller number of Tokelau emigrants had reached Samoa and come under the influence of London Missionary Society teachings. Only a few of these overseas Tokelau Catholic and Protestant converts can be securely identified, namely those who returned sooner or later to Tokelau and are remembered as ancestors.

By the end of 1861, the three atolls, long politically united in an atoll empire and joined in worship of Tui Tokelau, were each worshipping differently. The Atafu people were meeting in prayer morning and afternoon with their Protestant teachers; the people of Nukunonu were being taught Catholic prayers by Takua; and in Fakaofo Tui Tokelau was still receiving offerings and prayers, though some people gathered at the shore to pray to another god.

Some reflection clarifies the politics of the 1861 situation. Nukunonu had long been subject to Fakaofo domination. Views differ about the exact nature of this subjugation, but on two points there is consensus: (i) Nukunonu annually sent offerings to Tui Tokelau in Fakaofo, and (ii) the Fakaofo *aliki* was overlord of Nukunonu and appointed a deputy there through whom Fakaofo exercised its *pule* 'rule' in Nukunonu. People obeyed the edicts of Fakaofo because they feared the wrath of Tui Tokelau and sent tribute to Tui Tokelau to ensure the god's blessings. Yet, while Nukunonu people acquiesced to the *pule* of Fakaofo, obeying the 'words' (*kupu*) that emanated from there, they still gave local precedence to the senior man of their indigenous *aliki* stock. When Takua returned in 1861, his father, Hoifua, was regarded by Nukunonu people to be their indigenous *aliki* and Ulua was there as the Fakaofo *aliki*'s appointed deputy. Now Ulua certainly had Nukunonu ancestry, but he was identified with Fakaofo, and he was not of local *aliki* stock. The Protestant missionaries judged Hoifua to be 'second in rank to the King', i.e., to Ulua, but at the same time they wrote: 'The real authority evidently rests exclusively with Takua, Oulua [sic] is *King only in name*' (Gill and Bird 1863).

Takua had returned to Nukunonu not only as a worldly-wise native son and Christian convert, but also as an *aliki* son and successor to his aged father. In Nukunonu accounts of conversion, Ulua does not hesitate to decree that all Nukunonu will henceforth be Catholic, though conversion obviously compromised his authority. He continued to be called 'king' by visitors and is referred to as *aliki* by Nukunonu sages, yet he is portrayed by foreigners as a jovial, comic character and discussed in Nukunonu with a good deal of ambivalence.[13]

In Nukunonu Takua is hero, his return the turning point in their history. As their teacher, he released them from obligations to Tui Tokelau. No longer would they send offerings to a heathen idol in Fakaofo. As their spiritual leader, he had the stature of a revered *aliki* and, even if he was not formally designated *aliki* for several decades, his very presence reasserted the pre-eminence of the indigenous *aliki*. It was through him that Nukunonu claimed its independence from Fakaofo authority, in the first instance by espousing Christianity. And through him too Nukunonu articulated its representation of its place in the wider Tokelau polity.

Takua's father's father's sister was the founding mother of Atafu, consequently he, the embodiment of Nukunonu's indigenous *aliki* stock, was categorically the 'mother's brother' of Atafu. In addition, his *aliki* ancestors before him were allied to Fakaofo by the unions of their sisters and daughters with Fakaofo men, all following the 'path' of Nau, and therefore Fakaofo too harboured his sisters' children. Even Olohega could be included in this subaltern logic of relationships that represents Nukunonu as the categorical 'mother's brother' of all Tokelau. This, of course, did not (and does not) equate with Fakaofo's relational logic that privileges agnatic links and seniority. Nonetheless, Nukunonu could privilege its own representations and maintained its own logic of its relations with Fakaofo based upon enduring bonds of kinship rather than an imposed bondage of conquest. Of course, changes in the relationship of Fakaofo and Nukunonu did not happen in a moment, nor were they uncontested, as will become apparent.

Atafu had been settled as a colony or outpost of Fakaofo only a half century or so before Faivalua arrived. Tonuia, the founding father of Atafu, had been directed by Fakaofo's *aliki* to stay in Atafu as leader of the nascent polity, but before long he challenged the power of Fakaofo by transgressing a prohibition, and retribution was supernatural and swift. This version of the story was noted in Nukunonu (for Atafu versions, see Macgregor 1937:61, *Matagi Tokelau* 1991:44).

> *Before Tonuia left Fakaofo to settle Atafu, he was warned not to fell the bush of Togaleleva, meaning the* kānava *trees at the site of the ancient village at the Koko o Vao. When Tonuia transgressed this prohibition it was at once known afar in Fakaofo. When he voyaged there, not a word was said about what he had done. But upon his return, he encountered two female spirits at sea who capsized his canoe. He clambered upon the overturned hull and cried in despair.*
>
> > *Only now I know my punishment—only I felled the bush of Togaleleva Fakaofo stands apart—its censure is bitter, is harsh.*
>
> *Tonuia disappeared at sea.*

Many of the elders of Atafu in 1861, including the chief Foli, were Tonuia's grandchildren. Atafu was a young and growing community, established and augmented by Fakaofo people, and Fakaofo regarded Atafu as an extension or outpost, subordinate as younger is to older, and continued to exploit its resource of *kānava* timber.

Yet Atafu was not a wholly subservient, dependent polity—witness Tonuia's unfortunate challenge. Atafu had developed its own character and was asserting its separate identity. The reported encounters of early visitors with Atafu and Fakaofo people attest to this contrasting character. At Atafu the people were curious and acquisitive, open and informal, most unlike their hostile and aggressive, and later staid and formal 'brothers' in Fakaofo.

A story, set at the time of Faivalua's arrival, encapsulates Atafu's new identity *vis-à-vis* Fakaofo and can be read as the statement of transformation of political authority (for a fuller version see *Matagi Tokelau* 1991:82).

Apprised that Christianity had taken hold in Atafu, the Fakaofo aliki *despatched a voyaging party led by his son, Loaloa, to Atafu. En route a prophetic female spirit appeared to Loaloa in the night, telling him that he would not succeed in reaching Atafu and repeatedly urging him to turn back. He ignored her words, and the voyagers repeatedly criss-crossed the central Pacific without glimpsing Atafu—again and again the atoll 'slipped past them'—and their canoe finally disappeared in the ocean wastes.*

Tonuia's disregard for the words of Fakaofo *aliki* and punishment by avenging female spirits is inverted in the story of an *aliki*'s son who heeds the words of Fakaofo but disregards the warnings of the prophetic female spirit. The power of the Christian message is greater than that of Fakaofo's *aliki*, and Atafu has gone its own way. The two narratives are mythic constructions, perhaps motivated by historic disappearances, and together they highlight a historical transformation. The theme appears again in Mafalā's story of the 1861 castaways, when Foli, in doubt, despairs: '. . . the heathen will rejoice and say their aitu (gods) destroyed us. . . . It was all lies about Jehovah. Tui Tokelau is the great & true god.' Again, Jehovah prevails, and in this story the voyagers do not disappear.

Atafu's distinctive history begins when they listen to the message of Faivalua. Fakaofo's 'rule' in Atafu was not predicated on conquest; it was simply given because categorically as a younger or junior sibling Atafu was naturally expected to obey and support Fakaofo as its elder or senior. Atafu people had no autochthonous heritage, no intrinsic distinctive identity, to reassert—so they had to create one, and this they did by accepting Faivalua's message. In so doing they challenged the authority of their Fakaofo 'brothers', because they would worship Jehovah and no longer give offerings or pray to Tui Tokelau.

The centre of all Tokelau was Fakaofo, where the *aliki* reigned and where the embodiment of Tui Tokelau stood. Fakaofo's *aliki ma faipule* repeatedly rejected the overtures of all Christian missionaries, and with good reasons: their pre-eminence and their livelihood would be jeopardised. Fakaofo's authority was sanctioned by Tui Tokelau as well as legitimated by ancient conquest, and as Stallworthy reported in 1858, they had 'an apprehension that their *pule* may be interfered with'. Tui Tokelau too was the font of *manuia* 'blessings', of abundance from the sea and land, of prosperity and well-being. Prayers and offerings were addressed to the god in appreciation of 'blessings' given and to ensure 'blessings' to come. The return of a few of their compatriots who had been wrested away and 'left to die of hunger' in Uvea served to confirm these beliefs.[14]

However in spite of these good reasons for rejecting Christianity, Christian converts were tolerated in Fakaofo and even welcomed back, and no definitive steps were taken by Fakaofo to counter conversion in Nukunonu and Atafu. This was in large part because the Tokelau polity was both dominated by Fakaofo and linked by kinship. Wherever they resided most people had both Fakaofo and Nukunonu forebears, and all regarded some residents of other atolls as kinsfolk. While Tokelau commentators readily acknowledge that there may be discord and dissension among kin, they categorically assert that 'kinsfolk do not wage war', and that kinship, in the end, necessarily entails *alofa* 'compassion'. Thus, in principle, though the Fakaofo *aliki ma faipule* had the means to compel converts who returned from abroad to abandon their new faith, their determination to do so was constrained because the people returning were inevitably kin to some of them, and people of their collective land. This was their dilemma, even as the *aliki ma faipule* became increasingly less tolerant.

Between 1858 and 1861 at least eleven adult Christian converts returned to Fakaofo in mission ships, and others must have returned by other routes. All were welcomed back, at least all accounts report that they were, because they had ancestral ties to the land and people of Fakaofo. In only one reported instance were converts accepted 'on condition'; and this incident of 1861 is particularly telling. Initially, Likā told the bishop that the converts returned from Uvea could stay only if they 'abandon the strangers' religion and live according to the customs of the land'. However, in the end Likā relented at the urgings or insistence of the 'civil chief' whose 'son' was to disappear again (see note 12). Even when these converts provocatively heaped rubbish beside the stone of Tui Tokelau, they were only verbally chastised.

There are no accounts of the reaction in Fakaofo to Nukunonu's swift conversion. Neither mission knew of this for well over a year, but Fakaofo surely did. Takua had gone to Nukunonu from Fakaofo and subsequently no offerings were sent to Fakaofo for Tui Tokelau. Of the Fakaofo reaction to Atafu's conversion, there are several stories. The story of Loaloa's futile search for Atafu is posited upon Fakaofo knowing of Faivalua's success and seeking to intervene; the account of the 1861 mission voyage mentions no opposition from Fakaofo to teachers being placed in Atafu; and the Fakaofo canoe-builders who were at Atafu—some 200 of them including Likā's son—did not overtly interfere with the teachers' activities. Surely, 200 Fakaofo people could have prevented the reported 140 Atafu people from meeting with the teachers twice daily. Reports by Atafu men who accompanied the Fakaofo party back to Fakaofo (related by Maka, in Gee 1862) indicate that the *aliki*'s tolerance of Christianity was waning. Yet if Likā was angry, the Christians converts in Fakaofo 'reviled' and 'threatened', and war on Atafu rumoured, the only authoritative action reported was that the converts, both Catholic and Protestant, were forbidden to pray in the village. By prohibiting Christian worship within the village, the Fakaofo *aliki ma faipule* asserted their authority and that authority apparently was not challenged. Thus the Fakaofo dilemma was resolved—for a time.

In late 1862, when Mafalā and twenty-two Atafu converts visited Fakaofo in an attempt to persuade Likā to accept a teacher, the *aliki* took a more determined stand. First, 'that whosoever embrace the Lotu of Jehovah *would get no food*', and later that 'all who embrace the lotu of Jehovah must leave Fakaofo', and 'were at liberty to go off to Atafu', while at Fakaofo everyone 'must worship Tui Tokelau' (Williams 1863, Bird 1863a). It would appear that the *aliki ma faipule* saw no way of preventing people from worshipping

Jehovah, and were resigned to Atafu's conversion. Fakaofo, however, could expel the Christians and the difficulties they engendered for Fakaofo, so that even though Tokelau was not united in the worship of Tui Tokelau, Fakaofo would be.

Among the Fakaofo people who left for Atafu were Likā's younger brother and Foliga's son. The missionaries interpreted their departures as defections, but there is a more plausible interpretation. Even if people in Atafu no longer worshipped Tui Tokelau, they were still part of the Fakaofo-dominated Tokelau polity. How better might the *aliki* and his principal spokesman monitor the situation in Atafu than by having their brother and son residing there as their respective representatives. Their juniors might worship the Almighty, but they would still loyally support and obey their senior kinsmen.

The incident of the 'sacred clams' is the only recorded instance of violence during this period of contestation. Recall that two young Atafu men collected and ate clams, and were beaten by outraged Fakaofo people. Though the two were young, they surely knew the clams 'were sacred to Tui Tokelau', so this was an act of youthful rashness, if not defiance. Youth who flaunt the authority of their elders could expect to be beaten. The Fakaofo people may well have been particularly outraged because the youths were Atafu Christians, but the punishment inflicted upon them is unexceptional in Tokelau terms.

The final resolution of the Fakaofo *aliki ma faipule* was not tested, for the worshippers of Jehovah did not reach Atafu. About a month later they were back at Fakaofo aboard the Protestant Mission ship. They and two Samoan teachers were allowed to remain and Christianity became a presence in Fakaofo. Mafalā optimistically told the missionaries upon the ship's return from Atafu and Nukunonu that 'no more offerings of food shall be made to Tui Tokelau', and the missionaries rejoiced when Foliga told them 'to tell the priests nevermore to trouble the natives of Fakaofo'. Neither of these statements was borne out by subsequent events, as will be seen.

What caused the *aliki ma faipule* to change their mind in January 1863, only a month after they had rid their immediate domain of all Christian converts? This turnabout was not motivated simply by their 'compassion' for their people who had been cast adrift after being expelled from their homeland; nor presumably did they believe the missionaries' claim that the voyagers had been saved by Jehovah — although the missionaries attributed their change of heart to both.

The Tokelau views of the world must have changed radically during the previous decade or so; Christian conversion is only the best-documented manifestation of that change. The comings and goings of both Tokelau and foreign persons to and from the atolls which have been recounted and documented here, certainly do not represent all of their cross-cultural encounters, and the impact of these encounters on Tokelau perceptions is nowhere detailed. What did they think about the foreigners in their midst? What did they learn from them? What did those who returned tell their compatriots about their adventures abroad; how did they explain what they had heard, seen and done? We may infer that a tremendous amount of new information was discussed and many new ideas were entertained in the atolls.

The reactions of Tokelau people varied according to their knowledge and perception of the world beyond, and their local concerns. Different motivations have been attributed to the three atoll communities in their reception of the Christian message, and these have necessarily been presented as uniform. Surely there were differences of opinion among the Fakaofo *aliki ma faipule* in the early 1860s, and the seemingly sudden turnabout in Fakaofo may have been no more than a change in the balance of opinion.

Foliga in 1858 asked the first missionary visitors 'if [they] had presents for the "aliki"' (they did not) and suggested the people might build a house for a teacher if the mission ship was 'quite full of property' (Stallworthy and Gill 1859) — a statement not very different from his last word to the missionaries in 1863, requesting 'a lavalava apiece to start the new faith with'. This time the missionaries at least 'delivered a few trifling presents', but these would have paled beside the goods the castaways had been gifted with in Samoa— estimated to have been worth 'about 100 stg.' (Gill & Bird 1863). More generally, people had bartered for or been gifted with foreign goods for decades. They knew how coconut oil was produced and sold for goods or money, though apart from Hula's brief oil-producing venture in Nukunonu there probably had not yet been any export of this commodity except from Olohega, where an American, Ilai/Eli Jennings, was settled, claiming the island as his own and employing Tokelau labour (see Hooper 1975).[15] Then there was William, the American who left Atafu with Mafalā in 1862 and did not return, who had been trading in Atafu. Traders were tolerated, if not welcomed, for the goods that they could provide. Christianity, particularly Protestantism, required that its converts be 'neatly and modestly attired', which in turn required imported cloth. All this had a bearing on the attitudes in Fakaofo, especially when the voyagers returned from Samoa displayed all the goods they had received; and Foliga's request is an indication of the benefits that Fakaofo *aliki ma faipule* expected by accepting the teachers. Having received a foreign faith, Tokelau was poised to engage the marketplace. But then commerce of a different sort made a sudden catastrophic impact on the atolls.

Taken into Slavery: February 1863

Faleata was a madwoman. . . . Despite her madness, everyone attended to her prophecies and her prophecies always came to pass; they are recalled in each generation. . . . She would shout out prophetic pronouncements as if she were of clear-mind and far-seeing that were difficult for people of her time to believe. This was part of her madness. One day she stood and shouted mightily as follows: 'Ten ships shall arrive from beyond the horizon and carry away a part of the village. There will be struggles that will carry away another part of the village.'

—Fakaofo n.d.

Faleata's prophecy is said to have foretold the coming of the *vaka kaihohoa tagata* 'people-stealing ships' (henceforth, following H.E. Maude [1981], referred to as 'slave ships'). Tokelauans today still tell stories of how the 'slave ships' took their forebears captive, either by enticing them into the hold and slamming shut the hatches, or by rounding them up on land with swords and guns and fierce dogs. From their perspective they are telling of a brief but calamitous episode of their past.

H.E. Maude's definitive study of this episode of Pacific history was published in 1981. His work has been invaluable to us, allowing us to place the evidence from and about Tokelau in a wider framework. Not wishing to reproduce what Maude has written about the 'slave ships' in Tokelau (see his chapter 7), we draw upon Tokelau narratives written and told many years after the events, and juxtapose them to his account. The fit is quite extraordinary.

Four 'slave ships' were active in Tokelau for only a couple of weeks in February 1863 and thirty-two ships all told were in the Pacific for less than a year. In Tokelau as in the other remote, small islands, where they sought their human cargo and where there were no Europeans resident to report their activities, they had devastating effect, 'recruiting' in all 3634 people— 253 of them from Tokelau (Maude 1981: Table 6).

The ships that converged on Tokelau in February 1863 had left Callao off the coast of Peru the previous December and may have arranged to rendezvous there. One of them, the *Rosa Patricia*, had paused for a day or so outside Apia harbour and its supercargo made no secret of the ship's past activities or future plans. He was seeking a guide for Tokelau and was directed to Ilai at Olohega.[16] Missionaries urged the consuls in Apia to do something, but the consuls possibly had no inclination and certainly had little means to do anything (Gee 1863a). Ironically, the LMS ship *John Williams*, just then taking up its aborted schedule upon its triumphal return from Tokelau, departed Apia simultaneously with this 'slave ship'. W.W. Gill on board the *John Williams* saw the ship 'about five miles from us, and right on our track', but later the two ships went their separate ways: the *John Williams* continued east to visit the northern Cook Islands, which had already been ravaged by two other 'slave ships' that were about to appear in Tokelau; the *Rosa Patricia* turned 'to the North, as we suppose for the Tokelau or Union group', noted Gill (1863).

The *Rosa Patricia* was the first ship to reach Tokelau, making Fakaofo on 12 February, just ten days after the *John Williams* had departed, reaching Atafu on 16 February, and probably calling at Nukunonu on the way. By the tactic of trapping 'recruits' in the hold, the ship took fifty-seven adult men. The other ships, two sailing west together from the northern Cooks and one coming north directly from Niue, were not far behind. The two from the west, the *Rosa y Carmen* and *Micaela Miranda*, were at Atafu on 18–19 February and proceeded southward to Nukunonu and Fakaofo, altogether taking 136 people, seventy-six of them women and children, by rounding them up on land. The ship direct from Niue probably went straight to Nukunonu, bypassing Fakaofo and getting there first and gaining, quite easily, sixty prime 'recruits'. Three of the ships left Tokelau waters straight for Callao; the other, *Rosa y Carmen*, diverted to Tutuila to take on water, and dropped in elsewhere, including Sunday Island (see Maude chapter 15 for this appalling tale). The ships that took captives from Fakaofo also took aboard virulent dysentery introduced from Samoa by the mission ship. This disease spread rapidly among the confined human cargo and the number of deaths from the disease exceeded the number of Tokelauans 'recruited'.

For Tokelau the depredations of the 'slavers' were catastrophic. Maude calculates that 47 per cent of the population vanished. How did the people act at the time and react immediately after? From each of the atolls there are accounts, a few first-hand and many told from generation to generation.

The Fakaofo manuscript account, written many years later, gives the inside story in detail and in most respects confirms Maude's reconstruction of the sequence of events based primarily on P.G. Bird's letter (1863c). We paraphrase it, parenthetically juxtaposing Maude's account.

> *When the ships came to Fakaofo, an American named Peni was already there as a trader for the German Company in Samoa,*[17] *and so were the two pastors, Mafalā and Sakaio. From the first ship some Europeans came ashore to Peni's house and told him to inform the village to go aboard the ship to trade because there were untold goods there which would be traded for anything. So some men went aboard and the captain told them all to go into the hold to do their trading. Most of the men were thus tricked into the hold and trapped there, at the same time the lines attaching their canoes to the ship were severed. Those still on the deck of the ship leapt into the sea. Ship's boats were lowered and pursued them. Only three managed to reach a canoe and escape to shore.* [This ship was the *Rosa Patricia* which captured sixteen men. The Fakaofo account contradicts the Bird account in the manner of their capture, and is more plausible. Only the first ship could use the 'goods in the hold' ploy and this ship used it in Atafu as well.]
>
> *Two ships together came next but left without taking anyone when Peni said that no one remained because all had already been taken.*[18] [Maude, relying on Mafalā via Bird, had no record of these unsuccessful callers. They could have been the two ships coming from Atafu making an initial foray. If so, they were not convinced by Peni.] *The next ship seemed to accept Peni's word too, sailing off towards Nukunonu and Atafu, but when the captain discovered that many men were away from the village cutting copra, the ship immediately reversed its course. When the copra-cutters returned to the village, the crew came ashore with nets and with the aid of fierce dogs herded most of the people into the nets. 'It was just like the dispersal of Israel by the Assyrians because of their disobedience to God and his Prophets.'*[19] *When the ship departed only Foliga and some few other men remained, together with the women.* [These ships were the two from the northern Cooks. They took forty-four men.] *Soon thereafter yet another ship came, and since no others were left took away Foliga and most of the women. Some ran off and hid. A few hid in Peni's house, and only they escaped. Of the men only Tenaka, Galu and Lea remained.* [This was the *Micaela Miranda* which returned to take off women and children—seventy-six of them—and gained four more men as well. All these captives were transferred to the *Rosa y Carmen*. To the list of who remained should be added the *aliki* Likā.]

The account goes on to relate that the second-to-last ship, i.e., the *Rosa y Carmen*, went to Tutu'ila where the captain offloaded the 'weak bodied [sick?] men' (*tagata tino vaivai*), among them Tui Apelaamo, Tetaulu, Vaiala and Vaopuka, all of whom returned to Fakaofo. Maude via Bird (1863c) via these men reports this incident more fully. They were put ashore to conciliate the Samoans who recognised the nature of the vessel and refused to allow it to take on water. Some of those released were sick and died of dysentery shortly after. Bird's letter and the Fakaofo text give different counts. Bird writes that six men were put ashore and three of them died; the local text lists four survivors, all of whom figure in subsequent local events—two become Fakaofo *aliki*. This suggests that it may have been rank more than illness that brought them freedom, given that they were released to appease the Samoans.

Altogether Maude calculates that Fakaofo lost 137 people to the 'slavers' (140 minus the three who returned) after having lost at least sixty-four in the mission-imported dysentery epidemic. Less than sixty Fakaofo people remained on the atoll: six men, thirty women and twenty-four children, not counting Peni and the two Samoan teachers and their wives.

In contrast to the Samoan teachers in Fakaofo, who apparently took no noticeable role in the whole episode and who left by different routes shortly thereafter, Maka, the Rarotongan teacher in Atafu, was very active, both in protecting his flock and in reporting what happened. His several letters to the missionaries in Samoa are poignant, heart-rending descriptions of what transpired, and were widely quoted and published to galvanise public opinion and persuade the British government to take action to end 'the melancholy and execrable traffic' (Bird 1863b). We quote selectively from translations of Maka's letters. The first dated 16 February 1863 (enclosure in Gee 1863b, see also *Sydney Morning Herald*: 5 June 1863 and *Weekly Review and Messenger*: 13 June 1863) describes the activities of the first ship (which would be the *Rosa Patricia* by Maude's account) and was written on the day of the event.

> Our land is in a very bad state. All the men have been taken away in a foreign vessel. It was the ship of the Roman Catholic Bishop. When the ship was near the land a boat was lowered & the crew came off to barter with us. The Captain of the ship said to me let the people take Cocoanuts and Fowls to the ship & sell them & they shall receive in exchange for them cloth, shirts & trousers. I said to him you had better come on shore and buy, and he replied I do not like bartering on shore; it is far better in the vessel. . . . Teacher they have taken away all the men from this island. They have taken the chief [Foli] that was in Samoa and 34 others beside. We have only women and children here with the exception of six men. . . When the natives reached the vessel the Captain bid them all go on deck and look at the barter goods, but this was a contrivance of the Captain of the ship. Some of the barter goods were placed in the cabin [hold] of the ship. There was fine cloth, red cloth, shirts, trousers, white cloth, and dark cloth. There were also some goods placed on deck. The Captain then said to the natives go and examine the goods on deck & those also below in the cabin. When they saw the fine cloth in the cabin they all went to look at it. The Captain then called to them & when every one had gone below, one of the crew clothed them all, giving to each a shirt, a pair of

trousers, and a hat. The natives were highly delighted at this and said to one another we have got clothing to go to Chapel with now. . . . At the time there was not one native on deck with the exception of the chief of this island who was sitting up there. He arose and called to his people saying do not stay any longer below lest you spoil the goods of the white men. When he said this he was standing at the door [hatch] of the cabin, & the crew of the vessel rushed upon him & pushed him down below & shut the door immediately. . . . The ship then quickly sailed away. There is nothing we can do here now on account of the crying and wailing because our land is wasted.[20]

Later letters (probably three of them addressed to different missionaries, e.g. Bird 1863b) were all written some ten days after the first. They repeat, expand upon and on some points contradict the first letter, and report on the second appearance of the ships at Atafu.

. . . then we saw another vessel—a two-masted vessel. It came near, the boat was lowered and the Captain came ashore to my house. . . . Then said the Captain to me, give me the other men and you shall be paid. I replied there are not men left all were taken away by the other ship. He said again give me men, I replied—there are not men, only women here. Our conversation was not finished when I saw another strange vessel with 3 masts. It was near dark then, and the Captain returned to the ship and said to me we shall return to take men. . . . That night we heard the noise of foreigners on the beach—the boats of the other ship. . . . In the morning the boats returned to the ship & then came ashore two boats. . . . The Captain said to me, go seek for men to go in the ship. When you have the men then you shall be paid in money. Then he put 4 gold shillings in my hand and said he would bring lots of clothes when I brought two or three men. Then I said—I don't desire this money & goods to sell men. I don't rule over them. Then he said—Come you go off with me to the ship to Fakaofo & Nukunonu to seek men, then we shall return and land you—I replied I shall not go, and throw up my work—Then he persisted saying—'you go'—but I said I shall not go. Then he asked, is there no teacher there. I said 'There are two teachers there'—Then he said, Write you a letter to the Teachers to seek men to be taken off by the ship. Then I wrote as follows. 'The Captain of this vessel is about to go to you two; to seek men. There is not man left in our land. Do as you please in the matter you and the chiefs.' When finished I put the letter in his hand. [original punctuation and syntax]

Maka's letters are understandably somewhat frantic and not always clear and consistent, yet several matters regarding the second appearance of the 'slave ships' in Atafu may be confidently inferred: (i) there were two ships together and they had come from the northern Cooks; (ii) Maka insisted that there were no men to be taken despite threats and attempted bribery, though 'two lads' were captured in the end—which brought the total taken from Atafu to thirty-seven; and (iii) Maka wrote a letter warning the two teachers in Fakaofo, which was not delivered there but in Nukunonu.

First-hand accounts of the 'slave ships' at Nukunonu are all but absent. Catholic records are vague and contradictory, and from unidentified verbal reports, Bird (1863b) wrote: 'Five Slavers had been there. . . . The first took off 60 people, the second six and the third ten leaving about 20 people in the land.' Fortunately, there are numerous oral narratives about the 'slave ships' and central to Nukunonu accounts is the delivery of Maka's letter to Takua. The following is a manuscript collectively composed by the elders of Nukunonu in July 1977, 114 years after the events.[21]

The first slave ship came here by way of Fakaofo. It took away a large number of the able men. Another day another ship arrived here from Atafu. It took away another large number of adult men and also women. That ship brought a letter to Takua from the Rarotongan teacher at Atafu, who directed the white-men to the person who brought the Faith to Nukunonu. So the white-men came and handed the letter to Takua. Takua read it, it was he himself who brought the Faith here and he immediately disappeared to Vao and hid there with a large number of men and young women. Still others swam out and sat upon the coral-heads in the lagoon. There is the coral-head known as Mele and Vaka, for that pair were taken by the slave ship. The name of the Pastor who sent that letter to Takua was Maka. . . . After that slave ship left, Takua went to the aliki Ulua and said to him that a voyage should be made to Samoa to appeal to the Bishop to save these Lands from total depopulation by the depredations of slave ships. Ulua replied: 'Fine, let us prepare the canoes and, as soon as that is done, the voyagers will depart immediately.' The village was called together and the decision of the aliki made known: A voyage must be undertaken to inform the Bishop in Samoa about the disaster that has befallen Tokelau. Tasks were quickly assigned: older men went and readied the canoes, women filled coconut shell containers with fresh water, and young men harvested provisions for the journey. As soon as the canoes were ready the aliki was informed and the voyagers prepared to depart. There were two canoes: the canoe of the Ulua and the canoe of Takua. . . . For three weeks the voyagers were at sea. They fetched up at Savai'i, at the district known as Faga, and people gathered at the shore thinking they were castaways. Ulua told Takua to stand up and announce that they were not castaways. So Takua stood and shouted that they were purposeful voyagers come straight to Samoa. The aliki of the place called out to them to rest there and they came quickly to shore, dragging their canoes inland. When three or four days had passed, Ulua appealed to the village: 'Please excuse us for our party wishes to go to Apia to take our message to the Bishop.' He explained to the chiefs of the village the intent of their journey and they replied: 'Very well, but let us prepare some provisions for the journey, and why not leave your canoes here and we will transport you all in the long-boat.' And so it was that they left their canoes and travelled in the long-boat. They stayed at Vaiusu and from there walked to Mulivai where they informed the Bishop, Monseigneur Enosi [Bataillon], of the disaster that had befallen the islands of Tokelau through the depredations of the slave ships. The Bishop responded that he would think of a way to stop the slave ships. He wrote at once to the British Monarch to please take note that the Tokelau isles were being completely depopulated by the Spanish Government. A letter received in reply from Britain said that the Spanish Government had already been instructed that they were forbidden to despatch any further ships to take people from Tokelau. So it all abruptly ended that very year. Never again did a slave ship come to Tokelau. From slavery the Tokelau isles were saved. If it had not been for that voyage to Samoa perhaps the Tokelau people would have been completely dispersed to the far reaches of the Spanish Empire.

Other Nukunonu accounts tell the familiar story of men being enticed into the first ship's hold and trapped there, and one tells how Takua saved Ulua from being taken by trickery. By Maude's count based on Bird, seventy-six persons, both men and women, were taken from Nukunonu, leaving an estimated sixty-four, which would have been further reduced when the voyagers left for Samoa.[22]

How did the people remaining imagine what had happened? Apart from Maka's frantic letters, there is no account of what they thought. Local stories of the episode have gradually changed character over the years. Though people still speak of the horror of the events, of how people were lured below decks by the promise of trade goods and trapped, of how people were threatened with swords and fierce dogs, the tragedy has also been transformed into farce. The 'slave ships' are a well-worn theme for *faleaitu* 'comic skits' in which the star performers are older women. In Nukunonu these performances have been a regular feature of New Year celebrations. The actors blacken their faces, arms and legs with a mixture of charcoal and kerosene, and don men's trousers and shirts. Their ship is outlined by a stout rope and in it they travel through the village taking prisoners. The performance is ad hoc and slapstick; there is much pushing, shoving, wrestling and tumbling, and many hilarious and improper gestures and phrases.

Aftermath

After the 'slave ships' had disappeared with their captives, the dysentery epidemic had taken its toll in Fakaofo, and the Nukunonu voyagers had set off for Samoa, very few people remained in Tokelau. Taking as a baseline Gill and Bird's population estimates of January 1863, the number of Tokelauans in each atoll a month later were: Fakaofo 57, Nukunonu 45, and Atafu 103. However, there were quite a few Tokelau people elsewhere who would return: the twenty-one castaways of late 1862 whose canoes had separated from the rest and landed in Tutu'ila and Savai'i, the four surviving Fakaofo men who had been put off the *Rosa y Carmen* at Tutu'ila, the nineteen Nukunonu voyagers to Samoa, at least six Tokelau Catholic converts from Uvea, and Ilai's Tokelau workers at Olohega (four couples and their children). Many of them returned to their homelands in the later months of 1863, so that by the end of the year the populations were a good deal larger: Fakaofo nearly 100, Nukunonu close to seventy and Atafu about 110.[23]

An unidentified ship must have been at Atafu shortly after the February debacle to have conveyed Maka's letters of alarm and distress (Gee 1863b, Bird 1863b), and another must have returned from Tokelau early in the last week of May after taking back the castaways who landed at Tutu'ila and Savai'i, because Mafalā departed on it and Bird reports that he had been back 'several days' in his letter of 29 May. Therefore, this vessel was other than the one on which Father Elloy sailed, departing Apia 9 May and returning 29 May. Elloy's letters (1863) and published report (1879) provide little information,[24] so it is other sources, mainly several Tokelau texts pieced together, which document who arrived, who left and what transpired.

At Nukunonu nobody was in evidence; Elloy 'found the islet deserted—

Monseigneur Louis Elloy, Titular Bishop of Tipasa, voyaged to Nukunonu and Fakaofo several times between 1863 and 1875, but unfortunately provided very little information about his visits— preoccupied as he was with their discomforts. Regrettably, he even neglected to record the baptisms he performed during these visits. Reproduced from Mangeret 1932:213

not a soul left on it,' wrote the Protestant missionary Bird (1863c). Neither Elloy nor Bird knew of the Nukunonu voyagers who had by that time probably reached Samoa, nor did they suspect that the people who remained had taken refuge on the eastern side of the atoll (across the lagoon from the village). In Nukunonu the tale is told of how Falekie and Telakau, who had joined the Fakaofo canoe that had been castaway and ended up at Uvea seventeen years before, were with Elloy and were left at Nukunonu. They found their compatriots in their hideout, but they were not immediately welcomed. At their approach, people ran off, thinking from their dress that they were foreign intruders intent on taking them away too.

Elloy named none of his fellow passengers, but evidence indicates that this vessel brought a number of people to Tokelau. Elloy was escorting several Catholic converts back to their homelands: at least four Fakaofo men, including Likā's son Tefono, as well as the two Nukunonu men. Atone, a trader for Godeffroy und Sohn (known as the German Firm—later the Deutsche Handels-und-Plantagen-Gesellschaft) in Apia, probably arrived on this ship too. These arrivals to Fakaofo joined a community depleted of mature people, particularly men, with the exception of the old *aliki* Likā.

Although the old *aliki* had permitted the Protestant teachers to begin their work, he himself had remained pagan, giving up none of his prerogatives. Indeed, Elloy noted that Tui Tokelau was 'draped with mats and coconuts' (Elloy 1879), and judged that Fakaofo was still heathen, as it well may have been except for Lea and perhaps a few others. The reluctance of the *aliki* and others to accept Christian teachings may have had something to do with the presence of Peni (Ben), as the following Tokelau text suggests.

After these troubled times had passed, then the making of oil was started, but the Island was very much depopulated through the epidemic and the pirates. What did Ben do in this time with this depleted population? He assumed the authority of King. He was overbearing and pressed the few remaining people to work. The king of Fakaofo at that time was Likā but he was lorded over by the strong power of Ben. (Solomona n.d.)

In these circumstances it is not surprising that the arrival of a strong contingent of Catholics, the *aliki's* son among them, would have lasting effects, particularly considering what Peni did shortly thereafter. It happened in the same month that Elloy visited, and possibly in connection with the same voyage, though Elloy records nothing about it.

The ship was the *Augustita* (according to Peterson, her captain) or the *Alexander* and her captain Peters (according to Solomona n.d.). It had come from Samoa to visit Peni, bringing as passengers three of the men who had been put ashore from the slave ship in Tutu'ila in February. Two of these men were of the *kāiga aliki* and closely related to Likā: Tetaulu, his son, and Vaopuka, his cousin. While the ship was at Fakaofo, Peni induced Likā to sign a document of sale granting him title to the islet of Fenuafala. The circumstances of this sale have been set down in numerous places, by the main participants, by witnesses, by those recording their evidence, and by others who learned of the event from other sources. A petition from 'the King and people of Fakaofo' composed in 1907 gives most of the detail.

Then Ben went to Likā the king in order that he should sell the islet of Fenuafala. But when the king would not sell the islet Ben still persisted that the islet should be sold. Ben used a great deal of threatening language, in order that the chief should be made afraid, thus: If Likā would not sell or let him have the island, then, when the man-stealing ships came again, the king and all the people of Fakaofo would be taken away. It ended in Ben forcibly seizing the hand of the king and holding it above the pen and paper. But the king did not know what Ben was doing with his hand. (Ielemia *et al.* in Newell 1907)

Another document states that 'the purchase of this island was not paid for in cash but in trade' and that the payment made was 'six large axes, and ten whole bolts of cloth' (Solomona n.d.). The goods were taken to Likā's house, and Peni then left on the ship to gather labourers and register his document with the American consulate in Apia, confident that he had acquired the islet.

It seems likely that, after the forced sale of Fenuafala, which, according to yet another account (Cusack Smith 1892a), had been abetted and witnessed by the Protestants Sakaio and Lea, Tefono easily persuaded his father to abandon his paganism and join him in the Catholic faith. At any rate, Likā converted, and was baptised by another visiting priest shortly after, together with his wife, three other elderly women and three younger women whom the priest then married to three of the men recently returned from Uvea (Schahl 1863:15 June).[25] Perhaps it was despair and desperation at this Catholic triumph that led Sakaio to depart Fakaofo by canoe with three other men to seek solace from his colleague Maka on Atafu, leaving Lea in charge of

whatever Protestants there were. This canoe missed its landfall and eventually fetched up in the Fijian Lau group, and Sakaio did not return to Fakaofo
until August 1863 (Bird 1863d). By then the Protestant ranks had been or
would shortly be bolstered by the four couples returned from Olohega, and
Peni's return with seven Polynesian labourers who were associated with the
Protestants.

Fakaofo thus came to have significant numbers of both Catholic and
Protestant adherents, each faction associated with a different trader and
having its own lines of communication with the outside world. But whether
Catholic or Protestant or still pagan, the people (excepting Lea and perhaps
a few others) did not support Peni or accept his purchase of Fenuafala as
valid. And when Tefono began to harass Peni, destroying his pigs and banana
plantations, nobody in the island, except Sakaio and perhaps Lea, came to his
defence. Where his imported workers stood in all this is not reported.

Peni and Lea went to Samoa together in May of 1864, leaving the
Fenuafala oil-making venture in charge of a Maori labourer. In Apia they laid
complaints with Williams, the British consul who was also Acting US consul,
alleging that they had been driven from the island, as had other Protestants,
by Likā and the Catholic party. This prompted Williams to send the teacher,
Sakaio, a letter to be read out on the island, denouncing 'the tyrannical chief
who desires to drive the Protestant religion from the place' and exhorting the
said chief to 'Give up such bad customs and allow everyone to choose for
himself the religion he likes best'. Williams also threatened fines and a visit
from a man-of-war (Williams 1864). When Sakaio read this letter to the
assembled populace, it was met with derision from the Catholics. They kept
up their threats against Peni, letting him know of their intention to 'make
him fast and throw him into the sea', or so Peni wrote to Williams (Hughes
1864). He went again to Samoa in June 1865 to plead his case before the US
commercial agent, Jonas Coe, and get his title to Fenuafala authorised and
look for a purchaser. This time Coe, after ascertaining what Williams had
done, sent a letter to Likā, threatening fines; but when it was read out in
Fakaofo it was greeted with the same derision as Williams's earlier letter, with
Tefono himself remarking 'that he desired to see the face of the thing that
wrote the letter, he would then tell him who he was' (Sakaio 1865).

The oil-making continued nevertheless, and Peni managed to get his new
deed signed by two local witnesses, doubtless Sakaio and Lea. With this in
hand, he then announced that he would sell the islet back to the people of
Fakaofo for forty barrels of oil. According to a local account, the majority
agreed, but some, including Likā's son Tefono, did not, saying that '"it would
be simple to get the islet back"' (Fakaofo n.d.). Peni apparently received no
oil, and he left for Samoa in January 1866 to deposit his deed with the US
commercial agency (Hughes Affidavit, 18 May 1866). A deal for the sale of
Fenuafala for $600 was concluded with Th. Weber of the German Firm in
September of that year, and Peni never reappeared in Fakaofo.

None of the Fakaofo populace knew anything of these arrangements. The
first indication that things had changed came when Atone starting visiting

Fenuafala to make copra during 1867, having quietly obtained the lease of the islet in March for $100 a year. What role Atone might have played in the earlier harassment of Peni is not recorded. But from what Father Schahl recorded four years earlier (1863:15 June), Atone was keen to remain in Fakaofo as trader for the German Firm, on the condition that Peni did not return, and further, the German Firm favoured Atone because, instead of making oil, he processed copra for export. A reasonable inference is that Atone encouraged the harassment of Peni and may even have advised Tefono that 'it would be simple to get the island back', knowing full well that Peni's only alternative was to sell it to the German Firm, and that the Firm would then lease it to him. In other words, Atone and the Firm were together manipulating the situation to their own ends. Thus, though Fakaofo got rid of Peni, the people did not thereby repossess Fenuafala. The German Firm owned it and Atone demonstrably had legal possession of it.

There is no record of any general outcry against this turn of events. Specifically, neither Likā nor Tefono protested. Whether this was because they stood to benefit from the new arrangement, or because of loyalty to their religious ally, or because they were as mystified as everyone else, and compromised as well, it is hard to say. The majority of the Protestants too had wanted Peni removed, and had, at least tacitly, supported Tefono in his campaign of harassment, or at least had done nothing to prevent it. After all, Tefono was at least a native son. In any case, since there were no visits from the LMS missionaries between 1863 and 1868, its adherents had no avenue for protest.

Sakaio and Lea carried on with their work, no longer compromised by Peni's presence; but then Sakaio 'fell into sin' and, trusting yet again to a canoe, fled to Nukunonu with a local woman, leaving Lea to carry on alone for another year. In the wake of these developments, Atone's deception and Sakaio's sin, both religions were compromised, and in response there were probably some religious realignments at the time. In any case, the Catholics lost a cause and their moral advantage, and whatever the proportion of Catholics to Protestants was in 1866, by 1868 the Rev. Murray, paying a long overdue visit to Fakaofo, reported with satisfaction that 130 professed Protestants well outnumbered the Catholics in a population of less than 200 (Murray 1868). Furthermore, the situation held great promise, for he returned Mafalā, now fully qualified, to shepherd the Protestant flock. Though the exact proportion fluctuated, from then on Protestants substantially outnumbered Catholics in Fakaofo. When old Likā died in 1870 or 1871, he was succeeded by a Protestant *aliki*. Never again would there be a Catholic *aliki* of Fakaofo. Also, in 1870, Atone left Fakaofo, leaving his business and property to his son, known in Fakaofo simply as Peleila. Though Atone reappeared from time to time, he largely left his son to his own devices (see chapter 7).

The disintegration of the Tokelau polity was brought about by the pressure of events from the world beyond the control of Tui Tokelau and the *aliki*: famine, Christian proselytising, epidemic disease, and rapacious 'slavers'. Behind this headlong rush of events, however, Tokelau did not simply disintegrate in a random or wholly contingent manner. Having been put together by Tokelau logic, it came apart in line with that same logic. That Fakaofo should have rejected Faivalua and his 'good news' is hardly surprising; nor is it surprising that Atafu listened to him and his message. Atafu was more open to new ideas, and its leaders had little to lose. And with Atafu turning towards Protestantism, it seems almost inevitable that Nukunonu would have avidly taken up Catholicism. A year or more before the slavers arrived, both the subject and tributary atolls had seized their opportunity to devote themselves to another god and throw off the domination of Fakaofo, and to align themselves with opposed churches of that new god. Tokelau once again became three separate polities, distinguished from one another by the same combination of religious and temporal power that had bound them together in the first place.

In Fakaofo the *aliki*, once the mediator between Tokelau and the divine world, found his authority confined to his own atoll domain and soon came to realise, in the wake of the slavers, that Tui Tokelau could not prevail. Confronted with the Protestant alliance of Peni, Lea, Mafalā and Sakaio, and pressured by Peni to sign away the land of Fenuafala, he accepted the urgings of his recently returned son and became a Catholic. Thus Fakaofo, whose ancient order had encompassed both Nukunonu and Atafu, accepted both Atafu's Protestantism and Nukunonu's Catholicism, and embarked on decades of internal divisiveness.

In contrast to Fakaofo, Nukunonu and Atafu in the half decade after 1863 appear to have been uneventful, even tranquil places. Each atoll was united in a single Christian faith; neither received a large number of returned compatriots nor hosted many foreigners, and none of the foreigners they hosted managed to gain real control of any lands. They may have been concerned about what was happening in Fakaofo, but they were not immediately affected by these events, and Fakaofo was in no position to exercise any influence over what happened in Atafu and Nukunonu. Three autonomous village polities had replaced the old atoll empire. Yet things were not exactly as they had been 'in the beginning'. The atolls were connected to one another both by the marked unions of significant forebears, and by subsequent union of their known ancestors. People had kin attachments to more than one atoll. The greater Tokelau polity had collapsed, but both ancient and more recent connections between its parts remained.

SEVEN

Parishes and Polities

The events of the early 1860s dismembered Tokelau. The population of the atolls was halved and the overarching political and religious order fragmented. The population would recover, probably exceeding its pre-'slavers' numbers by the mid 1880s,[1] but the old order could not be reconstituted: its underpinnings had vanished. Tokelau was fragmented not just into three village polities but into four parishes as well—the London Missionary Society (LMS) Protestants and Marist Catholic Order had each established two congregations by the late 1860s.

The story of Tokelau in the latter part of the nineteenth century and into the early part of the twentieth century could be told in terms of sectarian celebration and conflict; the written mission records which are the primary sources almost impel such a telling. Preoccupied as the recorders were with their own sectarian interests, they give prominence to matters of 'parish'—to relations between pastor and flock, to the morality or immorality of both pastor and flock, and to the perfidies of the other sect and its adherents. It is a rather boring and superficial story. Much more was at stake in the atolls. On the one hand, each polity was having to contend with new situations, both internally and externally generated. Within they had to resolve differences among themselves and cope with foreigners in their midst. They were practised at the former; the latter called for new strategies. Furthermore, the continuing presence of foreigners—specifically teacher/pastors and traders—tended to ignite or exacerbate differences among themselves. On the other hand, the polities had different agendas *vis-à-vis* one another which foreigners never seemed to understand. This story, while much more compelling, is a good deal more difficult to construct.

Central to such a story is the ethic of *māopoopo* 'unity'. Maintaining *māopoopo* is the pervasive preoccupation of a Tokelau village polity, and in the late nineteenth century this was particularly challenging. Nukunonu,

216

one in faith, small in number, and hosting few foreigners, appears to have been a relatively peaceful and contented place, although it faced other challenges. Atafu people were also of one faith, but their numbers were double that of Nukunonu and their cherished *māopoopo* was regularly compromised by internal factions, usually complicated by alignments with resident foreigners. Fakaofo was encumbered with two competing faiths at very close quarters, each championed by resident foreigners and by visiting foreigners more prone to exacerbate than calm the tensions. Yet in each place *māopoopo* survived.

In the following pages, each of the atolls is visited in turn, from the least to the most beleaguered—primarily to explore and explain their particular situations and to contrast the different situations. To be sure there are stories to be told—mainly set in the 1880s, the middle decade of the era. By that time Christian beliefs and institutions were fully established and had become thoroughly integrated into atoll life, and during that decade Catholic and Protestant missions showed heightened interest in their atoll parishes. Both missions despatched visitors to the atolls most years, and these visitors wrote comprehensively about the state of the parishes and polities as they perceived them, and about events they witnessed or heard about. Consequently there is an ongoing record, from two perspectives, which is augmented by accounts written by other less involved though equally opinionated visitors. In the 1890s the interest of the missions waned or was deflected by the political turmoil in Samoa, and at the same time British Protectorate officials began to visit the atolls occasionally. Inevitably the story of the half-century after Christian conversion overlaps for the last two decades (c.1890–1910) with that of the following colonial era. Even though protectorate visits were infrequent and the officials remained ashore at most only a few hours, their interests and powers were quite different from those of the missions. They brought a new dimension to Tokelau life, introducing a new set of issues and providing a new avenue to the outside world, and the polities responded accordingly. Protectorate officials' reports are included in this chapter when they impinge on events and issues that are central to this era; otherwise they are put aside for the moment.

Throughout this half-century when missionaries, protectorate officials and other foreigners were writing reports for their superiors about happenings that they had either witnessed or heard about in Tokelau, the significance that they attached to a particular event did not necessarily correspond with its significance locally, and their descriptions of the village polities were not in the least comprehensive or particularly accurate. But despite their biases and preoccupations, all were alike in assuming that each atoll was an autonomous polity. They had no inkling, it seems, of how the political relationships between the atolls were being reformed; still this can be glimpsed in what they wrote. That story concludes this chapter.

Tokelau stories of life and events during the half-century after conversion are told in relation to persons—in written accounts of the reigns of teacher/pastors and their 'good works', and in oral anecdotes about their ancestors.

Each village has its own repertoire of stories about incidents in which its forebears figured, and raconteurs of one village are hesitant to tell of events that occurred in another. Each community thus has its own history, or collection of anecdotes. Stories volunteered rarely say anything directly about religious differences or political dissensions within or between the atolls. Informed listeners may either read them in or elicit them by asking questions. Linking foreign reports with local stories is not difficult.

Older people frequently reminisce about the hardships and virtues of the Tokelau life of their grandparents and parents and of their own childhood, but it is difficult to pinpoint the years to which they are referring. They are recounting the past to comment upon the present and that past is an ideal—constructed as a lesson for the present—rather than a chronological record. Anecdotes are not fixed in time or told in a temporal series, but they do involve genealogical personages. They are about the ancestors and their doings, and about the relationships of kinship between their ancestors, their own forebears and themselves. In order to appreciate a story, one needs to know not only the relationships between the people involved in the account, but also their relationships to the teller and the listeners, for it is upon these relationships that the narrative often turns; and they give colour and meaning to its telling. Consequently, stories and anecdotes are embedded in a genealogical matrix which may be used to place the recounted events in approximate temporal order, even in some cases to date them.

Again, diverse sources are juxtaposed and inferences informed by our knowledge of past people and present places. Reading between the lines of the reports of foreigners to discover the dynamics of village life and of relations between the atolls, and approaching Tokelau anecdotes not as isolated incidents but as paradigmatic occurrences, we have built our story

Nukunonu's Catholic Parish Polity

The documentary record of Nukunonu in the late nineteenth century is sparse, except for the decade of the 1880s due primarily to the lively reports of the zealous and indefatigable Father Eugene Didier. The years leading up to the 1880s are particularly shadowy, even though Monseigneur Elloy (Bishop of Tipasa) visited Nukunonu several times. His accounts of events and conditions on shore are slim, confused and conflated. His comment, 'Nothing is more miserable than the people of Tokelau' (1879:71), rather sums up the tenor of his reports, and, though he performed baptisms, he neglected to record them. He did, however, fully relate the discomforts of his voyages to Tokelau—with 'boards for a bed, hardtack and salt beef for food, and foul water to drink' (Elloy 1879:75). The Marist fathers took passage to Tokelau on trading vessels that happened to be going there for their own commercial purposes, and these vessels had rudimentary amenities and were often unsafe with 'no instruments to fix . . . position' and 'a large crack in the stern' (Dolé 1885:393–94). Accordingly the priests' visits tended to be irregular, infrequent and brief.

Only three foreign catechist teachers, all Samoans, ever resided in Nukunonu. One was removed after a year, having created some difficulties, and the other two promptly married Nukunonu women, thereby becoming less foreign. The priests applauded their unions, but even they did not remain very long. The precise comings and goings of these catechists are not detailed in either mission or local annals; altogether they seem to have been in residence for less than eight years. Consequently, visiting fathers were little informed about the events and affairs of parish. They were ashore at the most a day or two, rarely was there a foreigner in residence who might relate to them what had happened, and Nukunonu people (whether by birth or marriage) would have been loath to report any but the most innocuous matters to their eminent visitors.

The vision of Nukunonu that is presented in the Catholic records of the 1880s onwards is in part attributable to this reticence, but also this small isolated parish struck a familiar chord. Here was an egalitarian, strictly controlled, materially impoverished but spiritually blessed community. All the reputed values of monastic existence were exemplified, save one—celibacy. The fathers could not help but admire the 'little people so good, so simple, so full of confidence . . .' (Didier 1886b) who 'are not particular and maintain that they are satisfied with their poverty . . .' (Dolé 1885). Nukunonu brims over with naive hilarity, innocent joy and childlike humour. Senior men gambol about; the 'king' entertains the visitors 'with an exhibition of his kingdom's singing', and wears 'royal robes' consisting of a 'long woman's dress which reached to his feet and an old felt hat on top of which a faded ribbon was attached which fell to his waist' (Dolé 1885). Songs are composed to beg sweets and to mock English intruders (see chapter 9). The picture is of a people peaceful and pious, joyful but shy, even timid, and acquiescent. Only Father Didier glimpsed something of their indomitable tenacity and ironic wit. Yet in all these pastoral vignettes, however patronising, the characteristic demeanour of Nukunonu people may be recognised—timid, acquiescent and ingratiating, even dissimulating, in the presence of strangers. The most remarkable aspect of the Marist mission reports, especially when put beside those of their LMS counterparts, is the absence of any condemnation of the behaviour and activities of their parishioners. They celebrate the singing and dancing, delight in the antics and humour, and find the faults inconsequential.

Mission supervision of the parish was sporadic and fleeting. Except for those estimated eight years, the parish was locally supervised and directed, and many years no priest appeared at all. For two decades after 1861 Takua tended, taught and led the congregation, and upon the departure of the last foreign catechist the mission decided that local leadership was more practical and less troublesome, and pious and upstanding elders were appointed spiritual leaders and given soutanes to wear. Not until after the turn of the century were Tokelau men trained as teacher/catechists. The upshot of this mission 'neglect' was that the Nukunonu polity reconstituted its own social order under its own leaders with negligible foreign interference.

Cast of Characters

AT FAKAOFO

Vaopuka: Son of Likā's father's brother, who was released from the 'slave ship' at Tutuila and returned to Fakaofo in the latter months of 1863. He is reputed to have had six wives, and became *aliki* in the late 1870s succeeding Logotahi, who was the son of another of Likā's father's brothers. Little is known of Logotahi. Vaopuka died of a gunshot wound inflicted by Emile, a relative of Peleila, in 1881.

Tetaulu: Son of Likā, who also was released from the 'slave ship' at Tutuila and returned to Fakaofo. He succeeded Vaopuka as *aliki* in 1881, was a stalwart Protestant and adversary of Peleila, and died c.1890.

Lea: Leader of the Protestant converts in many years during the later 1860s and 1870s in the absence of resident pastors.

Tefono (aka Oto): Son of Likā, who opposed Peni but then was compromised by Peleila and his father, Atone, when they began to appropriate land. He was the foremost local Catholic.

Traders

Peleila (aka José Pereira): Trader for the German Firm and stalwart supporter of the Catholic faith, though married to the daughter of Lea.

P. Paulsen: Trader for British Firm of Henderson and MacFarland, and aligned with Protestants, though not an active member of the church owing to his common-law union with a Fakaofo woman.

Protestant pastors

Mafalā: A Samoan teacher who had left Fakaofo in despair in 1863 and returned in 1868 as a qualified pastor. He was removed in some disgrace in 1874.

Timoteo: A Tokelau pastor trained at Malua who was appointed 'evangelist to the heathen' of Nanumanga (Tuvalu) in 1871 (Powell 1871b) but had no success, owing in part to one 'foe of the Gospel' reputed to be his countryman (Gill 1872). He was returned to Tokelau in 1874 and was appointed temporary pastor at Fakaofo to replace Mafalā. The following year he retired to Atafu, his wife's homeland. It is probable that he was a companion of Faivalua and became attached to the LMS mission in Samoa in the 1850s.

Apeau: A Rarotongan pastor who served from 1875 to 1878. He was 'mild mannered' and promoted the cultivation of *pulaka*.

Iapesa: A Samoan pastor who served from 1880 to 1887. He was vigorously anti-Catholic and very industrious.

Marist catechists
Matulino 1868–73
Aniseto
Luimili 1881
Seu 1882
Amiteo 1883–86

AT NUKUNONU

Takua (aka Susetino/Justin): Locally recognised spiritual leader and most prominent person until his death in 1914. Formal recognition of his position—his *aliki* status—was compromised until 'King' Ulua's death and contested by Fakaofo. His paternal forebears were of the senior Talafau stock and he headed the *toga* known as Fagaaliki. Didier called him the 'sole high judge' and after Ulua's death, he was called *aliki*.

Telakau (aka Paulo): Surviving elder of the multiply linked stocks of Tuipagai and Lua, he headed the *toga* known as Tefala. Didier called him a 'senator/ deputy'.

Falekie (aka Tavite): Surviving elder of the Letele stock, he headed the *toga* known as Tohua, which included his sister's husband, Falevai, and their issue. Didier called him a 'senator/deputy'.

Ulua (aka 'King John'/Ioane Papitiso): The acknowledged but apparently inactive 'King' or *aliki*, celebrated by visitors for his virtuoso singing and drumming. He died in the early 1890s.

Falevai (aka Mateo): Ulua's only son married Falekie's sister, and they founded the expansive *puikāiga* called Faleula. Falevai died in Samoa and may have pre-deceased his father. In any case, he apparently was never considered *aliki* or indeed heir to that position. Didier called him 'secretary to government'.

Hehe (aka Sese Perez): A Portuguese trader for the German Firm in Samoa, who arrived in Nukunonu c.1864. He married a Fakaofo woman with Nukunonu connections. He was not able to acquire any land himself, though his wife seems to have had some rights to land use.

Iakopo: (see below for Atafu) A half-brother of Ulua, who moved from Atafu to Nukunonu sometime in the 1880s with his wife and children. Although he and his wife remained Protestant, all of his children became Catholic. He died c.1905.

Hakaio: A son of Vaopuka (Fakaofo *aliki*) who also had a series of wives. His last wife was a Nukunonu woman and he was baptised Catholic in order to marry her, though soon thereafter rejected his apparent conversion. He held Protestant services in his wife's house, but their children were baptised and remained Catholic.

Marist catechists
Sililo 1883–85: Samoan who within a year had married one of Falevai's daughters.
Luimili 1886, 1890, 1896: Samoan who married Takua's brother's daughter.

AT ATAFU
Togia: A grandson of Tonuia who succeeded his brother, Foli, as *aliki*, but was 'removed' from that office in the late 1870s.

Ioane: A grandson of Tonuia who became *aliki* in 1881. He accompanied the crew of the shipwrecked *Ophelia* to Samoa in 1866, where he was admitted to the LMS church, and subsequently became senior deacon of the constituted Atafu church in 1868, and indeed leader of the parish for many years in the 1870s. Although he wished to maintain his senior position in the church when he became *aliki*, he was 'persuaded' to step down. The latter years of his 'reign' were contentious and he died c.1900.

Iakopo: A grandson of Tonuia, who with Ioane was a founding deacon of the Atafu church. He moved to Nukunonu in the 1880s (see above).

Protestant pastors
Maka 1861–67: A Rarotongan who was the original mission teacher but was removed from pastorate in 1868. He remained in Atafu until c.1872, when his behaviour compelled his removal.

Fataiki 1868–74: A Niuean whose behaviour was exemplary according to mission visitors, and whose removal was occasioned by unsubstantiated local complaints.

Tinei 1876: A Samoan whose brief stay in Atafu was deemed 'unfortunate'.

Lemuelu 1881–87: A celebrated and controversial Samoan pastor.

Fineaso (?1888): A Samoan pastor of whom little is told, and whose short period of service suggests that it was 'unfortunate'.

Tavita 1890–c.1898: A Samoan pastor, commended as 'of a new school' (Clark 1890), although he too was eventually rejected.

Traders
Unnamed, for the British Firm of Henderson and MacFarland

MISSION VISITORS 1868–91

LMS missionaries to Fakaofo and Atafu
A.W. Murray 1868 (August)
S.J. Whitmee 1870 (September)
T. Powell, J.C. Vivian and G. Pratt 1871 (September)
W.W Gill and G. Pratt 1872 (July)
G.A. Turner 1874 (May)
H. Nisbet 1875 (August)
G.A. Turner 1876 (May)
T. Powell 1877
G.A. Turner 1878 (May)
S.H. Davies 1880 (September)
C. Phillips 1881 (September)
S.H. Davies 1882 (August)
J. Marriott 1883 (August)
C. Phillips 1884 (July)
J.E. Newell 1885 (September)
W.H. Wilson 1886 (August)
J. Marriott 1887 (September)
A.E. Claxton 1888
A.E. Claxton 1889
W.E. Clarke 1890 (May)

Marist priests to Nukunonu and Fakaofo (from baptismal registers):
Msgr Elloy and And. Schahl 1863 (May)
And. Schahl 1863 (September)
Msgr Elloy 1868
Msgr Elloy . . . and Gavet 1872
Msgr Elloy . . . and Gavet 1873
Msgr Elloy . . . and Gavet 1875
Dolé and Gavet 1882
E. Didier and J. Henquel 1883
E. Didier and J. Henquel 1884
E. Didier and Hyacinthe 1885
E. Didier and Mennel 1886
E. Didier 1887
E. Didier 1888
E. Didier and Garnier 1890
E. Didier and Hyacinthe 1891 (they were lost at sea)

The transformed social order

The local accounts of this social order are factual and unembellished, but their successive tellers have been engaged in the inevitable circle of explaining the past in the present and the present in the past, and have certainly altered them somewhat over the years. Yet what is related a century later corroborates much of what the visiting priests wrote at the time, and indeed enriches and makes comprehensible their accounts by setting them in a broader frame. In what follows, the local annals are the primary source.

Ulua, baptised Ioane Papatiso (John Baptist), was identified as 'king' by all visiting foreigners, though his demeanour was hardly dignified or kingly. A visitor in 1887 described him as: '. . . a veritable King Cole, a merry old soul, playing a rude native drum with great skill, singing to his own accompaniment, full of life and action, and with a queen as fat and as merry and goodhearted as himself' (Moss 1889:128). This characterisation echoes that of Father Dolé (above), suggesting that the old *aliki* of heathen days had taken (or been given) the role of village host and entertainer. That his role was previously otherwise is suggested by Father Didier's description of him as 'the former sorcerer . . . today mild as a lamb. . .' (1886a: 195, cf. chapter 5). In any case, he does not appear to have engaged in any political activity and, on the face of it, seems a person of little consequence—even though he was called 'king'.

Four men were prominent in the polity: Takua/Susitino who had brought the faith, Telakau/Paulo and Falekie/Tavite who had been castaways at Uvea in 1846 and returned with Elloy in 1863, and Falevai/Mateo the son of 'king' Ulua.[2] These men are repeatedly named in mission records and figure prominently in local annals; in fact, they may have been the only senior, active men of Nukunonu at the time, and thus obviously the focal persons and leaders of the reconstituted village.

Even in the 1880s there were only about a hundred people in Nukunonu, and very few of them were able, active adults. Consequently subsistence production was reorganised to exploit local resources most effectively. Harvesting the abundant fruits of the land posed little problem as long as there were some men and older boys to climb for drinking coconuts, but to exploit the reef and sea efficiently numbers of people were required to drive fish and tend nets and crew canoes. For skipjack fishing, women were enlisted as crew, specifically to paddle the canoes, and women also joined reef netting expeditions. The polity was regrouped for practical reasons, but the strategy of regrouping smacked of the past. Cognatic links were extended to join the residual members of previously distinctive *kāiga* into more inclusive cooperating groups called *toga*, and the original division, predictable for Nukunonu, was into four, each focused on one senior man. Apparently the Nukunonu 'rule of four' did not altogether suit the situation and two of the *toga*, those led by Falekie and Falevai who were brothers-in-law, joined together, so there were three, each having in its ranks, in time, five to ten active adult men—many of whom were affiliated by marriage. This new organisational design, though it operated mainly on the reef, was marked on the land by allocating to each *toga* a small plantation section in the same area on the eastern margin of the atoll. The name of each *toga* and its designated land section were synonymous, and each was delegated oversight of approximately one third of the encircling reef. These divisions corresponded to—although they were not identical with—the ancient divisions of the atoll. Specifically, Takua's *toga* with the land and name Fagaaliki (lit. 'chiefly fish-trap') was responsible for the southern portion of the reef, the area long associated with the indigenous *aliki* line from which Takua issued; Telakau's *toga* with the land and name Tefala was responsible for the northwestern reefs, the ancient domain of Tuipagai, the old 'warrior' stock to which Telakau had multiple ancestral connections; and the northeastern reefs were in charge of the joint Falekie/Falevai *toga* named Tohua. This area comprised the ancient lands of Lua, the lineage of fishermen, and Letele, the line of *faipule*—in which Falekie had significant ancestors. Although the equations of past and present were not absolutely exact, and had to take into account the line of the 'king', they certainly were not inconsequential.[3] Nukunonu was not only dealing with practical matters, it was asserting its complete dominion over the atoll, large sections of which were still claimed by Fakaofo, and which Ulua and his son continued ostensibly to represent. The remembered structure of a distant past was a model for rearrangements not only to accommodate the present but to reassert an autonomous past.[4]

The overseeing of the three reef divisions by *toga* did not entail exclusive rights; rather it was an efficient way of exploiting resources for the benefit of all. Each *toga* was expected to monitor the movements of fish upon and across its section of reef, and to scan (or search) the seas beyond for the baitfish which foreshadow schools of skipjack. Pragmatically the *toga* structure combined depleted cooperative groups into more effective production units, and when, around the turn of the century, the Nukunonu population reached its pre-1863 numbers, equally pragmatically *toga* organisation was abandoned, since by then less inclusive *kāiga*, associated with land resources, again had adequate personnel to exploit both land and sea. Today the named plantation sections remain as testimony to a structure that had once been in place. Only Nukunonu historians tell of these *toga*; there is no mention of anything of the sort in other records, which dwell on matters of governance and faith. However, in Father Didier's description of governance, the presence of the *toga* organisation may be glimpsed.

When Didier first crossed Nukunonu's reef in 1883 to baptise, confirm, confess, give communion, and bless a parish that by then numbered just over one hundred, he also instituted what he claimed was a 'new government', in which he took great, but hardly deserved, pride. He described it as follows in its third year.

> There have been no changes in the government, nor in the dynasty, not even in the ministers; even the leoleo [watchmen] were those we had nominated. The old king Ulua . . . was there in the place of honour. . . . His son Mateo [Falevai], the permanent secretary of the kingdom and representative of all the ministries had placed me between the king and himself while the senators and deputies, repre-

sented by Te Lakau and Falekie were opposite with Susitino [Takua], sole high judge of the kingdom. They asked me questions about political and administrative matters; I had to decide at once and give the ultimate decision on the most difficult matters which had arisen during the last year and I could not make any mistakes because my decision would become the law and custom of the land (1886a:195).

Setting aside Didier's overweening pride, self-importance and sheer arrogance, as well as the overblown French political model of 'ministries', 'senators' and 'deputies', this political order is not an imposed model. Nukunonu pundits describe it in different but comparable terms. Didier's 'king' was the *aliki*, his 'secretary of the kingdom' a *failautuhi* 'scribe', his 'senators and deputies' two *faipule* 'rulers', and his 'sole high judge' the *fakamahino* 'magistrate'. The proper people were in their proper offices—given that Takua could not be named *aliki* since Ulua strategically had to be 'king', so he was 'the sole high judge' for the time being.

Recall that in 1863 the missionaries Gill and Bird wrote of Nukunonu: 'The real authority evidently rests exclusively with Takua, Oulua [sic] is *King only in name*' (original emphasis). In the years that followed, this situation certainly did not change, so it might be asked why Ulua was not 'dethroned'. Whatever power Ulua had before 1861 (and local accounts grant him a good deal) was thoroughly compromised by Nukunonu's total conversion of which he was a part (cf. Didier's reference to him as the sorcerer turned into a lamb), and by complying with, or acquiescing to, the projects of his reputed subjects, he retained his nominal role. As long as he continued in the office of *aliki* or 'king', he appeared to represent Fakaofo interests in Nukunonu, and he was tolerated in that office in Nukunonu because he did not in fact fill it, but was merely a figurehead. Ulua as 'king' was a strategic anachronism—he did no harm in his 'old King Cole' role.

When Takua returned to Nukunonu, bringing a new faith and initiating a new politico-religious order, he in effect replaced Ulua as *aliki*. Takua was *te aliki tonu* 'the rightful paramount' by virtue of his ancestry, not a 'stranger-king' from afar but a 'returned son' of indigenous *aliki* heritage; not a conqueror but a culture hero.

This new politico-religious order explicitly rejected Tui Tokelau as a false god, but did not directly challenge Fakaofo hegemony or assert Nukunonu autonomy, at least for several decades. Ulua continued to be 'king' until his death, shortly before the turn of the century. Only after that event did the Nukunonu people explicitly assert their political autonomy by proclaiming Takua their *aliki* without consulting Fakaofo. The consequences of this proclamation are another story (see chapter 8).

The new political order of Nukunonu was not Father Didier's creation, though its leaders might have strategically encouraged him to think so. It was a Nukunonu creation, a reformulation of their ancient, independent polity with some adaptations to accommodate Christian morality. The people of Nukunonu had reasserted their separate identity both in the structures of their society and in their Catholic faith, and the material symbols of their parish polity were a limestone church, built under the direction of Takua sometime in the 1870s, and 'a large flag with a cross and the emblem of Mary as coat of arms', presented to 'the government' by Father Didier in 1886.

Nukunonu was the most self-contained of the late nineteenth-century polities, the place where foreigners intruded the least. Mission intrusions were minimal, priests visited rarely and foreign catechist presence was shortlived. There was only one established trader, a Portuguese named Hehe Perez, who remarked to an offshore visitor in 1880 that he had lived on the atoll for sixteen years (Coppinger 1899:154). Like Atone, his counterpart in Fakaofo, he probably arrived shortly after the slavers as a trader for the German Firm of August Unshelm in Apia, but unlike Atone, he did not, or was not able to, cause remarkable disruptions in this tight little polity. Soon he was married to a Tokelau woman who bore him numerous children, who in turn gave rise to the *kāiga potiki* 'portuguese family' of Nukunonu. The peace and good order Nukunonu apparently enjoyed may be simply because few foreigners visited or resided there to create conflict and disorder. It was nevertheless a small, exclusive polity understandably reluctant to air its internal disagreements to foreigners, and it was a polity that showed itself in the decades that followed to be resolute and indomitable in the face of British colonial officers, Protestant missionaries and its former Fakaofo 'rulers'.

Atafu's Protestant Parish Polity

Only two or three years after the slavers departed with their human cargo from the shores of Atafu, the island received some unexpected visitors of quite a different sort. The *Ophelia*, a German ship carrying a cargo of rice, ran upon Atafu's eastern reef (*Matagi Tokelau* 1991:109–10). The community displayed true Christian charity and generously provided for the captain and crew for eight or nine months (Murray 1868), but their visitors are not reputed to have been as charitable: 'The Europeans were incapable of giving even a morsel to another', remarked an elderly man over a century later. A two-masted vessel was fashioned from the wreckage of the ship and two Atafu men escorted the shipwrecked party on their voyage to Samoa. The episode of the *Ophelia* was testimony to Atafu's commitment to Christian morality, both in its telling shortly after the event (above) and as it has continued to be told in Atafu.

Maka, the Rarotongan teacher, is celebrated in Atafu not only as their original 'teacher' but also as something of a saviour. He had advised them not to go out to the slavers' ships and later had stood firm against the slavers' demands and threats. Maka undoubtedly had much influence and authority in the years immediately after. The *aliki*, Foli, had been taken by the slavers; his brother, Togia, had not, but was so insignificant that he is rarely remembered as Foli's successor. However, new local leaders were already in evidence at the time of Murray's 1868 visit. He singled out Ioane—'a native of decided piety who was admitted to the church at Apia a few months ago when on a visit to Samoa' (Murray 1868), whence he had escorted the crew of the *Ophelia*. Several others are named in subsequent missionary reports, who were probably young to middle-aged men in 1863, but were not enslaved, probably because they were not in Atafu at the time.[5] They were collectively, in Tokelau terms, the village *pule* 'authority, power', and were usually referred to as 'chiefs' by outsiders. Though one of them was given pre-eminence as *aliki* and called 'king' by outsiders, this office had always been equivocal in Atafu's egalitarian polity, and had further lost whatever sanctity it had in pre-Christian times.

In this polity that was also a parish, sanctity was associated with God, and persons most closely associated with God were worthy of respect and honour. Much of the time these were foreign pastors, who are highly visible in the historical record through the reports of their mission mentors. Other foreigners were traders, shadowy figures, first noted in 1880 but only in passing until the 1890s, when two of them caused an inordinate amount of trouble. Difficulties with foreign residents appear to have been endemic in late nineteenth-century Atafu, though one must be wary of the impression conveyed in reports of short visits that relied on information provided by the resident foreigners involved, who exacerbated by their presence and exaggerated in their accounts the inevitable disagreements that arose between them and the forthright and outspoken Atafu populace.

Then there was the chronic antipathy between pastor and trader (see Moss 1889:160–2, Dana 1872), intensified by their common isolation at close quarters. The pastors, while disparaging the morals and behaviour of traders, depended upon them for imported appurtenances which marked them as more sophisticated than their flock, and which they bought with 'gifts' from their flock. The traders, while disparaging the sanctimonious pastors, depended upon them for custom, for what they paid out for local produce became 'gifts' for the pastors and the wherewithal to purchase the cotton 'cleanliness' required of Christians. Traders and pastors—commerce and Christianity—were economically locked together, and together established a market economy even in isolated atolls.

Early on, Atafu experienced problems arising from the presence of foreigners in their midst. But these foreigners were not summarily ostracised, since their continuing presence was regarded as beneficial. Instead, Atafu people tried to contain and control them, not always successfully. Of the shadowy traders and commerce we will say no more for the moment, but will focus on the Christian establishment, the central institution of the late nineteenth-century village—at least in record and memory.

Relations between Atafu parish polity and its foreign pastors were not always harmonious, but this was not from lack of Atafu's Christian commitment. Reports of LMS visitors record building and improvement of churches and pastors' compounds, gifts to the pastor and the mission, sales of bibles and hymnals, school examination results, and the number of children in school and of adults in the communicant congregation. A brief survey of these reports is ample testimony to Atafu's Christian devotion.

Three churches were built in the nineteenth century: the first in 1862 of

The coral stone church Atafu constructed c.1885 and its congregation arrayed before it in their Sunday best. Photo: Mr Andrew who travelled *Through Atolls and Islands of the Great South Seas* with F. Moss in 1886–87, courtesy of the Museum of New Zealand Te Papa Tongarewa [D465]

wood; the second 'a neat, comfortable, wattle and plaster building, sixty feet in length by eighteen feet in width' (Turner 1874a); and then in the mid 1880s a church of coral stone measuring 95 feet by 30 feet (Moss 1889:169).

When a pastor was installed in a parish, it was the Christian duty of its congregation to support him and his family by providing an appropriately furnished residence, continual donations of food and provision of services, as well as the annual collective 'gift'. When the congregation could make their gifts and contributions in cash (which both pastor and the Missionary Society greatly preferred), the amount provides a rough year-by-year measure of local regard for the pastor.

People admitted to full membership in the congregation had to be able to read the Bible. All children attended school as soon as they were eligible and often stayed until they were married. Visiting missionaries conducted annual examinations, and those visiting Atafu invariably praised the enthusiasm and capabilities of the pupils. Adults continued their commitment to Christian learning and were inordinately eager to obtain books. Phillips wrote in 1881: 'The demand for Bibles and other books was astonishing—far more than I could supply. One man even offered me a gold wedding ring for a Bible', and Marriott in 1883 commented in the same vein: '. . . they rushed to me with money to buy Bibles, Hymn Books or indeed anything in the shape of a book . . .'.

Samoan was the language of the Bible and consequently the language of education. So all Protestants were literate in Samoan and bilingual: '. . . people have adopted Samoan as their sacred tongue, they speak to each other in their own dialect but Samoan is used in their religious services' (Pratt 1872). A Niuean pastor lamented that his flock spoke Samoan better than he did, but this problem was unusual. Most pastors were Samoan and they rarely learned to understand, much less speak, Tokelauan, dismissing it as an inferior 'dialect' unsuitable for the expression of profound Christian ideas or for addressing the Almighty. They dictated that in their environs and in their presence people should speak only Samoan. Their parishioners willingly acquiesced and were little inconvenienced, but the pastors had put themselves at a linguistic disadvantage. Though many Atafu people accepted the Samoan pastors' disparaging assessment of their language, all of them continued to speak it, enriching it with Samoan borrowings. They had the advantage of bilingualism; they could always understand what was being said, but they could also speak to one another and not be understood by their foreign guests.

Men who had excelled at school and had demonstrated Christian moral conduct were taken for schooling in Samoa. Those that did not succeed returned to Tokelau and became lay preachers or deacons, and those that did succeed did not return, except in retirement. Church policy prohibited pastors from serving where they had kin connections, which effectively prohibited a Tokelau pastor from serving in a Tokelau parish. So Tokelau teachers went as 'missionaries to the heathen' in Papua and Tokelau pastors served Samoan parishes.

The indices used by visiting missionaries to assess the performance of a pastor and the state of his parish were the roll of church membership (proportional to the adults of the community), attendance at the pastor's school (proportional to the youth of the community), and the number of people who had 'fallen' into sin. In Atafu, where there was no competing faith and heathen beliefs had disappeared by 1863, everyone attended school in their youth and sought to be communicants as adults. Virtually all adults had the necessary educational credentials, but their conduct was another matter. If their conduct was judged satisfactory, they became communicants, and thereafter, if they lapsed into sin, they 'fell' and were suspended. Under these circumstances, the only way that Atafu's general state of grace could be assessed was by the number of church members who had 'fallen', and this was invariably recorded, in more or less detail, by missionary visitors. The assessments, on the surface, might lead to the conclusion that in one year not a sin was committed and in the next sin was rife, whereas what was really being reflected was the pastor's relations with his parishioners and his diligence in rooting out 'sin'.

Indeed, relations of the Atafu parish polity with its foreign teachers/pastors were rather volatile, and visiting missionaries reported them at length. Was this just an obsession of the missionary reporters, or a real dilemma in this particular place? An informed reading of the evidence suggests the latter. There is no need to recapitulate the full saga of pastor–parishioner relations in Atafu as it is recorded in mission documents, where its significance is amplified by its centrality to the mission. Rather, drawing upon local and other accounts of the times, and upon later ethnographic reports, the relations should be interpreted as they articulate with local issues and concerns.

This difficult relationship is most fully portrayed in the case of Pastor Lemuelu (1881–87), which deserves close examination as it exemplifies an endemic social drama. But before relating and commenting upon Lemuelu's pastorate, a brief narrative of earlier events and relationships sets the scene.

By 1868, relations between Maka and the Atafu people were somewhat strained '. . . on account of certain things into the particulars of which it would answer no good to enter', and so Maka was removed from his position as teacher though he remained in Atafu 'connected with the church' (Murray 1868). His replacement was a Niuean teacher who took charge of the newly constituted congregation. Four years later Maka, who had been removed (Vivian 1871–72), was called 'the notorious Maka' owing to scandals surrounding his last years in Atafu (Pratt 1872), and in 1874 the Niuean teacher too was removed, not because his missionary superiors judged that he had sinned but because some Atafu people thought he had (Turner 1874a). An injudicious Samoan pastor was removed after one year in 1876 (Davies 1880) and in 1878 the mission received a letter from Atafu stating 'that they did not wish any new pastor as the pastors they had formerly had been a continual source of trouble' (Turner 1878).

Between 1874 and 1881, aside from the year of the injudicious Samoan, the Atafu flock was shepherded by two local deacons, one of them the afore-mentioned Ioane, and he along with the *aliki* were the signatories of the letter received by the Rev. Turner. Yet when Turner visited, he 'got a unanimous vote in favour of [a pastor] being sent them at once if at all possible', although Ioane pointedly abstained (Turner 1878). A pastor was not found at once, and in the meantime, there were developments in Atafu. Ioane, who '. . . seemed to a great extent to occupy the position of chief' (Coppinger 1899:155), was confirmed unanimously in his position as senior deacon until a pastor arrived (Davies 1880), though the congregation's sentiments are not altogether clear. At about the same time, the *aliki*, described as 'a good-for-nothing sort of person', was 'deposed by his subjects' (Coppinger 1899:157) or 'forced to abdicate' (Davies 1880). Mission reports of the period refer unspecifically to '. . . petty quarrelling which seems very much the bane of this small community' (Turner 1878) and 'constant dissensions' (Davies 1880). More specifically, the missionaries were taxed with resolving a matter of land—land given to Maka in the late 1860s. Without going into any details of this assuredly very complicated land issue, there can be little doubt that it had something to do with the quarrelling and dissension.

Finally, the issue of Maka's land was resolved (Davis 1880), and when the Rev. Phillips arrived in 1881 to install Pastor Lemuelu the situation appeared to be most auspicious. The villagers confirmed that Ioane was fully supported as their chosen 'king', and Lemuelu was received by them with 'joyous unanimity' after the proprieties of 'the relationship of pastor & flock' were fully explained. Furthermore, Ioane averred that he valued being a deacon over being king, and upon promising that 'he would never retain his royalty at the expense of the happiness of those he ruled' was allowed to retain his deaconate (Phillips 1881).

The promise of this beginning seemed to be more than fulfilled in the first years, particularly in Pastor Lemuelu's estimation. As Phillips (1882) related: '. . . not eight months after his settlement there and the progress made has been such as to incline me to call it "Millenium [sic] Island". . . . The church now numbers 85 and the candidates 20. They include all the adults of the island. No one remains in the service of Satan.'

The mission visitor of the year following reported that the people 'look to [Lemuelu] as their leader in everything' (Marriott 1883), and again, a year later, Phillips (1884) reported that Lemuelu 'spoke with the greatest pleasure of his relationship to his people. He could not be treated with greater kindness & consideration. They will do anything for him to testify their appreciation of his services. Whatever the island produced they bring in abundance. No one, he says, could be happier than himself at his work.'

It is notable, however, that at the very time that Lemuelu was extolling the people's devotion to him he was also having problems with 'King' Ioane and asked Phillips to persuade the 'king' to relinquish his deaconate. Phillips did with difficulty, and he also had difficulty assembling the elders concerned with a matter of land which, according to Lemuelu, they had determined to transfer to the mission (see below). Here may be glimpsed another picture of Lemuelu—the martinet and tyrant, as he was portrayed by other visitors with other interests.

Father Didier paid a visit to Atafu with some Nukunonu companions in 1886 to 'show them the cassock . . . and try to establish the faith there'. He did not succeed, but he did write a vivid account of his visit. Ioane welcomed the visitors, but then was admonished by *leoleo* (wardens) as follows:

> 'We have not come to make a fuss, . . . we have only come to tell you that these strangers have broken the law and that you [Ioane] have also broken it with them. . . . You know that no stranger can come ashore at night or without having first been visited by the *leoleo* of the government; you know that it is forbidden to make a noise, talk on the roads or travel around at night, and these strangers have done all this; you know that it is forbidden to light a lamp at night, and yours has been lit for more than an hour in your house. . . . The law has been broken, and that means there should be some punishment; these strangers should return immediately to their *lualua* (ship); you should pay a fine.' (Didier 1886b:343)

The 'king' did not disagree and the *leoleo* allowed the visitors to remain ashore. The following morning the transgressions of the night were smoothed over, the visitors were brought 'enough provisions to feed a whole company of soldiers' and had a 'great meeting with the chiefs and king'. The adventure ended agreeably enough, though Didier wrote critically of 'the despotic way in which the aoao [Pastor Lemuelu] governed the land', contrasting the hospitality and openness of the king and people with the restraints imposed by the 'aoao and his minions'.

Frederick Moss visited Tokelau in the *Buster* in 1887 and at Atafu encountered Pastor Lemuelu, whom he caricatured in his pointed critique of repressive Protestant mission establishments. 'At Atafu I saw one of these

gentlemen dressed in ill-fitting black, with orthodox white necktie, creaking boots and white helmet, with Bible under arm and umbrella overhead, walking solemnly from his house to the church. The distance was about twenty yards; and his pompous look as he paced along was most curious to see' (Moss 1889:116).

It does appear that Lemuelu was a model pastor in his early years but became greedy and dictatorial later. Before interpreting appearances, Lemuelu's decline must be limned.

The pastor's reputation with his superiors and with his parishioners apparently waned simultaneously. When the Rev. Newell visited Tokelau in 1885, Ilai (in Olohega) complained about being arrested in Atafu for being abroad after curfew, prompting Newell to write of '. . . the frivolous laws in force' there, and at Atafu Lemuelu reported that 'fourteen church members had fallen . . . mostly for adultery and fornication', an indication that all was not well in Millennium Island. Newell suspected and quickly confirmed that this was the case when 'two long letters were put into my hands containing a number of charges against the Pastor of avariciousness and arbitrary conduct in relation to the chiefs and church members'. He rebuked Lemuelu; Lemuelu apologised; the 'king and people' were satisfied and asked that the details of the 'really private letters' be suppressed (Newell 1885). Notwithstanding this request, it was later minuted '[t]hat Pastor Lemuelu of Atafu be severely rebuked for his avariciousness and the many [. . .] things of which he has been guilty during the past year' (Wilson 1885; the section in parentheses is indecipherable).

Apparently the rebukes and apology settled the matters in Atafu for a while: a year later a new church was standing. But still Lemuelu was to be faulted by his superiors, for the next visitor questioned the church roll which '. . . contained more names than that of any other Pastor's in proportion to the number of inhabitants', commenting that it was '. . . an example of those who are demons to add to the Church roll without due concern as to the conduct of members' (Wilson 1886). Lemuelu was caught in a double bind:

if he was charitable about his flock's conduct, he was criticised by his superiors; if he scrutinised his flock's conduct, he was accused of 'arbitrary conduct'.[6] Lemuelu departed Atafu on furlough in 1888 and never returned. Though the furlough was ostensibly 'in the normal course of events . . . it was not the intention of the S.D. [Samoan District] Committee to send him back to Atafu' (LMS Samoa District 1888). It is not recorded whether this 'intention' had been formed before he departed on furlough or because action was threatened against him by the trader in Atafu (which is what occasioned the minute).

A postscript dated 1890 reporting on another mission visit to Atafu completes the story of Pastor Lemuelu. 'The pompous gentleman dressed in ill fitting black . . . of white necktie, creaking shoes & white helmet who was so distasteful to the keen but not unkindly critic of the "Buster" has long since been removed. Had Mr Moss been present here with me he would have rejoiced in the sight of a younger man of a newer school . . .' (Clarke 1890). An informed reading of the saga suggests that Lemuelu's dictatorial and self-aggrandising manner were tolerated in Atafu—even probably pandered to by some people—up to a point, and thereafter relations between pastor and flock deteriorated. But what surely precipitated Lemuelu's fall from grace was changed missionary attitudes—perhaps partially in response to Moss's indictment.

Lemuelu was a product and exemplar of an old school, preoccupied with the eradication of heathen practices and with rooting out sin, with rules, regimentation and repression as the hallmarks of Christianity. In a sense Lemuelu was a victim of his mentors' wider reassessments: initially they viewed approvingly his self-aggrandisement and domination of his flock, encouraged his self-righteousness and their exploitation, and then castigated him for 'avariciousness', 'frivolous laws' and 'arbitrary conduct' when they had begun to instigate positive programmes of Christian service and devotion.

A matter of land was being negotiated at the time—specifically, land within the village for the pastor's residence and church, and two islets for the pastor's use. Lemuelu informed Marriott (1883), 'The people are very anxious to give over to the L.M.S. the site on which the pastor's house and the chapel stands. . . . in addition they want to give over to us two islets in their lagoon

Atafu church auxiliary in their distinctive dress (with scarf). The hats were made of newspaper 'pasted together, sheet on sheet, till thick enough to form a narrow-brimmed, high-crowned head-dress' (Moss 1889:78). Photo: Mr Andrew, opp. p.78

for the use of the Samoan teacher. . .'. The Society had no hesitation about accepting the village sites, but reserved judgement about the two islets (Powell 1883b). The following year the gift was confirmed when a document (Phillips *et al.* 1884) composed by the Society was signed by 'Ioane the King', five 'chiefs' of Atafu, and the visiting missionary, who commented that it was rather difficult 'to get the chiefs together to sign the deeds by which they give over the lands mentioned in last report to the Society in London' (Phillips 1884). The chiefs apparently had become reluctant donors, and the Society, not satisfied with the document, had another one drawn up by a Sydney lawyer and taken by the mission visitor the following year. But that would not do either because the dimensions of the gift had changed, so a modified deed was hastily composed and signed, though again with some reluctance (Newell 1885). The matter was not pursued, and years later Newell, who had written and witnessed the final document, wrote that the land did not belong to the Society. These protracted and changing negotiations over land most certainly impacted upon relations between Pastor Lemuelu and his flock, reflecting differing, and perhaps changing, interests of members of his parish.

Pastor Lemuelu was a pastor who acted like a king. His counterpart was Ioane, a 'king' who yearned to be a pastor. Recall that Ioane as senior deacon appeared to a visitor 'to occupy the position of chief'. In September 1880, he had written a letter requesting that no foreign pastor be installed in Atafu, and had appealed to remain a deacon when he became 'king' promising that he would relinquish his kingship should it compromise his Christian commitment to the people. However, he had been pressured to surrender his deaconate, not by the people but by the missionary on behalf of the pastor, and he remained 'king' until his death after the turn of the century.

Turner, on receiving the aforementioned letter, wrote that 'Ioane's motive in wishing no new pastor appointed is that in that case he may eventually be raised to the full pastorate' (Turner 1878). Turner was right about Ioane's motive, but he did not appreciate the overall context. Ioane was in essence *aliki* through his position as senior deacon, because he was, as *aliki* had long been, the principal servant of God and therefore the validating authority. The 'king' was 'good-for-nothing' because he had not that role. Ioane, destined to succeed to the position of *aliki* and aware of the essence of that position, wished to enhance his sanctity in that role. However, just when he was acknowledged *aliki*, he was superseded in his role as God's servant.

That both Lemuelu and Ioane coveted dual roles, the former as pastor/king and the latter as foremost deacon/*aliki*, was a product of the situation as much as of their personalities. Neither succeeded, and this too had to do with circumstance. Lemuelu was dismissed; what happened to Ioane? Two years after he had ceased to be a deacon Father Didier paid his visit. He described Ioane as 'a large and handsome man already middle-aged and with a naturally forthright character' and a 'natural feeling for right and justice', whom 'the protestant aoaos, and chiefs indoctrinated by them, did not like . . . and even spoke of dethroning' (Didier 1886b:342). Ioane, having lost his *aliki* sanctity with the loss of his deaconate, had become a vulnerable king in a staunchly egalitarian though not compliant polity. Lemuelu's departure did not change this. Reports of the 1890s note conflict between 'the king' and 'the government' (Cusack Smith 1896a). It is tempting to speculate what might have happened if the missionaries had bowed to Ioane's 1878 request, thereby leaving the Atafu parish wholly under local control. In the event they did not; instead the Atafu polity devised strategies for dealing with semi-sanctified foreigners.

Setting the pastor apart conformed to Tokelau ideas of social order. The pastor's clearly bounded compound was sited on the village periphery—'at the ocean side'. Entry to his domain was restricted and behaviour within it prescribed. Conversely, pastors and their families were expected to venture outside their domain only for express purposes and to behave outside it with circumspection and restraint.

Not all pastors conformed to these expectations, however. What Atafu people viewed as their regulations for social order, pastors often saw as rules of Christian conduct, broadly applied. From time to time pastors succeeded in controlling, at least for a time, secular affairs, thereby blurring any distinction there might have been between parish and polity, or sanctity (*mamalu*) and governance (*pule*). Village governance in Atafu is now and surely was then a subtle business involving compromise, negotiation and a least the appearance of unanimity among a body of elderly men. Singular authority is not congenial to such governance and the role of the *aliki* therein was to validate the unanimity achieved. A 'king' without sanctity does not stand apart, cannot decree and may be subject to threats or even deposed, but a meddling, overbearing pastor might actually be banished. This was the Atafu strategy of last resort, not infrequently employed.

Early on, Atafu came to assert, and subsequently repeatedly asserted its social order. In fact, it was almost inevitable that a pastor would be removed from Atafu at the instigation of the village. Pastors were installed in the village for the benefit of the whole village, but few were able to maintain impartiality. When partiality led to the formation of factions identified as supporters and opponents of the pastor, the Atafu ethic of community unity, backed by intertwining networks of kinship, came to the fore. The meddling foreigner, the person who had 'split up the village' (*vevehi ai te nuku*), had to leave. This scenario, founded on ethnographic observation and local account and anecdote, may indeed be read between the lines of many missionary reports. Sometimes there is no need to read between the lines, as when the Rev. Newell (1906) wrote:

> . . . letters and reports I had had . . . of the persistent and slanderous attacks on [the pastor's] character by a section of the people led me to fear that [the pastor] would be compelled to leave. I found however that only a small section of malcontents . . . were concerned in the charges. . . . But after lengthened talk & investigation I found that the majority still clung to the Pastor & had renewed their confidence in him. . . . In my address to the people I recalled the history of past years & their relations to former Pastors in such a way that I am persuaded the people begin to realize what a reputation they have acquired. . . .

Despite Newell's admonishments, and indeed local recognition of their 'reputation', when strife within the community implicated the pastor, though he might have no active part in it, he had to go, and, before the middle of 1908 a new pastor was already installed at Atafu. He remained there for eighteen years; his long tenure indicates that he understood the local context, as does a remark he made to his colleagues when on furlough at Malua (Upolu) in 1916: "'One of the major difficulties facing our work [in Atafu] is the tendency of some people to discredit the pastor and denounce him to the government official'" (quoted from *Sulu Samoa*, June 1916, in Nokise 1983).

Other disagreements taxed Atafu's *māopoopo* too. By the 1880s the population was far larger than it had ever been, and fourth- and fifth-generation descendants of Tonuia were being born. Land planted and harvested by Tonuia's children and grandchildren became subject to contending claims by their numerous issue. No stories are told or recorded of land disputes between Tonuia's grandchildren, and there may in fact have been none, for they were few and still closely related, but there are numerous recountings of disputes between Tonuia's great-grandchildren, some of which are still being pursued by their own grandchildren. This was inevitable. When people pondered the future of their many children and grandchildren each bit of land assumed greater and greater value, and as kinship links became more attenuated people became more disputatious. Atafu was still essentially the progeny of Tonuia and of the 'Seven Houses' established by his offspring, but in the last decades of the nineteenth century there were quarrels within the 'Houses'. The 'Seven Houses' stood for the unity of Atafu, a community linked by many lines of ancestry to Tonuia, but now divided by more immediate links of kinship into less inclusive *kāiga* with more exclusive interests.

Still *māopoopo* prevailed, even though severely compromised at times. It prevailed because the polity invoked old ways and invented new ways of preserving it. One new way was to remove the point of contention, and right into the twentieth century every pastor that served in Atafu departed 'under a cloud' because he had become the point of contention, even though the God and church that he served were central to the identity and unity of Atafu's parish polity or polity and parish.

Fakaofo: A Generation of Conflict

Recall that after the last of the slavers had departed and the epidemic had run its course in 1863, there were only fifty-seven Tokelau people left in Fakaofo, and of these only six were adult men—Likā the *aliki*, Lea, Tenaka (who was closely associated with Peni) and three others. There were also a number of foreigners present, who had been untouched by either slavers or epidemic: Peni, the Protestant teachers Mafalā and Sakaio, and their families. During the next five years these outsiders were coming and going: Peni repeatedly voyaged to and from Samoa trying to secure and exploit Fenuafala, brought in foreign workers, but then left permanently in 1866 (though some of his workers remained); Mafalā departed in despair in 1863 and returned five years later; and Sakaio voyaged away by canoe twice and returned by ship

once. In addition, another acquisitive foreigner (Atone) with his family settled more permanently, and in 1868 Fakaofo received its first Catholic
catechist from Samoa. Tokelau people too returned from elsewhere, adding
at least fifteen adult men and eight adult women to the populace and almost
doubling the number of Fakaofo people. Many of the returning came with
agendas and projects of their own: Tefono and his fellow Catholics with the
intention of converting their compatriots to their faith (as had Lea as a Protestant some years before); others with ambitions for self-aggrandisement.
There are no accounts of the structure of village life during these years, or
of how the island was governed—or, indeed, whether the notion of a single
island polity still existed. There was no one who might rule Fakaofo as a
whole; Likā, the obvious candidate, had become a Catholic and no longer
held any legitimate authority over the whole island and all its people. He was
called *aliki*, as were his successors, but he and they did not stand for the
same things as had their predecessor. Of this more later.

The transformation of civil authority

It was in these circumstances that a decision was taken to do away with *aliki*
authority altogether and reconstitute government along gerontocratic lines,
phrased as rule by the *uluhina* 'grey-haired'. It is not clear when this change
was made—or even, in fact, whether it was the result of a single decision or
the end result of a series of piecemeal accommodations to the changing
situations of the time. The clearest account we have of it is in a recent
Tokelau manuscript history which draws upon the wide store of knowledge.

Characteristically, this change is portrayed as the result of a conscious
decision, one which was taken at a meeting of *aliki ma faipule*, the pagan
council established by Taupe (according to the same source, see chapter 5).
With so few men present on the island, this cannot have been a large gathering, or even, perhaps, a very representative one. But it was a body legiti-
mised by indigenous practice.

> It was Aliki and Faipule who made this decision, 'All men of Fakaofo shall be
> equal, in accordance with the wish of God that all men be equal.' And another
> decision which they made was this, 'As soon as a man is grey haired he joins in
> the governing of Fakaofo, without regard to his rank in Fakaofo.' Another deci-
> sion which they made was this, 'The oldest man, without regard to his rank, will
> be made the embodiment of the dignity and honour of Fakaofo.' (Perez 1977)

The account makes no reference at all to the political and social context in
which the decision was made. Instead, it goes to some pains to establish the
legitimacy of the decision, pointing out that the council of *aliki ma faipule* had
been established by Taupe years before the missions arrived in Tokelau, in
order to give those outside the *aliki* lineage a degree of conjoint authority in
political matters. Why Taupe should have done this is not fully explained,
except to the extent that he was somehow (presumably unconsciously) 'the
instrument of God's profound and serious purpose' (Perez 1977). Admittedly,
Taupe was a pagan *aliki*, but still God worked through him, and thus the coun-

cil of *aliki ma faipule* was legitimated by two sources of divine authority. The decision to establish gerontocratic rule is organically Tokelauan, a decision of an *aliki*, as well as in accord with 'the wish of God that all men be equal'.

Indeed, the change probably made little difference to the actual composition of the governing body of the island. Age had always been associated with status. There had been a preference for older men in the choice of *aliki*, and it is likely that the preference applied to *faipule* representatives as well. It was only the difference in rank between *aliki* and *faipule* that was formally abolished.

Other, more material changes followed from the conversion of the *aliki* and the loss of most of the able-bodied men from the population. In the old order, two islets were held by the *aliki*, with a further two the common property of the population as a whole, under the jurisdiction of *aliki ma faipule*. The two islets owned by the *aliki*, lying on the western reef close by Falē, passed into the hands of the two missions for use as cemeteries and to support church activities. The churches themselves, together with the Protestant teachers' establishment, were built on what was said to be Likā's land on the ocean shore of Falē. The two communally owned islets, also on the western reef, remained village property, and to these were added lands on the eastern side of the atoll that had been associated with the *falepā*.

The *falepā* were literally depopulated in 1863, and their specialised functions and exploitation of their lands across the lagoon were undertaken by whatever able-bodied men were in the village. As institutions, they vanished along with their totemic associations which were inimical to Christian teaching. Their house sites in the village were absorbed into adjacent *kāiga* domains or passed to the village as a whole.

The dissolution of the *falepā* probably had subtle social consequences. With the houses no longer maintained, and polygyny disallowed, men became more closely associated with their wives' households and dwellings, making uxorilocality a more salient feature of the local social arrangements. And if, as also seems likely, unmarried youths had formerly slept in the *falepā*, they could now be accommodated (and given appropriate instruction and discipline) in the pastoral establishments.

Protestants, Catholics, Peleila and consuls

Whenever the newly formed council of 'grey-haired men' came into existence, and whatever the balance of Catholics and Protestants in its membership, it at least provided a venue, legitimated by both God and past *aliki* authority, in which differences could be aired and some attempts made at concerted action on behalf of the population as a whole. Given the tiny, confined space of the village islet and the longstanding practice of centralised authority and necessity of communal enterprises, the religious factionalism must have been enervating—but it was generally contained, despite the provocations and agitations of outsiders.

Under the guidance of Mafalā, the Protestants built their church, which was dedicated by their mission visitors in 1871. It was evidently an impressive structure, built of coral block, with 'venetian windows' (Powell 1871b) and measuring an impressive 42 feet by 24 feet. Mafalā was well supported by his people, but he suffered from elephantiasis. To the missionaries he seemed a 'pitiable object of humanity' (Vivian 1871–72). However, despite his pitiable state he remained until 1874, when he 'fell', having compromised himself with a young Fakaofo woman, at some time in the early part of that year. Unfortunately he had to be removed (Turner 1874a) and was replaced by Timoteo.[7] Timoteo was a Tokelau pastor returning home and certainly had kinfolk in Fakaofo, and so could serve only temporarily. He was replaced the following year. After years of shepherding by Mafalā, all this was undoubtedly disconcerting for the Protestants, but it was nothing in comparison with the disturbances perpetrated by the Peleila.

Around the middle of 1874, while he was living in Samoa, Atone Peleila 'bought' the islets of Fenualoa and Nukumatau from two Fakaofo men named Hiva and Pou, both Catholics, who had either become indebted to him or had become destitute (the stories differ). While the exact nature of the transaction is not known, a witnessed document was registered with the British consul in Apia.[8]

The sale was obviously a fraudulent one. Fenualoa, a large islet forming the southwestern extremity of Fakaofo, was at the time divided into separate properties among several Fakaofo *kāiga*. Nukumatau, a much smaller islet on the reef adjacent to Falē, previously the property of the *aliki*, had passed into the control of the village council. Since he had lived in Fakaofo for extended periods, Atone was well aware of these arrangements.

He was also well aware of how to go about what he was doing. The Samoans had been engrossed in political conflict and war for several years, and in order to obtain arms they had sold large tracts of land to eager Europeans (Gilson 1970:281). There was at that time no system by which such sales could be legally registered, and no law governing the conveyance of interests in land. The most that a purchaser could do was to deposit a record of the transaction with a consulate, and then press his claim as best he could. Although a Portuguese subject, Atone had already sought and claimed British protection. Hence he deposited the record of sale with the British consulate, and shortly afterwards went to Fakaofo with his son Peleila to press the claim. Once there, they read out a letter which purported to be from Consul Williams, but the people did not believe it, and continued to go to the islets as usual. The visit of the missionary George Turner gave the people their first opportunity to seek advice as to what might be done. Turner advised them to protest the sale with Williams, which they did by a letter written in the names of the 'king and ruler' of the island.[9] The letter was probably drafted by Turner and perhaps taken with him when he left. The people eventually received a letter back from Williams, asking them to clarify whether Hiva was really a son of the king of Fakaofo (as he had evidently claimed to be), and asking what flag Peleila was flying on the land. To this they replied that Hiva was no relative of the king's, and that the German flag flew over the land.

Williams then sought help from the Protestant mission in clarifying the issues, but this could not be done until the next mission visit to Fakaofo, in the following year. The explanations were eventually delivered, but then Williams wrote again to the 'chiefs of the island' demanding to know why they disputed this act of sale when they had previously allowed the sale of Fenuafala to the German Firm. Again the people took no notice, and again Peleila protested, prompting a further letter from the consul enjoining the people to protect Peleila's claims from theft.[10] Peleila had this letter translated into Samoan, but did not make its contents immediately known on Fakaofo.

Early in 1878 Fakaofo sent a delegation of four men to Samoa to protest Peleila's claims. According to Turner's account (1882), two of these men were 'chiefs' and two were 'rulers', and a local account (Fakaofo n.d.) gives the further information that one of the 'chiefs' was a Catholic. Although Fakaofo tended to be factionalised by Peleila's actions, it is evident that, at least in this instance, the council of *aliki ma faipule* had sufficient legitimacy to encompass both Catholics and Protestants. Once in Samoa, the delegation sought the help of the Protestant mission and further representations were made to the British consul. The consulate by this time had the records of four years of claims and counterclaims. Some official letters had been sent in both English and Samoan; others had been entrusted to Atone to translate into Samoan; some had been delivered, others had not. The confusions might have been cleared up readily enough if only Atone and his son could have been called in. They, however, had just left Apia harbour on a ship belonging to the German Firm, bound for Fakaofo.

At this point the catalogue of inefficiencies, lies and prevarications turned to farce. Turner and the delegation of four set off for Fakaofo in another ship, and when they arrived a few days later, Atone and Peleila were already ashore, together with the captain, Nipua, who had read out a letter to the village (presumably in Samoan) to the effect that, 'It is forbidden for Fakaofo people to go any more to Fenualoa. Atone and Peleila now own Fenualoa' (Fakaofo n.d.). With both ships lying off the island, Turner went ashore and demanded to see the letter which Nipua had brought, and after comparing it with the copy of the English original which he had, he was able to expose the deceitful Samoan translation to the council. Atone still had, however, an earlier letter from the consulate proclaiming his protected status, together with the request that 'favourable consideration' be given to his claims. The claims had not been judged, and neither Turner nor the people of the island can have been certain what their legal status might turn out to be.[11] It was to be fourteen years before they found out.

In the meantime, the conflict between Peleila and the people of Fakaofo escalated. The Fakaofo (n.d.) manuscript gives a direct and vivid account of what happened on the island in the period immediately after Turner's visit.

Although this was a bitter blow to the true patriots of Fakaofo, they continued their attempts to hold on to the islet. People continued to go to their lands on Fenualoa. They could not obey the letter which came with Nipua. The village was divided in two, with the Catholics siding with Peleila, including Tefono, Akafi

(Kilino) and Vaea (Aniseto), but the majority of Protestants were steadfast and determined.

Peleila brought some Samoan men to help him, including Papu and Alipa and others, and they were taken by Peleila and put on Fenualoa to work. They were like Peleila's dogs, these Samoan fools. What did they do on Fenualoa? It was true that they worked and built houses. But there were other evil things which they did: (1) They would fire guns when they saw canoes coming to their lands on Fenualoa. (2) They would stand with nets to catch people who persisted in spite of the guns. (3) They used savage dogs that tried to attack people when they went.

In spite of all these things, by far the worst aspect was the disunity, because some people sided with Atone, as mentioned above. The abominable behaviour of those seeking to ingratiate themselves with Atone was the subject of a song written by the old man Peniuto:

Fakaofo loto kehekehe	*Fakaofo of differing wishes*
Kua takaitahi ma tona maene	*Each following his own mind*
Kae hē tū atu ke teteke	*So not standing forth to resist*

The song was very true, since the outcome was that Peleila gained control of the islet. The plantations were enlarged and houses were built, and flags were put up on Fenualoa, the Hakea islets and Nukumatau. It was like a picture of Germany, although the flags were not those of the German government, but merely pieces of cloth sewn by Tali, the wife of Peleila, and set up as flags. The people were determined to press on with their petitions when they thought of what would happen to the coming generations of Fakaofo. For this reason the old man Peniuto composed another song expressing the concern of the council for the coming generations of Fakaofo:

Te fiā la o aliki	*The true burden of chiefs*
e ute ko pō amuli	*Is making provision for days to come*
e alofa ki kau tamaiti	*Is concern for the coming generations*

The names of the pastor Mafalā and the catechist Matulino are still remembered because of their great efforts to get the islet back. . . .[12]

Atone and Peleila established control over Fenualoa mainly by their aggressive occupation of the islet, and consolidated it by bluff and the threat of arms. A truly effective council of *aliki ma faipule* might have prevented this, but then the council was disabled and powerless because there was no unanimity between its Protestant and Catholic members. The Protestants might have forced the issue, but then the population was still very small, probably well under 200, with Catholics making up about a third of the total. The Protestants also lacked an aggressive leader. The pastor was Aperau, a Rarotongan and evidently a peaceable and industrious soul who is remembered mainly for having introduced and promoted the cultivation of *pulaka* on the atoll. Then when his term was completed, in 1878, the congregation was left in the care of two local deacons. Again, an aggressive rival trader might have sought his own advantage by attempting to galvanise an opposition to Peleila, and by 1877 there was in fact another trader on the atoll, who was working for a New Zealand company and was associated with the Protestants through his local wife. But he was a peaceful, contemplative man, more interested in mathematics than in commerce.[13]

The Fakaofo people, then, could do little but rely on the visiting LMS missionaries to act on their behalf in bringing the situation to the attention of British authorities. The missionaries did what they could. Turner handed over all the documents relating to his 1878 visit and confrontation with Atone and Peleila to the British consul in Apia, and the consul duly forwarded them to Suva in November of 1878. In Suva, however, the newly established Western Pacific High Commission (WPHC) was immobilised by disputes between the Admiralty, Colonial Office and Foreign Office over the respective duties of commanders, commissioners and consuls (Scarr 1967: chapter 3) and was hardly in a position to take decisive action. The result, perhaps predictably, was that no action was taken at all. The British consul eventually wrote to the people of the island in late 1880 requesting them not to 'further interfere with Peleila, who is under British protection' (Hicks Graves 1880). And there the matter rested for the time being.

The death of Vaopuka

In 1880, the Protestants were unified and stirred into action by the appointment of the Samoan Iapesa as pastor of Fakaofo. He was not a peaceable or conciliatory man. The visiting Catholic priests of the time describe him variously as 'véritable énergumène (real ranter)', 'notorious', 'infamous' and 'cunning'. The Protestant missionaries, however, were 'exceedingly delighted' with his work, characterising him as 'a most diligent and successful teacher', 'a true leader of the people' and as having 'real and undoubted ability'. Iapesa arrived at Fakaofo in September and was installed in his position by Davies. Foreshadowing the conflicts to come, the report of this visit remarks that, 'The one cause of annoyance during our stay here was the constant ringing of the bell for Papist services' (Davies 1880).

Within a month there were open confrontations between the two congregations, and from that point on the hostilities steadily escalated towards the climactic event, which was the shooting and death of Vaopuka, the Protestant *aliki*. Members of each side reported it all to their respective mission visitors. Characteristically, the Protestant account, taken from Iapesa's written records, drily catalogues the events day by day; the Catholic account is based on eyewitness accounts recorded over a year later. Phillips (1881) gives the Protestant version.

> *Oct 6th/80* The bible of one of our deacons was seized & torn up because they said it was not the true word of God. No redress was possible for this.
>
> *Oct 28/80* Resolved by the Papists to kill some of the Protestants if they persisted in erecting their new schoolroom so near the papist chapel. In consequence the school had be erected elsewhere.
>
> *Nov 7/80* Windows of teachers house smashed by papists of Nukunonu.
>
> *Jany 26/81* A very serious quarrel between the two parties because a Prot. boy in throwing a stone at a fowl happened to hit the papist chapel. Compensation money was offered but refused.
>
> *Feby 12/81* Resolved at a meeting of the papists held in the Portuguese halfcaste's house to kill all the Protestants, but a sick papist to whom the plot was communicated prevented it.
>
> *May 7th* A very serious quarrel arose between the two parties. The church and king tried to prevent it but the papists seized guns and succeeded in wounding four men — one of whom *was the King* who died from his wound the month following.

The fuller Catholic account was written by Father Dolé (1885:398–9).

> The reason for this battle was the *lali* [the aforementioned 'bell']. The catholics sounded their *lali* for the Angelus, morning, noon and evening. A heretic teacher . . . allowed the children of his school to beat, at midday, on a tin box, to mock the catholics. For some time they were patient; but, one day, one of our catholics went up to the school master himself asking why this unwarranted mockery. Agreement was not possible; they resorted to fists; but no one was seriously injured. Anyway, only young men were involved in the incident. The king, a heretic, wished to bring our young catholics to judgement, accusing them of starting the disorder. The land was brought together in a general assembly. The king ordered the accused to place themselves in the midst of the enclosure;[14] but suspecting some trap, they refused to obey, while agreeing to answer all questions and thereby clearly showing that the responsibility rested with the heretics. The king thereupon began a speech, which ended with this cruel command: 'Attack the catholics!' Two camps immediately formed; seizing stones, clubs, spears, old guns. The catholic chiefs realised that they must protect their endangered lives; they were fewer, it is true; but they fought for their religion, and feared not. The king wished to be the hero of the battle; he threw himself into the melee; but soon a young man, named Émile, fired on him, and the ball hit him full in the chest; he fell on the body of a heretic, whose head had been split in two by a club-blow. The Protestant side, seeing their king dead, fled in disorder and retreated towards the sea. The catholics were victors; among them were some wounded, but none were dead.

What happened immediately after this violent outburst is not recorded. Dolé attributed the Catholic victory to the Lord's mercy. Phillips, for his part, claimed the moral victory: '. . . many of [the Protestants] would be faithful unto death—as firm in their refusal to compromise between popery & Christ as our forefathers were in the times of the Reformation'. If his converts were not the victors, they could at least be martyrs.

There are no formalised Fakaofo accounts of any of the incidents surrounding Vaopuka's death. This may appear strange, but it is also characteristic. It was a shameful occurrence, one which reflected badly on the entire village, and thus not to be in any way celebrated in either song or story. The Catholics, according to Dolé, composed a song about the 'war', but if they did, it has been long forgotten.[15] Besides, Vaopuka's death did not by itself effectively resolve anything. Nor did much else change. Tetaulu, Likā's elder son, who was a Protestant, became the new *aliki*. But there was little that he could do as long as the council was divided and the Catholics were armed. Formal channels also did little good. Phillips collected evidence on the case during his visit in September of 1881, and in due course the Samoan mission laid a complaint with the British consul in Apia. This was duly forwarded to Suva and by September of the following year Phillips had a reply from the Secretary of the Western Pacific High Commission to the effect that the 'islands will be at once visited by HMS *Diamond*. The Captain of that ship Capt. A. Dale, R.N., is a Deputy Commissioner for the Western Pacific and will at once take measures to prevent any proceedings such as those attributed by you . . . and if necessary to remove from the island those British subjects who may be dangerous to its peace and good order' (Secretary, WPHC 1882). However, the HMS *Diamond* never made the promised visit, and Peleila remained in effective control of both Fenuafala and Fenualoa.[16]

During the next two years there were no more major alarms reported from Fakaofo, although Iapesa, who seems to have had the full support of his congregation, continued to report troubles with local 'papists', who were 'circulating lying stories' and causing him endless troubles, and even 'perils'. Both Davies (1882) and Marriott (1883) give accounts, which must have come from Iapesa, of visits by French priests from Samoa who moved among the local people and 'circulated outrageous stories concerning the break-up of our mission in Samoa!' telling them that 'French man of war was to come and tie up our teacher and take him to Samoa'.

These stories may or may not have been true.[17] Eventually, however, the English missionaries seem to have decided that the time had come for reconciliation between the two sides, and Phillips, on his visit to the island in 1884, spoke to both the catechist and Iapesa to remind them of their one common saviour, the many points of doctrine which they held in common and that 'to live in hatred, envy and strife was to serve the devil, not God'. On this visit Phillips also took the opportunity to show Peleila the letter from the Western Pacific High Commission threatening a visit from the HMS *Diamond*. Peleila appeared to be 'anxious and conciliatory' at this turn of events, and it appeared that Catholics and Protestants alike were 'determined if possible to get rid of him' (Phillips 1884).

 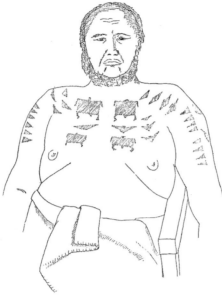

Tetaulu, the aliki *of Fakaofo (1881–c.1890), (*left*) wearing his emblems of office, and (*right*) 'showing the tattooing on his chest'.* In Lister 1892, reproduced by courtesy of the Royal Anthropological Institute of Great Britain and Ireland

Conflicts over land

For a brief period after Phillips's visit there was peace between the congregations. It was, however, a strictly local peace, one which did not involve a resolution of the differences between the larger church organisations and the British and French interests which they represented. Nor did it quiet Iapesa's ambitions for complete pastoral domination of the island.

Phillips, during this same visit, had learned, probably from Iapesa, that Tetaulu, the *aliki*, wanted to give land in the village to the Protestant mission. He had Tetaulu's intentions 'put in writing' and then delivered the letter to the Samoan mission.

July 15, 1884

> *This letter is to make known to you Missionaries the pieces of land set apart for the work of God that you may possess and protect them. On one of the pieces of land stands the house of our Pastor; on the other stands the Church. I have full power to give these* [lands] *up for the work. No other King succeeding me can have any authority over them.*

> *I am Teulu* [sic] *the King of Fakaofo*

The mission readily agreed and had a deed drawn up by a Sydney lawyer, which Newell took to Fakaofo for signing in September 1885. Iapesa greeted him with further tales of papist perfidy, which Newell appears to have taken at face value—while at the same time noting Iapesa's 'avariciousness and indiscretion' (Newell 1885).

Newell might also have experienced some disquiet when he realised that the proposed land gift was not a single plot and 'that one piece of land *included* the Roman Catholic Chapel which is *close* to the teacher's house'.[18] He did point this out to the king, only to be told 'that the land belonged to

245

the King, and has never been given over to the Papists'. 'Moreover', Newell's account continues, 'they desired to press the matter to a solution once and for ever' (Newell 1885). Newell therefore had the deed signed, taking the precaution of explaining it to all, including the Catholics and the 'Portuguese half-caste' (i.e. Peleila).

Newell heard no protest. Nevertheless, when Father Didier visited Fakaofo shortly afterwards he had a different story to tell: '. . . about a month before . . . the John Williams came here to Fakaofo with a certain little minister from Samoa called Newell. Now this little minister, no doubt tricked by the cunning Iapesa, had granted to him by the king Taulu [sic] and his chief minister Vaiala, not only the lands where the church is situated, the schools and house of the protestant teacher, but in addition our lands with our stone church, our schools and the house of the catechist . . .' (Didier 1886a:192).

Didier ridiculed the deed of gift, proclaiming it 'null and void' because '18 years before the old king Likā had given these lands to Mgr Elloy and the catechist Matulino, so that another king could not repossess [them]' (1886a:192–3). He then wrote to the *aliki* forbidding him to act until the French consul in Samoa had had time to consider the whole matter.

In Apia, once Newell had returned from his extended 1885 voyage, the topic was taken up by the missions and their respective consuls. Between them, they came to an amicable agreement whereby the Catholics would keep their rights to the land adjacent to the Protestant compound, which was occupied by their church and the catechist's establishment, and Iapesa was duly instructed by letter 'to give up the land on the side of [his] house' and 'not to precipitate matters by any unnecessary interference' (Claxton 1886).

Didier knew of this letter. But he also knew that Iapesa would probably not obey the instructions unless he were forced to. So he sought reinforcements, arranging for eight Uvean neophytes 'related to the Tokelau chiefs' (probably descendants of the 1852 exodus) to go to Fakaofo (Didier 1886c:297). He then went to Fakaofo himself in August of 1885, taking with him two strong young Samoan men. As he had predicted, Iapesa was still maintaining his garden on the Catholic land beside his house. So Didier took the two Samoans with him to pull up the plants and deposit them on Iapesa's land. To his obvious delight, the strategy worked: '. . . as soon as the task had begun, [Iapesa] ran around assembling all his followers and they arrived like an avalanche; I had told our catholics to stay in their houses. For about an hour we had the spectacle of the most mock-heroic scene I have ever viewed: the poor *aoao* [preacher] yelling, jumping about, exhorting his people, tearing his clothes, and calling me all the names imaginable; while at the same time, our young men were finishing their work and thereby establishing ownership of the land. For my part I kept the people in check and tried to pacify the *aoao*. . . .' (Didier 1886b:334).

In retrospect, Didier's move was as dangerous as it was audacious, since matters might easily have got out of hand. But it was in accord with local practices about land rights, and he excused his actions by claiming them to have been the only recourse he had. Once it was done, Didier wrote down

an account of the whole proceedings which he left on the island to be shown to the Protestant missionaries when they arrived (Didier 1886b).

Right on Didier's heels came Wilson, the secretary of the Samoan mission, who had been delegated to carry the news of the mission's decision to Iapesa because he was less personally involved with him than the regular mission visitors. Wilson listened to Iapesa's story, read Didier's letter, and came to the conclusion that Iapesa had 'acted very injudiciously and insultingly (but under provocation)' and reproved him severely. He did not, however, remove him from his post—mainly because the priests had predicted that he would. He also set the land problem straight by explaining to the 'King and chiefs' why the Society could not accept the gift as it had been offered, and the nature of the prearranged compromise with the Catholic mission (Wilson 1886).

Didier had the satisfaction of returning to Fakaofo soon after Wilson's departure and learning directly of what had happened. The Catholics were jubilant and the Protestants downcast, not only because they had lost out in the confrontation but because Iapesa had apparently led them to believe that they had the full support of the Society. Didier then pressed his advantage further by making formal complaints about Iapesa to the French government. Faced thus with the possibility of a minor international incident the British consul in Apia advised the Society to remove Iapesa and save further trouble. The task of going to Fakaofo and doing this fell to Marriott, and he dreaded it. But Iapesa apparently accepted his removal as being the 'wisest choice', although the *aliki* and chiefs were far from acquiescent. 'We assembled in a very hot room and for nearly two hours his highness reproached my brethren and myself. . . . They would allow me to rebuke him but they would not hear of my taking him away. When I told them I must take him away, the king declared in his wrath that they would become Roman Catholics' (Marriott 1887).

Oceanside of Fakaofo village islet, showing the Protestant pastor's compound at Maluatea (left) and adjacent Catholic compound (right). Somewhere in between is the area the Protestants and Catholics were contesting. Photo: Mr Andrew, courtesy of the Museum of New Zealand Te Papa Tongarewa [D460]

In order to gain the day, Marriott warned that if he did not remove Iapesa he might be forcibly removed by a French warship and taken to Samoa as a criminal. The parting was dramatic and tearful. Iapesa, in his final sermon, made the most of his accomplishments and the loss his congregation would suffer by his departure, and Marriott countered by publicly advising the new pastor not to follow Iapesa's intolerant ways.

Thus Iapesa departed, contentious to the end and adored by his congregation, but too provocative and ambitious to be tolerated by either the Catholic or the Protestant mission. Once he had left, an uneasy but lasting peace was established between Catholics and Protestants in Fakaofo.

It is obvious that Iapesa himself was in large part responsible for his removal. Yet the missionaries were responsible too—he was a product of their teachings and their prejudices. His predecessors had been mild and ineffectual, and they wanted a man of action and encouraged him in his actions. In 1880, when he arrived, Peleila and his workers occupied and used both Fenualoa and Fenuafala, and the Protestants appeared to be quietly acceding to this. Certainly, he harassed the Catholics, but he was also industrious and threw himself into various general improvements. Both Phillips (1884) and Newell (1885) praised him for overcoming the 'natural indolence' of the people, and Wilson (1886) gave him credit 'for the good road wh. circuits the island,[19] for a breakwater . . . & for sanitary improvements'. To be sure, there was an element of personal aggrandisement involved in all this, most particularly in his 'very remarkable house' (Phillips 1884) constructed of timber sawn from foreign drift logs, but even this could be seen as a success for his whole congregation and an emblem of their unity and strength. And what might be made of his large garden and poultry on Nukulakia, an islet immediately adjoining Fenualoa? Was he confronting Peleila or imitating him?

It was the French priest Father Didier, more than anyone else, who brought about Iapesa's downfall, which he engineered by the dramatic and well-timed removal of the garden, thereby provoking a minor international incident. Doubtless the local Catholics had cause to be extremely incensed, but it is difficult to see Didier simply as a heroic saviour of the oppressed when he and his brethren had for so long turned a blind eye to the activities of Peleila.

The respective governments involved—American, German, French and British (and especially the British, who brought Tokelau under the sway of the Western Pacific High Commission in 1877)—might perhaps have been expected to show something more than rhetorical concerns for justice. The consuls, however, all had greater difficulties to deal with, in larger situations closer to hand.

Control of conflict

The records and documents written by Protestant and the Catholic visitors to Fakaofo in the 1880s portray a village rife with strife. How accurate is that portrayal? First of all, the commentators had their own conflicting agendas, allegiances and selective sources of information, and, second, they them-

Pastor Iapesa, his wife, and attending members of his congregation in front of his house at Maluatea. Photo: Mr Andrew, courtesy of the Museum of New Zealand Te Papa Tongarewa [D461]

selves generated conflicts. In all of these accounts, 'the people' of Fakaofo, with the exception of the *aliki*, play no part except as 'factions' or 'parties', two 'camps' to be tallied by each visitor.

There is virtually no direct evidence of how 'people' in Fakaofo fared through it all. Yet they must have managed to feed themselves, raise their children and go about their daily lives, despite the conflicts and confrontations, and they might even have been working together and getting along with their neighbours who had different loyalties and religious convictions. After all, some 200 of them were all living on a village islet barely 100 metres in diameter, and in only one instance did one 'party' attack the other.[20]

Certainly, people were partial and looked after their own interests, but their very existence required accommodation and compromise. How else can the indirect evidence of what might seem improbable alliances be understood? Catholic baptisms recorded in 1882 include the only daughter of the recently slain Vaopuka (Dolé 1885:398), and those of 1883 include a daughter and son of Lea, the Protestant stalwart. The marriage of this same daughter to Peleila a year or so later might be cynically viewed as an opportunistic alliance—advantageous in different ways to both father and husband—but then, three other of Lea's children converted to Catholicism and married Catholics, as did a son of the *aliki* Tetaulu. Those who converted from one religion to the other (and we have evidence only of those who converted to Catholicism and have noted only the most striking) were not exiled from their natal *kāiga*, nor did such conversions lead to the division of *kāiga* lands along the lines of religious cleavage. Kinship ties must have been strained at times, but they were not completely severed. The general Tokelau strategy of establishing wide connections and maintaining all links to have access to all benefits was never abandoned, and the outcome was a dense network of overlapping interests. The tiny embattled polity would not have survived if

A son and daughter of the Fakaofo aliki, Tetaulu, *who was portrayed in mission records as a strong Protestant partisan. His son, however, wears a Catholic scapular. His daughter is wrapped in a mat of distinctive Fakaofo patterning.* Photo in Lister 1892, reproduced by courtesy of the Royal Anthropological Institute of Great Britain and Ireland

conflicts had not been moderated by the ties that bound the people to one another and to their land.

The authority of the *aliki* diminished sharply after 1863, but that was a conscious decision taken to accommodate Christianity morality, rather a result of religious factionalism. The office, however, was maintained well into the twentieth century, and all its incumbents, bar one, were drawn from the ancient *aliki* patrilineal line. *Aliki* were obviously no longer mediators between the people and Tui Tokelau, so what did they stand for? Reflecting back to Likā, the last pagan *aliki*, it seems that he stood for different things at different times. When Tui Tokelau was god of all Tokelau, he was the avenue of communication to the god, but when people began to embrace Christianity, he was the pagan *aliki* standing for the dignity or integrity of Tokelau against the outside world and its inroads in Atafu and Nukunonu. When he converted to Catholicism at the instigation of his son, he stood for the integrity of Fakaofo *vis-à-vis* Ben Hughes and Lea and Sakaio. So it was that when Peleila was the foreign agitator within, the *aliki* had to be Protestant, not just because the Fakaofo majority was Protestant, but because he stood for the integrity of Fakaofo *vis-à-vis* the Catholic intruder. *Aliki* still stood for something, even though Tui Tokelau had been toppled.

The respect and authority of elders was, if anything, enhanced by the patriarchal Christian order, whether Protestant or Catholic. These 'grey-heads', assembled as the council of *aliki ma faipule*, continued to meet, probably sometimes more regularly than others, throughout the conflicts.

'Nothing pleased these ladies better than to be summoned to the verandah of Mr Polsen's [sic] house and to be asked questions about the beliefs and customs of the people before the introduction of Christianity, which occurred about twenty years ago.' They were 'adorned with coconut leaves to show the decorations of the old times' (Lister 1892:45). Photo in Lister 1892, reproduced by courtesy of the Royal Anthropological Institute of Great Britain and Ireland

Evidence of their concerted action (aside from their delegation to Samoa in 1878) was a 'large leatherbound book of laws' which included among others the 'Law of the Year 1885' which was 'to the effect that if a native got into debt to a white trader his land should be given to the chiefs of his District and they would pay off the debt. The sale of land to foreigners was forbidden', witnessed by the *aliki*, the chief *faipule*, the secretary, *and* the two traders, Paulsen and J. Peleila (enclosure in Cusack Smith 1892b). Though the council of *aliki ma faipule* was certainly compromised at times by sectar-

Lister remarked of a performance he witnessed: 'The whole thing was, we understood, the revival of a "heathen" ceremony, permitted by the king for this special and so important occasion, when their island had become part of the British Empire' (1892:45). This photo apparently records this ceremony; many of those seated are attired as he describes. Photo taken by J.J. Lister in 1889 and reproduced by courtesy of the Royal Anthropological Institute of Great Britain and Ireland

251

ian conflicts, it emerged with its authority unquestioned when religious factionalism was put aside—which it was, more or less permanently.

Relations Between the Parish Polities

Sectarian rivalries at times transcended the fringing reefs of the atoll polities, as missionaries or converts of one denomination tried to gain converts where another held sway. On the one hand, in no instance did proselytisers prevail: once the three atolls had established their church affiliations, they effectively dismissed any others. On the other hand, the polities could not be completely self-contained, since people would not deny their common heritage and ancestry.

Take, for instance, the case of Pou. Protestant missionaries were fond of telling how Pou and his family abandoned their home in Nukunonu 'for conscience's sake', but these outsiders were seemingly unaware that Pou's conscience did not prevent him from leaving behind a daughter in Nukunonu, who was raised by his sister and who founded a large Catholic family. Pou himself disappeared in a 'slave ship', but his two sons carried on his Protestant commitment and both spent time at Malua, the LMS training school in Upolu. Yet the progeny of Pou maintain their kinship bonds despite their separate atoll affiliations and faiths to this day.

Incidents and their interpretation

In November of 1870, Mafalā with a party of sixty people in six large double canoes paid a visit to Nukunonu. There are no local accounts of this visit (from either Fakaofo or Nukunonu) and the references to it in mission records (Pratt 1872, Gill 1872) are slight. It was probably more than a social call on relatives, and had political and religious motives. With Likā's death and the succession of a Protestant *aliki*, the time would have appeared ripe for a reassertion of Fakaofo's traditional overlordship of Nukunonu. But Nukunonu was Catholic and could call upon the support and resources of the Marist mission, which would thwart reestablishment of Fakaofo overlordship. The success of the venture thus depended upon the Nukunonu people becoming Protestants—which would explain Mafalā's part in it.

What actually happened during the visit is not known with any certainty. Monseigneur Elloy complained that Mafalā had tried to persuade the chiefs of Nukunonu to 'leave the Papists and receive the word of truth' (Pratt 1872). In retaliation, Elloy later visited the Fakaofo *aliki* and attempted to persuade him to become a Catholic like his cousin Likā (Pratt 1872). The LMS missionaries denied that Mafalā's intent was proselytising. Whatever actually happened, Tokelau people probably drew their own conclusions about God's opinion of the whole venture when, on the return voyage to Fakaofo, the six canoes failed to make landfall, and, turning south for Samoa, fetched up on Olohega, whence they were taken back to Fakaofo by a German trading ship. Since this was Mafalā's second voyaging mishap, at least the Protestants on Fakaofo might have been persuaded that if they wished to attempt the conversion of any other islands, they should leave their pastor at home.

Again in the 1880s, there are Pastor Iapesa's reports to his mentors (Marriott 1883) of the proselytising activities of Catholic priests visiting Fakaofo. Recall that Father Didier did voyage to Atafu in 1886 to '. . . show them the cassock of a catholic missionary and try to establish the faith there' (Didier 1886b:339). He simultaneously warned of a 'conspiracy hatched by Iapesa and his minions, and the *aoao* [Lemuelu] of Atafu and some of his people' (1886b:346). Indeed, the LMS visitor of 1884 reported that Lemuelu had visited Nukunonu, stayed two Sundays, but had not been able to convert anyone (Phillips 1884a). These kinds of alarms and accusations were rife in the mid 1880s and seem to have had some substance at least in light of the stated intentions of Didier, Iapesa and Lemuelu. But what was the Tokelau perception of it all? According to Didier, the 1886 plot was that Iapesa's militant Fakaofo Protestants would voyage en masse to Atafu and there join forces with supporters of Lemuelu to overthrow 'king' Ioane and install another in his place. Then the combined forces of Protestantism would conquer Nukunonu. This scenario was certainly not without some foundation, though Didier was using it to undermine his arch foe, Iapesa, whom he characterised as 'far crueller and more wicked than ignorant savages' and a fanatic and tyrannous sectarian (Didier 1886b:347). Nukunonu's Catholic exclusiveness was undoubtedly an affront to the two Samoan pastors and their more avid parishioners, and from the perspective of Fakaofo, Nukunonu's autonomous stance, predicated on their exclusive faith, was surely an affront. There may well have been a lot of talk, but there appears to have been little action, for whatever may have been plotted never came to pass.

It was during this same decade that Iakopo, one of the original Atafu deacons, accompanied by his wife and at least four children, went to Nukunonu and made their home there. Whatever precipitated this move, it was not apparently seen in Nukunonu as a Protestant intrusion. On his father's side, Iakopo was a half-brother of Nukunonu's 'king' Ulua, yet his mother was the youngest daughter of Atafu's founders and he was married to 'king' Ioane's sister's daughter. Why did he leave Atafu and move to Nukunonu late in life? Did he see himself as a Protestant emissary with good connections and established rights, or did he shift to Nukunonu to assert his connections and establish his rights? The outcome provides no clues, since three of his children became Catholic—both sons even became catechists[21]—and married in Nukunonu, but his descendants have no property as their inheritance from him. If these were indeed his intentions, he was disappointed.

In any case, he remained in Nukunonu, and was joined there by another prominent Protestant, Hakaio, one of the sons of the late Fakaofo *aliki* Vaopuka by one of his several wives. Hakaio had a family in Atafu, but became a Catholic convert in 1892 to marry and father another family in Nukunonu. He quickly renounced his conversion and began holding Protestant services in his wife's house.

In order to complete the story, we must move forward to the next century. Hakaio and Iakopo and their families lived in Nukunonu for over a decade before the Protestant mission learned of this small Protestant congregation in an island they 'had understood was entirely Roman Catholic' (Newell 1904). Righteously invoking the principle of 'religious liberty', the Rev. Newell set about defending this 'interesting little community of twenty people holding the Protestant faith and maintaining it under severe persecution from the Roman Catholics who rule the Island' (Newell 1903).

At this time, Tokelau was being sporadically visited, when transportation could be arranged, by colonial officials deputised by the high commissioner in Fiji. It is not apparent whether Deputy Commissioner Hunter apprised Newell of the Protestants in Nukunonu after they complained to him that they were prohibited from establishing their own church (though they were allowed to hold services in their homes) (Hunter 1902), or whether Newell had an intimation of their presence and asked Hunter to investigate. Anyway, they were of like mind on the matter: the Protestant minority must be protected from persecution by the Catholic majority. Hunter was not certain that they were being persecuted, whereas Newell was certain that they were, though he had no direct evidence. He wrote to them; he arranged for a deputation from Fakaofo to visit them; he wrote to Hunter who '. . . visited them last year and insisted on religious liberty, which injunction has been ignored. . . .' (Newell 1903).

Both Hunter and Newell visited Nukunonu in July 1904. Hunter counted ten Protestants and considered that persecution had decreased. Newell reported on his first-hand visit at length. He claimed that Protestants numbered seventeen (eight of them children) and had 'at last been allowed to hold services in a small house . . .' without being disturbed, a concession he attributed to Hunter's recent visit. He was courteously received by the rulers and Takua (by now *aliki*), and when he 'stated our request for religious liberty for our people' was politely told that 'the little Protestant flock were not Nukunonu people and could hold services whenever they *visited* Nukunonu. Permission to build a little church at any future time could not be granted without the consent of the Priest . . .' (Newell 1904, original emphasis). Newell did not contest the statement, though he thought it incorrect, and deferred the matter of building a church to some future time. He conducted a service with the Protestants and departed on friendly terms with all, having been gifted with coconuts and fowls by 'the whole community united'. The Rev. Newell was somewhat placated, and surely must have appreciated that the Protestants were not an isolated or persecuted minority. Yet he continued to be misinformed, for example, that Iakopo, his wife and children had steadfastly refused to become Catholic for over twenty years, when their children and grandchildren were baptised Catholics, as were Hakaio's three children.

Newell chose not to contest the assertion that the Protestants were not Nukunonu people, though it is a statement that calls for some explanation. Certainly, the children with Nukunonu Catholic parentage would be considered Nukunonu progeny—perhaps they were not yet counted 'people'. The identified adults were Hakaio, Iakopo and his wife and another Atafu man,

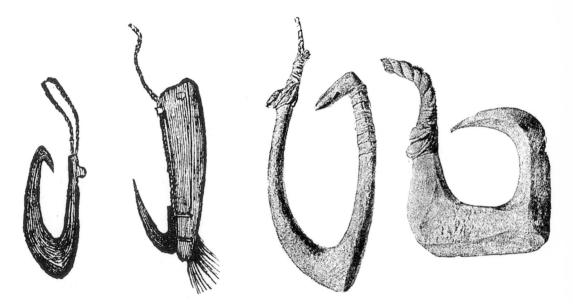

none of whom were Nukunonu people in the sense of uncontested ancestry and attendant property rights. Other adults would have been Iakopo's in-married children, who were baptised but had no real property in their own right.

Newell visited again the following year, again holding a service, but in 1906 only sent letters to 'the little flock. . . reported to be holding their own' (Newell 1906), an optimistic statement given his report that Iakopo had died and two others had returned to Atafu. He did not visit again, though the high commissioner in Fiji received a letter from him (1907) again appealing for religious liberty, and enclosing letters from Fakaofo (dated 30 July 1907). The beginning of one (in Newell's translation) reads:

Top left: 'Fish hooks of Union Islanders' collected by R.W. Coppinger, Surgeon, on the Alert in 1880. Drawing in Coppinger 1899:143

Top right: 'Fish-hooks used by the natives of Fakaofo. [left] A wooden hook. [right] A bone hook' (Lister 1892:63). Note: the wooden hook is twice the size of the bone hook.

> 1. To make known to your Excellency:—
> The instruction given in past years with reference to liberty to Protestants on account of hindrances which arose in Nukunonu. Now that hindrance has again arisen in Nukunonu. On July 27 some people from Atafu and Fakaofo were refused (a landing) unless they would return to Fakaofo and become Catholics, then they might go back to Nukunonu. The root of that action is they say that they have a revelation from heaven.
>
> We desire to remind your Excellency to again set that right. They have resisted your will and the rule of Fakaofo in that place. [our emphasis]

This last statement indicates that more than religious liberty is at issue, and an incident of that year recalled in Nukunonu suggests the immediate provocation. Here is the story.

> A young man from Fakaofo, named Sakalia, came to live with Hakaio and became enamoured of a Nukunonu girl, named Taugalea. Hakaio's attempt to wed them in a Protestant service was thwarted by the girl's father, and so the young man

255

resolved to become a Catholic in order to marry [he was baptised in 1906 or 1907], *and they were. But when a party from Fakaofo visited, he decided to carry his bride off to Fakaofo. His well-laid plan succeeded despite the attempts of his father-in-law to literally hold onto his daughter. There they joined the Protestant faith.*[22]

Carrying off a Nukunonu woman to Fakaofo was all too reminiscent of a well-remembered past, when Fakaofo men appropriated Nukunonu men. The Nukunonu polity, in closing its shores to all Protestants, was probably reacting to renewed threats of domination. Indeed, Fakaofo was being increasingly demanding and the demands were increasingly phrased in political terms. The episode that culminated in the mysterious disappearance of two canoes in 1902 marks a turning point, because it is here that the Western Pacific High Commission as 'protector' becomes involved (Huntsman and Hooper 1985). That story, however, belongs in the next chapter.

During the era of the parish polities, when religious commitment and political authority were bound up with one another as they had been before conversion, the relations between the atolls, and particularly the changed and charged relationship between Fakaofo and Nukunonu, were phrased, at least by ill-informed outsiders, exclusively in terms of sectarian conflict. However, beyond asserting that there was far more at stake than church affiliation, and glimpsing in some instances the intricacies of specific episodes and events, caution in interpretation is warranted. No mission visitors appear to have appreciated, or at least none of them remarked, that in the pre-conversion past 'rule' had been to some extent super-local, and Fakaofo had dominated a pan-Tokelau polity. Yet this past situation conditioned and motivated actions and reactions in Tokelau, as Fakaofo sought to re-establish precedence, and Atafu and Nukunonu in particular continued to assert autonomy.

How far did Tokelau converts of whatever persuasion share their teachers' and mission mentors' intolerance? People were visiting between communities and taking up more or less permanent residence in an atoll other than that with which they identified. Their motivations for doing so were undoubtedly various and not primarily determined by religious conviction.[23] Despite the sometimes contentious relations between the three parish polities, people were recognising and strengthening existing kinship ties and establishing new ones, in church-sanctified unions, that transcended the separate polities. Tokelau was both one and three.

EIGHT
Outposts of Empire

A colonial official wrote of Tokelau in 1920, '. . . the flag should never have been hoisted unless Great Britain was prepared to maintain some closer approximation to permanent government than has hitherto been observable', noting that the atolls being 'remote and valueless' could not 'pay their own way' and that 'the ideal officer would be a Medical Magistrate with a taste for anthropology, loneliness, and a fish diet' (Anon. n.d. in WPHC 1674/20).

Perhaps the Union Jack should not have been raised, but it had been. Tokelau came under the terms of the Imperial Western Pacific Order in Council of 1877, which gave the high commissioner in Fiji jurisdiction over all British subjects in all islands not already '. . . within the jurisdiction of any civilised Power'. The ritual of flag-raising was not performed until 1889 when a trans-Pacific cable was proposed and the atolls were a possible staging point, positioned as they were on a map of the Pacific near a straight line connecting Vancouver and Sydney (Morrell 1960:265). (The flag was raised in several of the uninhabited Phoenix Islands too.) High Commissioner Thurston, having been informed of his new domains, recommended that '. . . in the establishment of a recognised supervision and jurisdiction such islands be made a dependency of the Colony of Fiji' (some 1300 km away) and hastened to add, 'No establishment or expenditure would in my opinion be necessary; . . .' (Thurston 1889). His recommendation was quickly found impractical, and his opinion in time proved erroneous.

The story told in the first part of this chapter is essentially a colonial history from the perspective of the various protectorate or colonial administrators tangentially or briefly engaged in the 'supervision and jurisdiction' of Tokelau (or officially the Union Islands until 1946). From this outside vantage point, transportation was an administrative obsession. Those commissioned or delegated to oversee the atolls could rarely get to or between them, and when they did it was with some difficulty. Consequently, new arrangements were regularly devised for more effective administration, and these were equally regularly frustrated. Of course, this was related to 'expenditure' since the cost of transportation could hardly be met from trading licences or taxes on exports and imports, and of copra (which was frequently left unpaid). The story in full is a repetitive one, so it is radically abridged, and focuses on episodes in which the colonial frustrations are best documented and expressed. The second part of the chapter describes the institutions and arrangements that colonial administrations imposed upon the atolls.

The story of this era from Tokelau's perspective is very different—eventful and hardly concerned with transport at all. Within there were grand projects and new enterprises, times of hardship and times of plenty, and increasingly people travelled away from the atolls and returned by diverse routes. These local stories are told in chapter 9.

Outposts Viewed from Afar

The initial Fiji attachment

The HMS *Egeria* Log records, 'Hoisted Union Jack on shore and proclaimed . . . under British protection', three times on three successive days in June 1889 (Fakaofo was also treated to a *feu de joie*), before sailing north to proclaim British protection of the uninhabited atolls in the Phoenix group. The vessel returned to Tokelau waters for nearly two weeks in August of the same year 'sounding to North' and 'laying off'.[1] It was three years before any of the atolls saw anything further of their protectors, and Nukunonu and Atafu did not see them for seven. In all, three deputy commissioners, authorised from Fiji, paid seven brief visits from their posts in Samoa (to 1900) and Tonga (from 1901) in the two decades following 1889. During their few hours at each atoll, they could rarely resolve issues or take decisive action, constrained both by their circumscribed powers and their limited understanding of matters brought to their attention. They would warn and advise, but could neither follow up their counsel nor keep abreast of the issues.

It was difficult enough to arrange transport to Tokelau from Apia, but it was virtually impossible to arrange transport from Nuku'alofa. In 1908 after a four-year hiatus officials felt that a visit was a matter of some urgency, but, despite protracted negotiations, '. . . the provision of a man of war . . . has been found impossible to arrange this year and is yearly becoming more difficult' (Min. to Newell 1908b in WPHC 253/08). Some other arrangements had to be made and some kind of connection with the Gilbert and Ellice Island Protectorate seemed promising.

The Gilbert and Ellice attachment

A Protectorate deputy commissioner had favourably received an earlier proposal to extend his domain to Tokelau, provided that 'a fast and well-found steamer' was available, and funds and staff adequate (Min. to Cusack Smith 1896d). In 1908 a vessel, aptly christened *Tokelau*, was being acquired by the GEIP that might be able to pay annual visits to Tokelau, and the time seemed opportune to attach Tokelau to the GEIP. However, London, Suva and Ocean

Island had rather different ideas of what such an attachment might entail. The Secretary of State viewed the connection as replicating the previous arrangements in Apia and Nuku'alofa, that is, simply to facilitate annual administrative visits. The GEIP resident commissioner saw the attachment as increasing his domain, staff and revenues. The high commissioner just wanted to get something resolved.

By the time King's Regulation No. 7 of 1909 'to extend certain regulations [of the GEIP] to the Union or Tokelau Groups of Islands' was published (im Thurn 1909), an acting district magistrate was slowly proceeding to his Tokelau posting. He reached Nukunonu in March 1910, after a four and a half month journey from Maiana (Gilbert Islands), and his arrival inaugurated five years of 'direct rule'. On the one hand, 'direct rule' made Tokelau's remoteness more vexing; on the other hand, it firmly linked Tokelau with the colonial milieu of the Western Pacific.

The celebrated auxiliary vessel *Tokelau* did not solve transport problems. The atolls to windward were really beyond her safe range. So transport, and therefore communication, to and between the atolls was dependent upon trading and mission vessels whose itineraries did not conform to administration needs. Months might pass before a resident official could receive instructions or send off reports, or even shift from one atoll to another. The last resident officer was marooned on Atafu for nine months. A naval vessel deposited him there in March 1914; a trader called a month later before he was ready to move; a mission ship visited after calling at Fakaofo and en route to Funafuti—where he had no business going; and he departed permanently in ill health in December. Thus ended 'direct rule'.

Of the three officers posted to Tokelau, only the first initiated any changes of lasting significance. His name was Roderick MacDermot. He was a small, energetic, outspoken and impetuous man passionately committed to an ethic of industry and individualism, self-improvement and sanitation, and order. His achievements in imposing order and cleanliness in the villages were not matched by success in ordering civic affairs. Tomasi (as MacDermot is named in Tokelau) refused to acknowledge any *aliki* precedence; the subtle negotiations of village politics were both incomprehensible and inimical to him, and he simplistically viewed the mission establishments as dictating village affairs (MacDermot 1910). His superiors at Ocean Island and Suva were subject to his verbose and tactless reports and comments, and also to the repercussions of letters he fired off elsewhere (MacDermot 1910–11). His successor, Dr Hoare, appointed as both district and medical officer, was as tactless but could find nothing to do, so rather than 'simply wasting time' (Hoare 1913) he left for dental treatment in Sydney. His replacement, Lancelot Indermaur, was already in residence when he returned, and it was he who was marooned at Atafu while his superiors were devising other arrangements.

In early 1914 and only three months after the devastating 'Great Cyclone' (see following chapter), the captain of a naval vessel which had thrice visited the atolls wrote: 'I am of the opinion that the natives of the Union Group might very well be trusted to look after their own affairs *under normal con-*

Colonial Presences 1890–1947

(Note: Some visits may have been unreported or reports lost—but not many)

Visits from deputy commissioners of WPHC 1890–1909

T. B. Cusack Smith	1892 (Fakaofo only)
T. B. Cusack Smith	1896
T. B. Cusack Smith	1897(Fakaofo and Atafu only)
Ernest Maxse	1898
Hamilton Hunter	1900
Hamilton Hunter	1902
Hamilton Hunter	1904

GEIP deputy magistrates posted to Tokelau 1910–14

Roderick MacDermot	March 1910–May 1913
[Dr W. James	resigned in Suva when appraised of posting]
Dr Hoare	May 1913–April 1914
Lancelot Indermaur	April–December 1914

Other WPHC/GEIP/GEIC visitors

Quayle Dickson, RC/GEIP	October 1909
Arthur Mahaffy, Asst HC	September 1911 (Fakaofo and Atafu only)
Arthur Mahaffy, Asst HC	October 1913
Eliot, RC/GEIC	January 1916 (Annexation agreements signed)
Eliot, RC/GEIC	?1918
Wm Burrows, DC/Funafuti	September–October 1921
Cmd Sherston	1922
Cmd Sherston	1924
G. Swinbourne, DO/Funafuti	1925

Visitors from New Zealand Administration etc.

Richardson (Administrator)	September–October 1925
Ritchie (Med. Officer)	August 1927
Allen (Administrator)	August 1929
Turnbull (Secretary)	August 1935
Turnbull (Acting Admin.)	June 1937
McKay (Sec. Native Affs)	June 1937
Turnbull (Acting Admin.)	August 1938
McKay (Sec. Native Affs)	September 1939
Galway (Gov.-General)	?September 1939
McKay (Sec. Native Affs)	November 1940
McKay (Sec. Native Affs)	May 1941
McKay (Sec. Native Affs)	November 1941
McKay (Sec. Native Affs)	July 1942
McKay (Sec. Native Affs)	April 1943
Grattan (District Officer)	December 1943

US military presence begins

Grattan (Sec. Native Affs)	June/July 1944
Gov.-Gen. NZ	July 1944
Grattan (Sec. Native Affs)	October 1944

Fraser (Prime Minister)	January 1945
Thompson (Snr Sergeant)	June 1945
Grattan (Sec. Native Affs)	August–September 1945
Thompson (Snr Sergeant)	November 1945
US military presence ends	
Thompson (Snr Sergeant)	April 1946
Thompson (Snr Sergeant)	May 1946
Jessop ('new officer')	November–December 1946
Jessop ('new officer')	September 1947

ditions without a White Resident' (Ward 1914, original emphasis). The auditor (1914), who had just travelled to Tokelau on the vessel, concurred, and not a single official voice was raised against what in retrospect seemed an eminently sensible opinion. More problems had been generated by stationing 'White Residents' in Tokelau than by their earlier absence. However, the question remained: where might the atolls be 'indirectly ruled' or administrated from? Transport was again the central concern, so the question really was: from what place where a resident official was posted could a person get to Tokelau from time to time? The answer in mid 1914 was Funafuti. So the Gilbert and Ellice administrative connection was maintained 'for convenience' as the Secretary of State had first proposed, and Tokelau was included within the jurisdiction of the district officer stationed at Funafuti.

However, this apparently simple solution for administering Tokelau was immediately complicated because at that time the GEIP was being transformed into the Gilbert and Ellice Island Colony (GEIC). Tokelau, therefore, had to be included in the transformation, and this required that a document be signed by the 'chiefs' of each island '. . . agreeing to inclusion of islands in His Majesty's dominions' (Secretary of State for the Colonies 1915). All the Gilbert and Ellice Islands had signed deeds of cession by April 1914; signed documents from Tokelau were requested in October of the same year but were not obtained until January 1916. As a consequence, the Gilbert and Ellice Islands were declared a colony in late 1915 and Tokelau was added to the colony three months later. The Tokelau 'chiefs' readily accepted '. . . the rule of the King of Britain' and agreed that their islands '. . . should form part of the Empire of the King of Britain' (literal translation of document signed by Native Governments of the Union Islands on 25 and 26 January 1916; in the National Archives of New Zealand). The problem had been getting the documents to them for signing. The district officer in Funafuti had the documents but he could not get to Tokelau, which was not a very promising beginning for the new arrangement.[2]

What the arrangement in fact did was place Tokelau under the control of Captain Allen, Director of the Samoan Shipping and Trading Company, and owner of the steamship *Dawn*. Allen had begun shipping and trading in Samoa in 1900 and by at least 1909 had entered the Tokelau trade. By 1913 he was firmly and profitably involved in Tokelau. He had ingratiated himself with the 'White Residents', established patron–client relations with local traders who all became indebted to him, persuaded High Commission officials that he was a responsible and reasonable man and had been influential in the selection of some local officials. In 1914 Allen shifted his company from Samoa to Funafuti to avoid increasing German ill-will in Western Samoa and competition from American Samoa. Allen, in effect, created a monopoly not only on trade but also on communication between Tokelau and the world outside, specifically between the local polities and their colonial administrators. He alone tendered for Tokelau tax copra; he bought all other copra and supplied all imports. He transported all travellers in and out, ignoring port of entry regulations if it suited him (and vehemently supporting them otherwise). He had a captive labour force to recruit either for Olohega (where he had also insinuated himself) or the Phoenix Islands (where he acquired interests). People sentenced to serve time in the Funafuti gaol, often at the instigation of Allen, were conveyed to gaol on the *Dawn* and, after serving their sentences, returned on the *Dawn*.

In 1914 Allen was reputed to be calling at Tokelau every two months, but when tropical cyclones in 1914 and 1915 brought copra production to a halt, his calls were far less frequent, and they never seem to have been particularly regular. He visited when it suited him, despite disclaimers to the contrary. Though the district officer at Funafuti was officially responsible, Allen was in fact in charge. When an officer visited, Allen interpreted, transmitting what information it suited him to report and leaving the officials in the dark regarding his own activities, including his itineraries. He considered Tokelau his fief, and virtually did as he pleased and answered to no one.

British colonial officials might perhaps be excused for their inattention to this exploitation on the grounds that they were preoccupied with the Pacific echoes of the war in Europe. Or, perhaps, after having been plagued with the problems of Tokelau generated by the 'White Residents', they were relieved to hear very little. Official neglect during this period should not be called 'benign', however.

The *Ajax* episode and related matters

As early as 1919, the GEIC resident commissioner suggested that Tokelau might be transferred to the care of the New Zealand Administration in Western Samoa, specifically commenting on the increasingly irregular and inconvenient schedule of the *Dawn* (Eliot 1919). No notice appears to have been taken of the suggestion. Somewhat more notice was taken of a New Zealand request that Apia be made a port of entry for Tokelau which would allow a 'British' shipping company in Apia to trade there and in the northern Cook Islands. The High Commission secretary commented at first that Allen was already trading in Tokelau and doubted that there was enough business to justify another trader (Green 1921a). Yet eight months later the same secretary '. . . concluded that a little opposition was the only cure to Captain Allen's monopoly' (Green 1921b).

Captain Allen as a young man, probably about the turn of the century. Photo courtesy of his son, Ernest T. Allen

What brought about this change? To a large extent it was Captain Allen himself who overplayed his hand. Captain Allen had written two letters to the High Commission during the intervening months (Allen 1921), the phrasing of which was neither cautious nor reasonable. The letters were precipitated by the visit of another ship to Tokelau. The vessel *Ajax* had been approved to proceed there from Apia when the high commissioner received an urgent telegram from the New Zealand administrator in Western Samoa: 'Nukunonu reported starving no vessel 14 months do you approve *Ajax* proceeding to-day direct from Samoa. . . .' (Administrator Samoa 1920).[3] The customs officer

A village swept almost clean by the surging waves of the 'Great Cyclone' 1914. Photo: Captain Allen courtesy of the Public Record Office, London

sent along to 'watch native interests' reported on returning: '. . . the wildest imagination would hardly suggest starvation'. The people were healthy, the villages clean and orderly, and local foods abundant. Nukunonu, it transpired, was out of tobacco! The customs officer was rather bemused, but not so Captain Allen. He raged that the episode was a German-inspired plot, in collusion with the Catholic mission; that the Apia harbour master was a stooge of the owners of the *Ajax*; that his traders had been bullied and plied with strong drink; and that the *Ajax* had made away with thirty-nine tons of *his* copra. The *Ajax* did not trade again. The circumstances were indeed suspicious and the whole episode was smothered by official equivocation, but at the same time Allen's integrity was otherwise being questioned.

Reports of 'trouble' in Fakaofo had reached the High Commission through Mr Hough of the London Missionary Society. Allen had subsequently reported the 'trouble' settled. A newly appointed district officer, stationed in Funafuti, was determined to see for himself. It may be surmised that Allen did not favour an on-the-spot investigation, for the officer's attempts to get to Tokelau were thwarted for nine months—the *Dawn* was otherwise engaged—and he finally travelled '. . . by courtesy of the London Missionary Society'. At Fakaofo he found '. . . the state of the people being one of "armed neutrality"' (Burrows 1921a, the 'trouble' is presented in some detail in chapter 9). Though Allen was given benefit of the doubt in official reports, his interests were in fact served by reporting a settlement, and, though no direct complaints about Allen were contained in the officer's report, it concluded that when Allen arrived three weeks late he brought little in the way of stores— '. . . not nearly sufficient, in view of the fact that it is entirely problematical when [he] will again visit the Island'. In a separate note the unseaworthiness of the *Dawn* was remarked upon (Burrows 1921b). In addition, while the district officer was in Fakaofo, the High Commission secretary personally encountered Allen and judged him 'undoubtedly unscrupulous' (Green 1921b).

Many people in Tokelau had come to the same conclusion long before, but they had either not been heard or had kept publicly silent. Complaints were voiced the following year to the captain of a naval vessel and subsequently several other official visitors heard and recorded them. People who remember him remark that Captain Allen was *muliga ia Hatani* 'worse than Satan' and a *kuluku* 'crook', who absconded with monies, reneged on payments, marooned recruited labourers, ill-treated Tokelau people, and died suddenly—*nae mu i te ava* 'inflamed with alcohol'. But, before he died in 1924, his monopoly was broken when Apia was made a port of entry for Tokelau in early 1923.

The New Zealand solution

Meanwhile, the British colonial establishment was engaged in yet another round of debate on the 'insoluble problem' of administering Tokelau, raised in part by the proposed port of entry change. The New Zealand Governor-General pressed the case of New Zealand commercial interests; Suva offi-

Cast of Characters

AT FAKAOFO

Solomona (aka Teuku): As a labour recruit to Hawaii in the 1880s he seems to have become somewhat 'worldly' and appears as a signatory to a Fakaofo petition in the 1890s. He was appointed 'Magistrate' by MacDermot in 1910, dismissed locally in 1912, and then reinstated. Some years later he was again locally dismissed, then locally reinstated, and then officially retired in 1921.

Seanoa: Considered an agitator by MacDermot and Captain Allen, he was locally appointed to replace Solomona as Magistrate in 1912, and dispatched by Fakaofo to Suva to deliver complaints concerning MacDermot in 1913. His local appointment was officially overthrown in 1913, but, in 1921, he was officially appointed Magistrate by Burrows. Under the New Zealand Administration, he was appointed *Faipule*/Magistrate in 1926, a position that he held until his death in April 1942.

AT NUKUNONU

Samasoni: He was from Niutao (Tuvalu) and had been a crewman for Capt. Allen before settling in Nukunonu c.1911, and marrying a local woman. Dr Hoare appointed him Magistrate (probably at Capt. Allen's urgings) in 1913, a office he held for about ten years before he died at sea.

Alo: He was the eldest son of Takua and considered to be his successor. However, the position of *aliki* disappeared with annexation. He succeeded Samasoni as Magistrate and was appointed *Faipule*/Magistrate under the New Zealand Administration, a position he held until his death in October 1944.

AT ATAFU

Logologo Apinelu: He was taken to Fiji in 1911 to be trained as a native medical practitioner, entered the then Fiji Medical School in 1913, and returned to Tokelau as a qualified NMP in 1917. Although he was based in Atafu, he spent months at a time in Nukunonu and Fakaofo. He served as 'the doctor' in Tokelau for decades and died in 1962.

Nikotemo: He married the widow of Tanielu (below) and, though officially the trader, left the business to his wife. He was appointed *Faipule*/Magistrate under the New Zealand Administration and held that position until after the Second World War.

Tanielu (aka Daniel Jennings/Misikosi): He was the younger son of Ilai and established himself as a trader in Atafu some time in the latter years of the nineteenth century.

cials, fearing commercial exploitation, flirted for a while with the idea of direct High Commission supervision and even pondered re-establishing 'direct rule'; from London the Secretary of State telegraphed (1921): '. . . most convenient arrangement for Government of New Zealand to take charge . . .'. At first New Zealand resisted, but then reconsidered when Apia became a port of entry. Over two years went by while various contingent issues were resolved,[4] and in November 1925 Tokelau was excluded from the GEIC by proclamation and by another proclamation placed under the authority of the Governor-General of New Zealand, who might delegate defined powers under this authority to the administrator of Western Samoa ('The Union Islands (No.1) Order in Council, 1925' and 'The Union Islands (No. 2) Order in Council, 1925'). The official date of transfer, however, was 11 February 1926, when the first New Zealand Order in Council was gazetted.

In anticipation of relinquishing responsibility for Tokelau, the district officer at Funafuti paid a final visit to close the colony books. The most remarkable thing about his tour was its itinerary: he departed Funafuti on 31 March and reached Tokelau on 3 July, after being marooned in Nassau (northern Cooks) and from there conveyed to Apia. On reaching Tokelau, his pauses were brief. He did not even get ashore at Nukunonu where 'owing to the state of the sea . . . the natives were disinclined to land Europeans . . .' (Swinbourne 1925). So ended Tokelau's association with the Gilbert and Ellice Islands, in a replay of how it had begun—it had taken the first 'White Resident' four and a half months to reach his post in 1910.

The New Zealand attachment

Before assuming responsibility for Tokelau, the New Zealand administrator for Western Samoa visited the atolls personally to assess the situation.[5] He reported that the people were greatly pleased with the new arrangements. His round trip took nine days, five of which were spent in Tokelau itself— a promise of easier communication and more effective administration.

Though Tokelau was attached to the Western Samoan Administration as a responsibility of the Secretary for Native Affairs, its finances were kept strictly separate from those of Western Samoa. Tokelau was to pay for itself and not be a drain on funds of the Administration. Sources of revenue remained as before—twenty-five tons of tax copra, import and export duty levies and trade licence fees—and appeared more than adequate to cover costs, which indeed they did for over ten years. Overpopulation was a potential problem, and the obvious solution was controlled migration to Western Samoa.

Basically, conditions in Tokelau were deemed satisfactory and could simply continue as they were. Order, cleanliness, health and peace prevailed, and in the years that followed the atolls prospered. The three appointed *faipule* reported to their administrator in 1930: '. . . everything on their Islands is satisfactory, the health of the people very good, and no difficulties arising. Their islands are now well-provided for as to communication with Samoa, and facilities for shipping and receiving goods, as there are now two firms trading with them. The financial position of the Islands is satisfactory . . .' (Allen 1930).

Internally, Tokelau continued to thrive in the 1930s, but from the vantage point of its administrators transport and finance began to be troublesome when the world price of copra fell. This directly affected revenue from tax copra; indirectly it affected all sources of revenue—and transport as well.

Commerce in Tokelau became unprofitable when traders could get little return on copra bought, and the low prices to producers meant that they had little money to spend on trade goods. Import and export duty revenue declined as traders called less frequently. A drought in 1933–34 exacerbated the problem. Copra production halted and traders for a while stopped calling altogether. A nadir was reached in 1937 when the only vessel trading in Tokelau was wrecked in the Phoenix Islands. In many ways it was a replay of the late 1910s and early 1920s, except the reaction was different. Officials were concerned about the related problems of shipping and administrative bankruptcy. The acting administrator in Samoa wrote to the Minister of External Affairs, 'It is very much regretted, owing to no shipping contact during the last 18 months, the Island funds have been considerably depleted: a credit balance of only £73 being available at present. To meet the situation officers [in Tokelau] generously agreed to accepting only half-pay during the present year' (Turnbull 1938).

This plaintive report produced the desired response from the minister. To reduce the small remuneration of local officers seemed improper; it was 'our duty' to provide an outlet for produce; projects for 'the health and reasonable comfort of the people' should be pursued even in the face of insufficient revenues. Given the budgetary constraints, the only solution was 'a small grant from New Zealand funds' (Langstone 1938). The balance sheet for 1938–39 shows a debt to External Affairs of £179 15s. This little interchange and small amount was far more significant that it appears—it is a turning point in Tokelau's colonial history.

Though the wrecked vessel was replaced, Tokelau was not included in its itinerary. Officials from Samoa travelled to Tokelau on small vessels which could carry some trade goods but could not uplift bulky copra, which was virtually worthless anyway. With no ship to uplift copra, production again ceased, and without copra to sell people had little money to spend on goods. This time the officer in charge wrote: 'Two U.S. Naval Officers accompanied the visit and were affected, as I was, by the conditions of hardship which exist. I am sure that if these Islands were administered by any other Government conditions would not be allowed to remain so, and government assistance as to shipping communication would be provided' (McKay 1939).

This observation, like that the year before, was designed to prick the New Zealand Government's conscience, always sensitive to implications of neglect of duty. To it were added some vice-regal words: '. . . it is my personal opinion that some investigation should be made into their conditions of life with a view to affording them some much-needed assistance' (Galway 1939). It was the acting administrator, however, who made the direct request: revenue was less than regular expenditure, capital funds were needed, the Tokelau account was already in debt, and a grant of £500 was required (Turnbull 1939).[6] So Tokelau became a beneficiary after years of paying its own way. New Zealand accepted her colonial burden well before the international ethos of colonialism changed so dramatically after the Second World War; and would continue to carry this particular burden (see chapter 10).

During the early war years the Administration somehow managed to find some vessel to travel to Tokelau twice each year. Commercial trade was not profitable, but by 1941 dual administrative–trading voyages were breaking even by buying mats and other 'curios' for resale in Samoa and selling what 'needed commodities' could be obtained from Samoa. The situation had improved from the 'hardship' of 1939 and under adverse circumstances. The previously critical official now tendered praise, '. . . even though the Tokelau Islands under present conditions produce no revenue to cover their permanent charges in the way of salaries, we are serving them without any cost [to us] for transportation, which no other Administration could do' (McKay 1941).

After Pearl Harbor transport gradually improved as United States ships and planes were used for visits, and, in the latter years of the war, communication became overabundant, at least from the Administration's point of view. All the atolls received visitors from the sky, some official and some not; Atafu was blessed with a United States Coast Guard Loran installation (see below). They enthusiastically welcomed their generous visitors, causing one exasperated New Zealand officer to remark '. . . the minds of the people had strayed from New Zealand' (Grattan 1944b). The contrast between the seven preceding frugal years and the prodigious abundance of 1944–46, between *oge utufaga* 'tobacco famines' and free American cigarettes, sugar-sack clothing and fathoms of 'excellent print material', defunct wireless sets and 'the silver screen', did indeed compromise New Zealand's image. Almost immediately New Zealand took steps to counteract the American impact, so Tokelau gained in double measure. Improved water supplies had been at the top of the list of village requests to visiting administrators for nearly twenty years and nothing had been done owing to insufficient finances. Two months after the Americans 'landed' at Atafu, New Zealand approved expenditure for the construction of new concrete cisterns at each island. Both the Governor-General and the Prime Minister paid calls, each making recommendations which could not be ignored. The Governor-General called for improved health services, provision of agricultural and woodworking tools, soil improvements, and dissemination of information about the British throne and constitution. Prime Minister Peter Fraser urged educational improvements, suggested that the regulations prohibiting canoe travel between the atolls might be amended, and promised '. . . at least a bugle issued to each island, and something in the nature of a drum and fife band provided for Atafu' (McKay 1945a) where American influences were particularly strong. Suddenly aware that local salaries had remained as they had been set in 1925, as of January 1945, all were raised at least 50 per cent and some as much as 300 per cent.

To Tokelau the later war years were a boon. The boon ended with the abrupt departure of the Americans in 1946, but they did at least have improved water supplies and higher salaries. Other benefits would follow in due course.

There were profound changes in New Zealand's administrative attitudes in the years following the war, presaged by the concerns expressed by administrators, the Governor-General and Prime Minister when American open-handedness made New Zealand appear negligent and stingy in Tokelau eyes. But, more importantly, New Zealand was caught up in the post-war changing colonial world, with Prime Minister Fraser at the forefront of these changes in his role as chairman of the Committee on Trusteeship during the drafting of the United Nations Charter in 1945 (Davidson 1967:163). It was no longer enough to protect dependencies paternally: it was the duty of colonial powers to promote welfare and prepare their dependencies for taking control over their own destinies. Tokelau had for some years been provided for at New Zealand's expense, but in this regard it was the least of New Zealand's concerns. Even so, things began to change, particularly when Tokelau's status changed yet again.

Since 1925 (officially 1926) New Zealand had administered Tokelau on Great Britain's behalf, the powers granted by the monarch to the governor-general had been delegated to the administrator of Western Samoa. This arrangement could not be sustained when Western Samoa, as a mandated territory under the League of Nations, became a trust territory set firmly on a course towards independence. Tokelau, though linked administratively to Western Samoa 'for convenience', had a different colonial history—they had ceded themselves to the Crown—and therefore a different colonial status. To resolve the anomaly and set matters straight—for some legal questions had been raised about the procedures used in 1925 which had bypassed the New Zealand Parliament (McKay 1945b quoting Crown Solicitor 1928)—the Tokelau Islands Act 1948 was passed by the New Zealand Parliament and came into effect at the beginning of 1949. By this Act, Tokelau became 'a part of New Zealand' and Tokelau people shortly thereafter became New Zealand citizens. Their future was set on a separate course from that of their Western Samoan neighbours. New Zealand had assumed sole and accountable responsibility for them, and they had been given a clear place of attachment in the neocolonial world.

Within the Outposts

Apparently all that was required of the atolls in the two decades following the 1889 hoistings of the Union Jack was to hoist it themselves whenever a foreign ship hove into sight, and to have it aloft particularly when any deputy commissioner called.

When Tokelau became attached to the GEIP there were initial attempts to replicate GEIP administrative patterns in the atolls, but these attempts were thwarted by transport problems. Nonetheless, arrangements for taxation and local governance, once set in place during the five years of 'direct rule', persisted. Local revenue had at least to cover expenses, so trading licence fees were collected and each atoll was levied an annual tax in copra.[7] Thus the burden of financing the Administration was carried by Tokelau, but to realise revenue the Administration was dependent on commercial interests to buy and uplift tax copra and to pay licence fees. The promotion of commerce led to exploitation, particularly when 'direct rule' lapsed and the affairs of Tokelau were placed unofficially in the hands of Captain Allen.

Antipathy towards mission domination and meddling was common among GEIP and other colonial officials. To counter it in Tokelau official recognition was given to local civil authority structures that were designed by MacDermot, the first resident district magistrate. They were modelled on those already set up in the Gilbert Islands. The government officeholders were 'native magistrate' (*fakamahino*), 'scribe' (*failautahi*), 'policemen' (*leoleo*), and what in Tokelau were called *faipule* (which MacDermot wrote 'vaipuli'). The office of *aliki* was expressly left out of this local civic establishment. There were some difficulties in equating or comprehending the new offices in terms of Tokelau concepts of authority and its delegation. For example, in Fakaofo petitions for years had been signed *aliki* ('king') and *faipule* ('ruler' or 'lawmaker'), so who and what was a 'magistrate'? The man who had signed as *faipule* was installed as 'magistrate', but then who might be *faipule*? More troublesome was the fact that these officials were appointed by foreigners and were to be paid. Though provision was made for a number of men to be locally designated *faipule*, only one among them was to be remunerated as *faipule hili* 'chief ruler'. So something of the complementary nature of authority was maintained, that is if the position of *aliki* was ignored—which was the intention. MacDermot spelt out the duties of each officeholder, the rules and regulations they were to uphold, and the fines to be imposed for their violation.[8]

An assessment of the success of the 'native governments' set up by MacDermot is difficult. Predictably, some officers abused their authority, and those responsible for what was called 'the island chest', where local government monies were kept, were often charged with misappropriation. However, the local governments appeared to function despite meddlesome foreign officials and traders, and what was indeed achieved was a clear separation in principle of religious and civil authority. A formal distinction between *te pule fakalotu* 'church authority' and *te pule fakanuku* 'village (civil) authority' came to separate church and state. This, though, was not a radical innovation: separation of sacred and civil authority in the positions of *aliki* and *faipule* had characterised the pre-Christian polities to some degree. During the mission era sacred authority, at least as exercised by foreigners, was or came to be set apart and civil authority rested largely with local elders. The polities apparently found the imposed 'native government' structure comprehensible and operable—after all, some local 'rulers' were being paid to do much the same things they had done before without payment. Anyway, no word of dissent was recorded at the time, though there were occasional objections to particular officeholders.

MacDermot's obsession, however, was village 'improvement', and in this too he followed the GEIP model established by his former superior, Telford Campbell (see Macdonald 1982:83ff.). Cleanliness, spaciousness, airiness, and regularity were to be achieved by rearranging, resiting and rebuilding. Systems of 'streets' (*auala*) were laid out, and redesigned airy residences were aligned to them. For adequate circulation of air, the dwellings were set a specified distance apart. MacDermot threw himself into the task and demanded that the villages did too. Whatever the obstacles and compromises, whether people were obstinate or enthusiastic, MacDermot's model villages were created. They disappeared not long after, in the 'Great Cyclone' of 1914, but the model remained and the villages were rebuilt more or less as MacDermot had designed them.

Just when Tokelau was attached to the GEIP, there were moves afoot to establish medical services. Consequently, an attempt was made to combine the positions of medical officer and district magistrate. The first appointee, on learning of his duties and location, resigned forthwith: 'he was not aware . . . that he would be the only white man . . . the loneliness of his position would be so intolerable that in a fortnight's time he would cease to be a rational being' (James 1912). The second was the aforementioned Dr Hoare, who never did any doctoring and was only briefly in residence. These were temporary measures, however, for three young Tokelau men were already in Fiji and in 1913 began medical studies. Two of them returned to Tokelau as 'native medical practitioners' in 1917 and one remained. He was assisted by 'native dressers' trained in Funafuti. Of course, they were paid. Also added to 'native government' establishments with small emoluments were a 'scribe', a chief of police and two police and two warders, one male and one female, to supervise prisoners (Swinbourne 1925). Though there was hardly anything for these appointees to do, the positions provided status and a bit of money.

As part of the GEIP Tokelau came under the effect (or effectiveness) of several extant regulations. The regulation prohibiting firearms etc. was surely welcomed, given Fakaofo's experience. The WPHC regulation to protect contract workers was applied to Tokelau after the fact, and whether it applied at all to Olohega was a matter of debate. In the early 1880s, three Tokelau couples had been contracted for labour in Hawai'i and returned, and in 1904 sixty-four Tokelau labourers were working in the Phoenix Group (Bennett 1976, Hunter 1908). Otherwise, there are no records of labour contracts until 1916, when men from all three atolls were contracted by the GEIC resident commissioner to work at Ocean Island. Subsequent labour contracts in the Phoenix Group involved mainly Fakaofo people.

When the atolls finally became part of the GEIC in 1916, many of the WPHC regulations were revised as colony ordinances and other ordinances promulgated that came into force in Tokelau. Ordinance No.2 of 1917 'To confirm the observance of the native law as of the Gilbert, Ellice, and Union Groups' was formally imposed though its 'schedule' had been more or less followed from the time MacDermot established the 'native governments' some years before. It set out the duties of the appointed local officials, and the laws and the penalties to be meted out for their infraction. This set of laws was intended to replace any other local rules and regulations, though in fact it was simply added to them. Some were meaningless in the Tokelau context, for example those prohibiting certain Gilbertese sexual practices; and others were repugnant, for example flogging as a punishment.

In the early years of the century members of the thriving villages did go to Samoa for work and education. MacDermot counted sixty-three there attending mission schools or working, and another nineteen in the Ellice Islands, probably all at school (MacDermot 1910). But when Funafuti alone became the port of entry for Tokelau (from c.1914–23), access to Samoa was restricted, both from Samoa to Tokelau and from Tokelau to Samoa, which was not to the liking of either the Tokelau people or their missions. The opening of Apia as a port of entry was therefore most welcome, and when the people were belatedly informed (in December 1924) of the pending transfer of administrative responsibility to New Zealand, 'They seemed very keen to be governed from Samoa . . .' (Stevens 1924).

Detachment from the GEIC and attachment to New Zealand via Western Samoa brought some changes to local structures of governance, with the replacement of the Gilbertese model with a Samoan one. The GEIC offices of magistrate and chief *faipule* were combined in the role of the *faipule* as 'chief representative of the Government' and the office of *pulenu'u* (Tokelau: *pulenū* or *pulenuku*) was created with responsibility for internal affairs. In addition, no less than six 'elderly men who are recognised leaders' were to comprise the village ruling committee (Richardson 1925 & 1926). The division of civic responsibility between two appointed and modestly paid officials and a formally constituted (but unpaid) ruling council of elders was more in keeping with Tokelau practice than the GEIC structure which included specifically appointed (but unpaid) subsidiary *faipule*, and it was flexible enough to be adapted to differing existing practices and changing circumstances. The slight restructuring of the paid and appointed positions permitted some subtle adjustments, and the men initially appointed to the new *faipule* position were to be able and longterm incumbents.

The administrator seconded the native medical practitioner's initiative to found Women's Committees, again on a Samoan model, dedicated to the improvement of health and sanitation in the villages, and in support of the health services. The committees and their meetings provided venues, other than church auxiliaries, for women's activities and initiatives. Other organisations proliferated in the villages; whether introduced from afar or created within, they all were moulded to their local situations.

How did the Western Pacific high commissioner and his deputies measure up as 'protectors' of Tokelau, or the officials of the GEIP and GEIC as 'administrators' of Tokelau, or the officers of the New Zealand Administration of Western Samoa as 'caretakers' of Tokelau? From a historical perspective, those concerned were generally of good will and good intentions, though they rarely understood and only sporadically paid much attention to what was going on. The colonial era, at least up to the Second World War, might again be characterised as one of 'benign neglect', and this neglect on occasion allowed exploitation. The situations that arose, the episodes and events, the consequences of decisions taken from afar, are now better told as farce than as critique. That is the way Tokelau raconteurs tell them, and probably would have told them at the time. Just as Tokelau people view their missions and missionaries as fundamentally benevolent, so they have generally viewed the *mālō* (governments) as well-meaning, if sometimes misguided, whether the *Mālō o Auhitalia* (literally 'Australian Government', a phrase they use for their colonial rulers before 1925) or the *Mālō o Niu Hila* 'New Zealand Government'. Tokelau ways of thinking and speaking rather reflect this assessment: these *mālō* have not 'ruled' (*pule*) in or over Tokelau, rather they have 'taken care of or looked after' (*tauhi*) Tokelau. In other words, the role of the *mālō* is to protect, support and provide. *Pule*, in the Tokelau view, has always remained within and the recurrent local issue was exactly where it was situated within. This concerned the atolls and their relationships with each other.

NINE
Colonial Villages

Colonial officials from the beginning assumed that each atoll was an autonomous polity. The flag was raised thrice, three Deeds of Annexation received signatures, and every resident and touring official wrote separate reports on each village. Nowhere is there any explicit statement about this; the three atolls were simply assumed to be separate and equal and were treated as such. The same policies were pursued in each, the same demands made and benefits granted, though in the absence of any enforcement each polity responded in characteristic ways. A striking example is the coast watch stations set up in 1941, for which '. . . the three villages . . . made different dispositions . . .' (McKay 1941a). At Atafu three watchers were assigned duty every six months on behalf of the village and payment was directed to the village. At Nukunonu, fortnightly or monthly duty was rotated among *kāiga*, whose heads chose the watchers and received payment on behalf of their *kāiga*. At Fakaofo, three men were selected by the elders each month and collected their own pay. Each polity organised the task and handled the rewards in its own way: at Atafu the village was served, in Nukunonu *kāiga* were supported, and Fakaofo coast watchers were individually rewarded. Each colonial village reveals its preoccupations and characteristic tone in this and other recorded events.

Fakaofo

In June of 1889, when the HMS *Egeria* stood offshore and the British flag was first hoisted over Fakaofo with a resounding *feu de joie*, the populace, some 250 or so, must have been both startled and puzzled, but two months later, upon the HMS *Egeria*'s return, 'they were evidently highly gratified' (Lister 1892:44). In any case they could not have done much about it if they were not, given that there can have been no more than forty or fifty able-bodied men on the island. The few elderly men formed the ruling council of *aliki ma faipule*, together with old, tattooed *aliki* Tetaulu. Yet Fakaofo maintained a clear sense of its integrity and its own historical importance. It was still the 'land of chiefs', and for the next thirty years or so, throughout the whole of the protectorate period, it sought to reassert its dominion over Nukunonu and to resist foreign interference.

From a political point of view, Fakaofo had every reason to be 'highly gratified' with the raising of the Union Jack and the declaration of the Protectorate. It left local government unchanged and free to carry on without interference, and also promised to be of substantial help in relations with the outside world and in dealings with resident foreigners. The Protestant majority may have seen some potential advantage in the Protestant sentiments of the British and the possibilities this opened up for gaining support in their dealings with Peleila. The council of *aliki ma faipule* could feel strengthened and assured of its legitimacy.

Fenuafala and Fenualoa (again)

Land alienations were the most pressing matter. By 1889, Fakaofo had already made a host of representations to both church and consular officials in Samoa protesting the alienation and occupation of Fenuafala and Fenualoa. With the Union Jack now raised, it was surely time for the protectorate officials to do something concrete. Their move was belated but decisive. T. B. Cusack Smith, British Consul in Samoa and a Deputy Commissioner for the Western Pacific, went to Fakaofo on a British warship, arriving at daybreak on 31 August and leaving the same evening for Samoa. It was a crowded day, and, as far as Fakaofo was concerned, one of mixed accomplishments.

Fenualoa was restored to Fakaofo simply by Cusack Smith's court of enquiry calling in Peleila and having him acknowledge that at the time of the transaction with Hiva and Pou, both he and his father, Atone, knew that Fenualoa was divided among many *kāiga* and thus not the exclusive property of Hiva and Pou. Cusack Smith forthwith declared the sale invalid and restored the islet to 'the original native tenure' (Cusack Smith 1892b).[1]

Fenuafala, however, was a different and much more complicated matter. Cusack Smith sought to establish two points: whether the original sale to Peni had been intended, and whether or not Peni, and later Atone and Peleila, had been in effective occupation of the islet since that time. The evidence showed that the sale had indeed been intended and that it had led to the loss of the Fakaofo's effective control.[2] In this case it was not Cusack Smith's place to pronounce a judgment. He simply reported the evidence to the Western Pacific High Commission in Suva, and they in turn conveyed it to the British Government. A letter from Whitehall dated 23 December 1892 reporting the facts to the German ambassador (Powles 1956) in effect acknowledged British recognition of the German claim.

The people of Fakaofo were unaware of the diplomatic, legal and commercial implications of Cusack Smith's enquiries; nor is there any evidence that he sought to explain them during his hurried visit. Fakaofo was at the time under the impression that Peleila 'owned' Fenuafala, and when the enquiry showed that the German Firm (Deutsche Handels-und-Plantagen-Gesellschaft) were the 'real' owners, Peleila lied, telling the people that he had recently sold his interests to the German Firm. This information compounded the confusion, as it was doubtless intended to do, making it appear that the British had allowed the sale in spite of Fakaofo's long-standing request to be allowed to buy the islet themselves. Thus two Protestant elders were sent to Samoa in August 1894, bearing the following poignant letter to Cusack Smith (in Cusack Smith 1894).

> *Sir, please do not be vexed at our making known our opinion about Fenuafala. The story of José is that he has sold Fenuafala to Mr Beckman. That is why we wish to make known to you our opinion. Why did Pereira sell this land whilst we have for a long time been appealing for an investigation of it. For if it is impossible to restore this land to us without payment after investigation according to British law, all the trouble of Your Excellency will be in vain. We get letters from Samoa re the investigation of land in Samoa and the procedure is this. If any land has been wrongfully bought that land is restored to the original owner. If it is not to be so with Fenuafala unless we give payment then we will seek payment for it, but we think that we might have been the first to give payment to José Pereira for that land. Probably Your Excellency is aware that the population of these islands is increasing. We therefore appeal to you on account of our food supply for it will not be sufficient for us. But José has his own lands in Samoa which are sufficient for the needs of himself and his family.*
>
> (Signed)   *David the King*
>   *Matthew the Ruler*

On behalf of the delegation, Cusack Smith wrote to the German Firm at the end of August 1894 offering £100 in cash and 100 tons of copra over the following four years. The offer was not formally declined until May of 1895; by that time, however, the elders had returned to Fakaofo, apparently with the news that Fakaofo should continue making copra every month until they had raised $3000 or £600 (Newell 1907). Where this information stemmed from is not clear, since there is no written record of it. But the people continued to make copra and gave money to Western Pacific High Commission officials who visited in 1896, 1900 and 1904 (in WPHC 174/96, 69/00, 177/02) for deposit in a bank account in Suva. In 1904, the amount on deposit was £142 19s 10d (Hunter 1904).

All this was, however, in vain, since in reality the German Firm had sold Fenuafala to Peleila in September of 1902 for £400 (Burrows 1921a, Powles 1956).[3] Not to be outdone, when the news of this finally reached Fakaofo, the island made a request to the London Missionary Society for help in applying the money to the purchase of either Hull or Sydney Island in the Phoenix Group (in WPHC 211/07).

The 'story of Fenuafala' at this point began another long drawn-out chapter. Atone had left Fakaofo together with his Samoan wife in the 1870s, and upon his death in the early 1890s his son Peleila became sole heir to his

Tokelau interests (Woodford 1895). Peleila had children by two Fakaofo women besides his wife. These 'irregular' unions produced two sons and a daughter, most of whose descendants moved away from Tokelau. By his legal wife, the daughter of Lea, he had three sons and five daughters, and one son and one daughter married in Fakaofo and settled there, raising substantial families of their own. They were thoroughly integrated into the village life. The son became a popular *faipule*, as did his son after him. Peleila willed Fenuafala to his two surviving sons, but from then on Tokelau custom prevailed, so that rights to the islet fairly rapidly became dispersed among a diverse group that included both Protestants and Catholics. Fenuafala became, in effect, the property of just another local *kāiga*.[4]

Dominion over Nukunonu

Besides Fenuafala and Fenualoa, the 'native government' of *aliki ma faipule* had one other score to settle—against Nukunonu, which had effectively freed itself from Fakaofo domination and claims of 'overlordship' by its conversion to Catholicism in the early 1860s and an alliance with the Marist mission in Samoa. Fakaofo had already attempted to reassert its control in 1887 when 'some chiefs of Fakaofo', together with the Protestant pastor Iapesa, had gone to Nukunonu to 'oblige them to have [their] King and government with Fakaofo' (Didier 1887, see also Didier 1886b). That strategy had failed. Now, however, the Protectorate gave Fakaofo another opportunity to reassert its dominion over Nukunonu.

Visiting officials of the Western Pacific High Commission eventually grew impatient with Nukunonu's intransigence and insistence on flying the Marist mission flag rather than the Union Jack (see below). On his 1898 visit to the group, Ernest Maxse learned from the secretary of the Fakaofo government that '. . . his Island has always claimed overlordship of Nukunonu, and that the latter island has acknowledged it'. Seeing an opportunity to exert some indirect pressure, Maxse agreed with the secretary's generous but entirely disingenuous offer 'to proceed to Nukunonu with the first fair wind, to point out to the inhabitants the error of their ways' (Maxse 1898). In Fakaofo's view the error of Nukunonu's ways was not a matter of flags. Some years later a party from Fakaofo visited Nukunonu to tell the people there of the Fakaofo decision to unite all Tokelau once again under the Fakaofo *aliki*. Nukunonu did not acquiesce, and the party returned to Fakaofo. Shortly thereafter, another Fakaofo delegation went to Atafu on a mission ship to raise allies against Nukunonu. Atafu, however, was divided about the enterprise. Those who agreed with Fakaofo set off with the delegation in two canoes with the intention of voyaging to Fakaofo, and there enlisting more men to go to Nukunonu and enforce their submission. The two canoes made a safe landfall on Nukunonu, but when they set out on the next leg of their journey to Fakaofo they met with contrary weather and disappeared, never to be heard of in Tokelau again.[5] Needless to say, the loss of the canoes and their crews put an end to Fakaofo's warlike designs. It did not, however, end Fakaofo's claims to overlordship, which continued to be made to the Western Pacific

High Commission (Ieremia *et al*. in Newell 1907, Ielemia and Solomona in MacDermot 1910–11, Mahaffy 1913).

The Protectorate government

The stalemate over Fenuafala and the setback over Nukunonu were doubtless chastening for Fakaofo. But they by no means extinguished the claims of the council of *aliki ma faipule* or its determination to prevail. Fakaofo waited, taking care of its own affairs, cutting more and more copra for the village fund held in Suva, and dealing with Peleila and the endemic church rivalries in its own way.

The incorporation of Tokelau in the Gilbert and Ellice Islands Protectorate in 1909, however, posed new threats to both local authority and established practices. All this might have been accomplished peacefully enough, and without local resistance of any kind, if MacDermot had been less impetuous in his judgements. His rapidly formed opinions of Fakaofo were as callow as those he formed of the other two islands. According to the General Report on the group (MacDermot 1910) the 'so called native government' that he found in place on Fakaofo was not very effective. It was, however, '. . . numerically strong composed of the usual "King" [*aliki*], a large Vaipuli [council of *aliki ma faipule*], several Scribes and Policemen . . . anyone well supplied with local currency (land), cunning or standing with the L.M.S.'. They had, he found, 'written native laws which the Vaipuli in the exercise of some semblance of power tried to put into force with I believe the best intentions. Unfortunately the Catholic element here is a refractory one as far as explicit obedience to a necessarily Protestant Vaipuli goes.'

MacDermot also noted the five islets 'held by the Native Government for its own purposes. The proceeds from which, after all hands have had a "blow out", only the august body of Vaipuli know.' Many of his other observations are of the same tenor. Of the water supply: 'One native well . . . into which the water percolates through soil polluted on the surface by a dense humanity, and beneath by generations of defunct Fakaofutiana.' Of the village: '. . . houses scattered about regardless of any order or regularity . . . too close together and surrounded by a quantity of debri [sic] and dirt.' And of the people: 'Their laziness is killing them, and while they will expend all the energy they can muster howling hymns, they nevertheless seem to have little perception of right and wrong.'

MacDermot's cannot have been a comfortable presence on the island. Nevertheless, he did enlist support for the construction of a regular path around the village islet, the realignment of houses and their reconstruction along more open, airy lines. And, although he stayed with Peleila (Perez 1977), he was acutely aware of the disruptions that his host caused, and sought to resolve them by shifting the whole Catholic population to Fenuafala. That, of course, was never accomplished. The most radical change that he brought about, however, was the ordering and appointment of a new 'native government', composed of 'one Magistrate, five Vaipuli, one scribe and three policemen'. He appointed the 'King' to his 'Vaipuli', telling him that although he had no objection to people calling him 'King' if they wished to, 'there is no such person as "King" recognised in the Government of the Island, and that when he departs for more regal realms there will be no successor to his throne'.

Fakaofo was doubtless pleased that some of the appointed officials were to be paid salaries by the Protectorate, but the new arrangements were also a direct blow to the established authority of *aliki ma faipule*. Given this, the 'native government' quickly ran into trouble.

The man appointed by MacDermot to the senior government position of 'Magistrate' was Solomona, whom he described as 'eminently qualified', hard-working, intelligent and familiar with the ways of the outside world from the time he had spent in Honolulu during the 1880s. Solomona's appointment, however, was apparently opposed by members of what MacDermot in his letters referred to as the 'King's side' (plausibly the old *aliki ma faipule*), and at some time in 1912, surely after MacDermot's departure, Solomona was replaced as magistrate by a young, energetic man named Seanoa.

Seanoa had what were, for the times, some radical ideas, and he agitated for higher copra prices, lower tradestore prices, tradestore credit, a locally run store and payment for labour on public works—all of which were blocked by MacDermot. Nor did Seanoa confine his activities to Fakaofo. In company with the village policeman, Poasa, he travelled 'through the group raising an agitation' so that 'very little copra was made' (Allen 1913). More outrageously still, in October of 1912, Seanoa and Poasa were delegated by 'the "King" and his set' to go to Suva bearing complaints against MacDermot's official and personal behaviour. They were joined on the way by a young Fakaofo man who was studying in Samoa and they took with them an introduction from the Rev. Hill of the Samoan Protestant mission. Once in Suva, they created some consternation. Mahaffy, the assistant high commissioner whom they had been sent to see, was away at the time, and the delegation was inter-viewed by his secretary through a Samoan pastor who knew Fijian and a Fijian (Ratu Sukuna) who knew English. In spite of these difficulties, their message was clear and direct enough to gain attention.[6]

In due course the complaints were transmitted to MacDermot, drawing a predictable response. However he was at the point of leaving Fakaofo when the letter came from Suva, so it was left to his successor, Hoare, to deal with the unrest it caused. Having just arrived in the group, Hoare was faced with what he took to be an ugly situation, with 'the natives just watching to see who would win' (Hoare 1913), and he summarily imprisoned both Seanoa and Poasa for six months—the charges being making untruthful statements, departing without permits, refusing to obey the native magistrate (Solomona had been reinstated in the position by January 1913) and 'attempting to set up an opposition government' (Hoare 1914). The imprisonments apparently did nothing to curb the dissension, and the village settled down to what a later commentator described as one of 'armed neutrality'.

It was not until 1918 that the village made another concerted move against the 'native government'. In that year, a couple who had been recruited for work on Banaba (Ocean Island) in 1916 returned with the surprising news (which they said they had gained from conversations with the Resident Commissioner, Mr Eliot, himself) that the people might properly depose the members of the government if they so wished.[7]

This was not of course true under protectorate law, but it was sufficient for the elders (those not in the government) to devise a characteristically Tokelau coup d'état.

> *Gathering together all the able-bodied men and youths, they went together to the village lands across the lagoon to make copra.*[8] *In the evening while the others were entertaining themselves at the lagoon shore, the elders held a* fono *on the secluded ocean side of the islet, then they called everyone together and announced their determination and plan. Early next morning, before the sun rose, the copra was to be quickly loaded onto the canoes and everyone was to return across the lagoon to the village to assemble—elders, men and boys all—for a grand meeting that would dismiss the whole government. They explained what Mr Eliot had said to the workers at Banaba about the people being able to dismiss members of government. Now this all came to pass because Fakaofo was dissatisfied with the attitude of those in the government.*
>
> *As soon as they reached the village, they gathered the old men of the village at the* fale fono *and informed them of what the people returned from Banaba had said about dismissing members of the government, and they simply agreed.*
>
> *Then they sent for the magistrate to come, and told him that he was deposed. Solomona did not demur. They then sent a messenger to the 'Chief Faipule' (because he had difficulty walking) with the same news, and he raised no protest either. Neither did the chief of police when he was called in and told to take off his uniform. Only the second policeman protested, and his uniform was taken from him by force. So it was done, and Fakaofo in the following days was ruled entirely by the elders in all matters, while Teuku* [another of Solomona's names] *and Lameko* [the 'Chief Faipule'] *just sat by.* (Perez 1977:17)

This state of affairs did not last for long, however. On the next visit of the mission ship the elders asked the Rev. Dr Hough for his opinion on the legality of what had been done. Hough told them, and advised them to restore the deposed officials to their positions and then wait for an authoritative judgment from the Protectorate government. This they did. Solomona returned in his position as magistrate and took up his autocratic ways again, interpreting the laws after his own fashion. Finally, toward the end of September 1921, William Burrows, Deputy Commissioner for the Ellice and Union Islands, arrived, together with an Ellice interpreter and a Gilbertese policeman. Burrows stayed in Solomona's house (Perez 1977), and since there was ample time available it was several days before he called a general meeting of all the people.

> *The day arrived to examine the issue. A spokesman for the village explained that they were not happy with Solomona's authoritarian rule, his partiality to his family and friends, etc.*
>
> *Captain Burrows replied: What you did was wrong because you dismissed a government official without the authority of the Commissioner for Tokelau to whom you must report upon a member of a native government. He only is able*

Fakaofo village dignitaries 1924. Seated third from the left is Seanoa, appointed Magistrate by Captain Burrows in 1921. To his right is the Chief Faipule, Apete, and to his left is Veniale, the acting pastor. Photo taken by and courtesy of E.H. Bryan jr

to dismiss a person from his office in the native government; the people may not do that themselves. Therefore, you are all guilty of transgressing that law.

He concluded the investigation with despatch saying: I leave you all with two alternatives. Either (a) one person of Fakaofo is taken to gaol to serve Fakaofo's sentence for breaking the law or (b) the penalty is imposed upon all of you. I will leave you to decide between these two options, to choose whichever you prefer. In the meantime I shall go and look around your village, and when I return, you tell me what the village wishes to do. So he went off and strolled around the village.

They sat and discussed what they should do. . . . Many people stood up volunteering to be taken to gaol to serve Fakaofo's punishment. But most were not happy with this. The two pastors [Protestant and Catholic] spoke together, and the resolution was reached: The punishment shall fall upon all the people of Fakaofo.

The Commissioner's interpreter had remained at the meeting and he said to the elders: I have stayed to hear your decision and to convey to the Commissioner what you have decided. I have not wished to speak, but now I shall say something. The resolution that you have come to with your pastors, I say to you it is 'Straight from the Heavens'. This phrase has become proverbial in Fakaofo. . . .
(Perez 1977)

Burrows reported that the elders gave a candid account of their complaints against the government officials, and freely admitted what they had done—which Burrows thought 'at the very least might be called "unconstitutional"' (see photo chapter 2, p.48). But he also recognised that the people had no legal redress against the magistrate's decisions, more especially because 'Every member of the Government, excepting one Roman Catholic Faipuli [sic], but including the Police, were relations of the Magistrate' (Burrows 1921a). Burrows returned, accepted the decision and fined the village five tons of copra. He also 'accepted the resignation of the Native Government' and, several days later announced the appointment of the dissident Seanoa to the position of magistrate, together with a new chief *faipule*.

It was thus a victory of sorts for the village. The elders and men divided themselves into five groups, each with the task of preparing a ton of copra. They worked day and night, competing to see which group would be the first to finish, and the entire task was completed within a month 'the work being enjoyable because everyone was of one mind' (Perez 1977). According to Burrows's on-the-spot and more specific account (1921a), which is probably also more accurate, the people made 'eleven and a half tons of copra, on the public land only, between 27th September and 8th October!'.

Burrows spent about six weeks altogether on Fakaofo, and he was an acute and diligent observer. His comments on life there have a ring of authority. He investigated Fenuafala, finding it to be well cultivated and fruitful, and recommended that it should be registered 'once and for all' as Peleila property. And he went round the whole island and saw, contrary to the impression the people sought to convey, that there was ample food. In the lands across the lagoon, where freshwater pits had been dug, plenty of *pulaka* was growing and bananas were luxuriant; there were 'large numbers of pigs and fowls', and 'quantities of fish are wasted daily'. Burrows also occupied himself 'recording Tokelau stories about the past told him by Peniuto, the oldest man in Fakaofo at that time' (Perez 1977), which he later published (Burrows 1923). And, finally, Burrows discovered that one half of Tui Tokelau's stone was in the oceanside reclamation of the pastor's compound, and 'he instructed that it be brought up and erected in the meeting house, and so the stone that had been previously discarded was again honoured' (Perez n.d.1).

The theme of Perez's local account is 'unity' and this is recognisable in Burrows's report. Fakaofo was 'united' in its transgression and its penalty— a penalty urged upon the people by the Protestant and Catholic pastors

The elder Peniuto (centre), composer of songs memorialising the appropriation of Fenualoa (see chapter 7), with his daughters and grandchildren, 1924. At the back is his son-in-law, Veniale, the acting pastor. Photo taken by and courtesy of E.H. Bryan jr

Fakaofo memorials 1971. At left, erected to mark the return of Fenualoa in 1892; at right, a portion of Tui Tokelau's stone retrieved and re-erected in 1921 by Captain Burrows. Photo: Marti Friedlander

together, 'straight from Heaven'. Furthermore, Tui Tokelau's stone was reinstated, not to be worshipped, but as a symbol of all Fakaofo, and of Fakaofo's pre-eminence. The bounty that Burrows describes was not simply 'subsistence affluence'. Copra prices had been buoyant for a number of years, and as older people recalled the situation, several families had houses that incorporated imported building materials. Swinbourne (1925), some years later, commented on both 'the prosperity of the natives and the contributions made annually to the respective missions'.

Village, administration and the churches

When Tokelau was formally detached from the Gilbert and Ellice Islands Colony and placed under New Zealand administration in 1925, the several changes made to the structure of local governance meant that the 'native government' was not as isolated from local opinion and authority as it had been under the Gilbert and Ellice regime. In Fakaofo the magistrate Seanoa, appointed by Burrows, became the first *faipule*, and he carried on very successfully in this position almost until his death in the 1940s. There were no recurrences of the conflicts that had beset 'village' and 'government' in Solomona's time.

Village and administration, *nuku* and *mālō*, were quite separate institutions, but as long as the administrative visits from Apia were brief (so that administration officials had no opportunity to look too closely into local affairs) and the village remained peaceful and orderly, there was little cause for friction.

The churches were also quite distinct, from one another as well as from the village and the administration. Here, though, accommodation continued to be difficult at times, particularly when overzealous Samoan Protestant pastors went against local practice and attempted to enlist either the village or the administration to their cause.

The interaction between village, administration and the churches thus followed no rigidly established pattern in the twenty years or so following 1925. Much depended upon on particular personalities, as well as the changes that were occurring in the institutions of the village itself.

The worldwide depression that began in the late 1920s brought with it a sharp reduction in copra prices that in turn reduced the number of trading ships visiting the atolls. People remember the 1930s as a time of poverty and isolation. Perhaps because of this, Fakaofo in the early 1930s turned to the expansion of its *pulaka* supply—characteristically, by decree of the elders. Each elder, man and youth had to dig 'one fathom per month' (Perez 1977), and the work was supervised on the spot jointly by the *faipule* and the *pulenuku*, together with the catechist and the pastor.[9] 'When the works came to fruit and the *pulaka* and *talo* gardens were established, it was just like Samoa, and Fakaofo was in a good position in those days' (Perez 1977).

Once this work was done, 'clubs' were formed by the able-bodied men of the island. The first was a self-help cooperative organisation, its members exchanging labour among themselves (perhaps because of the extra work involved in maintaining the new *pulaka* gardens) and doing good works for both of the churches, without discrimination. They also played cricket among themselves. Once this happened, two other 'clubs' were rapidly formed, mainly to compete in cricket matches. The clubs were occasionally delegated by the elders to do specific village works, which were invariably done with more vigour and despatch than those done by ad hoc groups organised by the elders which 'worked the old way, slowly and without effort' (Perez 1977). Later, in 1936, came the establishment of the local *Āumāga* along Samoan lines, an idea brought by a Fakaofo man who had long been resident in Apia. This was also a success, particularly during its early years.

While all this enthusiastic cooperation and spirit of progress was in the air, the catechist and pastor together first proposed removing some of the obstructing trees from the cricket pitch, and when that was accomplished, they proposed completing the large reclamation on the reef flat adjacent to the village that for a generation or so had been the task assigned to minor offenders against village regulations.

The elders agreed that all the people would work together to erect a hospital compound. This was their resolution: the men and elders will divide into two groups, one to be directed by the [Protestant] *Faipule and the Catechist and the other by the* [Catholic] *Pulenuku and the Pastor* [thoroughly crosscutting roles and affiliations]. . . . *Each side would organise the work as they wished. They divided the reclamation area into equal halves, with each group assigned one half and in competition to see which finished the task first.*

'*London Missionary Society church, with water-cistern attached, Fakaofo*' 1925. *This church replaced the one that was damaged by the 'Great Cyclone' of 1914. (Published in* AJHR *1926.)* Photo from IT,1, EX 94/1 pt2 Union Group—Tokelau, Swain's Island 1926–1930, National Archives of New Zealand

A house that had been built by a former Pastor was transported from across the lagoon for a 'doctor's house', and the hospital was better than any other in Tokelau, getting good breezes from any direction because it stood separate from the village. Three new hospital building were erected that made it even better.

When this great enterprise was finished, it was dedicated with a great celebration for the fine work done for the benefit of all the people of Fakaofo. (Perez 1977)

'*Typical household, Fakaofo*', 1925. *Thirteen of the twenty people assembled to depict a 'typical household' are female and all but two are dressed in their Sunday best. (Published in* AJHR *1926.)* Photo from IT,1, EX 94/1 pt2 Union Group—Tokelau, Swain's Island 1926–1930, National Archives of New Zealand

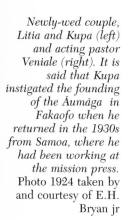

Newly-wed couple, Litia and Kupa (left) and acting pastor Veniale (right). It is said that Kupa instigated the founding of the Āumāga in Fakaofo when he returned in the 1930s from Samoa, where he had been working at the mission press. Photo 1924 taken by and courtesy of E.H. Bryan jr

The euphoria of *māopoopo* faltered in the late 1930s when the catechist and the pastor turned their attentions toward the improvement of their own establishments, and again a boundary between them was disputed. Though the judicious Faipule Seanoa called for intervention from afar, he orchestrated the compromise. Worse was to come, however. A militant Samoan pastor arrived on the island in 1940, and proclaimed that his mission was to straighten out the relationship between the two congregations and between the Protestants and the village authorities. It is uncertain whether this 'mission' was one of his own devising, or whether it had come from his superiors. In any case, the events that followed his arrival tested many local practices—as, indeed, they were intended to do.

Village guests at wedding feast of Litia and Kupa. Photo 1924 taken by and courtesy of E.H. Bryan jr

The pastor first forbade members of his congregation to play cricket for the club that the catechist held office in; he also told them never to stop a game while the Catholic participants took time out for the Angelus—as was the local practice. He demanded a larger share from village food distributions than the catechist received, on the grounds of the difference in size of the two congregations, and he questioned the Council's allowing Catholics to light cooking fires on the sabbath. He also attempted to persuade the elders to assert the old power of the *aliki* and go back to the 'rule of chiefs', following what was Samoan custom. Finally, when a youth of his congregation who had been particularly active in provoking the Catholics was killed by a lightning strike, he accused the catechist of witchcraft. These were all intensely local, parochial issues that severely taxed those who had endeavoured to overcome religious strife and disunity. Evoking the ethic of *māopoopo*, they prevailed in the end and the pastor soon departed. The village and its several institutions—the Council, the Āumāga, the Women's Committee—were non-denominational and had become pre-eminent. Conflicts between Catholics and Protestants were relegated to the past—related as cautionary tales. Henceforth, Fakaofo would celebrate its religious tolerance.

Nukunonu

Of all the Catholics in Christendom who are most deserving of their magnanimous courage, I put the . . . inhabitants of the atoll of Nukunonu in first place. They now have a church there, a beautiful and airy cement and coral-lime church that stands out like a sentinel, defying the turbulent waves that spend their strength against the nearby coral reefs. But it was not always so, and may not always be so.
—Father Joseph Diehl c.1935, in Tremblay 1964:96

Visiting priests invariably celebrated and praised the devoted Catholics of Nukunonu. Other visitors found them more difficult and attributed this to their obsessive Catholicism. Characteristic is the Nukunonu story of how they rejected British protection—a story that is at odds with the official record.[10] They told it to Father Didier in 1890 (1892:365–7) and they tell it still. The following version was composed by the elders of Nukunonu in 1977 at the request of Peato Tutu Perez (Faipule ma Toeaina 1977).

Two British Men-of-War came to Tokelau intending to hoist British Flags. What Atafu and Fakaofo did or what transpired there, is not known. But in Nukunonu, when the first Man-of-War came, the elders objected, refusing to hoist the British Flag above Nukunonu. So the Man-of-War departed.

Shortly thereafter, another British Man-of-War came yet again intending to hoist the Flag. That Man-of-War came via Samoa bringing the Samoan man named Luimili who was sent by the Bishop to tell the elders to raise the British Flag in Nukunonu together with the Flag of the Faith.

Recall, only one Flag flew in Nukunonu, the Flag of the Faith upon which was written the letter M (Mary). That was why the elders were afraid to hoist the British Flag in Nukunonu when the first Man-of-War came.

At the coming then of the second vessel it was still the same. The Man-of-War arrived and the soldiers came straight ashore with the Flag, forgetting Luimili, the Samoan who had been sent by the Bishop to tell the elders to raise the Flag. The soldiers came ashore and stood side-by-side to hoist the Flag. Paulo [Telakau] and Falekie came forward and told them not to raise the Flag, and Falekie told the soldiers to take their Flag and hoist it on a palm. To this they objected. They fastened the Flag and started to raise it aloft, but Paulo reached up and pulled it down, and so they continued to struggle.

Then Luimili saw from aboard the Man-of-War what the elders and the soldiers were doing beside the flag. He leapt off the ship, swam to shore, and said to the elders that he had been sent by the Bishop to tell the elders to hoist the British Flag together with the Flag of the Faith. Finally then the elders agreed to raise on high the British Flag.

The story suggests acquiescence, but the reports of visiting deputy commissioners indicate overwise. Again and again they report that the Union Jack was not aloft. Some were tolerant, others indignant, and it was such indignation that provoked an episode related above: the attempt of Fakaofo to reassert its *pule* in Nukunonu and the mysterious disappearance of two canoes. In Nukunonu the story is embellished by the following conclusion:

Earlier the same day that the two canoes left Nukunonu for Fakaofo, another canoe with three Catholic men from Fakaofo had departed on the same journey with the wind behind them. The men in this canoe later told the story of sailing along, singing as they went, when suddenly the wind went crazy and the current changed, swirling around. They said their farewells. Now they had with them a bottle containing 'the water of Mary' [holy water]. . . . At dawn they found themselves offshore Nukunonu village and came ashore. By their surmise the other canoes sank for the current was something extraordinary, by their account swirling like a whirlpool. That was their story and the other canoes were never heard of again. (As told by Manuele Palehau 1981)

Some tolerance of contradiction is required if one is to comprehend the events, situations and the stances taken by the people of Nukunonu during the colonial era. The Catholic Bishop characterised his Nukunonu flock as timid and frightened (Broyer 1913a), and a letter they wrote at his insistence to the assistant high commissioner was indeed tentative and enigmatic, in contrast to the blunt, demanding petitions forwarded from Fakaofo. By others they were portrayed as docile pawns bowing to the machinations of Catholic priests: 'not disposed to talk freely' (Indermaur & Smith-Rewse 1915), and 'shy and suspicious' (Newell 1905). They discouraged some officials from coming ashore, claiming that the surf was too dangerous (Coppinger 1889, Mahaffy 1911, Swinbourne 1925), and others were clearly unwelcome even though they managed to get ashore (Maxse 1898, Newell 1904). Nukunonu people no longer hid or ran away when strangers appeared, yet they still tended to be aloof and elusive. On occasion they thwarted foreigners, official and otherwise, with their intransigence: for example, their stubborn refusal to fly the Union Jack, their stand against 'religious freedom' (see chapter 7), and their resistance to official dictates that sent elderly spokesmen to Funafuti's gaol in 1913 and 1917 (see below). These contradictory characteristics may be satisfactorily reconciled in light of their heritage and of specific situations and actors.

Autonomy recognised

For generations Nukunonu had submitted to Fakaofo domination while at the same time maintaining the integrity of its autochthonous *aliki* line and lands (chapter 5). When the opportunity arose to reject that domination, it was immediately seized. However, to impress self-determination upon their former overlords required a campaign of subtle and subversive action. The Nukunonu's rejection of British protection and their steadfast refusal to entertain Protestantism were part of this campaign, and indeed Fakaofo realised what they were about. The Fakaofo letters demanding that their *pule* be recognised (see above) were attempts to counter Nukunonu self-determination. However, it was not until 1913 that a commissioner really took notice: '. . . the natives of Fakaofo claim a large part of . . . Nukunonu which they declare, and the Nukunonu natives agree, was conquered after some sort of razzia carried out by a former "King" of Fakaofo'. He 'suggested, and they [Nukunonu] seemed inclined to agree, that . . . an annual payment made to the landowners from Fakaofo . . . could be arranged' (Mahaffy 1913a). What he proposed was that 'the people of Nukunonu shall pay to the natives of Fakaofo a certain sum in copra, . . . and that in return for this payment the natives of Fakaofo should undertake to abandon any claims to lands in Nukunonu' (Mahaffy 1913b).

On the one hand, Mahaffy is celebrated in Nukunonu for giving them a way out of their historic bondage. On the other hand, the issues were far more complicated than Mahaffy realised. When the complications became clear, the immediate and apparently unanimous reaction was to abandon the whole idea.[11] Yet on 22 February 1918, according to Nukunonu accounts, the GEIC resident commissioner consulted with twenty Nukunonu elders about 'removing the Rule of Fakaofo', and they agreed that Nukunonu would pay four tons of copra in compensation to Fakaofo and 'that would end it'. This they did, and the commissioner of the GEIC decreed: 'That matter is concluded; now you have your own government'. Nukunonu had effectively 'ruled' itself for over half a century; but now local autonomy was officially recognised. Fakaofo had acknowledged Nukunonu's redefinition of their political relations by accepting the token payment of four tons of copra.

Another imposition

With foreign visitors too, Nukunonu adopted a mien of timid acquiescence that was not only deceptive, but also masked any local contentions. Disagreements are recorded only rarely by visitors, and none was ever brought to their attention (except by people considered to be not really of Nukunonu). This reticence may be linked to the nature of the Nukunonu polity, to the stable, delicately balanced coalition of separate yet closely interrelated *kāiga*. Within this polity disputes were absorbed or submerged by strategies of mediation, negotiation and dissimulation. They were definitely not aired outside.

Recollections of elderly people who were young adults in the years immediately following the period of 'direct rule' when, as they say, '[Captain] Allen alone looked after us', supplemented by an informed reading of documentary accounts, illustrate Nukunonu strategies at work. The final days (in late 1913) of the splenetic and tactless Dr Hoare in Nukunonu were memorable. On the pretext that the appointed magistrate was remiss in his accounting of public monies, he dismissed him and appointed in his place an Ellice Islander named Samson/Samasoni, who had crewed on Captain Allen's ship and been in and around Tokelau for a number of years before marrying and settling down in Nukunonu. Samson by all accounts merited his name: he was large, powerful, and forceful. He probably owed his appointment to the diplomacy of his former employer, Allen, who had ingratiated himself easily with the discontented Dr Hoare and could see the profit of having his own man in charge at Nukunonu.

Hoare also fell out with the appointed chief *faipule* on an issue of commerce, and on unclear grounds placed him in handcuffs aboard Allen's ship and sent him off to gaol in Funafuti. This time, however, he left the choice of the exiled *faipule*'s replacement to the village elders, and they selected a retired local catechist.

Though Samson had local support from the kin of his wife, whose interests he was bound to promote, he was Allen's crony, and usurped the authority of local leaders. He had a gaol constructed adjacent to his wife's house where those who broke the law were imprisoned at night. Those who resisted his judgments were shipped off to Funafuti on Captain Allen's vessel, and in this even the chief *faipule* chosen by the village was not exempt. He resisted Samson on an issue of land and was hauled before a visiting deputy from Funafuti for trial. Samson and Allen interpreted, and predictably he was sentenced to a gaol term in Funafuti. Samson's wife's sister's husband insisted on accompanying his elder in exile, evoking in so doing the essential social order of Nukunonu. Great significance was attached to this act of compassion and statement of autochthonous unity in the face of injustice, and the event was marked by naming two male infants Kave 'Taken', one for each of the exiles.

Nonetheless, people recalling the days of Samson speak with some ambivalence; as they do about the era when Fakaofo reigned supreme. On the one hand, power and strength are admirable: just as people take pride in their Fakaofo connections, people of the *kāiga* into which Samson married and those who are offspring of his adopted children speak of him with pride. On the other hand, Samson, like Fakaofo, usurped the authority of indigenous rulers.

Samson dominated the Nukunonu polity for ten years or so, yet on only one occasion did criticism of him reach the ears of colonial officials. A naval commander paying a call in 1922 reported complaints of one Willy Johnson (Sherston 1922). Willy could speak reasonable English and took the opportunity, in Samson's absence, to say that Samson was an unpopular foreigner who took gifts meant for the village as his own, was dictatorial and made unacceptable rulings in land disputes. These complaints are recalled, but only Willy voiced them at the time. He was an outsider, and perhaps had ambitions himself; still he was voicing wider discontent that the commander sensed even while dismissing Willy's remarks as self-serving.

Nukunonu's silence might simply be attributed to the absence of any channels of communication for expressing discontent. No resident, aside from Willy and perhaps Samson, could speak English to the infrequently visiting officials who understood neither Tokelauan nor Samoan. Allen could communicate in Samoan, but he was unlikely to pass on complaints about his former crewman. Nukunonu's alternative link with the outside world was virtually severed during those years, since no priests were visiting from Samoa. Allen's hostility to the Catholic establishment, official antipathy towards the Bishop, and port of entry regulations combined to prevent contacts between the Nukunonu people and their mission. Yet Nukunonu people were employing a characteristic strategy: patiently waiting, apparently acquiescing in their domination, while at the same time subtly and stubbornly resisting it.[12]

The waiting ended not long after 1922, when Samson disappeared. The story, expressing grudging admiration, is that he was injured in a heroic action on shipboard and died of his injuries. Allen too disappeared from the Tokelau scene shortly thereafter, and at the time of the 1925 visits of Swinbourne and Richardson, Alo, the son of Takua, held the office of magistrate. He was subsequently appointed to the senior office of *faipule*/magistrate by Richardson, and that office he held with distinction until his death in the 1940s. Again, an *aliki* son had been installed as the 'voice' of Nukunonu; authority had returned to where it belonged.

The village transformed

Nineteenth-century visitors did not describe Nukunonu village in any detail and local reconstructions are unspecific and surrounded by controversy. However, by piecing bits of information together its major features may be defined. A low wall set the limits of the village on three sides and the lagoon shore marked the fourth. Just inside the western wall was the Kalevelio (Calvary) cemetery and beyond that wall were the carefully nurtured stands of *kie* pandanus. Beyond the eastern wall were small *kāiga* plantations. The enclosed area was bisected by a shallow channel, through which canoes could be drawn at high tide and which served to divide the village into two parts. Viewed from the ocean shore, to the left of the channel stood the lime-faced church, an open *malae* and two residential compounds associated with two *puikāiga*; to the right were residential clusters associated with the two others.

Roderick MacDermot had been directed to attend to 'the state' of Nukunonu village as his first duty upon reaching Tokelau. From his description, it needed attention.

> The whole people, a much overcrowded cemetery, and a church were walled into a bit of land about two acres in extent. Over this wall any superfluous dirt that realy [sic] had to be shifted went. The chief features of the restricted space were

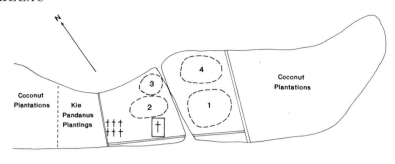

Schematic reconstruction of the layout of Nukunonu village c.1910. The reconstruction is based on MacDermot's description (1911a), residential histories, names associated with village sections at present, etc. Nos 1–4 indicate probable locations of compounds associated with the 'Four Houses'.

houses which would be shamed by the edifice a nomadic Australian aboriginal considers not too good a provision for one night's shelter, ruins of old structures and boundaries which they have not mustered enough energy to remove, pigs mingled with people, and dirt, and rubbish with everything. (MacDermot 1910–11a)

Older people agree that the village of their youth was crowded and dirty. Yet there was also evidence of prosperity. Eleven imported vessels and seven two-storey European houses were part of the clutter, and the community was amassing funds that would soon amount to over £1000, to build a concrete church. Having dwelt within those walls that had marked the limits of their village for generations, perhaps its inhabitants never thought of living beyond them. But when the newly arrived, energetic MacDermot proposed the creation of a new village, extending well beyond the eastern wall, they concurred, apparently without much argument—except over carving up the irregular holdings of coconut palms into standard, square residential sections. The officer laid out a grid, asserting that '. . . ownership of different plots of ground cannot be recognised if a neat village is to be made' (ibid.), though people negotiated among themselves so that the grid sections remained in recognised ownership (see map chapter 1, p.30).

Possibly some Nukunonu people shared the deputy's sentiments about the desirability of a new, orderly, clean village; in any case they knew that residential rearrangements would be inevitable when they built their new church. In the event, the village was extended, realigned, and rebuilt—and was much praised in October 1913 by Assistant Commissioner Mahaffy.

Bishop Broyer was in Nukunonu at the time to initiate the church-building enterprise, and he remained for two months (Darnard 1921). He had earlier expressed reservations about the village renewal project, which he regarded as interfering with higher designs, but then he discovered that the Nukunonu people had further plans in mind for their village that he found very agreeable. Imbued with enthusiasm for their mission, and now with a spacious new village and a substantial church being built, the elders asked the Bishop for a resident priest and some teaching sisters 'to teach our boys and girls, particularly to teach our children English'. The Bishop responded that he would 'send us two priests and two or three teaching sisters'. Twenty-one 'heads of families' and the Bishop signed an agreement whereby 'we who control [*pule*] the lands of Nukunonu atoll' would give the mission control of three specified sections of land on the village islet to house and provide for the priests and sisters, and, in addition, lands in the northeast islet of Tokelau to support the schoolchildren, on the condition that the promised priest(s) and teaching sisters were in permanent residence (Broyer 1913b).[13] The Bishop more or less promised that he would fulfil his part of the agreement in two to three years' time.

At the very beginning of the following year the walls of the church were standing. Boxing still enclosed the last section poured, and timber and barrels of cement to complete the structure were neatly piled at the ocean-side.

The Afa Lahi 'Great Cyclone' struck Nukunonu on 7 January 1914. All the atolls were devastated, and Nukunonu suffered the greatest losses (see *Matagi Tokelau* 1991:115–18). Seven people were swept away, though three returned to the village the following day, having clung to flotsam as they were propelled by the high waves right across the lagoon to the far side of the atoll. The aged and venerated Takua was severely injured by a falling palm and died shortly after. Ocean swells surged through the village, carrying away houses, felling trees, scouring the ground and filling in the shallow channel. Drums of cement lifted by the raging surf battered the walls of the church and reduced them to rubble, and those who had taken refuge inside were only spared by leaping into two commodious vessels that had been tethered to sturdy palms immediately outside.

In the calm of the following morning, what had been the village was now debris and destruction, dominated by the concrete columns of the church standing 'like leaning towers of Pisa . . . to bear mute testimony to the terrific violence of the sea. Everything was lost; every penny had been spent in vain' (Diehl, in Tremblay 1964:96). What had been so laboriously created on a small sandbank during years of prosperity disappeared in a few hours—the old church, the new church, the fine European houses, the new village. Only the vessels, which had provided refuge for many, remained.

Though the village was a debris-strewn sandbank, for the people it was still there and would be recreated as they envisaged it. The grid of paths was remeasured, houses were rebuilt, and those who had lived on the northern side of the now invisible channel joined the new village. The *kie* pandanus garden was gradually replanted from shoots retrieved from the devastation and seed nuts set in the ground to replace the palms that had fallen.

Prosperity, however, did not quickly return. There was no copra to be made and therefore no way of acquiring money to rebuild European houses or a concrete church. Another storm a year later again damaged coconut palms, delaying recovery. This time the people, forewarned, took refuge on the opposite side of the atoll, but the sea did not rise as before.

Nukunonu did not begin to amass funds again to build their church until 1924. They might have begun earlier if they had had some way of getting their copra to their mission in Samoa. The Bishop attempted to arrange transport with Captain Allen in 1916, and though he was not rebuffed out-

What remained of the imposing concrete Nukunonu church for which the cornerstone was laid in 1913 and which was almost finished when the 'Great Cyclone' struck in January 1914. Photo by Captain Allen courtesy of the Public Record Office, London

right, the prescribed itinerary via Funafuti was so roundabout that the venture was abandoned. So it was not until Apia was made a port of entry and another vessel was trading in Tokelau that copra production for a building fund began in earnest. The people were 'reticent in the matter' to official visitors (Swinbourne 1925).[14] Those who were younger men at the time reminisce about how they spent weeks at a time encircling the atoll again and again gathering and cutting copra from everyone's lands. This time is remembered as one of communal euphoria that culminated in 1930/31 when the church was finally built in eleven months, ending over twenty years of patient and frustrated devotion.

Changed and unchanged

With Takua's death the last real witness to the slave ships had passed away. Their children were now the elders of Nukunonu. They were not particularly worldly. Few of them had even the rudiments of a formal education, and those had lived abroad under the paternal auspices of the mission. Otherwise, they were little tempted to travel abroad, and given their atoll's abun-

Remains of church and village avenue eleven years later. (Published in AJHR 1926.) Photo from IT,1, EX 94/1 pt2, Union Group—Tokelau, Swain's Island 1926–1930, National Archives of New Zealand

dant resources, they had no need to. They were suspicious of the world outside and what it proposed (see *Matagi Tokelau* 1991:121–2), but their lives were altered by that world nonetheless.

The relative prosperity they had enjoyed in the years before the 'Great Cyclone' was based on copra, produced from the coconut palms on their lands. Land had acquired new value and questions of land use and ownership arose, complicated by happenings of the past centuries. There were the lands claimed by Fakaofo and the lands always controlled by Nukunonu; properties that had been replanted and properties that 'had always been recognised'; holdings that had changed hands when people had been carried off in 1863; and gifts and other transfers of rights outside *kāiga*, which were eventually and inevitably challenged by those within. For decades everyone of Nukunonu had had more than sufficient resources for subsistence and Nukunonu *kāiga* happily took in affiliate members who had either married into the community from Atafu, Fakaofo, Uvea and Samoa, or simply taken up residence on the basis of some kinship connection. Again, there were wide variations in the extent of property holdings, and since these holdings would pass to the burgeoning present and future generations, questions of rights and the basis of rights generated contention.[15]

Nukunonu was socially a changing place in the later 1910s. Much of this change may be related to the village transformation. The old residential compounds or clusters were broken up when people built their houses on sections in the demarcated grid. These sections did not accommodate compound homesteads and the compromises of arriving at rights to plots meant that former co-residents were not necessarily neighbours. People who had once resided in a single named homestead now occupied several separate houses, and as the population grew more separate houses were built. The *kāiga* continued to work together and share, but the immediacy of joint daily living was gone and the homestead names ceased to be of real houses, but continued to be applied to people whose ancestors had been of those 'Houses'.

Population growth, the copra cash economy, new residential arrangements—all contributed to a proliferation of propertied kin groups, which was reflected in the political structure, irrespective of what offices and bodies were officially decreed. Signed documents of the 1910s bear twenty or so marks or signatures, and the inclusion of an identifiable female signatory confirms that the majority of marks were made by representatives of landholding *kāiga*. The four 'Houses' of the mission era were already divided in 1913. Elders born around the turn of the century recall two to four elders meeting regularly with Takua to discuss village affairs—an arrangement not unlike that described in the 1880s (Didier 1885, 1892), and the named men indeed represented the same 'Houses'. But this soon ended. We cannot date exactly when the property divisions that created new *kāiga* occurred, and in any case they would have involved protracted negotiations. However, the outcome was that ruling body of the village greatly increased in membership, since there were more *kāiga* to be represented. The central organising struc-

'Chiefs in gala dress, Nukunonu', 1925. The group is posed before the pillars of the demolished church. They are wearing fringed malo plaited from Nukunonu's kie pandanus. Their choice of dress is indicative of Nukunonu's celebration of Tokelau 'tradition'. (Published in AJHR 1926.) Photo from IT,1, EX 94/1 pt2 Union Group—Tokelau, Swain's Island 1926–1930, National Archives of New Zealand

ture of the Nukunonu polity was retained as a coalition of *kāiga*, and the local government structure officially decreed by the New Zealand Administrator in 1925 was compatible with local practice. The heads of *kāiga* became the village committee '. . . of not less than six of the elder men who are recognised leaders in the village' (Richardson 1926).

In the old village, the canoe channel had served to divide the village residents into two more or less equal sides and these sides formed competitive teams for work and recreation.[16] The new village did not have a natural dividing line, though a logical one was the central street of the grid that might be, and sometimes was, used to divide the village into 'ocean-path' and 'lagoon-path' sides. This division would have thoroughly confounded the old one by running at right angles to it, and it was soon replaced for most purposes by a division that more or less reduplicated the old one. Those who dwelt in the northern portion of the new village still occupied part of the *kakai tuai* 'old village', and called themselves Egelani/'England'; those who dwelt in what was formerly plantation and was now the *kakai fou* 'new village', called themselves Niu Hila/'New Zealand' and later Amelika/'America'. Appropriately, 'England' had stayed in the old place while 'New Zealand'/ 'America' had shifted to a new place. The dividing line between the two was not marked by any path of the grid, since no path marked where the old wall stood. The new division in fact mirrored the old, except the spatial relations had been inverted.

In other respects too, the spatial relations of Nukunonu village had become the inverse of those in other Tokelau villages. There was no provision in the grid layout for public places, so village gathering places came to be located at the margins. The village was turned inside out simply by its rigorous, orderly design.

Protectorate and colony officials commonly despaired of the 'pervasive influence' of the Catholic mission in Nukunonu, but their words reflect British antipathy to the 'foreign mission' rather than speaking to its real presence. From 1900 to 1945 priests paid only twenty-two visits; for eight years after 1913 no cleric crossed Nukunonu's reef. Certainly some younger people attended mission schools in Samoa in the early years of the century and a few girls received a convent education in the later 1920s, but the numbers are

Virtually all the children of Nukunonu in 1925 are probably included in this photograph. (Published in AJHR *1926.)* Photo from IT,1, EX 94/1 pt2 Union Group—Tokelau, Swain's Island 1926–1930, National Archives of New Zealand

small in comparison to the number of Protestants from Fakaofo and Atafu who were sponsored for mission schooling in Upolu and Vaitupu.

Indeed, Nukunonu people had very little contact with their mission mentors, and visiting priests had little idea of the intense internal concerns of their Nukunonu parishioners. True, the priests' brief and busy visits would have provided little chance for them to build up rapport and understanding, and furthermore the catechists, who might have provided inside information, were themselves of the village and as reticent as their fellows.

What then was this 'pervasive influence'? Surely it came from Nukunonu people themselves. Their intense devotion to their faith had a political tinge, for it was closely linked with their self-asserted autonomy. It buttressed their self-determination and they used it with political cunning. With apparent naïveté they would deflect recrimination by pronouncing that the bishop 'would not allow' or had to be consulted (see, for example, Hunter 1902 and Newell 1904).

Catholic fathers were appropriately paternalistic but they could not be domineering. They left their flock to their own devices as long as these did not compromise church dictates. Nukunonu consequently became the conservator of items and practices banned elsewhere, and tended to resist innovations. Samoan influences in particular were viewed with suspicion. Āumāga organisation was summarily rejected as compromising elder authority and village unity, and Samoan forms of speech and etiquette were not pervasive. Birth, marriage and death were marked by Tokelau rituals as well as Catholic ones, and the Tokelau arts of song, dance and narrative were performed and taught. Nukunonu became consciously the living archive of *na tū ma aganuku anamua* 'ancient traditions and customs'.

Preoccupied with local matters, conservative in attitude and insular in outlook during the colonial era, Nukunonu was often portrayed as 'backward' by visitors and the other atolls. Yet the elders had proposed the establishment of a school to teach English as early as 1913. The cyclones, severed communication with Samoa and the First World War scotched this plan, though the promise remained. When the church was finally built, the precondition of the plan was met, but again it was thwarted by drought, depressed copra prices and erratic transport in the 1930s, and then the Second World War. Still, the

Hiva anamua *'ancient dance' in 'traditional' costume being performed for a priest visiting Nukunonu, c.1950.* Photo probably taken by Father A. McDonald, courtesy of A. Thomas

promise was not forgotten. Within two months of the Japanese surrender, a priest was in Nukunonu confirming the boundaries of the land promised to the church to support a local mission and school. Before another year had passed he was in residence and a year later his successor founded the school on the site of the first Catholic church.

Nukunonu's population exploded in the 1930s and the many children born in that decade and later had a very different education from their parents and grandparents, and correspondingly different visions of their immediate surroundings and of the world beyond. In addition to this, the mission and school brought foreigners, many of British heritage, into the community. Belatedly, Nukunonu was exposed to new (and predominantly metropolitan) ideas and attitudes, and new ways of doing things. The elders generally trusted their resident mentors to mediate for them with the outside world. That trust was for the most part well founded; however, it tended to make the polity dependent on their religious advisors. Nukunonu, with the advantage of having people who could speak on their behalf, could maintain their timidity and shyness towards outsiders. However, occasionally resident priests saw the determined intransigence that lurked beneath that apparent docility.

Atafu

The meeting house is all decorated with green leaves. The Union Jack is flying gaily on a respectable flag pole. As we come ashore guard of honour with guns carved out of wood salute and sing 'God Save the King'. All line up in double row—men first then women and then children. The Captain tells in simple words that His Majesty the King has sent his battleship to visit these distant islands as loyal subjects. . . . The sound of music comes from a distance. Long queue of performers appear headed by two men carrying a pig roasted whole followed by women carrying live fowl and others with bunches of cocoanuts. All food offerings put down in a heap. Children give song then gaunt native speaker leaning on staff thanks N.Z. for her wise administration. Captain replies, promises to let chief men visit his ship. . . . Soon [after vessel departs] boys go around street and pull out palm leaves which had been stuck in ground to line paths with greenery.

—Thomson 1928

This is how Atafu would present itself to colonial visitors if forewarned. If not, they would still informally express their loyal enthusiasm. 'In the last canoe that left the Ship they stood up and sang two verses of the National Anthem before leaving for the Shore. . . . A searchlight was used and the natives were seen to be dancing on the beach when we left' (Sherston 1922). When the HMS *Egeria* visited in 1889 to hoist the Union Jack, presumably it was likewise farewelled, though its log reports nothing of the occasions and there are no local accounts of the event.

For the most part, colonial officers briefly visiting Atafu described the people as '. . . most friendly, hospitable and cheerful' (Mahaffy 1911), 'happy and contented . . . well nourished and happy-looking' (Sherston 1922), living in a beautiful village and in good health (Allen 1929). This is how Atafu as the unified Falefitu wanted to be seen, and this is why they assiduously tended their village and their own relationships. For most of the colonial era they seem to have succeeded, but when the village was not 'happy and contented' it was readily apparent—the aggrieved were not inhibited about expressing their discontent to visitors, despite the ethic of unity. Documents picture Atafu in some turmoil both at the beginning and the end of the colonial era, and those writing them would have taken issue with the supposition made in more contented times that the people 'must be very easy to deal with' (Mahaffy 1911). However, the turmoil never got beyond local control and reports of it were probably exaggerated to or by visitors; and even in contented times disputes, infidelities and youthful erring strained community unity from time to time but were not brought to the attention of visitors lest the image of happy contentment be tarnished.[17] None the less, the two periods of turmoil have features in common: contentions were apparent to visitors; and they have not been forgotten. More important, they involved significant others residing in the atoll—not pastors (though pastors might be implicated) but outsiders who had not been inculcated with the Christian Atafu ethic.

Difficulties at the turn of the century

Six years after the Union Jack was raised at Atafu, a mission visitor was asked 'many questions as to the meaning of the English protectorate' (Marriott 1895). No one representing the British Protectorate had appeared since it

'Reception to Administrator at Atafu', 1925. This flotilla of substantial canoes coming out to meet visitors was the characteristic Atafu welcome from the earliest encounters. (Published in AJHR *1926). Photo from IT,1, EX 94/1 pt2 Union Group—Tokelau, Swain's Island 1926– 1930, National Archives of New Zealand*

'During the field trip on Atafu an exhibition of ancient dances was given, accompanied by singing of the performers. The dancers stood abreast in a single line throughout the dancing. They moved 1 or 2, or sometimes 3 steps; but the principal movements were made with their arms or canoe paddles. . . . The exhibition was led by a woman who had learned the songs and movements from her father' (Macgregor 1937:74). Photo: G. Macgregor

had been declared, and the Atafu people had good reason to ask questions. The deputy commissioner who finally did appear in the following year was deluged with complaints and appeals, some of which were stimulated by uncertainty and rumour; but he had not the time, authority or background to arbitrate on these. Old 'king' Ioane, whom missionaries called a 'warm friend', was described as 'a tyrant' who asserted that absolute power was given to him at the time the Protectorate was declared. 'The government' (presumably the Elders' Council) did not accept this, and determined to banish him and his family. The deputy phrased the dilemma thus: the "King" appealed to deport "the government" and "the government" appealed to deport the "King"' (Cusack Smith 1896a). Two property disputes which had been locally arbitrated were connected with this state of affairs. The deputy could only uphold the local rulings on these issues and advise constraint and patience to 'government' and 'king'.

Two traders, one a son of Ilai named Tanielu (Daniel) and the other an American-Portuguese,[18] were resident at Atafu in 1896. The latter was married to a local woman and was not disinterested in the property disputes, as indicated by a letter sent him by the deputy threatening deportation should he continue to interfere in government matters by '. . . talking unwisely and untruly about the decisions I made at Atafu' (Cusack Smith 1896b).

'Farewelling visitors at Atafu', 1925. Again, the exuberant farewelling of visitors with many people assembled at the ocean shore. (Published in AJHR 1926). Photo from IT,1, EX 94/1 pt2 Union Group—Tokelau, Swain's Island 1926–1930, National Archives of New Zealand

The deputy's numerous reports of his 1896 visit make no mention of the pastor. However, the record of contributions to the church supplied him by the Samoan mission show that support of the pastor was paltry in 1896 and in the previous year the visiting missionary was shocked at the long list of those who had been expelled from the church, a sure sign the relations between pastor and flock were strained.

In the following three years or so, these troubles faded into the background (one of the traders having shifted to Fakaofo), but they were replaced by others, specifically by difficulties with Tanielu, son of Ilai. Every visiting deputy between 1897 and 1900 heard complaints against him. He was said to be 'interfering and bullying' and 'making himself obnoxious'—so much so that seventy-six people had voyaged to Fakaofo to escape his 'overbearing conduct'. Yet his influence was sufficient to dissuade the 'chiefs' from signing a document giving the high commissioner jurisdiction over foreigners—that is, the authority to deport him (Cusack Smith 1897). Another deputy the following year heard more specific charges against him but was not inclined to act on the request for his deportation. His attitude towards the reprobate was chari-table—true, he seemed to covet the wives of others, but he was hard-working, had a good house and was generally sober (Maxse 1898). A woman visiting for the mission was not at all charitable: she wrote that he 'is a constant agent of evil among the natives' (French 1899). Another litany of complaints was re-corded in 1900 (Hunter 1900), but thereafter his name disappears from offi-cial correspondence until 1908 when he applied for a licence to trade in Atafu (Hunter 1908) and was encountered by the Rev. Newell 'ill from . . . degen-eration of heart—perhaps also cirrhosis of liver' (Newell 1908a). He died soon after, and Atafu was rid of its last disruptive foreign resident trader.

His trading concern remained, however, in the care of his Samoan widow, who had probably run it all along. She is remembered as kind and generous, the antithesis of her profligate spouse, and she joined the village by marrying an upstanding local man in whose name the business was licensed. It was the sole trading operation in Atafu and was run more for convenience than for profit, nicely serving a community that did not countenance personal profit at the expense of others. Those who had *koloa* 'goods', including the store-keeper, were expected to be generous to their less fortunate compatriots. Her reward was to be remembered as a *fafine alofa* 'compassionate woman'. Her able husband, Nikotemo, was later and for many years Atafu's *faipule*.

Atafu 'happy and contented'

When the Union Jack was raised at Atafu, the white-helmeted, booted and pompous pastor (see chapter 7) had been succeeded by 'a younger man of a newer school . . . [who] has done a good year's work' (Clarke 1890). After another eight years he was found wanting by his superiors and replaced by another pastor, who encountered some criticism but served his ten-year *feagaiga* 'covenant', and following him was the long-serving Pastor Tanielu. Atafu's relations with its pastor were not always smooth, but the conditions and rules of the 'covenant' between pastor and flock were firmly in place.

The pastors had their defined and elite place, insulated and protected, and their part of the 'covenant' was to keep within these boundaries. Strict rules governed people's interaction with the pastor, and violation of these brought quick and severe punishment. On neither side was the relationship seen as an easy one; it required careful tending. The reward was a 'covenant' fulfilled or even extended; the penalty a departure embarrassing to all.

Atafu was the administrative centre and port of entry for all Tokelau from 1910 to 1914, simply because it was marginally closest to Funafuti some 1000 km to the west. Viewed from Ocean Island, another 800 km away, it appeared the logical place for all outside contact with Tokelau to begin and end. This administrative centre had a house and office, containing a safe, and most of the months when Protectorate officers were at the remote Tokelau post they were resident at Atafu. Yet Atafu hardly figures in the reports, communiqués and correspondence generated by these same officers, so apparently their months in Atafu were relatively peaceful and uneventful. Even when Tokelau was put under the jurisdiction of the Funafuti district officer and the port of entry shifted there, Atafu, as the closest Tokelau point, continued to be viewed as 'central'. This perception was bolstered by Atafu becoming the medical centre for Tokelau, in part fortuitously.

Of the two qualified native medical practitioners returned to Tokelau in 1917, only Logologo Apinelu stayed. He was *te fōmai* 'the doctor' in Tokelau for decades, shifting between the atolls when transport was available but based at Atafu, where his hospital and his home occupied land that had been set aside for 'their doctor' by the village. Atafu enjoyed his medical services and also his guidance, for unlike any others of his time he was truly worldly, well educated and, most important, the only Tokelau resident who could speak English fluently. Visiting colonial officers had Samoan-speaking interpreters, and Logologo was the only person who could communicate with them without a mediating interpreter. Atafu was where English-speakers went when they planned to stay a while—for example, a meteorologist in 1928 (Thomson 1928) and an anthropologist in 1932 (Macgregor 1932).

The first resident officer wrote of Atafu: 'The people are all living on the N.W. Island which provides ample space for an excellent village. . . . The village has been kept fairly clean, but plenty of room remains for improvement' (MacDermot 1910). This was high praise compared to his scathing descriptions of the other villages. Furthermore, Atafu was very willing to improve. His call for an orderly, immaculate village appealed to civic pride and the people willingly devoted two days a week to public works. Streets were laid out with coral slab kerbs and smooth sandy surfaces. Houses were torn down and rebuilt further apart, aligned with the streets. Pigs were moved out of the village and a long road was cut through bush to the site of a new graveyard above the ocean beach to the north of the village.

Not much of these public works survived the 'Great Cyclone' of 1914, but the plan was recreated on a surface swept clean by the scouring waves. The people had all taken refuge near the protected bay at the north end of the village, and on their return found their church and the pastor's compound

*Logologo Apinelu,
doctor to Tokelau from
1917, and his wife,
Emilia, c.1946.* Photo:
G. Macgregor

had disappeared along with all but seven houses. They also found their village bigger. The waves and currents had deposited sand and rubble at its southern end, adding some acres that were soon divided and allocated, planted and peopled. Although an immediate disaster, the cyclone brought longterm gain.

Civic pride was coupled with Christian devotion when the congregation decided to rebuild their church not of local 'limestone' but of imported cement, not at the back of the village adjacent to the pastor's compound but at its centre. The demolished church was not be replaced as quickly or easily as the demolished houses: it took fifteen years. It probably would not have taken so long had the elders not been persuaded by Captain Allen in 1916 to invest an accumulated £500 in his Samoa Shipping and Trading Company at three per cent interest, with the additional agreement that all building materials would be ordered through him. By 1922 '[t]hey were inclined to be suspicious that Mr Allen was doing them out of their money and wanted to see it there in the Island in hard cash' (Sherston 1922). Subsequently they petitioned repeatedly to retrieve their investment, but never saw the money again. Yet they were building their concrete church in the midst of their village in 1927. It was opened in 1929 and stood until 1970, a magnificent testament to devotion and craftsmanship. In relation to its surroundings its

'*The modern village was laid out when the island was under the administration of the Gilbert and Ellice Islands Colony. The paths, the arrangement of the modern, cooler types of house, the segregation of pigs from the village, and the clearance of all undergrowth was planned and accomplished. . . .*' (*Macgregor 1937:56*). Photo: G. Macgregor

303

Funeral procession through village to the burial ground, established some twenty years before. Before this, burial was on the village land of a kāiga of the deceased. These graves are still a feature of the Atafu village landscape. Photo: G. Macgregor

dimensions were imposing; within it was glorious. The lofty pure white interior was mellowed by beams and pillars, rails and posts lovingly hand-adzed out of dark local hardwood, and rosy light filtered through a large red stained-glass window, emblazoned with the words SIONA FOU 'New Zion', high above the pulpit. The *vi'i* 'song of praise' (in Samoan) composed for its inauguration glorifies Atafu, the church and the polity founded less than 150 years before, which had created their 'New Zion'.

Aue tagi e ma fa'avavau	Alas oh lament and mourn
Manatua o uso ua i tu'ugamau	In memory of compatriots in graves

The Atafu burial ground above the ocean beach north of the village. A low wall surrounds it, and within graves are marked by upright slabs of coral rock. Photo: A. Hooper

O e na latou fa'avaeina	For it is they who began it
Le galuega o latou lima	The work of their hands
Ua latou le silasila	May they view
I lenei fa'atasiga	In this gathering
I le fa'ai'uina o lenei fe'au	The completion of this task
Ua tu i Atafu To'elau	Standing in Atafu Tokelau
Muliselu e, lo'u sei	Ah Muliselu [Atafu], my blossom
I lenei vasa Pasefika	In this vast Pacific

The ideology of civic pride and service was again articulated with the founding of the Āumāga in 1939, and the anchor of the *Ophelia* became a symbol of the new organisation and the ethic it embodied. The anchor had lain for over seventy years off Atafu's northeastern reef, where the *Ophelia* had run aground in 1865. Everyone knew it was there and several attempts

Atafu concrete church three years after its completion. The stark exterior contrasts with the elegant interior of dark wood and white surfaces infused with a rosy glow from the stained-glass window above the pulpit (see photo, chapter 2, p.93). Photo: G. Macgregor.

'Meeting house (Fale loa) at Atafu of type with low eaves used formerly for men's houses' (Macgregor 1937: Plate 5c). The structure was centrally located just inland from the lagoon shore. Here the elders gathered, village fishing nets were stored, and important catches, such as turtle, were brought to be butchered and distributed to the village. Photo: G. Macgregor

had been made to raise it without success. The village manpower, mobilised as the Āumāga, brought it up and ashore and deposited it in the centre of the village. There it lay, rusty and unobtrusive, yet always a visual testimony to what collective will and effort can accomplish.[19] The Āumāga, referred to as *te mālohi o to tātou nuku* 'the strength of our village', became a dominant institution of Atafu, with its distinctive form and practice.

The Āumāga's counterpart was the Komiti Fafine 'Women's Committee', instituted some years earlier by Logologo. It too was modelled on a Samoan institution (introduced from New Zealand), was devoted to the civic good and took on a characteristic Atafu cast.

Village pride did not inhibit Atafu people from voyaging away from their homeland. When the Union Jack was raised, Atafu had the largest population of the three atolls, about 300, and 375 Atafuans were counted in 1900. Thereafter, until the Second World War, the population fluctuated between 350 and 400 persons, falling behind Fakaofo and nearly being overtaken by Nukunonu (see Hooper and Huntsman 1973:380). Natural causes may have had something to do with this lack of growth—for example a dysentery epidemic in 1914 that carried off thirty-four persons (Thomson 1928). However, the mobility of the people themselves was the major factor. As early as 1902, twenty Atafu people were reported absent in Olohega, and two years later eight were reported to be at Olohega and sixty-four at the Lever plantations in the Phoenix Group (Hunter 1902). While recruiting for the Phoenix commercial plantations was intermittent and subject to licence regulation, the Olohega connection was informal and continual. This was administratively disturbing, but since Olohega's proprietor, the namesake and son of the original Ilai, purposely kept the national status of his island domain equivocal, not much could be done. The Atafu–Olohega connection was probably initiated by Ilai's trader son, Tanielu (see above), was maintained by Captain Allen, and continued thereafter despite official discouragement. The second Ilai ran his establishment 'on unbusiness like and semi-native lines' encouraging Atafu (and Fakaofo) people 'to make a sort of second home there' (MacDermot 1910). The work routines were not strictly regimented, and ample time was allotted for communal and family activities. Ilai took the role of benevolent patriarch, and was in fact linked to many of his workers by kin and affinal ties. Wages were small, but Olohega was attractive for other than monetary reasons. The provisions were ample (see Strum 1918) and the accommodation was agreeable. A further attraction was that Olohega residence might give access to American Samoa and ultimately to Hawai'i. If Apia or Funafuti were the front door of Tokelau, through which Tokelau people and their visitors officially arrived and departed, Olohega was the back door for many unofficial departures. People departed Atafu by the front door too, going for schooling to Samoa or Tuvalu and to Samoa for jobs. A substantial number returned home sooner or later, but others stayed in Samoa and acted as hosts for schoolchildren and others. Although the Atafu population counts fluctuate within a narrow range, they do not represent a particularly stable population. People were going and returning, the going outnumbering the

Supercargo of trading vessel weighing copra ashore at Atafu.
Photo: G. Macgregor

Manhandling sacks of copra to lighter.
Photo: G. Macgregor

Bucking the incoming surf at the reef edge, lighter transports copra to trading vessel standing offshore at Atafu.
Photo: G. Macgregor

returning enough to mask natural increase. It was not until the mid 1940s that Atafu's population was solidly above 400 (442 in 1944, 451 in 1945), but then there were major attractions at home (see below).

Some Atafu men journeyed abroad to avoid the strict regulation of activity and the rigid codes of behaviour in Atafu—particularly those who had violated these codes. This regulation was true of the other atolls too; but in one

Fishermen back from the sea: left with skipjack casting rod, right with skipjack in hand. They are standing at the ocean shore with the exposed reef, reef shallows, and breakers at the reef edge in the background. Most of the fishing crew disembarks at this point so that the canoes can be guided unburdened through the shallows to the lagoon.
Photo: G. Macgregor

important respect Atafu was constrained unlike its neighbours. It had easy access to subsistence resources, but in limited supply. In imposing a copra tax levy of nine tons in 1910, MacDermot noted that 'it will be some months before they will be able to collect 9 tons' (MacDermot 1910–11). A year later, an official visitor remarked on the variability of copra production and entertained a request that the tax be adjusted to yearly fluctuations (Mahaffy 1911). Not until 1925 was it suggested that perhaps the tax was excessive following 'observation of outlying islands . . . [where] all the nuts were harvested and the trees were bearing very few nuts' (Richardson 1925). Tax tonnage was originally assessed roughly on the basis of human population instead of palm population. At that time Atafu did have the largest population, but they were harvesting from the fewest palms. After 1925, Atafu frequently requested tax relief and usually all or a portion of the assessment was remitted. A thorough evaluation was finally made in 1944, and the officer who made it readily confirmed what Atafu people had been saying for years—the tax burden was excessive (Grattan 1944b). Besides having fewer palms than the other atolls, Atafu suffered more frequently and severely from droughts, so that productivity varied significantly from year to year and consequently Atafu people were never able to rely on copra as a source for cash. In many years, after cutting tax copra, and cutting and selling copra for

Well-filled vaka malaga *'harvesting canoe' returned to village with provisions from* kāiga *lands across the lagoon. In the coconut frond baskets are husked drinking coconuts* (hua), *under them in the bow are two pandanus fruits. The little girl is perched on mature coconuts that nearly fill the hull.*
Photo: G. Macgregor

annual contributions to the pastor and mission, the elders prohibited all further copra cutting to preserve subsistence supplies. Money for essential
imports such as tobacco, soap and dry goods, or to pay Samoan school fees,
could only be earned elsewhere, and even if the earnings were paltry, the
absence of wage-earners removed consumers, and the coconuts not consumed could be made into copra by those who stayed home. Limited resources and uncertain productivity meant that Atafu could not be as
commercially prosperous as the other atolls. None the less a plentiful supply
of food was assured by careful monitoring of resources that, combined with
the ethic of generous sharing, meant that all were more than adequately
provisioned. As the unified Falefitu they thrived, celebrating their village in
feast and song.

Extraordinary visitors

In January 1944 the Allied War Cabinet selected Atafu as the site of the
southern end of a Loran chain otherwise located in the Phoenix Group. What
prompted the choice of Atafu rather than Nukunonu or Fakaofo? At
Nukunonu it was believed that Logologo, 'the doctor', had promoted his
home atoll to officers of a naval ship that called at Nukunonu while he was
there in 1943. Nukunonu felt cheated. New Zealand officials in Apia certainly had no voice in the choice: 'the thing was already arranged and . . .
when we [the district officer and administrator] were made aware of it the
negotiations had ended' (Grattan 1944b). The Governor-General had questioned the choice of Atafu, wishing, as did others, that the choice had been
otherwise. The choice was probably made on technical grounds—by ruler
and compass—but, given Atafu's characteristic open hospitality, in a way this
was the logical atoll to play host to the Americans. The War Cabinet inadvert-
ently selected the atoll that would be most congenial to the easy-going, fun-
loving young Americans. The Atafu people were ecstatic (see *Matagi Tokelau*:
128–30).

A United States Navy float plane dropping into Atafu apprised the villagers of their good fortune and established warm relationships some time before a survey party arrived by air in May 1944 to mark the area required for
the station. The district officer was left the unenviable task of sorting out
tangled claims to trees and compensation. When he arrived in June he was
dismayed not by that task but by the transformation of Atafu.

Vaka alo 'skipjack
fishing canoes' with
rods set to be taken up
for casting at sea. This
communal fishing is
surrounded by strict
etiquette. Photo: G.
Macgregor; see Hooper
1985, Hooper &
Huntsman 1991

309

Nearly all the villagers were arrayed in excellent print material. . . . There was so much of this that even the eight chairs in the Fono House were draped with a fathom each. Nearly all the men, and some of the women, were wearing what appeared to be servicemen's undershirts, and shortly after our arrival the new Pastor . . . was presented with half a dozen . . . even members of the [administrative] staff were presented with them. Gift of paint had been brought down from Canton Island and more had been promised for the painting of the Church. Tools had already been distributed in fair quantities and more of these had also been promised. Most of those seen smoking were using American cigarettes. A Doctor had paid a visit . . . and promised to perform a number of eye operations. He actually arrived the next day and performed the first operation. . . . (Grattan 1944c)

Atafu and the Navy were on marvellous terms. Atafu had opened its village to its open-handed visitors and both sides were engaged in active trade. Atafu was producing 'curios' for returns previously undreamt of (a foot-square mat inscribed 'USN' fetched six shillings, compared with seven shillings that had been the rate for a twenty-four square foot mat), and high-quality goods were offered at incredibly low prices. An anonymous local wrote: 'America is now looking after us very well indeed', and a diplomatic blunder was narrowly averted when 'the Native Magistrate [was persuaded] that it would not be proper to display on the arch of welcome [for the New Zealand governor-general] an enormous Stars and Stripes. . . .' (Grattan 1944c).

All this was only preliminary to the real American presence. When the construction crew landed in late July, 'the Polynesian village elders insisted upon vacating and making available to them eight native houses, for use until a camp could be set up. . . . Their hospital was gratefully accepted for the four days of unloading operations, during which the natives' amazement shown toward our mobile equipment and other gear was almost unbelievable' (US Coast Guard 1946:97). Construction took four months or so, and thereafter rotated Coast Guard detachments manned and operated the station.

Atafu people still regale themselves and visitors with recollections of 'the days of the Americans'. They tell of the unending supplies of candy, chewing gum and cigarettes; of the miraculous *katapila* 'caterpillar tractor' that cleared vegetation, transported harvesters over land and water, and began a road around the atoll; of the vast stores of canned provisions, especially canned hams, that filled the commissary shelves; of the marvellous visions on the 'silver screen' at the Quonset hut camp, and the truck that would pick them up for the show and return them to the village. More recent American visitors are repeatedly asked the name of their *hitete* 'state' in hopes that they might know something about some family's 'friend', for to prevent local jealousies and to promote an equal distribution of largesse each Atafu family was assigned its American 'friend', and their names and home states are well-remembered. American slang and profanities still feature in Atafu jest and comedy, as do memorable situations and movie episodes.

While people frequently reminisce about the wonder and glory of 'the days of the Americans', they are reticent about the troubles that eventually arose. New Zealand officials were not silent about the difficulties, even though they were not fully informed. Just before the Americans descended, the district officer praised the 'vigour' of the Faipule and 'the support his people gave him' (Grattan 1944a). A year and a half later, an official reported 'the Faipules [sic] authority very limited' (Thompson 1945a).

Initially the village was united in its euphoria, but when the Americans had encamped to man the station, difficulties arose. Some Atafu men were hired, at hourly wages set by the Administration, to work at the camp, where they received substantial bonuses in goods and provisions and established special friendships. The Americans did not have onerous duties and sought fun and diversions, like wandering around the village at night and setting up a distillery, contrary to long-standing parish and village regulations concerning evening curfews and prohibition. The pastor and deacons tried to enforce the rules in an effort to 'institute some measure of control' fearing that the situation was getting out of hand. Consequently, the pastor became 'rather unpopular' with some segments of the community. The village was split between those who sided with the pastor and those who wished to accommodate their exuberant American friends. The pastor's supporters included the Faipule, while the Americans' supporters were primarily their employees who agreed 'to work for no pay at the American Camp'. The village was in an 'upset state' (Thompson 1945a).

A climactic confrontation between the two parties arose when the Americans heard news of Japan's surrender. Jubilant, they raced to the village to proclaim victory in their cultural manner by tolling the church bell. The pastor, long taxed by their ebullient presence, righteously ordered them to desist on the grounds that the bell was under his jurisdiction and his permission had not been asked. The celebrants irreverently answered back and angry words were exchanged. Stories of the confrontation at the church spread rapidly and were elaborated on. The following day, perhaps prompted by their American friends, some of the camp employees verbally abused and threatened the pastor. While the supporters of the pastor might admit that he had acted injudiciously, they were fearful that the 'covenant' of village and pastor might be broken. The immediate crisis passed, but the village remained divided.

Two months later an administration officer was greeted with blank stares and inaction when he asked for labour to work the ship and was not accompanied by local officials when he boarded the ship to depart as was customary (Thompson 1945b). The officer was certainly not apprised of what had transpired—nobody was telling tales—but what he reported reflects the tale that people now very occasionally tell and more often elliptically cite. With the village disunited, labour could not be mobilised and the tension between factions made local officials loath to depart the village even briefly.

The abrupt departure of the Americans in the early months of 1946 eased the tensions, as evidenced by the report of the same officer visiting after their evacuation: 'the people were also found in a pleasant mood and all assistance given us in unloading and loading again' (Thompson 1946). The Americans

Memento of the United States Coast Guard presence incorporated into a 'modernising' house. Photo: J. Huntsman

had said they would return, and their loyal supporters had every reason to believe they would—the equipment and stores they left behind were testimony to that promise, so the Atafu people waited and watched over the stores, but nobody came. Their disillusionment is expressed in the stories of how shelves and shelves of tinned food in corroded containers had to be dumped in the sea—this unbelievable waste of good food was the outcome of their blind loyalty. The equipment remained, and with it some hope of a return. New Zealand officials were confronted with a difficult situation that is encapsulated in a suggestion for the wording of a telegram to be sent to the New Zealand Ministry in Washington: 'In as much as these installations have caused considerable unsettlement in the life of the Islanders it is preferred that they be removed, but on the other hand the personnel stationed there have been so liberal in material things that there would be reaction unfavourable to New Zealand if the Islanders were informed by anyone that the installation was being removed at the request of the New Zealand Government' (McKay 1947). No practical response appears to have been made to this diplomatic probe, but the installation was eventually dismantled, and some equipment and materials were removed several years later, despite Atafu objections. Then, or perhaps some time before, tired of waiting, they dismantled the abandoned camp. Houses sported 'pin-up girls' on wall panels, and pieces of metal were transformed into coconut graters and fishing sinkers.

Near the Atafu seaside landing, hidden within a grove of pandanus, stands a small concrete monument recording the presence of the US Navy. More conspicuous was a tall mast standing in the midst of low scrub at the site where the camp had been, an area where the ownership of all useful trees was precisely determined so that their owners could be compensated for their removal. They were compensated: forty-six separate claims were adjusted within an eighteen-acre area. Once the trees were down nobody was sure where the boundaries of the forty-six plots were, and now the communal pigsty takes in a portion of it—including the overgrown tennis court! As for the radar mast: when foreign ships came by and asked what it was for, they were told that it was a lookout for fish. The loyalty of the Atafu people to their generous American friends remained.

The village, of course, was reunited, but there were subsequent changes that echo an American political ideology. These were not immediate, but were in place by the early 1950s, some time after the death of the Faipule of some twenty-five years who, along with his brother and a few other elders, had long been the *taupulega* 'rulers' of Atafu. First, the constituted membership of this 'elders' Council' was made more representative, and consequently not so elderly. Second, all men in the 'Council' were excluded from the membership list of the Āumāga and thereafter were not eligible to hold office, though they could continue to join in Āumāga activities. Thus, the two bodies became discrete and the Āumāga became semi-independent with its own organisational structure. Finally, the incumbents of the offices of *faipule* and *pulenuku* were elected by universal adult suffrage every three years, rather than appointed for an indefinite term. The last innovation was extended to the other atolls following New Zealand's ready approval. All these changes might be characterised as 'more democratic' than previous arrangements, and indeed this is how they are viewed in Atafu. If the Americans did espouse 'more democratic' procedures, their teachings were congenial to Atafu, where an ideology of unity and equality is so pervasive, but they were nevertheless implemented cautiously.

New Competitions and Old Relationships

The Western Pacific High Commission officials had belatedly recognised that Tokelau in the past had been more than just three villages (Indermaur and Smith-Rewse 1914); but then officially proclaimed Tokelau to be just three villages, each separately annexed to the British Empire with the king or queen of England as the remote sovereign or *aliki*.

Atafu had been treated as central, being the closest atoll to Funafuti and having the main medical facility. Now and again there are hints that this may have been something of an issue at the time, when people talk about which atoll might be the *laumua* 'capital' of Tokelau. To officials from Ocean Island or even Fiji, Atafu could well have seemed an appropriate choice for an administrative centre in the 1910s, for aside from being closest to Funafuti, it had the largest population. Fakaofo, for good historical reasons, did not accept this, but then it did not mean much and came to mean nothing when Apia became the port of entry for Tokelau and New Zealand became responsible for Tokelau's administration. The new New Zealand administrators had seemingly no awareness of the old relations between the atolls, and apparently Fakaofo voiced no claims of supremacy to them. Perhaps this was in

Fakaofo versus Atafu cricket test, Atafu 1967. Top left: Atafu side, uniformed in white lavalava *and singlet, marching onto the* malae kilikiti *'cricket pitch'. Right: Fakaofo cricket side, dressed in new uniform* lavalava *and matching neck-scarf, presenting a challenge to their Atafu opponents at the* malae kilikiti. Photos: A. Hooper

consequence of the Nukunonu copra payment, or because Tokelau people no longer acknowledged any *aliki* now that the atolls were part of the British Empire and they were subjects of the British monarchy.

The silence about the issue of historical precedence did not end competition between the atolls, but competition took new forms: civic pride in village amenities and beautification, glorification of God by church-building, celebration of atoll home in song and dance, and atoll prowess in what had become the Tokelau national sport—*kilikiti* 'cricket'.

The first inter-atoll *kilikiti* 'test' was played in 1931 between Fakaofo and Atafu. It was a memorable event. A brief commentary on the event is a fitting conclusion to Peato Tutu Perez's account of Fakaofo (1977). A more fulsome account was published in the Atafu School newspaper, transcribed from the words of Taupe Alesana who had been the captain of the Atafu team (*Te Vakai* 1970). The highlights are paraphrased below, and direct quotations (in translation) are so marked.

> The Atafu team, numbering 110, arrived in Fakaofo with gifts of some 500 tamu [dry-land taro] *and a substantial six-seat canoe, 'because timbers to make such a canoe are unobtainable in Fakaofo'. As we approached our destination, we sounded our trumpet and all Fakaofo rushed to the shore in delight. Feasting and speeches and gift-giving followed.*
>
> *Play began the following day. After some contestation about which side would bat first, and what balls would be used—Atafu had brought 'nearly 60 hardwood balls' that Fakaofo rejected, the Pastor intervened and the match proceeded.*
>
> *The fielding of Kolo Alefaio was remarkable as he threw the ball straight to the wicket from far afield—'just like the straight shooter of Buffalo Bill'. None the less, Fakaofo scored nearly 400 runs, and Atafu was unable to beat that score.*
>
> *The next day the Atafu team was discouraged at first, but when the game began Fakaofo was transfixed by Kolo's fielding, and '. . . the ball hardly ever touched the ground, despite ricocheting through the high trees and palms, it suddenly appeared in the hand of a fielder.' Again Fakaofo scored nearly 400 runs, but in this match the batting of the sons of Atafu was amazing. We struck boundaries to the canoe channel, to the reef-flat. One remarked afterwards that as the ball came towards him down the pitch, 'it was as if he saw a tiny basket floating towards him'. Some never got a chance to bat because Fakaofo's score was topped with nine wickets still left.*
>
> *'The third day, we were like iron-men . . .'. But then an elder put an end to the competition. 'You may well ask why.' Anyway, it was stopped so we went*

314

fishing and in that too Atafu excelled, providing great quantities of fish for every-one and celebrating their fishing prowess, to which Fakaofo responded by giving them a great quantity of clothing.

Just before we departed, one Fakaofo man said to us, 'It was just as well the competition was not concluded, for if it had been, they would not have known what to do. It was unfortunate that you were unfamiliar with the field on the first day.'

On the way back to Atafu, they played a match at Nukunonu, and triumphed there, and as they came offshore of Atafu, all those who had 'eggs', i.e., made no runs, leapt into the sea and swam ashore—perhaps from embarrassment.[20]

Top left: *Fakaofo fielders celebrating the dismissal of Atafu batsman with 'routine' to the accompaniment of drumming.*
Right: *Atafu fielders arrayed on the pitch as Fakaofo batsmen* tuli te kai lit. *'chase the score' made by Atafu.*

Darkness fell before the Fakaofo batsmen were all out, and the imminent departure of the ship returning the Fakaofo team meant that the test was again a draw. Photos: A. Hooper

The account concludes with appeals to remember the Almighty—that 'He created the world that his children might enjoy life'.

The story as told from a Fakaofo perspective would be different, but whatever the tale, the cessation of the competition with one victory to each side would be crucial to the story. Tokelau people now carefully tended the peace and enjoyment of life, granted them by the Almighty, while they also competed.

In November 1967, Fakaofo travelled to Atafu for a one-day match that was not too different in spirit from the contest some thirty-six years before. The match was a draw!

315

POSTSCRIPT
'Part of New Zealand'

Our intention in this brief postscript is to sketch the changes that came to Tokelau in the years between 1949, when the Tokelau Islands Act 1948 came into effect, and c.1970. This brief narrative completes the story of how Tokelau came to be what it was then, but it could equally well be the beginning of another story of how Tokelau as we knew it then was embarked on yet another transformation. In that case it would be of rather different character—more detailed and searching. What is here a postscript may in good time appear as a preface.[1]

Tokelau's political status changed yet again with passage of the Tokelau Islands Act 1948 in the New Zealand Parliament. By this Act, Tokelau was incorporated as 'part of New Zealand' and, as a consequence, later in the same year Tokelau people became in effect New Zealand citizens.

New Zealand accepted Tokelau as part of its dominions at a time when relations of political dependency were being re-evaluated. No longer were dependent territories simply to be protected and provided for. They should be prepared to take charge of their own destiny and adequate provision should be made for their development and welfare regardless of cost. Though Tokelau at the time was New Zealand's dependency of least concern, these changes in attitude were still weakly reflected.

In fact, Tokelau's new status was a direct consequence of New Zealand's greatest concern—Western Samoa.[2] A radical reorientation of the New Zealand policy in Western Samoa produced a step-by-step programme leading to independence, which was achieved in 1962. But where did this place Tokelau, which for over twenty years had been linked with Western Samoa for administrative convenience? Tokelau's political status and political sentiments were utterly different from those of Western Samoa. The atolls had been annexed by Britain in 1916 and administered by New Zealand on Britain's behalf since 1926, and Tokelauans had never expressed any wish for independence. Fur-

THE POTENTATE

N.Z. HERALD 22-10-48

Political cartoon by Minhinnick: an ironic New Zealand reaction to the inclusion of Tokelau within its domains. (Original drawing given to the authors by Cluny Macpherson).

thermore, when the position of Tokelau was scrutinised, questions were raised about the legality of the procedures by which the atolls had been placed under New Zealand's care.[3]   In the event, when the Tokelau Islands Act (1948) was put before it, the New Zealand Parliament assented, and Tokelau was added to New Zealand's domains. People in Tokelau were agreeable to being 'part of New Zealand'.

In the years that followed, as Western Samoa and New Zealand were gradually disengaging, Tokelau became more and more firmly linked with New Zealand. Tokelau's choice was not clearly voiced at first, though it is certainly implied in a statement made sometime in the 1950s: '"I was every-where struck with their loyalty to New Zealand and their evident pleasure that they are now regarded as New Zealand subjects. . . . The Tokelau people in no way admire the Samoans"' (Ma'ia'i 1957:159, quoted without attribu-tion). Samoans, for their part, characteristically viewed their atoll neighbours as backward and unsophisticated, disdainfully mocking them as *Ko'elau 'ai popo* 'Tokelau coconut eaters'. It is neither appropriate nor necessary to explore Tokelau–Samoan relations here; what is notable is that New Zealand officials were unaware of Tokelau antipathy. They viewed Tokelau as a tiny, simpler Samoa and the Tokelau language as an impoverished dialect of Sa-moan. Well-trained by Samoan pastors, Tokelau people tended to use the Samoan language and protocol in formal encounters with outsiders. This had long been their strategy for dealing with people of whom they were wary and from whom they were seeking benefits.

Had New Zealand officials appreciated Tokelau views they would not have been confounded by a decision taken by Tokelau in 1964. Two years before, it had been conjectured that Tokelau might like to become part of independ-ent Western Samoa or of the Cook Islands, soon to become self-governing.

Leaders of both these countries were approached about the possibility, and were mildly agreeable. So New Zealand put it to Tokelau to choose one or the other. The Tokelau response was less than enthusiastic. Nevertheless, they were persuaded to assess the New Zealand proposals personally with a fact-finding tour. The nine-man delegation from Tokelau returned to regale their compatriots with tales of their experiences, but Tokelau opinion did not change. Their Cook Island hosts were open and friendly, and the way of life in the northern atolls was familiar, but, as they phrased it, there was the problem of the Bible—by which they meant language differences and mission affiliations. Linkage with Western Samoa did not pose these problems and Samoan leaders were genial, referring to the long-standing *mahani* 'familiarity' of Tokelau and Samoa. But, as one person ruefully commented: 'You can't eat *mahani*', which succinctly sums up Tokelau perceptions. Whichever of the options they chose, Tokelau would be a remote appendage, the last in line to receive whatever benefits might come the way of the new nations. So Tokelau chose neither option and opted for a third. They would stay as they were, part of and dependent on New Zealand, which though even more remote had more benefits to offer. New Zealand could not but accept Tokelau's clear choice, even if it was not among the options given.[4]

Thereafter, some New Zealand officials reasoned that if Tokelauans were so keen to be 'part of New Zealand' they might all in time settle there. This belief was thoroughly scotched at yet another meeting to discuss Tokelau's future some seven years later. On behalf of the Tokelau delegates, the following question was put to the honourable Minister: 'Do you intend that all Tokelauans should eventually migrate to New Zealand, or do you intend us to stay here and develop our islands with the help of New Zealand. . .?' The Minister referred the question to the delegates and the answer was ready: 'The [Meeting] has decided that we want to stay in the Tokelau, and wants New Zealand to help to develop the islands . . .' (General Fono 1971). By this time Tokelau people saw two continual and non-exclusive options for their future: (i) living in Tokelau and benefiting from aid which New Zealand would provide, and (ii) living in New Zealand with all the benefits of citizenship. Their vision was accurate; that was how things were in 1971. An abbreviated chronicle of how they came to be that way begins in the early 1950s.

When New Zealand gave some attention to its new responsibilities for Tokelau, first priority was given to education. Government-supported schools were to be established, and promising Tokelau students were to be sponsored for teacher training. In no time, seven or eight students were at Teachers' Training College in Western Samoa, and two qualified Tokelau teachers, with Samoan counterparts, were setting up schools in Tokelau. Further developments in education and training would build upon this substantial beginning.

After some years of consideration, 1955 saw the nucleus of a separate Tokelau office established in Apia with the appointment of an executive officer responsible to the New Zealand High Commissioner (also Administrator of the Tokelau Islands). The new administration did not have an auspicious first year. Again the difficulty was transport. Six months after the new appointee took up his post, a Sunderland flying boat[5] struck a reef in Nukunonu lagoon and further flights were suspended until lagoon landing areas could be surveyed and marked. The new Tokelau officer was distressed about the lack of direct communication, but the only charter he could arrange was for a 70-foot unsinkable motor vessel which had been at anchor in Apia Harbour for some time. She left her moorings on 3 October and was next seen on 10 November in Fiji waters '. . . drifting and water-logged, without trace of any of her people' (McKay 1968:152). What became of her captain, crew and passengers (which included the newly appointed district officer and six Tokelauans), and what transpired aboard her has been officially investigated (McKay 1968:152–5) and widely speculated about.[6] The *Joyita* 'mystery' remains, in the words of the official enquiry, 'inexplicable'.

The lost officer's successor was a more prudent man who responded, in the absence of any policy or programme, in sensible, low-key and ad hoc ways to changing situations. The absence of policy was consistent with New Zealand's intention that Tokelau would join one or another new nation and a preoccupation with getting those new nations launched. Yet something was happening in Tokelau that could not be ignored. The 1961 census showed that there were 252 more people there than in 1956 (1618 in 1956; 1870 in 1961), whereas the increase between 1951 and 1956 had been only 47. Overpopulation in the atolls had long been a matter of concern, but the most recent increment was cause for alarm. The explanation for the 'explosion' was Samoa's pending independence, which ended a long-standing pattern of Tokelau migration. As long as Western Samoa was a New Zealand administered territory, Tokelauans could come and go as they wished, or stay as persons for whom the governing power was also responsible. With independence Tokelau people in Samoa would become aliens, disadvantaged with regard to opportunities for employment and access to services, their presence or entry permitted (or not) by the Western Samoan government. Some took up their rights as New Zealand citizens and moved another step away from Tokelau, while others with secure jobs, solid Samoan connections and property remained. Still others returned to Tokelau, accounting for most of the dramatic intercensal increase.

Fakaofo people in Samoa had an additional attraction to return home. After nearly 100 years of pleas, petitions and disappointments, a portion of long-alienated Fenuafala was recovered by the Fakaofo polity, when about 50 acres were purchased with Fakaofo and New Zealand monies from the Pereira estate. How the repossessed land was to be apportioned and used was uncertain and controversial, and people wanted to be present to get their share, so they returned.

Irrespective of the circumstances that brought people back to Tokelau, the fact remained that Samoa would no longer accept that small influx of people which partly compensated for the natural growth of the atoll populations. Some other outlet had to be found, and New Zealand was the obvious one. A few Tokelauans had managed to get there, but more would have to be established before 'chain migration' could effectively counteract

The first students brought on scholarship from Tokelau to New Zealand, photographed at the Auckland Zoo with the Tokelauan teacher who accompanied them. The 'exotic' young Tokelau boys are framed by an 'exotic' llama. New Zealand Herald, *January 1963*

population growth. The Labour Department was persuaded to include some Tokelau girls in its programme for assisting workers from overseas to immigrate to New Zealand. Ten girls arrived in New Zealand in January 1963 to work as 'domestics' in hospitals and hostels. By the end of 1965, thirty other single people had been similarly assisted and, in addition, scholarships for post-primary schooling had brought a dozen students to New Zealand.[7] All these young, unmarried migrants were selected on the basis of their school records; good students, it was presumed, would be best able to adjust to life in New Zealand, and by and large they did. Unlike those who had preceded them, often after some years in Samoa, who were older and had families to support, the young workers had very immediate ties back to Tokelau and fewer demands on their pay packets. They wrote enthusiastic letters home about their life in New Zealand, and sent money and parcels to their families. Their elders in Tokelau were impressed and appealed for an expansion of sponsored migration, in particular for its extension to 'families'.

The New Zealand government was not averse to this appeal, especially since Tokelau had so clearly affirmed its attachment to New Zealand in late 1964. Even though fifty-two young people had moved to New Zealand with some kind of official assistance and others had migrated on their own (it was reported that forty departed Apia in the first six months of 1963), the population in the atolls was still increasing. Something more had to be done.

Thus was the scene set for the Tokelau Resettlement Scheme. It was formulated in Wellington in 1965, approved in principle by Cabinet at the end of the year, and presented by the Minister of Island Territories to Tokelau delegates at another meeting about their 'future status' held 22–25 January 1966. The Minister reported, '. . . it was clear from these discussions that the people ardently desire to retain a close and direct relationship with New Zealand [p.37]. . . . At each Island they expressed the wish for further Government assistance to resettle some of the people in New Zealand and a scheme had been prepared to assist annually a selected number from each island to migrate [p.43]' (*AJHR* 1966, A3).

After being endorsed by Tokelau and Cabinet, the Scheme was dramatised by nature. Four days after the Minister's departure, a cyclone struck. The storm was mild compared to the 'Great Cyclone' of 1914, but circumstances had changed since then. The event was immediately known and widely publicised; humanitarian organisations and the government quickly responded with relief. The storm provided an immediate rationale for the Scheme both to Parliament, which approved it in June, and to the New Zealand public, who might otherwise have been sceptical about its merits. Obviously no one doubted it would be approved since twenty-eight young, unmarried adults arrived in New Zealand at the end of March under the provisions of the Scheme. Three families and twenty-two girls arrived at the end of the year, and their trip was documented on film (National Film Unit 1966).

The aim of the Scheme as widely reported was '. . . resettlement of 1,000 of the Islanders in New Zealand over the next five years, with others to follow' (*Pacific Islands Monthly* 1966). In some quarters such grandiose statements caused disquiet, a fear that this scheme of humanitarian assistance might be misinterpreted as intentional depopulation.[8] Consequently, statements became more muted and a balance was struck by emphasising humanitarian programmes in Tokelau itself.

So it was that the ad hoc arrangements and responses of the previous ten years gave way to enunciated programmes: the Resettlement Scheme directed towards facilitating the movement of people to New Zealand, and a Building Programme and Educational Development directed towards improving conditions in the atolls. Inevitably, however, the explicitly stated plans were amended as time went by. The number of persons resettled in New Zealand rarely reached 100 in a single year, let alone 200 per annum as had been grandly announced. An economic downturn in New Zealand, delays in providing housing for families, and difficulties experienced by some migrants slowed down the pace in the late 1960s. The appeal of government sponsorship waned in Tokelau, despite increasingly open eligibility and more flexible employment and residence arrangements, and this slowed the pace in the

Nukunonu performs an ancient action song for National Film Unit photographers. Sticks on weaving boards provide the drumming, and some of the performers wear coconut-frond crowns. The meeting-house roof has been extended with aluminium coconut palm banding material fastened to a frame of poles. Photo 1966, courtesy of New Zealand Government Publicity Division, now in National Archives of New Zealand, Wellington (AAQT 6401)

321

early 1970s. Five years after its inception 356 people had been resettled under the Scheme (*AJHR* 1971, A3: 40). The total number approaches 450 if those who were assisted outside the Scheme, for example under scholarships and before 1966, are added. This number does not include the relatively large number of people who went to New Zealand without assistance or sponsorship, except from their Tokelau kin, nor does it take account of the few who returned to Tokelau. Yet by 1971 there were some 1500 Tokelauans in New Zealand and 1640 in the atolls, whereas ten years before there were perhaps 30 in New Zealand and 1870 in Tokelau. Leaving aside the apparent 'explosion', largely attributable to the uncounted Tokelauans in Western Samoa in 1961 who later went to New Zealand (see Huntsman 1975:186–7), the 1971 situation attests to the perspicacity of Tokelau's 1964 determination to retain its New Zealand connection.

In Tokelau the anticipated benefits were forthcoming too. An ambitious building programme was instigated in 1966. Building overseers with appropriate qualifications were recruited from New Zealand to direct local 'work gangs', whose members, contrary to long-established practice, received hourly wages. Tokelauans were naturally not averse to being paid for work that they had previously done for nothing, but this departure from precedent presented problems. The intention was that in each atoll 'work gangs' of ten regular workers would acquire skills on the job. This violated the Tokelau ethic of equal opportunity: why should one man be paid and trained and not another who was equally unqualified? Yet if the Tokelau ethic were to be served by rotating 'work gang' membership and thereby sharing the benefits, the rationale for having a paid 'work gang' would be compromised. So paid permanent 'work gangs' were formed, not without some rancour between Tokelau elders and New Zealand overseers, and between those selected and those not.

The policy of Educational Development was implicated in both the Resettlement Scheme and the Building Programme. A 1965 report by education experts questioned the adequacy of the local schools in meeting local needs and especially in equipping young people for life in New Zealand. Raising the level of education was urgent, and the way to do this was to recruit qualified New Zealand teachers. Of course, New Zealand teachers required proper New Zealand houses and educational development required proper schools, so these were the first structures erected under the Building Programme. Teaching couples were posted to each atoll in early 1969 and were enthusiastically welcomed by their Tokelau hosts.

Meanwhile, life in Tokelau went on much as before. People departing for New Zealand were feted with farewell feasts, and those remaining in Tokelau settled back into their daily chores. Travellers who returned were besieged for news of kin and friends, and people would listen for hours as they told and retold stories of happenings in New Zealand. There was constant talk of visiting or settling in New Zealand, and kin already there arranged airfares for siblings and parents to visit and perhaps stay in one of the growing Tokelau enclaves in New Zealand. By 1969 people settled in New Zealand were paying visits back home. New Zealand was no longer remote or unknown to

Schoolroom 1966. Village public structures were converted to classrooms during the day, with the children seated on coconut frond mats. Photo 1966, courtesy of New Zealand Government Publicity Division, now in National Archives of New Zealand, Wellington (AAQT 6401/ A81175

those in the atolls, and virtually anyone could journey there. The earlier enthusiasm to emigrate had abated and more people went for a holiday, or to work for a while and accumulate goods and money to take home. Instead of seeing it as the place where a person might *hakili tona lumanaki ma te lumanaki o na fanau* 'seek his future and the future of his children', people viewed New Zealand as offering one kind of 'future' and Tokelau another. A person could even travel back and forth and benefit from both.

Even in the late 1960s when many people spoke of their intention to emigrate, and enthusiasm for resettlement was at its height, the people were still committed to solid achievements in their atolls. When Fakaofo's new Protestant church was dedicated in September 1967, the biggest bell ever cast in New Zealand summoned the celebrants to the ceremony. The bell was a gift from the Fakaofo people in New Zealand. The Atafu church-building enter-

Schoolroom 1971. A special purpose furnished classroom in a new concrete block, iron-roofed school. Photo: Marti Friedlander

323

prise again illustrates this commitment and the close attachment of Tokelau and New Zealand. In 1966 a decision was taken to replace the old church with a larger structure, because 'the people did not fit into the old one', and five years later the new church was dedicated. Large delegations from Nukunonu and Fakaofo and smaller ones from Hawai'i, American Samoa, Western Samoa and New Zealand arrived to celebrate. They feasted on local foods and were presented with locally manufactured mats, fans, baskets, shell necklaces, wooden boxes and model canoes. The guests brought barrels and stacks of food, and presented their hosts with gifts and money. No visitors were more enthusiastically received than the Atafu people who had journeyed from New Zealand. They were not really guests; they were sons, daughters, brothers and sisters. Arriving before the others, they were recruited to help put the finishing touches on the new church, to which they had generously contributed. Doffing their New Zealand clothes and donning *lavalava*, they willingly pitched in. Indeed, the links between Tokelau and New Zealand had become 'close and direct'—woven by ties of kinship and village which transcended more than 3000 km. As these Atafu-New Zealanders were reincorporated into their homeland during their week-long visit, so any compatriot arriving in New Zealand could be incorporated into New Zealand-Tokelau communities of kin and fellow-villagers, where migrants from each atoll tended to gather together, replicating the separate communities of their homeland.

Songs composed for that reunion at Atafu in 1971 expressed the new dual location of Tokelau. They are an apt closing to this Postscript.

Ia au kua mao	Overwhelmed am I
I toku fiafia	With joy
Ka ko au e puli	Yet I forget
E feiloaki kae toe tēteka	We meet but again part
Maumau ake te alofa	Would that love
Ke fai kapahau	Would give wings
Ke fanatu au	That I might
Momoli koe ki tō kāiga	Convey you to your family
Oi auē! te faigatā	Alas! the anguish
Te kokona o te alofa	The bitterness of love
Hau lā koe keinā fano	Come then you must go
E hē tiakina atu koe	You shall not be forgotten
Fakahao tonu mai ki luga i Atafu nei	You are securely again upon Atafu's shores
Oku tuāgane oku uho ma oku kāiga	My brothers my sisters my kin
Nae tāhe mai koutou i nā nuku kehe	You have wandered in foreign places
Tenei lā kua feiloaki fiafia	Here we meet joyfully
Fakafetai ki te tupu i te lagi	Thanks to the Almighty
Kua pā mai koe	You have come
Toe kikila ki to nuku moni	To again gaze on your homeland
Tenei au nae fakatali atu i Atafu nei	I have awaited you here in Atafu
Te tia ō tamana	The graveyard of our fathers.

CONCLUSION

We might end here, as Tokelau raconteurs do, with the brief phrase: *Ko te tala kua uma* 'the story is finished', but there is still a bit more to be said about this particular story.

Silverman and Gulliver draw a distinction between what they call 'historical ethnography' and 'anthropology of history' (1992:16-20). Historical ethnography, in their words, 'provides a description and analysis of a past era of a people of some particular, identifiable locality, using archival sources and, if relevant, local oral history sources' in order either to trace 'how the past led to and created the present' or to 'explain the present through understanding the past'. The anthropology of history, by contrast, focuses 'primarily on the ways and the cultural rationale by which a particular people have envisioned, created and recreated their own past and related it to their perceived present. . . . Its concern has been to record and describe the insiders' views, assumptions and perceptions and to show them in the insiders' own socio-cultural terms.'

The distinction is a useful one, both for general heuristic purposes and because it points up the differences between the interpretive modes of ethnography and history. Historical ethnography is a negotiated stance, one which might be congenial for either a historian willing to supplement archival sources with a few oral ones, or an ethnographer working among a people whose views of the past have some historicity and little of the fantastical about them. By contrast the anthropology of history is a hard-line ethnographic stance, which might be adopted out of either theoretical conviction or simple necessity—as in seeking to understand peoples whose material and ritual lives are bound closely to ancestors, spirits and timeless mythical notions of the world, but for whom few relevant archival sources are available.

In narrating the Tokelau past, we have taken both stances, always mindful of the differences between them. In essence we have written a historical ethnography of Tokelau. Yet it is a historical ethnography guided by Tokelau representations of the past, so it is also an anthropology of Tokelau history. Quite simply, the documented, archival sources bearing on the Tokelau past make most sense when they are interpreted in the light of what some might consider the 'softer', inherently 'less reliable' sources of myth, historical *tala* and genealogy. This does not mean that we have accepted the data of myth, *tala* and genealogy as 'facts' of the same order as archival records or eye-witness accounts, and then used them to push the historical record back before the time for which archival records are available and 'real history' can begin. Tokelau history, or the past as it is recalled and related in Tokelau, is little concerned with establishing causal chains of events in the past; like other 'ethnographic histories', it recounts events that are set in the past to construct and reiterate cultural verities, schemes of significance encompassing both the past and present. Interpreted in the light of these schemes, the outside archival sources add considerably to the depth and detail of what Tokelau itself has 'always known', and also give a new perspective on the social differences between the atolls.

At the core of the anthropology of Tokelau history, and therefore the central problematic of its ethnographic history, is the construction of a social and cultural unity from three separate, geographically dispersed atolls. What the narratives of Tokelau's past (chapter 4) essentially 'do' is to bind the atolls together in a structured set of relationships which is proclaimed in the separate idioms of myth, historical *tala* and genealogy.

As with all such bricolage, the central message is a highly redundant one. The tale of reciprocal theft sets up several basic categorical elements. Fakaofo, as aggressor, steals Nukunonu's water, a source of its fertility, leaving just a token bit behind; Nukunonu in turn steals all of Fakaofo's *kie* pandanus, the prime women's valuable. Thus a relationship is set up between male and female, in at least one of its canonical Tokelau forms. Fakaofo invades Nukunonu, subduing it because the members of Nukunonu's fighting force are preoccupied with domestic, *kāiga* tasks, and then proceeds to march around the island claiming large areas of land until halted by a cast-off woman's skirt—representing another canonical Tokelau male–female relationship, that of brother and sister, and also a reminder of Nukunonu's women and their *kie*. The rest of the land is left for Nukunonu, more than a token but to be harvested for tribute to Fakaofo. There follows the taking of a Nukunonu woman as a spouse by the Fakaofo *aliki*, establishing a line that would provide the Fakaofo overlords with apt deputies in Nukunonu (and a Nukunonu presence in Fakaofo). Atafu is the third original player, its autochthons portrayed as undisciplined and barbarous—utterly inhuman, in a Tokelau sense. They completely disappear and are replaced by the issue of a canonical couple, a Fakaofo man and a Nukunonu woman. Thus is set up a pattern of relationships between the atolls in which the idiom of kinship reiterates that of myth and the *tala* of war. But the overarching genealogy that posits these patterns may be read different ways: Nukunonu and Atafu agree that their own relation is one of mother's-brother and sister's-children, but do not concur with Fakaofo views of their respective relationships. Fakaofo claims precedence on the twin principles of agnation—as wife-taker/father to Nukunonu, and of seniority—as elder brother to Atafu. These views are fully in keeping with Fakaofo's internal genealogical predispositions, and both have to do with exclusivity and hierarchy. Nukunonu has its own reading whereby its position is that of mother's-brother to its Fakaofo sisters'-sons. These readings are not contradictory but are from different perspectives, and Nukunonu's subtly counters Fakaofo's assertions of masculine superiority by its preoccupation with the sister–brother 'covenant'. Atafu characteristically contests Fakaofo's assumed seniority. This is not another perspective but a contrary assertion, again in keeping. All the atolls tell essentially the same myths, *tala*, and genealogy, but they do not agree, and their disagreements too follow the pattern.

As historical 'facts', these narratives of the past are inherently implausible: water supplies are not so readily uplifted; Nukunonu men cannot have been so uxorious, devoting themselves to domestic concerns in the face of battle; and a woman's skirt, though a potent symbol, is unlikely to have had such a dramatic effect on an invading party. It is also inherently unlikely that the genealogies at this level of remoteness are records of *actual* ancestry. What these Tokelau accounts of the past establish is not 'facts' at this level at all. What they do set up, in the idiom of basic cultural categories, is a distinctive character for each of the island's polities, and a structured relationship between them.

It is this structure which guides our interpretation of many archival 'facts'. It explains, for example, the different kinds of reception accorded to the earliest explorers—Atafu outgoing, expansive, egalitarian; Nukunonu timorous and retreating; Fakaofo at first overbearing and later restrained and menacing. It also made us doubt the locations given in Paulding's account of USS *Dolphin*'s visit. It seemed most unlikely that the ship was first at Nukunonu, and very probable that it was at Fakaofo. A full investigation of the evidence showed that this was indeed the case (Huntsman and Hooper 1986). Again, in a broader perspective, it is possible to appreciate that in the dramas of the early 1860s, there was a Tokelau cultural logic: Atafu rapidly converting to Protestantism, Nukunonu instanteously embracing Catholicism, and Fakaofo determined to retain Tui Tokelau as its god. Thus even before the 1863 'slaver' incursions, the subject and tributary atolls had in effect rejected the domination of Fakaofo, and asserted their distinctiveness from one another. Yet though they were once again three separate atoll polities, they were still bound to one another by much of what had brought them together in the first place. Their relations were transformed by their own actions, but their cultural order persisted.

We now appreciate why the strategy of controlled comparison that underlay our initial research agenda proved to be inadequate, if not misguided. Certainly there *are* ecological distinctions to be made between the atolls and variations among them in terms of the number, frequency and intensity of various social phenomena—*kāiga* size, the use of available resources, the proportions of time devoted to communal as distinct from domestic affairs and so forth. Some correspondences between and among ecological and social factors may even be statistically significant. They are not, however, the differences which create the distinctions between the Tokelau atolls. Controlled comparison as a tool of social analysis has been used productively in several ways and in many places—including island Polynesia. However, it is a method which has a logical 'in-built' temporal assumption, in that differentiation is presumed to have taken place from a more unitary, more homogeneous state of affairs some time in the past.

Past homogeneity is not necessarily the only basis for unity. It may also be created by taking originally differentiated elements and forming them into a structured set, which can then be maintained so long as the relationship between the elements remains somehow 'the same'. The unity of Tokelau is predicated on, indeed created and maintained by, the structured differences between its three parts. This structuralist reading of the evidence is not dictated by adherence to any of the well-known forms of structuralist theory. Its plausibility depends ultimately on the internal coherence and the suggestive power of its patterning in time and space. The structures are there in the narratives and documents.

Further, we contend that certain contemporary social differences between the islands (particularly the way their village institutions are organised and operate) are reflections of this structural set. Such an interpretation might be faulted for denying people control over their own destinies, portraying them as locked forever within the confines of a particular *pensée sauvage* which condemns them to mere stereotypic reproduction of their own pasts. This is not at all what we mean to imply. The general debate over the relationships between 'agency' and 'structure', 'history' and 'culture' has had a good airing in recent years, and is seen to have involved too rigid antinomies. People live their lives and make decisions that change their lives, but always, inevitably, by reference to culturally ordered schemes of things. History, then, 'is culturally ordered, differently so in different societies, according to meaningful schemes of things. The converse is also true: cultural schemes are historically ordered, since to a greater or lesser extent the meanings are revalued as they are practically enacted' (Sahlins 1985:vii).

In proposing that some of the significant differences between the atolls are analogues of a far more ancient scheme of social and cultural differentiation, we need not imagine that they have been brought about either by conscious decision or by atavistic, hidden impulse. They are, most probably, simply the outcome of a series of changes, conscious and unconscious, made by people of the three communities, acting in terms of their own ideas and responding to the demands of circumstance, to create local ways of doing things which have local legitimacy and significance in terms of their separate pasts.

We have looked to Tokelau's culturally ordered views of the past to interpret both its 'real' history and features of contemporary life, and beyond this suggest that other Polynesian pasts and presents may be ordered by more than their adaptation to their particular island world and their simple, familiar historicity. As Dening remarked in a quite different context (1991:350), 'the most powerful structures have trivial, particular expression'—perhaps as in the 'just-so' story of Hemoana and Fenū.

NOTES

1 Atolls and Villages

1. A fourth atoll, named Olohega in Tokelau and Swain's Island elsewhere, is not included here. This is not because we do not support the Tokelau claims to it, but because it has, for good reasons, not been part of our ethnographic study—although it figures in our historical research.
2. Formerly the Ellice Islands.
3. This collective name was given them by Captain Hudson of the US Exploring Expedition in 1841 (LMS Samoa District 1841: Harbutt 1847) and generally used during the period the islands were under British jurisdiction.
4. Fakaofo also suffers from the smaller night-flying *Aedes vexans nocturnus*, which is confined there to the village area.
5. Accidentally introduced into Nukunonu in 1964, the beetle did a lot of damage in the late 1960s, but is now controlled there and has been kept out of the other two atolls.
6. Turtles are classed as 'fish' in Tokelau.
7. Furthermore, with this usage the unwieldy terms 'Atafuans', 'Nukunonuans' and 'Fakaofoans' can be avoided when referring collectively to the people of a particular atoll-village.
8. We refer here to the published accounts of the US Exploring Expedition (Wilkes 1845, Hale 1846).

2 Te Nuku—*The Village*

1. *Te nuku* is both the place and the people of that place, both village and villagers.
2. The classic formulation of banishment is setting a person adrift upon the sea in a *vaka-ama*, i.e. a raft, but there is no record of this ever having been done.
3. The intense local nature of the humour makes it incomprehensible to persons unfamiliar with the language and culture, and almost impossible to explain. One has to know the village and villagers past and present to understand, though the slapstick nature of some performances allows some of the humour to transcend this.
4. The gloss 'dowager' as 'an elderly woman of imposing appearance' would be appropriate, as would 'dame' as 'a woman of station or authority', but the former is a colloquial usage while the latter has slang connotations which have rather overtaken its standard meaning (see *Webster's Unabridged* 1959).
5. Also known as the *Taupulega* 'Ruling body' and *Fono Matai* 'Meeting of Family Heads'.
6. Also referred to as *tamana* 'fathers' of the extended family and as *matai* following Samoan usage.
7. Another designation of this group is *taulelea*, or for one of its members *taulealea*, which is derived from the Samoan *taulele'a/taule'ale'a* 'untitled men/man'. Since Tokelau has no system of titles, the term is used for males without elderly status and is synonymous with *tagata*.
8. Richardson (1925) regretted the absence of any 'healthy' competitive sports, at a time when *kilikiti* was surely being played.

NOTES

9. A similar vagueness is characteristic of responses to enquiries about the beginnings of the *fātele* 'action songs', which are the Tokelau national art form. All agree that *fātele* came from Tuvalu, but when and how is 'unknown' (see Thomas 1986).

10. Atafu *faitū* have undergone two more transformations since; the Āumāga was divided into four 'companies' for a while, and then the whole village was again divided into 'Argentina' and 'Great Britain' at the time of the Falklands war, a division that more or less corresponds to the 1960s territorial one.

11. An entrepreneurial club, known as the 'bank', is unique. A number of salaried people formed it and deposit varying sums of money in its treasury. The 'bank' club makes loans to others at a flat rate of 10 per cent, on the understanding that both the principal and the 10 per cent interest on it will be paid when the next three-monthly ship arrives. Not only do the club members, i.e. depositors, receive an excellent rate of return, they also have no money in hand to meet requests from friends and relatives, and refer them to the 'bank'. Yet Tokelau ethics prevail when it comes to sharing the profits. All club members, regardless of the amount they have deposited, receive an equal share of the profits.

12. Schooling in Tokelau for nearly a century was an activity of the churches. Secular, administration-funded schools replaced the church schools in the 1950s. However, children still required religious instruction: Protestant children to read the Samoan Bible and Catholic children to recite the Samoan catechism. So the Tokelau schoolteachers and others assist in teaching this essential Christian knowledge outside the secular school on the sabbath.

13. That sexual derelicts are so frequently brought to court is not surprising considering that (i) sexual dereliction may be very broadly defined, particularly in cases where at least one party is married; (ii) it is very difficult for any sexual dereliction to go unnoticed in a Tokelau village; and (iii) any pregnancy out of wedlock must come before the court so that paternity can be established. In this last circumstance, if neither party is married the court enjoins them to wed with the incentive that they will be excused their fine if they do. This is a way for young people who wish to marry to put pressure on their families who object.

3 Kāiga: *The Kinship Order*

1. We have over the years written a number of articles on aspects of *kāiga* and kinship, which which contain fuller discussions of many matters covered in this chapter. We cite them as appropriate, in the interests of brevity here.

2. *Kāiga* has other meanings as well, besides that of corporate stock. Rather like the English 'family' and 'familial', it may denote progeny, relatedness, households, kinship, intimacy, as well as certain relationships in the conceptual ordering of the natural world. For all of these senses of *kāiga* we use the appropriate English glosses. For other referents of *kāiga* as well as for fuller treatment of what follows, see Huntsman 1971.

3. For an extended discussion of this problem, see Huntsman and Hooper 1976.

4. These sections are marked by blazes on the trunks of the palms at their margins, so that a boundary passes between blazed palms. These marks are a statement rather than a guidepost, for harvesters know exactly which trees are theirs.

5. These terms which have other referents are often followed by 'of the *kāiga*'. The Samoan term *matai* is sometimes used for this role too, though almost everyone is aware that the role of Samoan *matai* is very different. Some people stress the absence of *matai* titles in Tokelau, and the much less hierarchical nature of the local system.

6. *Fofou* is 'sexual desire'. While persons who feel *fofou* may also express *alofa*, kinship and *fofou* are antithetical.

7. See Huntsman, Hooper and Ward 1986 on how genealogies are ordered.

8. Slippage of reference between these two contexts may be avoided when necessary by distinguishing those relationships which are *moni* 'real/true', e.g. the *mātua* who bore one, from other *mātua* who are same generation female kin of one's parents.

9. See Huntsman 1971 (especially pp.34–50) and 1981.

10. See Huntsman and Hooper 1975:416. The pair with equal effect may be close cousins, and, even in single sex gatherings, often much of the humour turns on the relationships of the performers or of the performer to the person being parodied.

11. The term *mate* is comparable to the Tongan *mateaki* 'bodyguard, or person devoted to and ready to die for one . . .' (Churchward 1959:344). The Tokelau mother's-brother/sister's-child relationship is, however, rather different from the Tongan *fahu* (and Fiji *vasu*) because the onus is upon the younger of the pair.

4 Tokelau Formed

1. Lister wrote Fakaofo 'Fakaofu'. To avoid confusion and a profusion of [sic], we have corrected, without comment, all misspelling of place names.

   Tokelau's place in the greater Polynesian culture history is not our concern here. Nonetheless, we note that preliminary archaeological investigations (Best 1988) suggest c.1000 BP [AD 950] as the earliest certain date of human presence and about 1600 BP [AD 350] as a possible date. The material recovered does not indicate a source homeland, but does show contacts with neighbouring island groups. Best summarises his findings as follows: '. . . several hundred years ago, in conditions far more difficult than those of today, thriving communities existed in the Tokelaus . . . permanent settlements of some size were established and maintained. Contacts between these and other countries, such as Samoa and Fiji, show that Tokelau was not just three isolated atolls, but part of a wider Pacific community'. Languages of Tuvalu appear to be most closely related to Tokelauan (Hooper and Huntsman 1992), but again this does not necessarily point to an original homeland.

2. According to the Fakaofo (n.d.) manuscript:

   Two stories show the origin of the people of Fakaofo; though it is certainly the same story, differing only in small details.

   1. Long ago there was washed onto the beach at 'The Malae' (at Afekē) a large ulua *(Jack fish). There flew down a bird from heaven known as the 'sacred bird' and pierced the body of the dead fish with its beak, and two maggots grew from it. From these two maggots grew two people, both of them boys, Kava being the elder and Sigano the younger.*

   2. The bird that flew down from heaven was called a tuli *(golden plover), and the* tuli *pierced the body of the* ulua *and from it grew the two boys Kava and Sigano.*

3. This rendition of the myth told in 1968 was transcribed by Toloa Poasa. The translation is ours. For another version see *Matagi Tokelau* (1991:16–17). We have heard this story again and again, yet it is recorded by only one other visitor (Burrows 1923:185) in a very abridged form. Others may have thought it inconsequential as we did at first.

4. This account told in 1970 was transcribed by Maselino Patelesio. The translation is ours. For other versions see *Matagi Tokelau* 1991:28-36, Burrows 1923:148–9 and Macgregor 1937:19–22.

5. This version of the narrative was told in 1970 and transcribed by Toloa Poasa. The translation is ours. For other versions see *Matagi Tokelau* 1991: 33–36, and also Burrows 1923:148-9, Macgregor 1937:20–22 and Newell 1895:606 which are less detailed but include the same core episodes. The teller positioned himself where he was in Atafu ('here') in relating the story, while the transcriber from Fakaofo unconsciously repositioned the story so that Fakaofo was 'here'. The translation retains the teller's perspective. Speculating beyond the narrative, people claim that the Atafu autochthons reached various of the Polynesian outliers and settled there, e.g. Sikaiana, Tikopia and Nukuoro.

6. In Tikopia, Nau is the generic title of a married woman, e.g. Nau Porima as the wife of Pa Porima.

7. The links between Pio Toevave and Pio Tanuvalevale are set out in a Nukunonu genealogy which counts some six generations separating them. Atafu accounts tend to confound the two Pios, thus truncating the time during which Atafu was uninhabited and nothing memorable happened there. Fakaofo accounts are little concerned with any Pio, though two published 'lists of *aliki*' contain two Pios, separated by two or three generations. The events that follow from Pio Tanuvalevale are predictably differently evaluated and interpreted in the three atolls. Our basic text is from Nukunonu.

8. So too did Macy, captain of a whaler out of Nantucket, who 'saw natives on it' in 1825, according to Reynolds (1835:19). Reynolds's report of the '. . . islands, reefs and shoals in the Pacific Ocean' was gathered from log books and the first-hand accounts of American whaling captains. He evidently placed some faith in Macy's observation. Unfortunately, Macy's journal of this voyage is lost, probably destroyed by fire in 1846 (Stackpole, pers. comm. 1969).

9. Whereas this encounter replaces Paulding's as the earliest account of Tokelau–European meetings, it is doubtful that it is located in Fakaofo as Gunson suggests, for the following reasons: (i) relatively few canoes and one a double canoe—versus the many canoes at Fakaofo, (ii) the one-day transit from Sydney Island, and most especially (iii) the estimated size of the island. Richardson 1926 gives the circumferences of the atolls based on a thorough survey as: Atafu 8 miles, Nukunonu 24 miles, and Fakaofo 16 miles. From the sea, Fakaofo and Nukunonu appear comparable in size, but Atafu is definitely smaller.

10. The published account of this voyage by the First Officer Hiram Paulding (1970 [1831]:76–93) describes the two islands which the *Dolphin* visited as being the Duke of Clarence's (Nukunonu) and Duke of York's (Atafu), the only two atolls which had been reported at that time. Evidence that the first island was in fact Fakaofo and the second Nukunonu is contained in Paulding's published account. The first island visited is described as having a 'beautiful little bay' close to the southwest point of the island. This could well be a description of Fakaofo, but it is most unlikely that it could be Nukunonu, which had neither a clearly defined southwest point nor any 'little bay' along its southwest coast. Again, the second atoll visited is described as being very similar to the first, and as 'comprehending . . . a lake of many miles in circumference'. Since Atafu is very much smaller than Nukunonu, and has a much more landlocked lagoon, it would be strange if this fact was not noted. Finally, the *Dolphin* is reported as having made the passage between the two atolls in about eight hours and as having come upon the second '. . . much sooner than was expected . . .'. The distance between Fakaofo and Nukunonu, 64 km, is considerably less than the 92 km which separate Nukunonu from Atafu. This could account for the *Dolphin* having made a faster passage between the atolls than had been expected. (For further discussion of these points and others see Huntsman and Hooper 1986.)

11. The longitude and latitude reported by Broughton correspond more closely with the readings of voyagers that viewed Fakaofo as a 'discovery' than those generally given for Nukunonu.

12. It is unclear whether the Fakaofo traders or the whalers were offering pearlshell. Other evidence supports the Fakaofo location of the first island. A third island was seen to the northwest at daylight in the morning after departure from the second—thought to have been Duke of York's. This was noted in the log with the observation, 'suppose it to be the same one we saw yesterday' and it was not investigated further. If this third island had in fact been Atafu (which is supported by the decreasing latitude recorded), the first must have been Fakaofo.

13. This speculation is repeated again and again in the Expedition's publications and journals (see chapter 5).

14. Within the house were rough benches, which Hale learned were called 'seats of the god'. More tantalising, but less explicable, was the 'windlass of a vessel . . . much worn' that Hale made some inquiries about. At first they replied that it came 'from the sea', but when pressed told of how 'a vessel was lost in the surf . . . two men got ashore, one of whom was named *Fakaaukamea*'. *Ukamea* is iron, and the gloss of the name might be 'Iron-like' or again the word for iron might have come from the name of the man. This latter speculation might be supported by Hale's observation that iron tools had been used to cut and plane crossbeams, and these were said to come from the same source (1846:157–8). From the names given the two men, Hale assumed that they were Polynesians rather than Europeans. No Tokelau story harks back to any of this.

5 The Ancient Orders

1. On the basis of his few hours at Atafu and Fakaofo he sorted out one of the trickier aspects of Tokelauan phonology and produced a brief syntax and word list of 214 items (Hooper and Huntsman, with Kalolo 1992:345–6).

2. The Perez manuscripts are particularly remarkable in this regard. The author was both deeply interested in Tokelau's pre-Christian past and a Catholic catechist. In his writings he customarily uses *aitu*, but in a single passage he also uses synonymously *atua* and *tupua* 'guardian spirit'.

3. There is no evidence to suggest that warring parties from what is now Tonga ever reached Tokelau. Tonga here perhaps refers to the general southerly direction rather than a specific place.

4. There are striking parallels here, as elsewhere in the Fakaofo accounts, with some of the beliefs, idioms and ritual paraphernalia of *The work of the gods in Tikopia* (Firth 1967).

5. Sigano, the other original man, is simply elided: 'Concerning the issue of Sigano we have no record' (Fakaofo n.d.).

6. The idiom is also used (see Fakaofo n.d.) to distinguish between the issue of Kava-vahe-fenua by his two wives, those by the Fakaofo wife being the *lātūpou* as distinct from those by the Nukunonu woman, the *lāfalala*. This usage remains a sensitive issue to this day in

relations between Fakaofo and the other two atolls, especially when reference is made to it on formal occasions.

7. *Polo* may be glossed 'intermediary'. The lexeme is no longer used, but its meaning may be inferred from the verbal form, *poloaki* 'send a message, command, order', and corresponding nominative form, *poloakiga* 'message, commandment'.

8. *Vaka-atua* carries a connotation of the individual as a vessel, or *vaka*, of the *atua* or god. This suggests that they could serve as mediums — an inference which is supported by Turner's account of a medium's role in the curing of sickness, which involved summoning the spirit of a deceased person to speak through his mouth (1861:530).

9. A 'civil chief' is also mentioned by Catholic visitors in 1861 (Poupinel), and Foliga is referred to as 'the principal counsellor of the King' in 1863 (Gill and Bird). No more is heard of him thereafter, apart from the observation that he was taken by slavers (see chapter 6).

10. Some accounts give ten or more, together with an explanation of how some came to be abandoned.

11. Another possibility is that there was a system of double descent, with *falepā* and their associated goods passing in the agnatic lines, and houses and house sites in the uterine lines. However, since there is no evidence of any kind to support such a view (and some which contradicts it) it seems more likely that the *puikaīga* were structured as the present-day *kaīga* are, with complementary *tamatāne* and *tamafafine* divisions.

12. The distinction between 'line' and 'stock' is necessary to capture the cognatic aspect of Nukunonu genealogies. 'Line' emphasises the exclusive linear aspect of the early generations. 'Stock' emphasises the inclusive, proliferating quality of later generations, and the complex interlinkages between the genealogies, so that, as a Nukunonu pundit explained, 'everyone is really *aliki*'.

13. This kind of duality is a feature of other Western Polynesian social orders, e.g. Samoan chiefs as *ali'i* and *tulafale*, Tongan paramounts as Tu'i Tonga and *Hau*. The further addition of two more to make four recalls the four clans and chiefs of Tikopian, and their entitlements are not dissimilar.

14. The absence of any godly presence was yet another feature of Nukunonu's subordination, and is further supported by the story of Teatua, a deputy of Fakaofo's *aliki*. He brought with him a small stone and set up his own god-house where he entreated Tui Tokelau's blessings. The logic of conquest suggests that the conquerors would appropriate the god of the defeated. As has been previously suggested, perhaps the smaller stone slab standing next to Tui Tokelau outside Fakaofo's god-house, 'partially covered with mats—as though . . . fallen into disrepute' (Hudson 1840–42), reported to represent Hemoana (Lister 1892), was Nukunonu's appropriated god (see story of mutual theft, chapter 4). Further, a Nukunonu ancient chant to Hemoana was directed to a blossoming tree, which might well have been an alternative instantiation.

15. The latter observation, we hasten to add, is not a categorical statement nor a statement made by Nukunonu commentators. Rather, it is a statement of tendency based on our inspection of genealogies.

16. His father's father was of Tuipagai, his mother's mother of the senior Talafau stock, his father's mother of Letele and mother's father of Lua, and his spouse is identified in the junior Talafau stock. He was appointed *aliki* by Fakaofo decree and held that office in the early 1850s as a very old, crippled elder (see *Matagi Tokelau* 1991:79–80).

17. H.E. Maude (1959) and others (Becke 1897:105–7) have identified Rakahanga in the northern Cook Islands as Quiros's 'Gente Hermosa' and thoroughly debunked its identification as Olohega. Quiros wrote that the people were 'the most beautiful white and elegant people that were met with during the voyage', thus accounting for the island's name. Not surprisingly, this identification was appealing, even if those so identified were no longer present.

18. In his reconstruction, Macgregor confuses Togia, Tonuia's companion, with Togia, Tonuia's grandson. The earlier Togia had no issue and it is probable that his name was given to Tonuia's grandson, who was called *aliki* in the 1870s, to carry on the memory of his companion.

19. In some accounts Laua appears to be eldest; otherwise Vaovela is given the senior position. The ambiguity was nicely resolved in a characteristic Atafu way by the explanation that Vaovela was indeed the eldest, but since he was a persistent voyager or man of the sea, the role of senior was taken by his brother, Laua, who was in constant residence as a man of the land.

20. If there was a linkage, it located the *aliki* stock in one and all the others in the other.

6 Tokelau Transformed

1. Captain Zerbrandts of the *Paradise* from Hamburg later in 1841, Captain Morvan of the French barque *Adolphe* in 1844, and Captain Guedson of the *Salamandre* out of Le Havre in 1950. Adding these claims of 'discovery' to the earlier ones of Americans Smith and Hudson, and of Captain Watson of the British ship *Tuscan* in 1838, Fakaofo has the distinction of being claimed as a 'discovery' six times by captains of four different nationalities (see Ward ed. 1967).

2. The Pacific Manuscripts Bureau bibliography of whaling logs and journals in New England collections (Langdon 1979:145) lists sixteen sightings of Tokelau atolls between 1842 and 1857. Only five of them report encounters with the people. While there were certainly other whalers in Tokelau waters, there is no reason to believe that they were any more interested in the inhabitants of these little reef-bound islands.

3. A common motif in Tokelau stories is that of an aggressive male being lulled to sleep by a maiden searching his hair for lice. He is then despatched by the maiden's brothers. One tale tells of a long-haired ogre who spirits the maiden away. While he slumbers, her brothers tie his locks to coconut palms, and upon awakening his furious struggles bring the palms down upon his head—and he is finished. The Tokelau accounts of this event echo this particular narrative motif.

4. In this synthetic narrative, the written documents of both European and Tokelau authorship are cited, oral accounts, all of which are from Tokelau, are not, because they themselves are synthetic accounts told on different occasions by different people. For other written accounts of many of the same events see *Matagi Tokelau* (1991:99–105).

5. The captain of the *Kate* (see below) told Father Padel (Padel:13 February 1852) that in 1848 the LMS mission ship *John Williams* had visited Clarence Island (perhaps Nukunonu but also possibly Fakaofo).

   > The Captain of the mission ship saw the chief and said that if a house were built he would bring a missionary to them, to which the chief replied that if a missionary were brought then a house would be built for him. Then the Captain instructed the chief that he should be very wary when the Papists come for they are tyrants who will carry off your women and take your land. Several months thereafter the same ship returned with five Tokelauans which a whaler had picked up at sea and brought to Samoa in October 1846. They were brought as teachers. For some inexplicable base reason the Captain placed them not in the native village but on a small islet called Puka some distance away and departed. These bogus teachers made themselves detested by their dissolute ways and their greed.

   There is a story in Nukunonu about a LMS convert being present before 1861 that might have something to do with this story, which is being told by one captain about another captain to ingratiate himself with a Marist father, who is the recorder. For all that, it is entirely possible that people who had gotten to Samoa were returned in 1848, i.e. some of those who had abandoned Olohega in the same year and the surviving 1846 castaways.

6. Here and elsewhere in the Marist records, Fakaofo is referred to as Clarence. We hesitate to attempt to explain this misappellation, noting only that Jules must surely have known that Nukunonu was the atoll named Clarence.

   Piastre in French usage is simply 'coin', but may refer to Spanish 'coins' used in Latin America and the Philippines.

7. These parish records, courtesy of Th. Cook SM, merit detailed study. A superficial perusal shows that many of the Tokelau evacuees were baptised *in extremis* and buried in 1852, having arrived when 'malades de la grippe' were widespread (Padel:17 February 1852).

8. In October 1851, the whaler *Oliver Crocker* 'fell in with a canoe with 8 persons on board in a starving condition. 3 men, 3 small children, and 2 women 1 with a broken leg bound to Swains Island [Olohega]. We took them aboard and found that they had been 3 days in canoe with only 10 coconuts when they left the land. . . .' The whaler shipped the party to Olohega and sent them ashore there with their canoe, commenting: 'Cannot find words to express the misery of those poor [beings] that we took off from the canoe. They were all alive and that is about all' (*Oliver Crocker* 1851–52).

9. Faivalua and his companions may have gone to Olohega because of the Fakaofo famine, they may have found Hula and his fellow beachcombers there, and they may have been among those that were transported to Apia in 1848. Such a neat scenario is appealing, but uncertain.

10. LMS sources for the following narrative are Williams 1863, Gill and Bird 1863, and Bird 1863a, enclosing Mafala's account.

11. The primary document of the voyage (Gill and Bird 1863) has one or more pages missing though they are sequentially numbered. There is discontinuity between the pages numbered 6 & 7 and the missing narrative covers the two days at sea after the observation that many Tokelau passengers were suffering from dysentery. Their absence raises suspicions that they were deleted either because they did record the missionaries' qualms or because their contents would have brought the voyage into question. In the event, the voyage was reported an unblemished success.

12. Foliga is not named in this document, but genealogies suggest that he was the person referred to as the 'civil chief'. Father Poupinel (1882: 170) described how the man, identified as the father of one of the young men brought back to be a teacher, continually stroked him and 'repeated endlessly: "Soon I will die, leave me my son."' Lua, the young man referred to, was not Foliga's son, but his brother's son, and they would have called one another 'father' and 'son'. This would explain why the usually recalcitrant Foliga challenged Likā's decision, saying 'that if his son would not stay, he himself would leave', and, having persuaded the *aliki* to relent, went in pursuit of the mission vessel.

　　The bishop had at the outset decreed very strict conditions for allowing 'his converts' to stay but the converts pleaded with him to allow them ashore despite the *aliki*'s rejection of these conditions. The Catholic record of the voyage of course considers the bishop's restrictions reasonable and the *aliki*'s misguided, attributing them to earlier encounters with Protestant missionaries. Indeed, the Catholics and Protestants damned one another in their attempts to gain a foothold in Fakaofo, and their mutual recriminations were used by the Fakaofo *aliki ma faipule* to reject them both.

13. Attitudes towards Ulua depend upon relationships (see chapter 5).

14. If Fakaofo people were dependent on tribute from Nukunonu and the resources of Atafu to maintain their accustomed lifestyle, then in a very pragmatic sense their livelihood was threatened too.

15. Jennings landed at Olohega in October 1856, having learned that Europeans who had been there had left, and having been 'given' the island by an Englishman (extract from journal kept by Jennings courtesy of H.E. Maude). Of other Europeans who might have been there between Jules Tirel's departure in 1849 (Padel:17–18 November 1849) and Jennings's arrival seven years later we have no information, but, despite continuing assertions to the contrary, it is certain that some Tokelau people were always there when foreigners arrived, and that though many left, some always remained (as in 1848). Jennings himself noted that 'a few natives' were in residence, but maintained that they had recently 'drifted there' and were not really settled—'they made no attempt to cultivate anything at all but simply [were] living on cocoanuts' (Journal entry for 13 October 1856). These notes might or might not support the assertion that Olohega was uninhabited and therefore claimable as an individual property. Irrespective of any foreign assertion, Tokelau people have always claimed that Olohega is part of Tokelau (see *Matagi Tokelau* 1991:39–43 for a lengthy narrative of comings and goings between Fakaofo and Olohega, and Hooper 1975), and that people were living on coconuts cannot be taken as testimony of temporary residence.

16. Jennings is implicated in several accounts of the slavers. According to Atafu reports he was on board the first ship there, which was indeed the *Rosa Patricia* according to Maude and had called at Olohega before beginning its activities in Tokelau. What puzzles us is the subsequent favourable attitude of LMS missionaries towards Jennings, if indeed he colluded with the slavers.

17. Peni was Ben Hughes, and the time and context of his arrival in Fakaofo are somewhat mysterious. He himself claimed to have arrived there in February 1863 after spending some time at Swain's Island [Olohega] (Hughes 1866). The missionaries take no note of the presence of a trader in January 1863. Fakaofo accounts have him there at the time of the slave ships in February, but imply that he is already well established. The evidence points to his being present in February, but in what context? Did he join the *Rosa Patricia* when it called at Olohega, bringing his labourers from the northern Cooks with him? The only matter now clarified is that he was not the same 'Peni' who collaborated with the slavers at Penryn (*pace* Maude 1981:53). The Penryn 'Peni' was Thomas Payne, a 'leftover' from the wreck of the *Chatham*, who did indeed collude with the slavers (pers.comm. Wilkie Rasmussen from local accounts and LMS South Sea Letters).

18. Suggesting that Peni was protecting his labour supply. The captain was said to have learned otherwise from the son of a Manihiki man married to a Fakaofo woman, who was aboard

the ship, but it is not clear whether he joined the ship or had arrived upon it.

19. The reference is to Kings II (ch. 17:6 ff. and ch. 18:11 ff.) and views the slave ships as punishment for Fakaofo's persistent heathenism.

20. In the published versions, a sentence implicating the Roman Catholic bishop was expurgated—the LMS missionaries knew better. Nonetheless, the statement was not outrageous bearing in mind that the only comparable event in Tokelau history had been the 1852 Fakaofo 'exodus' in which the same tactics had been used. Maka, by his own account, was suspicious of the visitors' intentions from the outset, but apparently could not dissuade the eager Atafu traders from going aboard the ship.

21. We are grateful to the late Peato Tutu Perez for a copy of the letter (dated 14 July 1977), written to him in New Zealand at his request for the information. We have been told many of the same stories in Nukunonu and this letter is a useful collection of them.

22. Estimates of Nukunonu's population before the slave ships are very rough, being based on Gill and Bird's impressions during their very brief visit in January 1863. The number removed is more secure and represents virtually all able-bodied men and a number of women. Nineteen persons voyaged to Samoa—Takua and eighteen who were baptised while there, including women, children and infants.

23. Births and deaths during 1863 are not known and therefore cannot be included.

24. Elloy was not a good reporter. The several documents he wrote about visits to Tokelau (Elloy 1879; Elloy 1863, 1871–75, 1874) are vague, even contradictory concerning the dates of his visits and his activities, and he rarely names ships or the people he travelled with or encountered.

25. Schahl's journal records these baptisms on 15 June 1863; however, the baptismal register records the same day and month three years later, i.e. 1866. The earlier date is assuredly the correct one.

7 The Parish Polities

1. Each population had a different growth pattern. Nukunonu's increase was slow, though steady, and the population did not reach pre-1863 numbers until the turn of the century (see Molloy and Huntsman 1995). The Atafu population grew rapidly at first, undoubtedly because no women had been lost to the slavers, and then increased less dramatically until the 1890s, when another marked increase tripled it from what it had been after the slavers. Throughout the latter part of the nineteenth century, the greatest number of Tokelau people were in Atafu. Fakaofo's numbers rose sharply in the later 1860s, largely through in-migration, remained at about 200 throughout the 1870s and 1880s, and then increased markedly in the 1890s. These differing patterns may be attributed to the demographic character of the populations remaining after the slave ships, to patterns of migration into the atolls from afar and between them, and to unrecorded variations in morbidity and mortality. Emigration was probably insignificant until after the turn of the century.

2. Falevai was the only son of 'king' Ulua and probably younger than the other three men. Strategically, he had to be accommodated as the 'king's' heir, but both his ancestry and his youth must have compromised his status.

3. By linking Ulua's son and only child, Falevai, with his wife's brother, Falekie, in the *toga* structure, the 'rule of four' was perhaps compromised, but more significantly the whole atoll was symbolically and structurally under authentic Nukunonu control. Testimony that the practical three-way division was in principle a division into four are the four sections of named *toga* land. The four 'encompassing stocks' (*puikāiga*) cited in Nukunonu today are indeed derivative of this nineteenth-century division, but they have no common property.

4. When Nukunonu is formally greeted as the Falefā, the ancient stocks of Talafau, Letele, Tuipagai and Lua are usually invoked. At one period, not too long ago, it was proper to include Ulua and his descendants, so Tuipagai and Lua were together addressed as the Gafalua to accommodate this addition without compromising the 'Four Houses'.

5. Some had been aboard the castaway canoe that landed at Tutuila and did not return until mid-year. Others were at Malua in Upolu training as pastors. These men were all of the second and third generations from Tonuia. No women are named in the LMS mission reports. As far as they were concerned, this was a village of men, though most of the elder members of it must have been women.

6. Definitions of adultery and fornication were sweepingly ambiguous in Atafu nearly a century after Pastor Lemuelu was there, so there is ample reason to assume that they were

equally so then. Intention was not distinguished from act, and sexual congress might be as broadly defined as kissing or meeting at night.

7. This was an ad hoc arrangement. Timoteo was an early Fakaofo convert in Samoa and had been trained at Malua and then posted to Nanumanga in 1871 (Powell 1871b). Despite missionary hopes, he had little success there, and was being brought home—whether to Fakaofo or Atafu is not known. In any case, when Mafalā had to be removed, he was installed 'as his substitute' (Turner 1874b).

8. The document, witnessed by Francis Milford and Wm Allen, was recorded in the Archives of Her Britannic Majesty's Consulate for Samoa, Printed Record Register No. 108, dated 4 August 1874.

9. This is the English rendition of the Tokelauan *aliki ma faipule*, the name of the council created by Taupe and later reconstituted to include all the 'grey-haired men'. Both the *aliki* and the senior *faipule* at that time were Protestants. Presumably they spoke on behalf of the whole council, that is 'all the people', but it is not known whether any of the Catholic congregation participated in the decision to send the letter. The Catholic members were always in a minority in the council.

10. The letter did not state that the islets were in fact Atone's property, but referred to them merely as 'claims'.

11. Tokelau by this time lay within the bounds of the Western Pacific High Commission, which had been set up by Imperial Order in Council in 1877, and which had its headquarters in Suva, Fiji. Tokelau was not one of the newly formed Commission's most pressing concerns at the time, and the British Consulate in Samoa had no jurisdiction in the atolls.

12. This last sentence pointedly includes the Samoan catechist among those who resisted, stressing unity, despite the earlier statement of Catholic support of Peleila and the strong statement of it lack in word and song. In fact, both Mafalā and Matulino had left Fakaofo before the events herein related.

13. This man was named Paulsen, a native of Schleswig-Holstein. Although never a church member, because he was not married to the local woman he lived with, he did help the Protestants with translations and formal testimonies. Lister (1892:44) remarks on his interest in mathematics, and records that, 'It was curious on going into his house in this out-of-the-way island to see the familiar backs of Todhunter's 'Euclid' and 'Algebra' and Tables of Logarithms arrayed along his bookshelf.' Phillips (1884) also mentions that he was a good linguist and 'was quite ready to discuss with me "The Differential Calculus".'

14. Some sort of civil authority evidently still existed, even if it extended only to calling an assembly together. The gathering could have been either *aliki ma faipule* or one of the entire population. In either case, if we can assume that such matters were arranged then as they are today, the elders would be seated foremost in a U-shaped line, and the 'accused' brought into the open space between them. If that were the case, the young accused Catholic men would have been surrounded on three sides.

15. People today know about the guns and the shooting, but little about the immediate circumstances, and they tell about it simply as part of the accounts of how bad things used to be, in more ignorant days, between the two congregations.

16. The Catholic mission must have been at the very least discomforted by Atone's extra-legal dealings and Peleila's tactics at Fenualoa, and by the complaints made by the Protestants to the Western Pacific High Commission (WPHC). There is, however, no evidence of this in Catholic records. To the contrary, Father Didier in 1884 wrote that Peleila was a 'devoted host . . . who received us with the same affability and enthusiasm as he had the preceding year . . .' (1885:514), and four years later witnessed a deed by which Peleila gained another piece of land in satisfaction of a debt, and himself, from the same party, acquired in return for a double-barrelled gun a piece of land, which he later exchanged with Peleila for a piece of land on Upolu (Cusack Smith 1892a). In all this, Father Didier was, it seems, following the example of his 'devoted host'.

17. Catholic fathers did indeed visit Fakaofo in 1882 and 1883. The 1882 visit was the first in seven years, and the 1883 visit was Father Didier's first. Quite understandably they mention no such threats.

18. The two pieces of land involved were, firstly, that on which the Protestant church stands today, in the southeastern quarter of the village islet, and secondly, that on the ocean shore of the islet occupied today by the Protestant pastor's establishment of Maluatea and the adjoining Catholic church. A low stone wall now divides Maluatea from the site of the Catholic church.

19. By which he means the village islet.
20. Even in that confrontation a 'person' of Fakaofo did not pull the trigger. Émile, the slayer of Vaopuka, was a relation of Peleila, and it was he who provided the guns.
21. The eldest son was baptised in 1892 and soon thereafter was selected for training as a catechist. The other son and a daughter were baptised in 1902, before marrying, and this son too later became a catechist. Both had the advantage of literacy, gained in pastors' schools, which made them promising candidates for pastoral roles. The other daughter married a Fakaofo Protestant, but her daughters were raised by her elder brother as Catholics.
22. The Nukunonu account goes on to tell of how six of the eight children of that union returned to their mother's homeland, where they converted to Catholicism, married and raised Catholic families. This ending of the story is told with smug satisfaction if not moral superiority.
23. Catholic baptismal records record numerous adult baptisms of Atafu and Fakaofo people who came to reside in Nukunonu, as well as of people who changed affiliation in Fakaofo.

8 Outposts of Empire

1. Why did the *Egeria* return in August and loiter around Tokelau for two weeks? Surely it was not just to accommodate the scientist J.J. Lister who had come aboard to investigate an emerging volcano in the Tongan archipelago. Other documents and stories suggest that perhaps the Union Jack had to be raised a second time in Nukunonu (see chapter 9) but this is not divulged in the log. It has been written for years that Comm. Oldham was in charge of the *Egeria* at the time, when he did not take command until 1890. Instead, it was Capt. Pelham-Aldrich, though Oldham may have been the one who reported to the High Commission. (*Egeria* 1889).
2. The saga of getting the annexation documents to Tokelau for signing is tortuous. Letters and cables of increasing impatience were received from London, intentions and hopes were expressed back that the mission would be soon accomplished, but getting the documents, a proper authority and transport together could not be arranged for well over a year
3. The diverse documents relating to this minor but telling incident are in WPHC 3209a/20.
4. The major issue was whether Olohega was to be included as part of New Zealand's responsibility for Tokelau. There ensued much communication between Apia and Wellington, between the prime minister and governor-general in Wellington, between Wellington and London, between London and Washington in 1923–24. The upshot was that it was not, at least in Washington and London. The arguments and counterarguments will not detain us here, but see IT-1 EX94/1 pt.1 in National Archives of New Zealand.
5. One published report (*AJHR* 1926:A4D) and two draft reports (Richardson 1925 & 1926) document the visit. They differ somewhat in detail and arrangement, though their contents are essentially the same.
6. A side episode of 1939 had a part to play in this. The High Commissioner in Fiji wrote to the Secretary of State for the Colonies in mid January suggesting that Tokelau might be moved back under the WPHC auspices for 'administrative convenience' along with the Gilbertese settlements in the Phoenix groups (Luke 1939a & 1939b). The Governor-General was not officially apprised of this suggestion until May, but rumours had reached the atolls already in January and the reaction was resoundingly negative (Turnbull 1939: 30 January, with enclosure from Alii & Faipule, Nukunonu). From the Administrator of Western Samoa to Prime Minister Fraser to Galway and hence to the High Commissioner diplomatically and firmly the proposal was rejected, primarily on the grounds that 'they would be guided in their consideration of this matter largely by the wishes of the inhabitants . . .'.
7. This was assessed per head (excepting the Peleila 'estate' at Fakaofo which was taxed separately), rather than on the basis of available resources, which might have been equitable if the two corresponded. They did not. Atafu, at the time had to largest population and Nukunonu the smallest, but Nukunonu had the most resources and Atafu the least. Problems would ensue.
8. Documents pertaining to the establishment of local governments are in WPHC 609/11.

9 Colonial Villages

1. Fakaofo did not in fact restore Fenualoa to *kāiga* control, perhaps seeking to avoid disputes over boundaries. Instead the islet became village property, under the control of *aliki ma*

faipule. A small stone monument commemorating the recovery was later set up by the village meeting house and 'The Day of Fenualoa' is still commemorated annually by a day of village celebrations.

2. The evidence of Lea, who was one of the witnesses of the original transaction between Peni and the *aliki*, Likā, was that, although Likā had been threatened, he had agreed to the sale. According to Cusack Smith's report, other elderly men, including the 'king', agreed with Lea, although younger men were dissatisfied with this evidence. The report also notes that, at the time of the enquiry, Lea was 'under German influence', since he was Feleila's father-in-law.

3. This episode involved many interests—mission, commercial and consular, as well as Fakaofo's and Peleila's—and thus multiple complications, dissimulations, and suspicions. WPHC documents concerning it are 254/94, 180/95 (in HBM Consulate Tonga, misc. papers) enclosing five letters between the British consul in Apia and Mr Beckman of the German Firm in a single day and five letters signed David (or Tavita) the King, 284/95, 414/95, 101/96, and 174/96 containing documents up to 1910 including a note dated late 1901 to the effect that Peleila 'had purchased it in good faith'. This is the first indication, five years after the fact, that Peleila truly owned the islet, and is contrary to dates later reported.

4. Fifty-three acres of Fenuafala were bought by the New Zealand Tokelau Administration in 1956 and vested in the people of Fakaofo for the establishment of a new village. Perhaps it would have been easier to let demography take its course; eventually virtually everyone would have entitlement in Fenuafala. However, politics and principle militated against the natural solution.

5. See Huntsman and Hooper 1985 for the texts and a close analysis of this incident.

6. The document complained of taxation, labour demanded without pay and MacDermot's relations with his cook/housegirl, and was signed by seven *faipule*, including the Aliki Ielemia, and Seanoa himself as Faamasino.

7. Eliot may have been speaking of parliamentary elections in Britain.

8. Appropriately enough, the lands which had previously been controlled by the *falepā*.

9. If this meant a fathom *square*, it was a not inconsiderable labour. The *pulaka* gardens were dug on several islets on the eatern shore to the depth of the freshwater lens, or approximately 2 metres. 'One fathom' thus meant the excavation of c. 6 cubic metres of sand and coarse coral rubble.

10. See chapter 8 for the colonial account. It seems in this case that the local narrative has more 'truth' than the official record (see *Matagi Tokelau* 1991:111–12 for yet another version).

11. The complications need not be detailed here. They are documented in reports and attached minutes of WPHC 207/11, 2138/13, 2518/13, 1337/14, 2937/14, 1561/15. One point is worthy of note, however. When officials began to take their claim seriously, Fakaofo rejected a 'quit claim payment' and wished 'to be allowed to have the same rights as they used to in former times' (Indermaur and Smith-Rewse 1913). This would have been completely contrary to the WPHC policy that prescribed colonies within a colony (Min. to 211/07). Fakaofo had been too demanding and almost forfeited the token four tonnes of copra.

12. With their accustomed ironic bemusement, people tell the storyn of one recalcitrant youth whom Samson could not contain within his gaol. Nightly, the young man would find some way of escaping, to the frustration of this gaoler. This story encapsulates this subtle defiance.

13. The document, which was transmitted to the WPHC for approval, is written in Samoan with an English translation; the translation here is ours. The agreement begins with the appeal from Nukunonu for residenbt priests and teaching sisters, then specifies the lands that will be transferred to the mission in return, and emphasises that the transfer is conditional on the continuing presence of the priest(s) and sisters. It ends by reiterating the initial request: 'we have appealed to Monseigneur Broyer for pastors/missionaries [*faifeao*] to care for our souls and some teaching sisters, and will freely place our lands in the control [*pule*] of the Bishop to provide for the pastor(s) and sisters and schoolchildren.' Officials of the High Commission were suspicious of the bishop's intent and dubious about the whole undertaking. The priest who accompanied the bishop implied that having priests and sisters in residence was the bishop's idea: 'Monseigneur believes that the time has come to provide them with priests and sisters' (Darnard 1921:461). What was later appreciated was that the lands that Nukunonu would transfer to the *pule* of the mission were lands that were claimed by Fakaofo to be in their *pule*.

14. The disputes of this era have never been fully resolved, even though those who cleared, planted and harvested plantations were rarely effectively challenged. Inevitably, the divi-

sions and coalescence of holdings render all inequalities transient in the long run. Holdings which were by far the largest at the turn of the century have been repeatedly divided so that today they are part of the properties of fourteen separate *kāiga* and well over half the population have rights by birth to them.

15. Longstanding administrative antipathy to their mission, expressed with vehemence by several officials in residence in the 1910s, was probably the reason for this reticence.

16. Elders insisted that cricket was played in nineteenth-century Nukunonu, having been introduced by Samoan catechists. Of this there is documentation, but it is conceivable that Catholic tolerance of frivolity may indeed have meant that Nukunonu people enjoyed this diversion well before their Protestant neighbours.

17. They were, however, sporadically recorded in the pastors' parish records and in the magistrates' *Tusi fa'amasino* 'Book of judgments'.

18. So Tokelau people refer to him to distinguish him from the 'black Portuguese' in Fakaofo and the 'white Portuguese' in Nukunonu. It is probable that he had come to the Pacific from a New England seaport.

19. In the 1970s it was moved, silvered and mounted on a concrete plinth to stand at the entrance to the new Atafu school, a striking monument to the value that Atafu most cherishes for its *tupulaga fou* 'younger generation'.

20. A *huamoa* or 'egg' is a common metaphor for zero. A person will be asked: 'How many runs did you score?', and the reply may be: 'An egg.' Sometimes such non-scorers are penalised by their teammates, and in this case those who scored 'eggs' may have been 'punished' by having to swim ashore—a rather non-triumphant route of return.

Postscript: 'Part of New Zealand'

1. See Wessen *et al*. Part II for more detail.

2. Western Samoa was quickly set on the course towards political independence. Western Samoa was a mandated territory under League of Nations, and such territories were the first to be considered under the United Nations trusteeship provisions. New Zealand was fully committed to the principles of trusteeship, Prime Minister Peter Fraser having chaired the committee on trusteeship during the drafting of the United Nations Charter. Most importantly, however, Samoans had long agitated for independence and were set to take that road (see Davidson 1967, particularly p.163).

3. This had been accomplished by Orders in Council, thereby avoiding parliamentary assent (or dissent). It could be doubted '. . . whether the New Zealand Government has any power of acceptance of such duties without the assent of the Parliament of New Zealand' (McKay 1945 quoting Crown Solicitor opinion dated 10 October 1928).

4. For a description of that tour by one of the participants see *Matagi Tokelau* pp.136–38. Some months before the tour, a Fakaofo delegation visited the Governor of American Samoa and offered to cede all Tokelau to the US. They viewed a US connection as highly beneficial in light of earlier experience, but when the governor explained that it was not a simple matter, they did not pursue it (Tokelau accounts and letter written by H. Rex Lee dated 14 July 1975, courtesy of H.E. Maude).

5. The Sunderlands had been flying to the atolls from Laucala Bay, Fiji at three-month intervals and in emergencies for some years.

6. These speculations include Robin Maugham's *The 'Joyita' Mystery* (1962), John Harris's *Without Trace* (1982), and more recent work by Robert de Zoete (1985).

7. The story of 'Tokelau Scholars to New Zealand . . .' has been told (see Sallen 1983), and will not be pursued here except as it is embedded in wider projects of 'resettlement'.

8. The Minister of Maori and Island Affairs in reply on 1 October 1967 spoke as if depopulation was indeed intended (*New Zealand Parliamentary Debates* 1967:2117), and this intention is confirmed by an article in the *Evening Post* (May 1969) in which the minister, then retired, stated that this was the purpose of the Resettlement Scheme—a 'thrilling experiment'. This report was in turn cited by the administrator who shared the late minister's view and questioned if 'the interests of the Tokelauans [are] being served by their continued residence on their atolls' (Taylor 1970). Intentions aside, the Department of External Affairs had already put the brakes on the more grandiose statements in mid 1966, concerned that the United Nations might charge New Zealand with 'depopulating' the atolls and that questions that might be raised when a UN delegation visited some time in the future to 'verify' the wishes of the Tokelau people.

REFERENCES

Abbreviations

AJHR	*Appendices to the Journals of the House of Representatives*
AMO	*Annales des Missions de l'Océanie*
JPH	*Journal of Pacific History*
JPS	*Journal of the Polynesian Society*
LMS SSL	London Missionary Society South Seas Letters
LMS SSJ	London Missionary Society South Seas Journals
NZNA	National Archives of New Zealand
OMPA	Marist Oceania Province Archives
PMB	Pacific Manuscripts Bureau
WPHC	Western Pacific High Commission

° indicates unpublished text

AJHR. 1927, 1948–55, 1959–72. [Annual Reports on the Union Islands/the Tokelau Islands/ Tokelau]. In *AJHR*, A3. Wellington: Government Printer.

° Allen, Captain. 1913. Letter re activities of Seanoa and Poasa, and in support of MacDermot and Hoare. In WPHC 1337/14.

° — 1921. Letters to Resident Commissioner of Gilbert and Ellice Island Colony, dated 31 May and 6 June. . . . In WPHC 3209a/20.

° Allen, S. S. 1929. Memorandum for—. . . Minister of External Affairs, dated 22 August. NZNA IT-1 EX94/1 pt2.

° — 1930. Memorandum for Minister for External Affairs dated 13 May. . . . NZNA IT-1 EX94/ 1 pt2.

° Anon. n.d. Notes on the Union Islands. In WPHC 1674/20.

° Auditor, WPHC. 1914. [Letter reporting on situation in Atafu when Indermaur arrived there.] WPHC 1047/14.

Becke, L. 1897. *Wild life in southern seas.* London: T. Fisher Unwin.

Bennett, J. A. 1976. Immigration, 'blackbirding', labour recruiting?: the Hawaiian experience 1877–1887. *JPH* 11:3–27.

Best, S. 1988. Tokelau archaeology: a preliminary report of an initial survey and excavation. *Indo-Pacific Prehistory Association Bulletin*, 8: 104–118. Canberra: ANU.

° Bird, P. G. 1863a. Letter dated 9 February . . . enclosing narrative by Mafala of events in late 1862. LMS South Seas Letters.

° — 1863b. Letter to Dr Tidman dated 30 March . . . enclosing letter from Maka. LMS South Seas Letters.

° — 1863c. Letter dated Safotulafai 29 May. . . . LMS South Seas Letters.

° — 1863d. Letter dated Safotulafai 5 August . . . LMS South Seas Letters.

Broughton, C. F. 1838. Report by . . . of encounter of whaleship *Admiral Cockburn* in Tokelau. *Sandwich Island Gazette*. Reprinted in Ward, R. (ed.) 1967, *American Activities. . . .*

° Broyer, M. P. 1913a. Letter to A. Mahaffy on 'Condition of the island of Nukunono [sic]' dated 27 December. . . . In WPHC 207/14.

REFERENCES

° — 1913b. *O le feagaiga nei na osia i le va o Moseniolo P. Broyer S.M. epikopo o Samoa ma le Atu Tokelau ma le Ekelesia katoliko o Nukunonu.* . . . WPHC 2518/13.

° [Burrows, W.] D. C. & D. O., Ellice and Union Islands. 1921a. . . . to Acting Resident Commissioner, Ocean Island, dated 28 September. . . . WPHC 3262/21 but enclosed in 609/11.

° — 1921b. . . . to Resident Commissioner dated 29 November. . . . WPHC 3265/21.

Burrows, W. 1923. Some notes and legends of a South Sea island. *JPS* 32:143–73.

Churchward, C. M. 1959. *Tongan dictionary.* London: Oxford University Press.

° Clarke, W. E. 1890. Voyage to North West Is. 1890 deputation report. LMS South Seas Records 3/172.

° Claxton, A. C. 1886. Minutes of Special Committee Meeting held at Malua 18 October . . . and accompanying letter dated 8 November . . . to Rev. Thompson. LMS SSL.

Cohn, B. 1961. The past of an Indian village. *Comparative studies in social and history* 3:241–9.

Communicate New Zealand photographic collection 1996. AAQT Series 6401. National Archives Head Office, Wellington.

Cook, Th. B. SM, 1984. Catholic Diocesan Archives in the Pacific: . . . *Journal of the Polynesian Society,* 93:227–29.

Coppinger, R. W. S. 1899. *Cruise of the* Alert: *four years in Patagonian, Polynesian, and Mascarene waters. 1878–1882.* London: Swan Sonnenschein.

° Crocker, S. R. 1836–1839. Journal of the *General Jackson.* Nicholson Collection, Providence Public Library [PMB 862].

° Cusack Smith, T. B. 1892a. Letter from . . . to Sir John Thurston, High Commissioner for the Western Pacific, dated Samoa, 7 September. WPHC 190/92.

° — 1892b. Letter from . . . to Sir John Thurston, High Commissioner for the Western Pacific, dated Samoa, 9 September. WPHC 191/92.

° — 1894. . . . to Sir J. Thurston, dated 6 September. WPHC 254/94.

° — 1896a. Report of visit to Manua and the Union islands, dated 3 July. . . . WPHC 230/96.

° — 1896b. Enclosure in letter to Sir John Thurston, dated 11 September. WPHC 368/96.

° — 1897. Report of . . . visit to Tokelau (Union Group), dated 9 July. WPHC 293/97.

Dalton, W. 1990. *The Dalton journal: two whaling voyages to the South seas, 1823–1829. Edited by N. Gunson.* Canberra: National Library of Australia.

Dana, J. D. 1872. *Corals and coral islands.* London: Sampson Low, Marston, Low & Searle.

Darnard, J. SM 1921. Extrait d'une lettre . . . à un confrère, Noukounonou [sic] 9 décembre 1913. *AMO* XIII (4):460–62.

Davenport, W. 1959. Nonunilinear descent and descent groups. *American Anthropologist* 61:557–72.

— 1963. Social organization. In *Biennial Review of Anthropology,* ed. B. Siegel, 178–227. Stanford: Stanford University Press.

Davidson, J. W. 1967. *Samoa mo Samoa: the emergence of the independent state of Western Samoa.* Melbourne: Oxford University Press.

° Davies, S. H. 1880. Journal of Missionary Cruise in the Tokelau, Ellice, and Gilbert Groups during Sept., October, & Nov. 1880 (64 days). LMS SSJ.

° — 1882. Report of a voyage made in *John Williams* to outstations of Samoan mission in the Tokelau, Ellice and Gilbert groups during August, September and October 1882. LMS SSJ.

Dening, G. 1980. *Islands and beaches: discourses on a silent land: Marquesas 1774–1880.* Melbourne:Melbourne University Press.

— 1991. A poetic for histories: transformations that present the past. In *Clio in Oceania: towards a historical anthropology,* ed. A. Biersack, 347–80. Washington & London: Smithsonian Institution Press.

de Zoete, P. 1985. The *Joyita. MORE* September: 66–70.

Didier, E. 1885. Le P. Didier au R.P. Procureur des Missions, 14 septembre 1884. *AMO* 5:509–17.

— 1886a. Lettre du P. Didier au R.P. Assistant pour les missions, 10 décembre 1885. *AMO* 6:189–97.

— 1886b. Lettre du P. Didier à son frère, curé de Hesse, dans la Lorraine allemande, dated 18 octobre 1886. *AMO* 6:331–47.

— 1886c. Lettre du même au révérend Père Assistant pour les Missions, dated 25 Mars 1886. *AMO* 6:293–300.

° — 1887. Copies of letters from Catholics in Nukunonu and Fakaofo forwarded by . . . to British Consulate [and hence to LMS Samoan District Committee]. LMS Samoan District Correspondence, PMB 141.

Didier, R. P. 1892. Lettre du . . ., au R.P. Jeantin, n.d. *Annales de la Propogation de la Foi* 64:344–68.

Diocese of Wallis and Futuna. various. Liber Baptisatorium Matauta, Mua, Hihifo. Oceania Marist Province Archives, Uvea.

Dolé, E. 1885. Lettre . . . au R.P. Procureur des Missions de la Société de Marie. Apia, le 10 juillet 1882. *Annales des Missions de la Société de Marie [AMO]* 5:392–402.

° *Dolphin.* 1825. Logbook. US National Archives, Washington.

° Edwards, E. n.d. Papers 1789–92. Microfilm A 797, Mitchell Library, Sydney—FM4/2098.

— & G. Hamilton. 1915. *Voyage of H.M.S.* Pandora . . . with introduction and notes by Basil Thomson. London: Edwards.

° Eliot, E. C. 1919. [Advocating transfer of Union Group to Administration of late German Samoa.] In WPHC 1711/19.

° Ella, S. 1861. Letter dated Fasitootai 27 November. LMS SSL.

° — 1861–1863. Tokelau /or Union/ Group of Islands, South Seas. [Extracts of letters from Maka.] LMS SSL.

° Elloy, F. L. 1863. Letters to Rocher [from Apia, dated 24 Jan., 20 Mar., 9 May & 29 May 1863]. Archivio Padri Marissi [Rome] VM 223.

° Elloy, M. 1871–75. Journal, pp.219ff. Archivio Padri Marissi, Rome.

° — 1874. Letter to Rev. Germain, Mission procurator at Lyon, dated Apia 25 November. Archivio Padri Marissi OC418.1, Rome.

— 1879. Rapport de . . . à MM. les Membres des Conseils centraux de l'Oeuvre de la Propagation de la Foi. III. Iles de Tokelau. *Annales de la Propagation de la Foi* 51:70–76.

Errington, S. 1979. Some comments on style in the meanings of the past. *Journal of Asian Studies* 38:231–44.

° Faipule ma Toeaina. 1977. [The 1889 raising of the British flag in Nukunonu.] Narrative composed by elders of Nukunonu at request of Peato Tutu Perez.

° Fakaofo. n.d. Handwritten exercise book.

Firth, R. 1957. A note on descent groups in Polynesia. *MAN*, o.s. 57:4–8.

— 1963. Bilateral descent groups: an operational viewpoint. In *Studies in kinship and marriage.* RAI Occasional Papers, ed. I. Schapera, vol.16:22–37. London: Royal Anthropological Institute of Great Britain & Ireland.

— 1967. *The work of the gods in Tikopia.* London & New York: Athlone Press, University of London & Humanities Press.

Freeman, J. D. 1961. On the concept of the kindred. *Journal of the Royal Anthropological Institute of Great Britain and Ireland* 91:192–220.

° French, M. A. E. 1899. Visit to N.W. outstations in the *John Williams* dated Papauta 7 September . . . LMS SSJ.

Gallagher, R. E. (ed.) 1964. *Byron's journal of his circumnavigation 1764–1766.* London: The Hakluyt Society.

° Galway, Gov.-Gen. NZ 1939. Memorandum for Prime Minister dated 18 October . . . NZNA IT-1 EX94/1 pt3.

° Gee, H. 1861. Minutes of special meeting held 21 October. . . . LMS SSL.

° — 1862. Letter dated Apia 31 August . . . reporting on four letters received from Maka in Atafu. LMS SSL.

° — 1863a. Letter dated Apia 26 January. . . . LMS SSL.

° — 1863b. Letter dated 20 March . . . enclosing letter from Maka, teacher on Atafu, dated 16 February 1863. LMS SSL.

° General Fono. 1971. Transcript of proceedings of General Fono held in Nukunonu—April 1971. Cyclostyle.

° Gill, G., and P. G. Bird. 1863. Journal of third missionary voyage to the Tokelau or Union Group of Islands, January 1863. LMS SSJ.

° Gill, W. W. 1863. Journal of . . . 9 February–23 March . . . LMS SSL.

° — 1872. Diary of a tour of the Gilbert, Ellice, Union and Loyalty islands in the *John Williams* . . . 21 May–11 October. . . . Mitchell Library, Sydney B1444.

Gilson, R. P. 1970. *Samoa 1830 to 1900: the politics of a multi-cultural community.* Melbourne: Oxford University Press.

— 1980. *The Cook Islands 1925–1950,* ed. R. Crocombe. Wellington, Victoria University Press.

Goodenough, W. 1955. A problem in Malayo-Polynesian social organization. *American Anthropologist* 57:71–83.

REFERENCES

° Grattan, F. J. H. 1944a. Report on 'Tokelau malaga' of December 1943 dated Apia, 4 February. NZNA IT-1 94/1 pt3.

° — 1944b. Memorandum for the Administrator: United States activities—Atafu, Union Islands—dated 17 July. NZNA IT-1 94/8A pt1.

° — 1944c. Letter dated 31 July . . . to 'Mac' [McKay]. NZNA IT-1 94/8A pt1.

° Green, R. 1921a. [Minute re. Capt Allen and proposal to change port of Entry]. In WPHC 1674/20.

° — 1921b. Report of tour. WPHC 2965/21.

Hague, J. D. 1868. Some coral islands and islanders. *Atlantic Monthly* 22 (129) (July):36–51.

Hale, H. 1846. *United States Exploring Expedition . . .: Ethnography and Philology.* Philadelphia: Lee & Blanchard.

° Harbutt, W. 1847. Letter dated Lepā, Samoa, 22 February. . . . LMS SSL.

° Hicks Graves, J. 1880. Letter from HBM Consul . . . dated Samoa, 18 November. . . . In WPHC 67/84.

° Hoare, D. 1913. Letter dated 18 November. In WPHC 1333/14.

° — 1914. Letter dated 21 March. . . . In WPHC 1333/14.

Hocart, A. M. 1952. *The northern states of Fiji.* London: Royal Anthropological Institute.

° Hooper, A. 1968. An outline of the social organisation of Fakaofo. Unpublished report to Department of Maori and Islands Affairs at the request of John Springford.

— 1969a. 'Land tenure in the Tokelau Islands'. Symposium on land tenure in relation to economic development. Working Paper no.11. Noumea/Suva: South Pacific Commission.

— 1969b. Socio-economic organization of the Tokelau islands. In *Proceedings of the 8th International Congress of Anthropological and Ethnological Sciences, 1968*, ed. H. Befu, 238–40. Tokyo: Science Council of Japan.

— 1975. A Tokelau account of Olosega. *JPH* 10:89–93.

— 1985. Tokelau fishing in traditional and modern contexts. In *The traditional knowledge and management of coastal systems in Asia and the Pacific.* K. Ruddle & R.E. Johannes, eds. UNESCO, Jakarta.

Hooper, A. & J. Huntsman. 1973. A demographic history of the Tokelau islands. *JPS* 82:366–411.

— 1990. History and the representation of Polynesian societies. In *Culture and history in the Pacific*, ed. J. Siikala, 9–24. Helsinki: Finnish Anthropological Society.

— 1991. Aspects of skipjack fishing: some Tokelau 'words of the sea'. In *Man and a half: essays in Pacific anthropology and ethnobiology in honour of Ralph Bulmer*, ed. A. Pawley, 249–56. Auckland: Polynesian Society Memoir 48.

Hooper, A., J. Huntsman & K. Kalolo. 1992. The Tokelau language 1841–1991. *JPS* 101:343–72.

Howard, A. 1963. Land, activity systems and decision-making models in Rotuma. *Ethnology* 2:407–40.

° Hudson, C. W. L. 1840–1842. Journal of the U.S. Exploring Expedition, 11 August 1840 to 19 February 1842. PMB 416.

° Hughes, B. 1864. Letter from . . . to Mr Williams, dated Bowditch Island 4 July. Despatches from U.S. Consuls in Apia, 1843–1906, Roll 2 Volume 2. Microfilm Publication No. T-27, US National Archives.

° — 1866. Affidavit by . . ., dated Apia 18 May, before Jonas M. Coe, U.S. Commercial Agent in Apia. Despatches from U.S. Consuls in Apia 1843–1906, Roll 2, Vol. 2. Microfilm Publication No. T-27. US National Archives.

° Hunter, H. 1900. Visit to Tokelau islands of Deputy Commissioner in H.M.S *Pylades*, August 1900. WPHC 69/00.

° — 1902. Report of visit to Union islands in July. In WPHC 177/02.

° — 1904. Report of a visit to the Union Group, July 1904. WPHC 177/02.

° — 1908. Union Islands—license to recruit labour from. . . . WPHC 169/08.

° Huntsman, J. 1969a. Food distribution on a Polynesian atoll. Paper delivered at Northeastern Anthropological Associations Meetings, Providence, RI. May 1969.

— 1969b. Kin and coconuts on a Polynesian atoll: the socio-economic organisation of Nukunonu, Tokelau Islands. PhD dissertation, Bryn Mawr, Pennslyvania.

— 1971. Concepts of kinship and categories of kinsmen in the Tokelau Islands. *JPS* 80:317–54.

— 1975. The impact of cultural exchange on health and disease patterns: the Tokelau Island Migrant Study. In *Population change in the Pacific region*, ed. Y. Chang & P. J. Donaldson, 183–92. Vancouver: 13th Pacific Science Congress.

— 1981. Complementary and similar kinsmen in Tokelau. In *Siblingship in Oceania*: . . ., ed. M. Marshall. ASAO Memoir 8. Ann Arbor: University of Michigan Press.

— 1994. Ghosts of hierarchy II: transformations of the wider Tokelau polity. In *Transformations of hierarchy*, ed. M. Jolly & M. Mosko, 321–38. Cambridge: Harwood Academic.

Huntsman, J. & A. Hooper. 1975. Male and female in Tokelau culture. *JPS* 84:415–30.

— 1976. The 'desecration' of Tokelau kinship. *JPS* 85:257–73.

— 1985. Structures of Tokelau history. In *Transformations of Polynesian culture*, ed. A. Hooper & J. Huntsman, 133–49. Auckland: Polynesian Society Memoir 45.

— 1986. Who really discovered Fakaofo . . .? *JPS* 95:461–67.

Huntsman, J., A. Hooper & R. H. Ward. 1986. Genealogies as culture and biology: a Tokelau case study. *Mankind* 16:13–30.

° Ielemia et al. 1907. Petition signed by . . . dated 14 October. . . . In WPHC 211/07.

im Thurn, E. 1909. [Publication of] King's Regulation no.7 of 1909. Published and exhibited in the Public office of the HC for the Western Pacific, 24 December. . . . By Command. A. Montgomerie.

° Indermaur, L. & G. Smith-Rewse. 1915. Report of . . . Commission. WPHC 1561/15 (see also 1562/15).

Island Territories Department Registered Files, IT Series 1. Photographs of Tokelau, 1925, in EX94/1 Part 2 Union Group—Tokelau, Swains Island 1926–1930. National Archives of New Zealand, Wellington.

° James, W. 1912. Dr W. James announces his resignation from Goverment service. WPHC 1478/12.

° Jennings, E. 1856. Diary entry for 13 October. . . . location unknown—courtesy of H.E. Maude.

Journal de la Société des Océanistes. 1962. Wallis et Futuna. . . . . xviii (18 Décembre):1 ff.

LaFontaine, J. 1973. Descent in New Guinea: an Africanist view. In *The character of kinship*, ed. J. Goody, 35–51. Cambridge: Cambridge University Press.

Langdon, R., ed. 1979. Thar she went: an interim index to the Pacific ports and islands visited by American whalers and traders in the 19th century. Canberra: Pacific Manuscripts Bureau.

° Langstone, F. 1938. Memorandum for: Acting Administrator, Apia, from Minister of External Affairs. NZNA IT-1 EX94/1 pt3.

° Lee, H. R. 1975. Letter to Mark Seidenberg [copy]. Courtesy of H.E. Maude.

Lister, J. J. 1892. Notes on the natives of Fakaofu [sic] (Bowditch island), Union group. *Journal of the Anthropological Institute* 21:43–63.

° LMS Samoa District. 1841. Minutes of a meeting held at Manono, 10 May. . . . LMS SSL.

° — 1858. Minutes of a meeting of LMS mission, Safotulafai, 16–17 June. LMS SSL.

° — 1888. Minutes of Special Meeting 23 July/22 August. . . . LMS SSL.

° Luke, S. H. 1939a. Letter to Secretary of State for the Colonies, dated 17 January. . . . NZNA IT-1 EX94/1 pt.4.

° — 1939b. Memo to NZ Governor General, dated 2 August. . . . NZNA IT-1 EX94/1 pt.4.

° MacDermot, R. 1910. General Report: Union Islands, dated 1 December. In WPHC 609/11.

° — 1910–11. [Reports, letters, enclosures]. In WPHC 609/11.

Macdonald, B. 1982. *Cinderellas of empire: towards a history of Kiribati and Tuvalu*. Canberra: ANU Press.

° Macgregor, G. 1932. Tokelau Islands field notes. Bernice P. Bishop Museum Library.

— 1937. *Ethnology of Tokelau Islands*. Honolulu: Bernice P. Bishop Museum Bulletin 146.

° Mahaffy, A. 1911. Report on cruise in Ellice and Union islands in August–September. WPHC 1567/11.

° — 1913a. Report of visist . . . WPHC 2138/13.

° — 1913b. Report on land registration. . . . WPHC 2253/13.

Ma'ia'i, F. 1957. A study of the developing pattern of education and the factors influencing that development in New Zealand's Pacific dependencies. MA thesis in education, Victoria University of Wellington. Islands Division of the Department of Education.

Mangeret, R. P. s m. 1932. *La croix dans les îles du Pacifique: vie de Mgr Bataillon de la Société de Marie évêque d'Enos, premier vicaire apostolique de l'Océanie centrale (1810–1877)*. Troisième ed. Lyon: Procuré des Missions d'Océanie.

Markham, S. C. 1904. *The voyages of Pedro Fernandez de Quiros, 1595–1606*. Vol. 2 vols. London: Hakluyt Society.

° Marriott, J. 1883. Journal of a visit to the Tokelau, Ellice & Gilbert Groups in the *John*

REFERENCES

Williams in August, September, October . . . LMS SSJ.

° — 1887. Report of Voyage to Tokelau, Ellice & Gilbert Islands, 1 September to 4 November. LMS SSJ.

° — 1895. Report of the first voyage to the Tokelau, Ellice & Gilbert islands of the s.s. *John Williams*. 4 June to 18 July. LMS SSJ.

Matagi Tokelau. 1990. . . . . Tokelau ed. Apia (Western Samoa) & Suva (Fiji): Office of Tokelau Affairs & Institute of Pacific Studies.

— 1991. . . .: *history and traditions of Tokelau*. English ed. Translated from Tokelauan and edited by J. Huntsman & A. Hooper. Apia and Suva: Office of Tokelau Affairs & Institute of Pacific Studies.

Maude, H. E. 1959. Spanish discoveries in the central Pacific: a study in identification. *JPS* 68:284–326.

— 1981. *Slavers in paradise: the Peruvian labour trade in Polynesia, 1862–1864*. Canberra, Stanford (CA), Suva: ANU, Stanford University, USP.

° Maxse, E. E. B. 1898. Report on tour of Tokelau group, dated 25 June. . . . WPHC 213/98.

° McKay, C. G. R. 1939. Report on visit to Tokelau islands, September 1939. NZNA IT-1 94/1 pt3.

° — 1941. Report on visit to Tokelau islands, November 1941. NZNA IT-1 94/1 pt3.

° — 1945a. Memorandum for Administrator of Western Samoa: Visit of the Rt. Hon Prime Minister: Business arising from, dated 6 May. NZNA IT-T 1/–.

° — 1945b. Letter from . . . to Secretary of External Affairs, dated Department of Island Territories 10 July. . . . NZNA IT-T AO 35/14/3.

° — 1947. Memorandum dated 13 February . . ., for the Secretary of External Affairs: 'United States Installations at Atafu'. NZNA IT-1 94/8A pt1.

— 1968. *Samoana*. New Zealand & Australia: AH & AW Reed.

° Mills, W. 1841. Letter dated 10 February. . . . LMS SSL.

Molloy, M. and J. Huntsman. 1996. Population regeneration in Tokelau: the case of Nukunonu. *JPS* 105:41–61.

Monfat, F. A. 1890. *Les îles Samoa ou archipel des Navigateurs: Étude historique et religieuse*. Lyon: E. Vitte.

Morrell, W. P. 1960. *Britain in the Pacific Islands*. Oxford: Clarendon.

Moss, F. J. 1889. *Through atolls and islands in the Great South Seas*. London: Sampson, Low, Marston, Searle & Rivington.

° Murray, A. W. 1868. Report of a Visit to the Out-stations of the Samoan mission in the Tokelau group in the month of August 1868, enclosed with a letter to Dr Mullens dated 2 November . . . LMS SSL.

National Film Unit, New Zealand. 1966. *Atoll people*.

Nautical Magazine. 1861. A cruise in the Pacific—the Tokolau [sic] group. . . . vol. 30:470–74.

° *Nautilus*. 1835–1838. Logbook. PMB 354, 883 from New Bedford Public Library, New Bedford, Mass.

Newbury, C. 1980. *Tahiti Nui: change and survival in French Polynesian 1767–1945*. Honolulu: University of Hawai'i Press.

° Newell, J. E. 1885. Voyage to the Tokelau, Ellice and Gilbert Isl in the *John Williams*. LMS SSJ.

— 1895. Notes, chiefly ethnological, on the Tokelau, Ellice and Gilbert islanders. *Australian Association for the Advancement of Science* 6:603–12.

° — 1903. Report of visitation of the Gilbert, Ellice and Tokelau islands by JE Newell and Mose, assistant tutor at Leulumoega high school. 24 June to 5 August . . . LMS SSL. Mitchell Library FM4 395.

° — 1904. A brief report of the visitation of the Ellice and Tokelau Island stations . . . July. LMS SSL, Mitchell Library FM4 395.

° — 1905. A missionary tour in the outstations. LMS South Seas Odds, Mitchell Library M656/011–018.

° — 1906. Report of the visitation of the north west (Ellice and Tokelau) island district, 16 June to 16 August. LMS South Seas Letters, Mitchell Library FM4 395.

° — 1907. Letter from . . . on subject of island of Fanuafala [sic] and land Fakaafo [sic], also complaint by native Kalepo, dated 17 December . . . WPHC 211\07, filed with H.B.M. Consulate, Tonga, set 43, item 39.

° — 1908a. Diary. Newell Papers, LMS South Sea Odds, Mitchell Library FM4 3026. [National Library of Australia accession number M 654].

° — 1908b. Union Group: notes on visit to and affairs at . . ., dated 7 July. . . . WPHC 253/08.

New Zealand Government. 1948. *Tokelau Islands Act*. No. 24 of 1948. Government Printer, Wellington.

New Zealand Parliamentary Debates. 1967. Tokelau Islands Amendment Bill. Government Printer, Wellington.

Nokise, U. F. 1983. The role of the London Missionary Society Samoan missionaries in the evangelisation of the south-west Pacific. PhD thesis, ANU, Canberra.

° *Oliver Crocker*. 1851–2. Logbook. PMB 832.

Oliver, D. 1974. *Ancient Tahitian Society*. Honolulu: University of Hawaii Press.

— 1981. *Two Tahitian Villages: a study in comparison*. Hawaii: Institute of Polynesian Studies.

Pacific Islands Monthly. 1966. N.Z. plan to resettle Tokelauans. . . . 17 (February):17.

° Padel, P. 1845–1852. Journal du. . . . 4 vols., Archivio Padri Marissi, Rome.

Paulding, L. H., US Navy. 1970 [1831]. *Journal of a cruise of the United States schooner* Dolphin. Reprint of original published by G. , C. & H. Carvill, New York, with new introduction by A. Grove Day, ed., Honolulu: University of Hawai'i Press.

Pearson, W. H. 1969. European intimidation and the myth of Tahiti. *JPH* 4:199–217.

° Perez, Peato Tutu. 1977. [Narrative of events in Fakaofo: 1928–41.] MS provided by author.

° — n.d.1. Fakamatalaga na mea tau ki te tuakau / Tokelau ma te kaloa: fakamatalaga mai toku tupuna ki Mikaele Kauai. Photocopy of typescript courtesy of author.

° — n.d.2. Tala fakaholopito o Fakaofo mai anamua. Photocopy courtesy of author.

° Phillips, C. 1881. Journal of a voyage to the Tokelau, Ellice & Gilbert Islands during the months of September, October and November 1881. LMS South Seas Journals.

° — 1882. Letter to Rev. R.W. Thompson dated 21 September. . . . LMS SSL.

° — 1884. Report of voyage to the North West Outstations of the Samoan mission from 8 July to 15 September. . . . LMS SSJ.

° Phillips, C. et al. 1884. Agreement with Atafu 'chiefs' regarding transfer of land to London Missionary Society. LMS Samoan District Correspondence, PMB 141.

Poesch, J. 1961. *Titian Ramsay Peale: 1799–1885. And his journals of the Wilkes Expedition*. Philadelphia: American Philosophical Society Memoir 52.

Poupinel, V. 1882. Au Révérend Père Mayet. En mer, le 23 décembre 1861. *AMO* 2:160–74.

° Powell, T. 1871a. Journal. . . . LMS SSL.

° — 1871b. Report of a visit, in the *John Williams*, to the Tokelau, Ellice and Gilbert groups, Sept., Oct. & Nov. LMS South Seas Journals.

° — 1883b. Letter to Rev. R. Wardlaw Thompson dated Malua 2 November. . . . LMS SSL.

° — 1883a. Report of the sub-committee on the North West Outstations dated Malua 1 November. LMS SSL.

° Powles, G. 1956. Letter to Secretary of Island Territories, dated Apia, 17 July. . . . Seen 1968 Tokamin, NZ High Commission, Apia.

° Pratt, G. 1872. A yatching excursion to the Tokelau, Ellice and Gilbert groups. LMS SSJ.

Radcliffe-Brown, A. R. 1950. Introduction. In *African systems of kinship and marriage*, ed. A. R. Radcliffe-Brown & D. Forde, 1–85. London: Oxford University Press.

Reynolds, J. N. 1835. Letter to the Secretary of the Navy enclosing 'Report in relation to islands, reefs, and shoals in the Pacific Ocean, &c'. US Navy Department, House Document 105, 23rd Congress, 2nd Session. Washington, Government Printing Office.

° Reynolds, W. n.d. Journals on board the *Vincennes*. MSS in Franklin & Marshall Library, Lancaster, Pennsylvania.

° Richardson, G. 1925. Union Group (Tokelau Islands). NZNA IT-1 94/1 pt1.

° — 1926. Report of visit to the Union Group (Tokelau Islands). NZNA IT-1 94/1 pt2.

Rieu, E. 1936. *Centenaire des missions Maristes en Océanie*. Lyon: E. Vitte.

° Rocher, J. L. SM. 1856. Letter to Mgr. P. Bataillon dated Sydney, 6 August. . . . PMB, OMPA Microfilm 26, 1.6.

Sahlins, M. 1957. Differentiation by adaptation in Polynesian societies. *JPS* 66:291–300.

— 1958. *Social stratification in Polynesia*. Seattle: University of Washington.

— 1985. *Islands of history*. Chicago: University of Chicago.

— 1990. The return of the event, again: with reflections on the beginnings of the Great Fiji War of 1843 to 1855 between the kingdoms of Bau and Rewa. In *Clio in Oceania: towards a historical anthropology*, ed. A. Biersack, 37–99. Washington & London: Smithsonian Institute Press.

— 1992. *Anahulu: the anthropology of history in the kingdom of Hawaii*. Vol. 1. Chicago: University of Chicago Press.

REFERENCES

° Sakaio, T. 1865. Letter from . . ., Samoan L.M.S. teacher on Fakaofo to Jonas M. Coe, U.S. Commerical Agent, Apia, dated Fakaofo 21 September 1865. Despatches from US Consuls in Apia 1843–1906, Roll 2, Vol.2. Microfilm Publication No. T-27, US National Archive.

° Sallen, V. 1983. Tokelau scholars in New Zealand: experiences and evaluations. MA thesis, University of Auckland.

Scarr, D. 1967. *Fragments of empire: a history of the Western Pacific High Commission 1877–1914.* Canberra: ANU Press.

° Schahl, A. various. Extracts from letters and journals. Typescript from original in Archivio Padri Marissi (Rome), courtesy of Th. B. Cook SM.

° Secretary, WPHC. 1882. Letter dated 21 September. . . . WPHC 134/82.

° Secretary of State for the Colonies. 1921 . . . to High Commissioner for the Western Pacific dated 26 August. . . . In WPHC 1674/20.

° Sherston, C. G. 1922. Report of visit to Union Group, 11–12 June . . ., dated HMS *Laburnum* at Pago Pago, 14 June. WPHC 2035/22.

Silverman, M. & P. H. Gulliver, eds. 1992. *Approaching the past: historical anthropology through Irish case studies.* New York: Columbia University Press.

Smith, S. P. 1922. A note on the Tokelau or Union Group. *JPS* 31:91–93.

° Solomona, the witness. n.d. Story of the taking of the island of Fanua fala [sic], Fakaofo (Tokelau), by a whiteman known as Ben. Translation of original document written in Samoan, seen 1968 in Tokamin, NZ High Commission, Apia, Western Samoa.

° Stackpole, E. A. pers.comm. 1969 . . . to J. Huntsman re. loss of Macy journal in Nantucket fire.

° Stallworthy, G. 1858. Letter dated Raiatea 2 November . . ., enclosed in Chisholm to Rev. A. Tidman. LMS SSL.

— & G. Gill. 1859. Ethnology of Polynesia—xviii. *The Samoan Reporter* 20 (January):4–5.

Sterndale, H. B. 1890/91. A lone land and they who lived on it. *Monthly Review.*

° Stevens, A. O. 1924 . . . to Collector of Customs, Apia, dated 11 December. . . . NZNA IT-1 EX94/1 pt.1.

° Strum, L. C. L. W., USN 1918 . . . on Swain's Island, reports on treatment and conditions of Natives and gender conditions on the Island. Letter to Governor [of American Samoa?]. Copy in NZNA IT-1 94/1 pt1.

° Stuart, F. D. n.d. Journal of . . . aboard the *Peacock,* 19 August 1838–18 July 1841. Records of the Hydrographic Office—RG37, US National Archives, Washington, DC.

° Swinbourne, C. A. 1925. General report on visit of inspection to the Union Group. NZNA IT-1 EX94/1 pt1.

Sydney Morning Herald 1863. [Letter from S. Ella re. 'slavers', reproducing Maka's letter from Atafu, dated 16 February.] 3 June.

Taupe Alesana. 1970. [The first inter-atoll cricket match.] *Te Vakai* 2 (3):1–2.

° Taylor, R. B. 1970. . . . to Secretary of Maori and Island Affairs, dated 20 April. . . . NZNA IT-1 94/23 pt1.

Thomas, A. 1986. The 'fatele' of Tokelau: approaches to the study of a dance in its social context. MA Thesis, Victoria University of Wellington.

— E. Tuia & J. Huntsman. 1990. *Songs and stories of Tokelau: an introduction to the cultural heritage.* Wellington, Victoria University Press.

° Thompson, E. 1945a. Report re. 'Tokelau voyage' of 9–26 June . . ., dated 29 June. NZNA IT-1 94/1 pt4.

° — 1945b. Report re: 'Tokelau voyage' 11–26 November, dated 28 November. . . . NZNA IT-1 94/1 pt4.

° — 1946. Report re. 'Tokelau voyage' 16–24 April, dated 2 May. . . . NZNA IT-1 94/1 pt4.

Thompson, E. P. 1977. Folklore, anthropology, and social history. *Indian Historical Review* 3:247–66.

° Thomson, A. 1928. Notes during meteorological research at Atafu, 18 June–20 July. . . . Original notebooks in authors' possession.

° Thurston, J. B. 1889. Letter to the Secretary of State. WPHC. Despatches to Secretary of State, vol. 1887–1893.

Tokelau Dictionary 1986. Office of Tokelau Affairs, Apia, Western Samoa.

Tremblay, E. A. 1964. *God's redhead: a life sketch of Father Joseph Roch Deihl, S.M. (1895–1948).* Honolulu: 93–105.

° Turnbull, A. C. 1938. Memorandum for Minister of External Affairs dated 24 October. . . NZNA IT-1 94/1 pt3.

° — 1939. Memo to Minister of External Affairs, dated 30 January . . ., enclosing letter from Alii & Faipule, Nukunonu. NZNA IT-1 94/1 pt.4.

° — 1945. Memorandum for the Secretary, Department of Island Territories dated 23 March . . . re. Visit of the Rt Hon. Prime Minister—business arising from. NZNA IT-1 94/1 pt4.

Turner, G. A. 1861. *Nineteen years in Polynesia*. London: John Snow.

° — 1874a. Report of a voyage through the Tokelau, Ellice and Gilbert groups in the *John Williams*. LMS SSJ.

° — 1874b. Voyage through the Tokelau, Ellice and Gilbert Islands in the *John Williams*. LMS, PMB129.

° — 1878. Report of a missionary voyage through the Tokelau, Ellice & Gilbert Groups. LMS SSJ.

° — 1882. . . . to High Commissioner of the Western Pacific. In WPHC 144/82–1.

United States Coast Guard. 1946. *The Coast Guard at war, Loran IV*. Vol. II. Washington: Historical Section, Public Information Division, US Coast Guard.

Valeri, V. 1985. *Kingship and sacrifice: ritual and society in ancient Hawaii*. Chicago: University of Chicago Press.

— 1994. Review of *The Apotheosis of Captain Cook: European mythmaking in the Pacific*, by G. Obeysekere. *Pacific Studies*, 17(2):124–36.

Verne, R. P. 1895. Extrait d'une lettre du R.P. Verne à M. Giroust, curé de Reyrieux (Ain), dated Futuna, 10 décembre 1846. *AMO* 1:517–22.

° Vivian, J. C. 1871-2. Voyage of the *John Williams* from Tahiti to Sydney calling at numerous islands en route. LMS SSJ.

° Ward, C. 1914. Letter dated Suva, 28 April . . .: Administration of the Union Islands . . . suggestions for. . . . In WPHC 1045/14.

Ward, R. G., ed. 1967. *American activities in the central Pacific*. 5 vols. New Jersey: Gregg.

Weekly Review and Messenger. 1863. Slavers in the South Seas. . . . 1 (13 June):2.

Wessen, A. F., A. Hooper, J. Huntsman, I. A. M. Prior & C. E. Salmond, 1992. *Migration and health in a small society: the case of Tokelau*. Oxford: Clarendon Press.

° Whitmee, S. J. 1870. Letter to Dr Mullens, dated 23 December . . . LMS SSL.

° Whittle, J. S. n.d. Journal as surgeon of the 'Vincennes' and 'Peacock', 1838–1841. University of Virginia Library, Charlottesville, VA.

Wilkes, C. 1845. *Narrative of the United States Exploring Expedition during the years 1838, 1839, 1840, 1841, 1842*. Vol. 5. Philadelphia: Lea & Blanchard.

° Williams, J. C. 1863. Minutes of Special Meeting of Samoan mission held at Apia, 5 January. . . . LMS SSJ.

° Williams, S. F. 1864. Letter from . . . British Consul in Apia to Sakaio, the Samoan LMS teacher on Fakaofo, dated Apia, 14 June. Despatches from US Consuls in Apia, 1843–1906, Roll 2 Volume 2. Microfilm Publication No. T-27, US National Archives.

° Wilson, W. H. 1885. Minutes of special meeting of the S.D.C. 24 November. . . . LMS SSL.

— MS 1886. Visit to N.W. Out-stations 11 August–25 October. LMS SSJ.

Wodzicki, K. 1969. Preliminary report on damage to coconuts and on the ecology of the Polynesian rat (*Rattus Exulans*) in the Tokelau Islands. *Proceedings of the New Zealand Ecological Society* 16:7–12.

— & M. Laird. 1970. Birds and bird lore in the Tokelau Islands. *Notornis* 17:247–76.

° Woodford, C. M. 1895. Return of probates of: Antonio Pereira, R.L. Stevenson and George Pritchard. WPHC 280/95.

Yaldwyn, J. C. & K. Wodzicki. 1979. Systematics and ecology of the land crabs (Decapoda, Grapsidae and Gecarcinidae) of the Tokelau islands, Central Pacific. *Atoll Research Bulletin* (235).

YANKEE. 1835. D'Wolf's Island. *Bristol Gazette and Family Companion* III, no.11, Nov. 21.

INDEX

affines 120-1
Ajax visit 262-4
Akafi (Kilino) 241
Alefaio, Kolo 314
Alesana, Taupe 314-15
aliki ma faipule 160-1, 203-4, 237, 251-2; *see also* councils of elders
aliki (sacred chiefs) 128, 136-9, 150-1, 153, 155-61, 163, 166-7, 168-70
Allen, Captain 261-4, 290, 291, 303, 306
Alo 265, 291
alofa (affection) 115-16, 119, 330
Amiteo 220
animal life 22, 329
Aniseto 220
anthropology, ethnography and history viii, ix, 1, 5, 7, 10-12, 325-8
Aperau (Rarotongan) 220, 241
Apete 281
Apinelu, Logologo 265, 302, 303, 306, 309
archeological findings 331
Atafu: abandoned by first inhabitants 133-5, 138, 170-1, 331; as administrative centre (1910-14) 302; Anniversary Day 61, 65, 75; burial site 302, 303; character 180, 192, 298-9, 309; Duke of York's Island 139-40, 142, 332; features of village 302-3; 'flight of' 129, 133-5; food supply 309; 'Great Cyclone' (1914) 302-3; maps 18, 20, 142; plan of village 29, 172; as Protestant parish 226-36; resettled 5, 171, 180; Seven Houses (*Falefitu*) 139, 153, 170-4, 178, 236; size 331; uninhabited 139, 140, 180; village 28-29, 32-35, 40-121
Atone (Antonio Pereira) 184, 188, 211, 213-14, 220, 237, 239, 240, 241, 275-6, 337
āumāga ('strength of village') 59, 60; Atafu 60-63, 305, 313; Fakaofo 59, 60, 63-66, 284
authority 46-49, 115; among women 49-50; of chiefs 159-61; and equality 46, 50; *see also* councils of elders; elders

Avafatu 157

banishment 41, 329
Bataillon, Mgr Pierre 182-3, 186, 187, 188, 189, 191, 197, 209, 335
beachcombers 184-93 *passim*, 204, 212-13, 227, 300-1, 334-5
birds 22, 25
boundaries 21, 34, 35, 107, 112, 330
Bowditch Island *see* Fakaofo
British and French interests 245-8; *see also* churches, disputes
brother-sister *see* sister-brother
Broyer, Bishop 288, 291, 292-3, 297
Burrows, William 260, 280-3

Campbell, Telford 270
chiefs 132, 133, 136-9, 144-5, 146, 148, 333; authority 159-61; duality 163, 333; Fakaofo 'land of chiefs' 153-63; as priests 150-1, 158-9, 173, 250; *see also faipule*
children: in churches 96, 97, 98; discipline 48, 56, 83, 96; in *inati* 81-83; in Nukunonu 297; parentage 118; seniority among 174, 333
Christianity, conversion 183, 194-5, 198-215 *passim*, 336; *see also* churches
churches 92-101, 216-52; affiliation 2, 93-98, 252; in Atafu 93-94, 226-36; buildings 35, 99, 228, 238-9, 285, 286, 292-4, 303-5, 323-4, 339; catechists 101; children 96, 97, 98; communicants and non-communicants 94, 96, 97; covenant with pastor 301-2; deacons 95; definitions of 'sin' 229, 230; disputes on Fakaofo 238-52, 286, 337; disputes on Nukunonu 252-6; dress 93, 94, 95, 233; in Fakaofo 93-94, 236-52; intermarriage 249-50; men 97; in Nukunonu 93-94, 218-26, 296-7; priests and pastors 41, 94-95, 99-101; reaffiliation 249, 338; Samoan influence 100, 222, 228; seating 93, 96; and village 94-96, 270, 283, 286;

309-13; waiting for return 312
United States Exploring Expedition (1841) 5, 14, 144-7, 148, 159, 160, 172, 173, 181, 329
Uvea, Tokelauans at 36, 187, 188, 191, 198-9

Vaea (Aniseto) 241
Vagi 182
Vaiala 207, 246
Vaopuka 207, 212, 220, 243-4
Veniale 281, 282, 287

wages, introduction (1960s) 322
warfare and warriors 129-31, 163-4
water: containers 28; supply 1, 27-28, 51, 128-9, 268, 278
wealth goods 137
Weber, Th. 213
Western Pacific High Commission 244, 254, 256, 257-72; attachment of Tokelau 36, 257, 258-62, 269-71, 278-83, 313, 338; and Captain Allen 261-4; claims Tokelau (1889) 257, 258, 274-5; detachment of Tokelau 265-6, 283, 338; finances 256-7; founding (1877) 242, 257, 337; native government 265, 278-81; officials in Tokelau 259, 270-1, 302; represented in Western Samoa 262; Tokelau administered from Gilbert and

Ellice Islands 36, 257, 258-62, 269-71, 278-83, 302; visits from officials 260, 275-6, 277
Western Samoa: and government 2, 39, 101; influence on churches 100; migration to 266, 306-7; preparation for independence 316, 340
William 195, 204
Williams (British Consul to Samoa) 189, 213, 239-40, 242
Wilson, W. H. 222, 247
women: church groups 69; clowning 73-74; committees 68-76, 306; and division of food 113-14, 116; *fakamua* 44; Fakaofo 75-76; fishing 23; household rulers 285; inspections 70-71; and male elders 49, 69; mat-making 27, 44, 71-73; 'matrons' 69, 71, 98; Nukunonu 75; play 72, 73; proper spheres 49-50, 113; residence 110, 111; as resource 137; 'sacred beings' 131; unmarried 70; valued as sisters 178; *see also* marriage; sister-brother
work groups 45; in Nukunonu 66-67; *toga* 223-4; *see also āumāga; faitū; fakatahi*
World War II: coast watchers 274; New Zealand policy 268; US presence 260-1, 268, 309-13

DATE DUE
